THE *RESOLUTION* JOURNAL OF JOHANN REINHOLD FORSTER

1772–1775

VOLUME IV

EDITED BY
MICHAEL E. HOARE

THE HAKLUYT SOCIETY
LONDON
1982

ISBN 0 904180 10 7

Printed in Great Britain at the
University Press, Cambridge

Published by the Hakluyt Society
c/o The Map Room,
British Library Reference Division
London WC1B 3DG

CONTENTS

ILLUSTRATIONS, SKETCHES AND MAPS

All sketch maps are taken from J. C. Beaglehole's edition of *The Journals of Captain James Cook on his voyages of discovery*, II. *The voyage of the* Resolution *and* Adventure, *1772–1775*, Cambridge, 1961, by kind permission of Dr T. Beaglehole, Wellington. All such maps are indicated by an asterisk * and the numbers in brackets refer to the figure number in that edition.

July ye 13th ☿ The breeze somewhat abated. Brought to during night. Stood on at daybreak. Saw a Procellaria Gavia & several Tropicbirds. The Thermometer at 74½, in my Cabin 77. A few drops of rain fell on the preceding Evening.

This day two year we left Plymouth; & are now probably gone through the greater part of those disagreable circumstances, which we must undergo. The Almighty keep us all alive & healthy & free from too great difficulties, & give us still opportunities of making useful & interesting discoveries in these Seas, especially wish I come to a Country where I may get a good Quantity of new & interesting plants & birds, fish, & other productions of nature, & then after all may the same providence bring us safely home to the shores of old England, where I may enjoy ease & rest after these fatigues, in the bosom of my family, in the company of my friends, & under the Approbation of my Patrons.[1]

July ye 14th ♃ The breeze gentle. The weather fine. Made Sail all night. Saw several Tropicbirds. The Thermometer 77°, in my Cabin 79°. Today a Saylor offered me 6 Shells to sale, all of which were not quite compleat, & he asked half a Gallon brandy for them, which is now worth more than half a Guinea. This shews however what these people think to get for their Curiosities when they come home, & how difficult it must be for a Man like me, sent out on purpose by Government to collect Natural Curiosities, to get these things from the Natives in the Isles, as every Sailor whatsoever buys vast Quantities of Shells, birds, Fish etc. so that the things are dearer & scarcer than one would believe, & often they go to such people, who have made vast Collections, especially of Shells viz. the Gunner & Carpenter, who have several 1000

[1] George, in mock humorous vein, records the celebration of this second anniversary 'by the sailors with their usual mirth'. One, 'of a fanatical turn', even composed a hymn for the occasion before, like his mates, sinking under 'the powerful influence of his adversary', grog, *Voyage*, II, 196. Cook was silent.

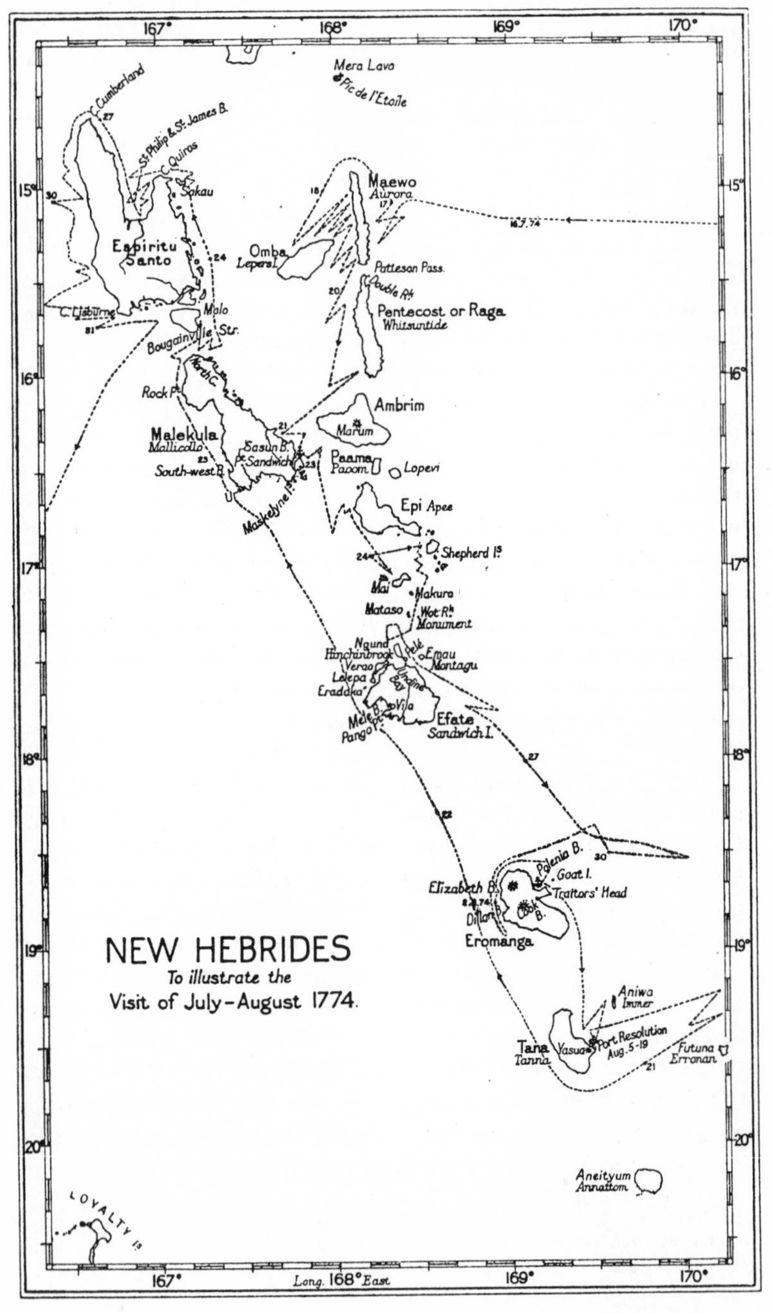

Figure 34. New Hebrides, to illustrate the visit of July–August 1774 ★(66).

Shells: some of these Curiosities are neglected, broke, thrown over board, or lost.[1]

*July y^e^ 15th* ♀ The breeze fresh, tacked from 11 o'clock to 5. Saw in the Evening a Man of war bird & several flying Fish & Tropicbirds. The Thermometer at 76½, in my Cabin at 80°.

*July ye 16th* ♄ The course changed from NWbW to W & at last to W.bS. Saw flying Fish. The Thermometer at 78°, in my Cabin 80°.

*July ye 17th* ☉ A little after noon a Calebash was seen a head drifting & we passed it. The Gale strong, hazy, now & then Squalls & rain. After 2 o'clock Land was seen on our starboard Bow. It is high & of a good extent, & in the Evening we saw land a head. We tacked all night, had rain & several Squalls. The Gale strong. The Ship works much. The long Isle we saw seems to be M. Bougainville's *I. de la Pentecôte.*[2] All night the water entered my & my Son's cabin, just as if we were quartered on deck, all our bed swims, all our cloths, & books are wet, & we are deprived of sleep. My Son's cabin is however infinitely more leaky, than mine; for his matrass is wet quite through, as if it had been steeped in water.[3] We stand continually on & off. The Thermometer at 74½, in my Cabin 80° because I must keep the Skuttel shut, to keep the rain out, which makes it very hot.

*July ye 18th* ☽ The gale very strong, a high sea, continual rain. Foggy & a rolling leaky Ship, all disagreable circumstances to people that have so long been used to the gentle weather to the East of this place between the Tropics. We have upon the whole a sound Ships-Crew; & a few only have had fevers, but are recovering. The worst is we have hardly any thing to give them, to restore their former Strength with. We have hardly any Hogs left, & eat allready all Salt Meat; the only comfort are the fine Yams we got at *Anamocka* & which still last till now, & are the best we ever tasted. If this rainy & stormy Season should last long, it will do no good to our Crew & ill prepare them for the next Southern cruize, which will of course be the most fatiguing in our

[1] This is interesting comment and provides further food for speculation on the amount of natural history curiosities brought home from this and other voyages. For the shells see S. Peter Dance, 'The Cook Voyages and Conchology', *Journal of Conchology*, XXVI (1971), 354–79.

[2] It was, in fact, Bougainville's Aurora, the island of Maewo. Cf *Journals*, II, 457.

[3] '. . . the rains were incessant at the same time, and coming through the decks into our cabins, thoroughly soaked our books, cloaths and beds, depriving us of rest', *Voyage*, II, 196.

circumstances; all the provisions having lost their nutritive quality by keeping, mould, vermin etc; the Ship & its rigging being worse than before, & the most stormy Sea to encounter. But we hope it will soon settle into fair weather, & the country before us will prove beneficial to us with its refreshment, & the Natives prove friendly & hospitable & supply us with hogs. I wish besides to find a good many new plants & Animals here, & some of them that may prove beneficial & usefull.[1]

It is however remarkable *Bougainville* met with storms & rainy, foggy weather, off the coast of the *Louisiade*, as he calls it; & *Quiros* had here stormy weather & Squalls with rain & fogs; so that it seems this weather is peculiar to this part of the world.[2] Capt *Cook* in the *Endeavour* had allways blowing & foggy weather on the coast of N. Holland.

When we were about 2 or 3 miles off the Land at 4 o'clock P.M. we saw the breakers towards the Shore. We stood on & off all night & in the morning we saw again the Land & go along its shores, it lies nearly NW & SE & has a high land to the South of it, which seems to be *M. de Bougainville's* I. de *Pentecote* & the long Island we now run along is to all appearance his *Aurora* Island. We saw a good many Coconut Trees, on the very ridges of the hills, & white flowers on its shores. I observed likewise by my Glass a Tree with yellow Flowers on its top. By the help of the Glass I discovered likewise two Natives on the Shore after we had made the N.W. point, & a little after we heard them calling out. We might see many things more if the weather were not so hazy & if the Squalls came not so often on. The Thermometer at 76½, in my Cabin 79.[3]

*July ye 19th* ♂ We see Land right a head, which is the Island of *Lepers*[4] of M. de *Bougainville*. Upon the whole not having a good special map or a more detailed account of *Quiros's* Expedition we cannot compare every part of his acc^t^ with that of M^r^ de

[1] Cf. George's summary of the past two years of 'visiting the discoveries of former voyagers, in rectifying their mistakes and vulgar errors' and his more hopeful prospect of a third year 'term in new discoveries, and to make amends for the first two', *Voyage*, II, 197–8.

[2] The weather in the New Hebrides in June and July – the SE trade wind season – is commonly rough and unpleasant.

[3] *In margin:* When we were off the point of Aurora I. I saw a high peak on the Starboard side, at a great Distance – v, f.79. This was Bougainville's Pic de l'Etoile or Mera Lava. *Journals*, II, 581, n.3. See fig. 34 for this complicated navigation.

[4] Aoba, usually pronounced Oba or Omba, a massive island peak rising to 4000 feet and visible on a clear day at a distance of 50 miles.

Bougainville & with what we saw. However I believe the first Isle after *Quiros* left *Tucopia* & which he called in the Memorial St. *Marcos*, is the same with the *Pic d'Etoile* of M. de *Bougainville;*[1] the Great Land to the West is called by Quiros *el Vergil*[2] & is probably the Land *Bougainville* saw to the West of this *Pic:* the next to SE. or S. is called by *Quiros N^ra^ Sen^ra^ de la Luz*, & seems to correspond with the Island of *Aurora.*[3] I suppose the Isle of *Lepers* is *Quiros's Las Lagrimas de. S. Pedro.*[4] The next lands which *Quiros* names[5] his St *Raymunda*[6] is the new Peak; & next to it follows *la Isla de la Virgin Maria*[7] which seems to be the Isle in the Gap & next to this he mentions the 3 parts of the Country called *Australia del Espiritu Santo,*[8] in which was found the bay St *Philip & James* & the port of *Vera-Cruz* with the two rivers *Jordan* & *Saviour.*[9] This *Tierra Austral del Espiritu Santo* he mentioned before to be called by the Natives *Manicolo* & it is by him described as very large, extending westwards 8 days sail, though M. *Bougainville* seems nothing to have seen of it, probably on acc^t^ of the thick fogs that hide it from the sight at a few miles distance.

If but the winds would abate & the weather become clear we

[1] This is a correct deduction. It is Mera Leva or Star Peak, most southerly of the Banks group. Tucopia is Tipokia Island, a Polynesian outlier, northeast of the Banks Islands in 12° 18′ S, 168° 55′ E.

[2] The islet of Verjel or Merig and scarcely a 'Great Land', although easily so interpreted from Forster's Dalrymple text. See below.

[3] This, of course, is completely erroneous. It brings us to the heart of the problem Forster realised himself if he had only Dalrymple's *Historical Collection of... Voyages* (London, 1770), vol. I, upon which to rely as a source for Quirós' voyage of 1606. San Marcos is in fact identical with Torquemada's Nuestra Señora de la Luz (Mera Leva). Dalrymple (I, 6) pointed out the anomaly which is certainly not clear from the longer account of the voyage. See *Collection*, II, 131–2. Aurora is probably the Spaniards' La Margaritana. The best guide to Quirós' island identifications is Table A 'Islands Discovered by Quirós in 1606' and other associated maps, tables and notes in Celsus Kelly (trans & ed.), *La Austrialia del Espíritu Santo...* (Hakluyt Soc., Ser. II, Nos 126 & 127, Cambridge, 1964 & 1966), I, opp. 39 and 47–9.

[4] Forster compounds the error. The reference is to Quirós' *La Clementina.* Quirós' 'Las Lagrimas de San Pedro', the modern Mota with Mota Lava in the background, lies to the north, in the Banks group.

[5] *In margin:* are *Los Portales de Belen & el Pilar de Zaragoza* which probably are Whitsunday & the first new Isle after it to the South – v, f.79. These are respectively Vanua Lava and Ureparapara or Norbarbar Island.

[6] San Raymunda, Lathi-hi or Sakau Island. See Kelly, I, 203, n.

[7] Santa Maria or Gaua Island. Quirós' La Virgen María.

[8] Not, of course, Australia but La Austrialia del Espiritu Santo, the general name given Cardona – the modern Espiritu Santo – and La Clementina, to the south and southwest.

[9] According to Pedro, a Sikaianan slave, seized by Quirós at Taumako, Manicolo lay ten days' sail to the south and southeast. Its chief port, moreover, was both narrower at the entrance and larger than Big Bay (the Bay of St Philip and St James). The evidence would therefore suggest Vanua Levu in Fiji rather than Malekula or Espiritu Santo. See G. S. Parsonson in Kelly, II, 378–9.

certainly should get an opportunity of comparing all these accounts & ascertaining their authority & how far they can be relied on: though it is now certain, that it can hardly be a very great land, or Continent as *Quiros* thinks, for to the North are other Islands *Tucopia, Taumaco, St Cruz, Guaytopo, Chicayana, Mecayraila* etc.[1] to the East *Bougainville* sailed; we came from the S.E; *Bougainville* sailed to the W.; & Capt Cook in the *Endeavour* found the E. Shores of *N. Holland:* it can therefore extend only to the S. & S.W. This, time must soon disclose.

We saw at four o'clock the W. part of the *Isle of Lepers* at about 1½ miles distance before us. We saw a Turtle sleeping on the Sea. The Land was here steep & very high; the tops of its hills involved in clouds & fog: we observed in 2 or 3 places considerable Cascades rushing down the precipices & lastly into the Sea. The sides of the hills were all covered with verdure & trees, especially with numberless Coconut-Trees, which had a very yellow foliage, & might therefore be of another kind of Palms, though I am inclined to believe them to be Coconut-Trees.[2] We sounded with 120 fathoms line & found no bottom, & therefore put about Ship but the wind continuing high, we could not carry canvas & had double reefed Top Sails, which caused a great deal of leeway to our Ship, & we shall find enough to do, to get through the passage between the Isles of *Lepers* & *Aurora*, unless the violence of the winds abates, which would be very desirable.[3] We beat up to windward all night, standing on & off between the Isles of *Lepers* & *Aurora*. We were close under the land at 8 o'clock in the morning. After we had put about, we saw a small Canoe come off, with a single man in it. The weather foggy, with Squalls, & the wind high; but smooth water. We made but a short trip & stood in again, & observed another Canoe with 3 Men in her. On The Shore & the rocks were here & there Men, some of whom I observed through

[1] Respectively, as Forster lists them, Tikopia, Taumako in the Duff Islands, Santa Cruz (Ndeni), Vaitupu, Sikaiana or Stewart's Island, and Nukulaelae in the Ellis Islands. See Parsonson in Kelly, II, 377–8.

[2] The yellow foliage might seem to have been the result either of drought or potash deficiency and general overcrowding or of infestation of pets such as the red palm weevil (*Rhynchophorus ferrugineus*) or stick and leaf insects and locusts of various kinds (e.g. *Graeffea* sp. and *Tettigoniidae* long-haired grasshoppers). Cf. R. Child, *Coconuts* (London, 1964), pp. 104 ff. George Forster adds that the coconuts grew on the hills 'where we had never seen them in other islands', *Voyage*, II, 200.

[3] The coast in question is steep-to and difficult of access, though there are several reasonable anchorages. Strong streams and races are found in the channel between Aoba and Maewo and also along the north coast of the island. Cf. *Pacific Islands Pilot*, II (6th ed., 1932), p. 190.

the Glass to be blacked as far as the breast; they had something white on their heads & the greater part of them were nacked, except a kind of *subligaculum*,[1] one man had a cloth over one Shoulder, which came under the other arm in form of a Scarf & then round his thighs, it seemed to be of a dirty white, with a reddish border; these people were armed with bows & long arrows. They seemed all to be of a brown complexion.[2] The men in the Canoes came pretty near & talked a good deal, but would not come on board. We observed in several places reeds stuck in rows like hurdles between the rocks, probably in order to catch fish by this method. The North-East point of the *Isle of Lepers* is lower than the body of the Isle, & near the point is a bite which has to westward a bluff rocky point, it seemed to form a tolerable harbour, but we were not near enough to judge of its depth.[3] We took a trip to the Isle of *Aurora*[4] & saw when we were near it, all along a fine beach & the most luxuriant Vegetation, especially numberless climbers running up the highest Trees & forming various green Obelisks & Pyramids, & Garlands from one Tree to another. We could by the Glass observe a fine plantation hedged in on a Sloping Side of a hill, near a small hut. A Cascade was seen a little more to the SE. We then put about again. About noon we were about mid-channel between the two Isles. When we came thus far, that the force of the wind was no more broken by the *Isle of Aurora*,[5] we were thrown vastly to leeward; & thus we find that not the long trips are the most advantageous: the short ones under the lee of the high land would have brought us farther in less time. The Thermometer 74½, in my Cabin 77°.

*July ye 20th* ☿ We were near the Isle of *Lepres* at about 1 o'clock & put about again near *Aurora* I. something past 2 o'clock, for there is only about 4 or 5 miles from the one to the other.[6] We put about again & we now could fairly weather the point of the *Isle of Lepers*.

[1] A reference to the penis wrapper, the national costume of the male pre-Christian New Hebrideans, worn with a band of dyed coconut matting.

[2] The people of the north end of Aoba are much lighter skinned than the generality of New Hebrideans. Current evidence would suggest a major Micronesian or Polynesian influence of late date.

[3] Apparently Lolowai Bay, 15° 17′ S, 167° 57′ E, perhaps the best anchorage on the island.

[4] Maewo or Aurora, 15° to 15° 30′ S, 168° 09′ E, 30 miles long by 3 miles wide, rising to 2000 feet. The island is thinly inhabited by people of predominantly Papuan stock.

[5] According to the *Pacific Islands Pilot*, II, p. 189, though the water here is smooth in fine weather, strong puffs come off at an acute angle from the land.

[6] It is in fact seven miles.

When we were going about from *Aurora I.* 3 Canoes came off, but seeing us leaving their shore, they again paddled in Shore. We soon put about again & reached the Shores of *Aurora I.*, where we saw another Cascade[1] & on the beach 8 or 9 Natives, remarkably black; & a Canoe hauled upon the beach. The shores steep & bold, about 60 fathom soundings. The I. of *Whitsuntide*[2] is much lower on its NE. Point than this of *Aurora* on its SW. point, & the S. Eastermost part of the *I. of Lepers* is likewise of a gentler slope than the Westermost Side. We went about, again before 6 o'clock. We continued to stand on & off all night & in the morning. We saw *I. de Pentecote* & even a little of the Land behind it to the South, which looked very high.[3] All the N. Ends of these Isles are low & the Southern ones high. The passage between *Aurore* & *Pentecote* is in about 15°. 20′ S. whereas according to M de *Bougainville's* Map it is exactly in 16°. S. Lat.[4] The Extent of *Aurora* is about 11 Leagues length,[5] but *Pentecôte* seems to be still longer. In the Straights between *Pentecôte* & *Aurore* the wind & Current set us so much to leeward, that we gained very little by our tacks.[6] When we came under *Aurora* again, we made two short trips & came very near its point. *Aurora* has a few Inhabitants & a few plantations on the slope of the hill, but *Pentecôte* is all over planted on it Northermost End.[7] The Thermometer at 74°, in my Cabin 74°. At noon we were in the middle between the 3 Isles of *Lepers*, *Aurora*, & *Whitsuntide* & in 15° 27′ Latitude. The Gap between *Aurora* & *Whitsuntide* is about 4 miles.

*July ye 21st* ♃ The Isle of Whitsuntide has on it Westside by no

[1] In fact a double waterfall about a mile inland from Lakarere on the north-western end of the island in 15° 10′ S, 168° 10′ E.

[2] Pentecost or Raga, a densely wooded, well-watered, well-populated island, dominated by a mountain chain rising to 3065 feet.

[3] Ambrym, 24 miles from east to west and 16 miles from north to south, in 16° 06′ S, 168° 09′ E (North Point), a very mountainous island with an enormous volcanic complex in the centre rising to 4380 feet (Mt. Marum) and a smaller peak, Mt. Tuyio, near the northern end. George adds: 'Later in the day we discovered land to the Westward, which proved to be the south western most land seen by M. de Bougainville. We advanced towards it, overjoyed with the variety of new islands which presented themselves to our view. Having reached the NW end of the former island on which we suspected a volcano, we were convinced of its existence, by columns of white smoke, which rolled up with great violence from the summit of an inland mountain.'

[4] About 15° 23′ S. This is Patteson Passage. Cf. Cook, *Journals*, II, 458, on Bougainville's reckonings. Bougainville's chart (pl. 10) in the French edition is more accurate.

[5] George gives the dimensions of Maewo (Aurora) as twelve leagues 'but not above five miles broad in any part', *Voyage*, II, 202. Maewo is in fact thirty miles long by six miles wide, Pentecost 34 miles long. Cook, it seems, had little time to revise or enter his distances during this tricky navigation. See *Journals*, II, 458–9.

[6] Southeast winds give rise to a heavy swell in Patteson Passage.

[7] As Forster notes, Maewo is thinly peopled compared with Raga.

means such a sinuosity as Mr de Bougainville's Map represents, but it has on the contrary a bluff point projecting to the West,[1] & then all the following points & its whole Coast does edge away to the SSE. or thereabouts. We observed about noon the Land to the SW of *Whitsuntide* Island; it is very high & perfectly divided from the just mentioned Isle, there runs a low point a long way to the S.E. from it.[2] To the West from this Land, we observed two hummocks: but from the Mast head Land was seen in 5 different places, which at Sunset extended to W.bS.[3] In the Isle of *Whitsuntide* we saw in the Evening fires to the very top of the hills, & as we saw so many cultivated Lands & but few & bad Canoes, I think I may conclude from thence, that the Natives chiefly live upon Vegetables, & depend not so much upon Fishing, as in the *Society Isles*, where the Natives attend to fishing with a patience quite peculiar; but it must likewise be mentioned that the fine reefs including their Isles give them the finest opportunity of fishing, to which we may add the vicinity of some flatt Isles, where they resort to for fishings sake. The Land before us is all bold, without reefs & no low Islands in the neighbourhood, which is certainly against it, & must deprive them of the best opportunities of getting fish.[4] At noon we saw a Landbird fly very high near the Ship. I took the same for a Parrot. The day next will discover more.

We tacked several times during night, & in the morning saw a free & open Passage between *Whitsuntide* & the Land next to it of about 5 or 6 miles breadth.[5] *Mr de Bougainville* doubted whether it was a Passage & however laid it down in the Chart as one. We observed on some hills of the new Land a Haze, probably from Clouds, which was by some people construed into Smoke from a Volcano:[6] This however is true, we saw every

[1] The bluff referred to would seem to have been Lifu Point, 570 ft high, followed by Whale Point, Casuarina Point, Truchy Point and Fan-mara-mara Point to the south.

[2] The reference is to Selwyn Strait, 5½ miles wide. The 'point' is Southeast Point, an extension of the central range of the island, terminating in a bold, cliffy bluff 590 feet high.

[3] The 'two hummocks' would seem to have been Mt Tuyio (3280 ft) on the north side of the island and possibly Mt Marum (Bwe ma ope) (4380 ft). The land seen in five different places from the masthead all lay on the north coast of Ambrym which, as Forster notes, runs WbS. See also *Journals*, II, 459, n. 7.

[4] A sound observation. In general the New Hebrideans are not much given to fishing, particularly when compared with the Polynesians. The staple on Pentecost is *taro*, grown inland in irrigated plots.

[5] Selwyn Strait, between Ambrym and the south point of Pentecost. See n. 2 above.

[6] There are two major volcanoes on Ambrym, Mt Benbow, 3720 feet, and Mt Marum, 4380 feet, the latter more active than the former but usually covered with cloud.

where on the land Smoke arising from the Fires the Natives made to dress their victuals by, this Smoke had a blue appearance, & the Haze on the hill was more grey, which leaves the subject of the Volcano's on this land still dubious, till better proofs are alleged for their existence.[1]

We saw Land to the South[2] distinct from the new Isle, edging away to the NW. & we soon found that it was quite divided from the New Isle, which probably is *Quiros's* St *Raymunda.*[3] This latter is high on its Northermost point & gradually growes lower towards the South. The next new Land is low on the Southermost point & seems to increase in heighth to the North.[4] A little while after there appeared an Isle[5] in the passage between the two new Lands, & yet a little after another appeared[6] bearing with its Northermost point, when it opened with the Southermost point of the first new Land S77°E. This new Isle had a high peak like a Volcano, capt with clouds. The first new Isle,[7] whereon we suspected in the morning to see two Volcanoes, of which I then doubted, has certainly one, for when we came more to the South of its Southermost bluff point & could see the Windward side of the Isle, I observed plainly very white columns of Smoke roll out with great velocity & Strength out of the Summit of one of the Inland mountains. The windward Side is very sloping & bears a fine appearance & to judge by the numerous fires strewed over the Isle, it is very populous. The great Land a head, which I suspect to be *Manicolo*[8] is on this S.E. point, pretty gently rising, full of Coconut Trees, & has a fine beach. Saw several flying Fish. The Thermometer 75°, in my Cabin 75°.

[1] One of the people 'construing' volcanoes on Ambrym was Wales. See *Journals*, II, 849. The scientific gentlemen vied actively now to cast doubt on each others' opinions.

[2] Paama in 16° 25′ S–16° 31′ S, 168° 15′ E, 1490 ft on the north end, 1030 ft on the south.

[3] Forster is well out; Quirós' St Raymunda was Sakau, a small island lying off the eastern tip of Cape Quiros, Espiritu Santo. See p. 559, n. 6 above.

[4] Epi, 16° 42′ S, 168° 15′ E, a mountainous island rising between 2–3,000 feet. The southernmost point visible to Forster here is about 1200 feet, the land increasing northwards to Mt Lele Kera Vena, 2300 feet.

[5] Lopevi, 16° 30′ S, 168° 21′ E, a beautifully symmetrical occasionally active volcano cone rising to a height of 4755 feet.

[6] Forster repeats himself. The reference is again to Lopevi. One may suspect that the clouds shifted in the interim.

[7] I.e. Ambrym. The reference is to Mt Benbow to the East (3720 ft) and Marum to the west (4380 ft) surrounded by a great ash plain. There is a third peak (1190 ft) on the eastern end of the island, last active in 1886. The peak referred to here is clearly Mt Marum.

[8] Malekula. The reference is to that part of the coast lying between Cape Doucere, 16° 28′ S, 167° 50′ E, and Lamap Point, at the eastern entrance to Port Sandwich.

July ye 22^d ♀ We were at noon close in shore on *Manicolo;* we saw numbers of people wading into the water to their waist, having Clubs in their hands, & waving green boughs in sign that we should come ashore. One had a bow & arrows, & one a Spear. Some open huts were observed close in shore. But we put about against their Expectation. However we put about several times & at last sent two boats into a bay we observed, & as the anchorage seemed good, the Ship followed into the bay. In the mean time the whole beach on the South entrance of the bay was lined with people, & some few came off in boats, but would not come near us; Several a shore & in the boats presented green bows of plants especially the *Croton variegatum*[1] & *Dracæna terminalis* Linn: & waved with them towards us: nevertheless the greater part of the people were armed with bows & arrows, & some few with Spears. They came at last near the Ship & got a few pieces of Otahaitee cloth which they eagerly accepted, & afterwards they gave in exchange some of their blunt arrows, pointed with wood only & a little after they even parted with such arrows as were pointed with bones, some of them were daubed with a black stuff, for which reason we suspected them to be poisoned, & wounded a young dog in the leg with it in order to see, what effect it might take.[2] The anchor was here dropped in a fine sheltered bay, open to the north only.[3] We did nothing understand of the language, which seemed to be harsher than any we had hitherto heard; it has a great many *r*'s in its pronunciation. The people are slender, but finely proportioned, very black, with crisp woolly hair, all naked & have only a bag for the genitals, but the Scrotum is free. The have bracelets about their wrists of Shells & pieces of wood.[4] Some had a kind of club, & a few had a cap of mat on their heads.[5] When it grew dark, they all retired ashore & had there a good many fires. About 7 o'clock all the Canoes came off & wanted to trade for arrows & trifles, but went off a little while after, when it was ordered none should trade with them, in order to get rid

[1] *Cadiaeum variegatum* (L.) Bl., much used in these islands in connexion with mortuary and propitiatory rites.

[2] See p. 567, n. 3 below.

[3] Port Sandwich, 16° 26′ S, 167° 46′ E, probably the best harbour in the New Hebrides, 5 cables (1000 yards wide) between the reef, protected from all winds and heavily bushed to the water's edge so that, as Forster says, the villages do not appear.

[4] Worn to protect the wrist from the action of the bow string. George's remarks on the language are very apposite here.

[5] George expands this first description in *Voyage*, II, 204–6.

of them the sooner. The Evening was fine & the moon shone bright. They beat their drums[1] & sung Songs & danced ashore, allmost during all night. In the morning early their Canoes came off & began to trade: four or five of the people came on board & were as friendly & easy as possible & climbed like cats up the Shrouds. When they came down again the Capt took them into the Cabin & gave them presents of Medals & some red bays. They wanted to have allmost every thing they saw, but were easily satisfied at the least refusal. They have perforated Ears, & likewise the Cartilage of the Nose is bored & they put either a Stick or two Spar or Alabaster-Stones, which are tied together, into the Hole. I got many words of their language & two were drawn by Mr Hodges:[2] but on a sudden the first Lieut came in & mentioned, that one of the Natives being refused to be admitted into the boat, had pointed his bow with an Arrow at the Sailor in the boat alongside the Ship. The Capt immediately ran upon deck & one of our Indians jumped overboard through the Quarter-gallery window to hinder the fellow from shooting our sailor, which another of the Natives was likewise doing to prevent mischief, but the Fellow got rid of his Companion, when just the Capt appeared on deck & pointed a gun at him, but the fellow coolly pointed the Arrow at the Capt & then he got a charge of small shot into his head, he clapt immediately his hand to the head, but immediately pointed the Arrow again at the Capt, when the 3^d Lieut gave him a full charge of small shot into his Face, which caused him to lay aside his shooting Scheme, & he paddled astern as fast as possible, then another fired an Arrow from the Starboard side of the Ship at the Capt, which went into the Mizen Shrouds & dropt into the Sea & was afterwards picked up: but a bullet was sent after him for his too great officiousness, however he came off unhurt; all the Natives flew in Shore but only gently, which motion was vastly accelerated by the discharge of a large Gun over their heads, among the Trees of the Shore: & then all made off without

[1] Slit upright ancestral drums, *na-mbe*, raised to commemorate the dead. The Malekulans have a vast number of songs which they sing in a high pitched voice. See J. Layard, *Stone Men of Malekula* (London, 1942), p. 313.

[2] One of these drawings was engraved by J. Caldwall for Cook's *Voyage* (pl. XLVII) and drew a critical comment from George: 'It is very characteristic of the nation; but we must lament, that a defect in the drawing, has made it necessary to infringe the *costume*, and to throw a drapery over the shoulder, though these people have no kind of cloathing', *Voyage*, II, 209–10. One of Hodge's red chalk drawings is reproduced by Beaglehole, *Journals*, II, fig. 71a.

Exception & their Drums began to beat, by way of allarming Signal.[1] We went then peaceably to breakfast. During which time some Canoes of Natives came off again; we beckoned them & waved a branch of the *Dracæna terminalis.* They came nearer & rowed round the Ship & at last nearer & nearer. The Capt ordered two boats to be manned & armed with Marines. A great number of people went ashore, in order to cut & saw some wood. We landed without opposition in an immense croud of people, who behaved very friendly, & brought a middling pig, as a kind of Expiation for the illbehaviour of their Country man & in order to make peace.[2]

All was soon settled; we wanted wood, they shewed us some trees, which we sawed & cut; the Marines drew up on the Shore, we drew a line for the Natives, which they should not transgress & they complied. There were however immense Numbers of them, all armed with bows ready strung & Arrows, some of which were in Quivers, supposed to be poisoned,[3] for when we bought some, which had bone points smeared with a black Substance, they would not advise us to try the points against our fingers & gave by signs to understand, that with the common Arrows, one might be shot through the Arm without dying, but a little hurt caused by the other kind was lethal, & therefore in a friendly manner held our hands back. They would not part with their bows, & Spears & Clubs, & in regard to poisonous arrows, they parted difficultly with. None of their Arm-Ornaments or bracelets, Hogs-Tusks[4] & wooden ruffles on the wrists could be bought. They would us not allow to go into the woods.[5] Their women came at a distance

[1] Cf. *Journals*, II, 461 and *Voyage*, II, 210–11. Cook wrote that this incident 'put all to confusion but in the end I believe turn'd out to our advantage'.

[2] *In margin:* Their chief gave away his bow & arrows & came unarmed up to Capt Cook to shew us their open friendly disposition – v, f. 86.

[3] Some varieties of Malekulan arrows were indeed 'poisoned', apparently with vegetable substances, and painted to distinguish them. The poisoned arrows of Santa Cruz by contrast were commonly infected with tetanus spores and were, of course, invariably fatal. George (II, p. 213) says all these arrows were made of reeds 2 feet long and were provided with a point about 12 inches to 15 inches long, consisting of a polished jetty black wood, like ebony, but excessively brittle, and were pointed with a bit of bone, 2–3 inches long. The point of the bone was very sharp and smeared with a black resinous substance. Layard, 1942, p. 214 records poisoned human bone tips (*wuh-na-ta-mat*).

[4] The discarded tusks of circle-tusked pigs, sacrificed in great 'feasts' or *maki* rites, held to mark the progression of the men of a particular clan from a lower to a higher rank in the graded society.

[5] George and Sparrman, however, advanced unnoticed 'about twenty yards' into the woods and got two new plants. George's report (II, pp. 213–19) of this landing supplements his father's account with much useful information on weapons and tells us much about the Forsters' considerable success in gaining linguistic information from the islanders, whom

& were the most disagreable creatures I ever saw. Some had powdered their heads, hair & faces all over with the powder of Turmerick. Some carried their Children on their backs. The grown women had short pieces of cloth or rather Mats round their waists & half their thighs down;[1] but some young Girls were stark naked, & so were young boys. The Men had a string round their belly about the Navel, very strongly tied, or rather so as hardly any Man, not used to it, could bear, & their Scrotum was naked & the other part of the Genitals was wrapped in a cloth & fastened to the belt or String.[2] Some wore a Shell from a string round their Necks,[3] others had Bracelets of small pieces of Shell, black & white,[4] finely & closely worked, & round the left hand a kind of ruffle of light soft wood worked over with Straw to keep off the recoiling of the bow string: but with these ruffles, bracelets, Shells, beads of Shells, Stones to wear in the Noses, they never would part. Having stood on a sandy & hot beach, till 4 o'clock, we went on board again, having taken in some wood. The Thermometer at 78°, in my Cabin 78°.

July ye 23^d ♄ In the Afternoon I went ashore with the Capt for the Natives had stolen a buoy & we saw it by our Glasses ashore, & we got it as soon as the boat landed, but the strap was gone, & perhaps the Anchor rope cast off. We traded for some triffles, & went northwards towards the point where we saw some houses & an inclosure with plantains,[5] several breadfruit Trees etc. The houses were low, small, thatched hovels; round which we observed a good many hogs, small & great & a Hen. Further on to the point,[6] we saw all the 3 Isles & asked for their Names, which

they regarded as 'the most intelligent people we had ever met with in the South Seas', *Voyage*, II, 208. George's comment on Hodge's 'fine plate' of 'The Landing at Mallicolo' (Cook, *Voyage*, II, pl. LX) demonstrates his impartiality and concern for accuracy.

[1] A good observation. Ethnographers distinguish between two cultures on Malekula, the mat skirt people and the fringe skirt. Cf. A. B. Deacon, *Malekula, A Vanishing People in the New Hebrides* (London, 1934), pp. 10–13.

[2] The reference is to a narrow bark *belt*, wound six or seven times round the waist into which was tucked the end of a banana leaf penis wrapper.

[3] A piece of turtle shell in the shape of a gorget.

[4] So-called shell 'money', drilled and ground circular and strung.

[5] '...I prevaild on one man to let me see them, they suffered Mr F. to go with me but were unwilling any more should follow', Cook, *Journals*, II, 463. This adds to the evidence that Forster, a not unimposing figure or character, was certainly seen to have some standing among the European visitors by the islanders of the South Seas. His language researches on Malekula doubtless added to his authority. The co-operation with Cook here seems to have been excellent. See also Sparrman, *Voyage around the world*, p. 146 for more details on this visit.

[6] Lamap point. This account is best read in conjunction with Cook, *Journals*, II, 463–4.

we very easily got from the Natives, the Volcano Isle being called *Ambrrÿm;*[1] the Peak Isle *Pā-oòm,*[2] & the southermost *Apèe.* We embarked again & went to the bottom of the harbour, where we found a good many Mangroves, but no Water & lastly we returned on board,[3] tired with heat & weariness & had collected but a few plants. We found the edge of the curiosity of the Natives was taken off, & they were now it seems convinced, we meant to do them no harm at all, & they therefore dispersed again & went to their remoter habitations,[4] for we met in proportion with but few Inhabitants in the Afternoon. In one place we passed by in the boat & found the people dancing at the beating of the Drum, by their Fires. Next morning we unmoored, & hove the Anchor & set Sail, but were becalmed & obliged to be towed by our boats, & made but very little way.[5] In the mean time many Canoes with Natives came off & sold their bows, Arrows, & Clubs for pieces of old rags & other trifles.[6] The number of boats never exceding 14.

Their Canoes made several trips ashore & brought always new arrows & bows off. The night before, our people caught in the harbour a large red Fish[7] of the *Sea-Bream-kind* (probably the

[1] This is an error. There was no general native name for any of these islands in Cook's day. According to local legend six men from Fonah on Ambrym on a visit to Port Sandwich gave Cook a pig and a yam saying *Ama rem* – 'Your yam' – hence Ambrym, 'the name to be' of the island. Cf. W. F. Paton, 'The Tale about Ama rem (Your Yam)' in *The Language and Life of Ambrym; an Island in the New Hebrides* (Sydney, South Pacific Commission, 1956), p. 3.

[2] In fact Lopevi, not the modern Paama. George (II, p. 236) adds: 'Pa-oom, the high peak to the south of it, is of an inconsiderable size, but we were dubious whether the land which we saw before, or to the westward of it [i.e. Paama], and which was of moderate height, is connected with it or not'. George gives Lopevi in 16° 25′ S; it is in fact in 16° 30′ S.

[3] The head of Port Sandwich is divided into two long narrow coves with extensive mudbanks. There are in fact two local streams – Erskine river and Murder Stream, the latter navigable for nearly half a mile, *Pacific Island Pilot*, II, 201.

[4] There are half a dozen local villages, all well hidden, and all on Ashuk Head, the northern end of the eastern side of the bay, but otherwise the population here is far from numerous.

[5] George's account (*Voyage*, II, 219–23) of this expedition, upon which he did not go, is a good example of his ability to cull from and expand upon his father's notes. His writing on the events at Malekula is lively and perceptive.

[6] Several items are listed from Malekula in the Oxford 'Catalogue of Curiosities' (including a bow, a club and a bundle of arrows, items 142–4) and the Göttingen collection lists a sling and a bag with stones from the same island. Sparrman (p. 143) notes: 'I have augmented the collection of the Royal Academy of Science with bows and arrows from this place'.

[7] This fish is not described but an account of its toxic effects is given in *Descr. Anim.*, p. 249. There is no drawing. See Beaglehole's note and his reference to G. Whitley's opinion that it was the Chinaman Fish, *Paradicithys veneratus* Whitely, or Red Bass, *Lutjanus coatesi* Whitley, *Journals*, II, 469, n. 5. A. Sparrman, however, notes: 'we caught several red fish

Sparus Erythrinus or *Pagrus*, for I could not examine the fish, as they were cut open & mangled before I got up). The Dogs had eaten the guts of these fish, & one pig likewise. There was caught besides them a Rockfish, an Indian Sucking Fish (*Echaneis Naucrates*)[1] & a Shark[2] of about 9 foot long. Several people ate of the Shark, the Rockfish & the Sucking-fish, but were not at all affected by them, but those that ate the red fish got the next Evening, night & morning the most violent Symptoms. I do not in the least doubt, but these red fish are the *Pargos* of *Quiros*, who he says poisoned his Ships-crew. Several had violent vomiting & purging, great heat in the face & head-ache; others felt a benumbing pain in their Arms, knees & Legs so that they could scarce stand or walk; the salival-glandes were somewhat swelled & separated so much saliva, that it ran out of the mouth; all had gripes in the intestines, & a painfull erection of the penis. The Dogs had the same Symptoms; but the hog died next night after.[3]

*July ye 24th* ☉ In the Afternoon the breeze freshened & we stood out between *Mallicollo* & *Ambrrym*.[4] About 6 o'clock we saw off the South East point of *Mallicollo* 4 or 5 little Isles[5] in a kind of

(*Sparus erythr*. L.?) the poisonous paragus (pargos) of Quiros...' Sparrman, p. 147), which suggests either Lut red bass *Lutjanus coatesi* Whitley or, more certainly, the red snapper *Lutjanus Bohar* Forksal. Cf. Kelly, I, 233 and particularly A. H. Banner, 'Fish poisoning in the Tropical Pacific', *South Pacific Bull.*, XI, No. 4 (1961), 18–25 and Hawaii Marine Laboratory, 'Poison Fish Projects Report', ibid., XIV, No. 2 (1964), 51–4. Sparrman (p. 147) further suggests that the fish were made 'poisonous by consuming without harm to themselves, the poisonous mangrove fruit (*Phizorphora manglae*)', but modern research suggests that the true cause of *ciguatara* type fish poisoning is the ingestion of fine algae by herbivorous fish which are then eaten by larger carnivorous fish capable of storing the toxin. The toxin concerned is said to have a potency roughly comparable to the venom of rattlesnakes.

[1] A species of Remora (Echeneidae) mentioned but not described in *Descr. Anim.*, pp. 250 and 257. There is no drawing. See also p. 593, n. 1 below.

[2] *Squalus carcharias* of *Descr. Anim.*, p. 250 (name only).

[3] From Forster we get the best account of the progress, treatment and symptoms of this fish poisoning. George (*Voyage*, II, 237–8 and 244–5) drew extensively on his father's notes. See also *Journals*, II, 469–70, n. 2. Patten dined with Cook on this day and 'by that means escaped the fate of his messmates'. He was however free to treat them!

[4] Cook (*Journals*, II, 464–8) and George Forster (*Voyage*, II, 225–36) here brought together their summary of ethnographical and other findings on Malekula. Forster, Cook writes, collected 'about Eighty Words' of which 'hardly one bears any affinity to the language spoke at any other island or place I had ever been at'. George's summary is, of course, the more 'philosophical' of the two with full documentation on the possible origin of these Melanesian people who struck all the observers as 'a race totally distinct' from the other islanders of the Pacific. There was much discussion of this in the *Resolution*. Forster senior seems to have had an important part in the writing up of George's excellent ethnological account. See also *Observations*, p. 267, Wales, *Journals*, II, 849–51 and Beaglehole's annotations, ibid, 465–8 which it is here superfluous to supplement. Forster senior wove his observations on Malekula into later parts of the New Hebridean ethnographical exploration.

[5] Sakau, Kuliviu, Ko i vu, Wulei, a group of low islets on extensive coral reefs, apparently named by Wales the Maskelyne Islands. See *Journals*, II, 468, n. 3.

bay. The day when we went into harbour, there had been seen 3 peaks to leeward of *Apèe*. The next morning we saw them & several Lands more. The three Peaks formed one Isle.[1] We stood for it & saw several Natives on its shore, similar to those on *Mallicollo*, who had likewise bows and Arrows. There was a very long reef running out from its South point, with a couple of rocks on it.[2] Beyond this Isle a peak was seen to the SE.[3] & beyond them 3 other hummocks.[4] Between this 3 peaked Isle & *Apee* appeared likewise 3 Isles[5] & here & there small Lands between them.[6] We put about at noon & stood for the greatest of these Isles.[7] The Thermometer at 76°, in my Cabin 78°.

*July ye 25th* ☽ The greater part of our poisoned patients recover, but slowly: those that took Salts are pretty well, & also those are more easy, who took a Diaphoretic. The Dogs are still very ill & have violent reachings: the sound Dogs eating what has been thrown up by the sick Dogs, fall likewise sick. We saw several Booby's & a couple of Terns; the day before some Booby's had been seen. During night we tacked, & were at daybreak off the Southermost of this groupe of rocks,[8] & went towards the South more or less West, for the Land which is seen to the South.[9] We passed to

[1] I.e. Maunga, 2171 feet; and two other peaks 1504 and 1803 feet in height on the island of Emai.

[2] Pula Iwa or Cook Reef, a submerged atoll 2½ miles to the west of Emai, in 17° 03′ S, 168° 16′ E. The lagoon proper is about 7 feet deep. As Forster notes, a ten fathom spit projects nearly half a mile on the south side.

[3] Makura in 17° 0′ S, 168° 26′ E, 979 feet in height.

[4] Mataso or Two Hills, 17° 15′ S, 168° 26′ E, consisting of two peaks, the northern one 1643 feet and the southern 465 feet in height, separated by a low connecting spit not visible from a distance so that, as Forster says, it appears as two islands. The third 'hummock' is clearly Wot or Monument Rock, 17° 16′ S, 168° 28′ E, a massive inaccessible volcanic plug, rising precipitously to a height of 379 feet.

[5] Iwose, 16° 57′ S, 168° 35′ E, 1076 feet high; Tongariki, 17° S, 168° 38′ E, 1687 feet high, the second largest of the Shepherd Islands; and Tongoa, 16° 54′ S, 168° 33′ E, the largest of the group.

[6] Amora rocks, 112 feet; Valca, 352 feet; and Buninga, 723 feet.

[7] Cf. *Journals*, II, 469 and *Voyage*, II, 238–9. They now stood for the Shepherd islands off the south-east of Epi.

[8] Amora rocks, off Buninga.

[9] Off the Shepherd islands they were temporarily becalmed 'left to the Mercy of the Currants' (*Journals*, II, 470). George Forster makes more of this incident on which, surprisingly, his father is stoically silent: '. . . the darkness of the night, and several broken rocks close to us on all sides, rendered our situation extremely critical. The navigator, who means to explore new islands, and give an accurate account of their position, is often in danger of losing his ship. It is impossible for him to form a just conception of the coast, without approaching close to it; but he must necessarily be exposed to the dangers of a sudden storm, a sunken rock or a swift current, which are sufficient, in a few moments, to destroy all his hopes of glory. Prudence and caution are very necessary in the conduct of every great enterprize; but it seems, that in a voyage of discovery, as in every undertaking of consequence, a certain degree of rashness, and reliance on good fortune, become the principal roads to fame, by being crowned with great and undeserved success',

leeward of a singular rock, which was all striated in an irregular & broken manner, a few plants grew on it, & we saw some Booby's & Terns.[1] We saw a Sailing Canoe standing from the SW. for the Isle with 3 Peaks, under which we were the day before. The Thermometer at 77°, in my Cabin 79°.

July ye 26th ♂ Out Patients recover slowly, have still gripes & pains in their limbs, which are extremely heavy & weak; they find themselves better in the cold & painfull in bed & when warm: slept very little, have still a giddiness & stupidity in the head: of two that were worst, one had a continual secretion of Saliva as if he had taken Mercury, the other looses the skin from the thighs, Legs & Arms: the Dogs are still bad & groan very hard, all are heavy & drowsy, weak in their limbs & some are violently reaching. A little Parrokeet of Otāhāitee, that had eaten some Fish died of it today. Diaphoretics I believe will do the best to expell the virulent matter out of the bódy.

We came in the Afternoon pretty close to the new group of Isles & were willing to go to the windward of the Eastermost Isle,[2] but the wind fell & we were becalmed & drifted to leeward: at 10 o'clock we were very near the West-Isle[3] but however we fell clear of it. Next morning we were to the NW of the same Isle & made Sail, when a little breeze sprung up. In the Evening we had several large Boobies about the Ship. We now ran between the two Isles & opened a third[4] all lying north before a more extensive fine Isle. The small ones are steep & high, especially the two outermost ones.[5] The large Isle is very gently sloping & one of the finest Isles we have hitherto seen, woods & clear ground

Voyage, II, 239–40. Was J. R. Forster looking over his son's shoulder as he wrote this? Certainly George gave Cook, if it was to Cook he was alluding, a much more favourable credit for more considered navigation in his essay 'Cook der Entdecker' (1787). Wales (*Remarks*, p. 71) sprang to Cook's defence.

[1] Qat or Wat, Monument Rock, in 17° 16′ S, 168° 28′ E, 397 feet high, 1½ miles eastward of the southern point of Mataso, Cook's Two Hills.

[2] Emau or Cook's Montagu, an extinct volcanic island, 1493 feet high, 17° 28′ S, 168° 30′ E. See Beaglehole's note for the confusion concerning Cook's naming of Montagu and Hinchinbrook islands, *Journals*, II, 472, n. 2 and 509, n. 7.

[3] Which was Nguna or Cook's Hinchinbrook, 17° 27′ S, 168° 21′ E, 2013 feet high. George Forster (*Voyage*, II, 241–2) gives a somewhat heightened account of 'our situation this night' (Monday 25 July) as they were drifting towards Nguna, and remained 'in the most dreadful suspense till near ten o'clock' when at last 'we fortunately drifted clear of the point at a short distance'.

[4] Pele, a small island 662 feet high, a quarter of a mile off the eastern end of Nguna. The narrow channel between the two islands is blocked off to the north by an extensive coral reef.

[5] I.e. Emau and Nguna.

being mixed in the most romantic manner.[1] We passed the Eastermost high Isle & saw a good many Inhabitants running along shore with their bows, arrows & Darts. We saw huts & plantains, Coconuts, & some of their boats on the beach. The Thermometer at 79°, in my Cabin 80°.

*July ye 27th* ☿ Just behind the Westermost Isle[2] is on the larger Isle a bay,[3] but I believe it has no other Entrance than from the West, for the East Entry has several small Isles & reefs & breakers, however there may be a passage for all that, but we were a good way off.[4] Our poisoned patients are allmost all in the same condition, & if the pains are less, their weakness increases, so that they can scarcely drag their legs along. Some get small pimples & heat in their hands. The dogs are all ill & groan pitifully; drink much, pant & seem to be full of pain. Saw some Boobies & flying Fish. We stood all night on to the SE & SEb.S.½E & courses thereabouts. In the Evening a good many Boobies came near the Ship. The Thermometer at 74, in my Cabin 74°. At daybreak at SSE. one Island was discovered, about 14 leagues distance.[5] We were then at about 8 o'clock in the morning at 15 Leagues from the Groupe of Isles we passed through about noon last day, bearing from N.72W. to N.87E. The wind gentle, the weather mild.[6]

*July ye 28th* ♃ We saw a Tropicbird: At noon the new Isle bears from South till 16° W. about 10 leagues distance. Our patients are better, but weak, & some pain is still returning upon them.[7] The Dogs are allmost recovered & begin to eat, but now & then they have still pains; & lay down groaning very hard. We observed,

[1] It was Efate or Cook's Sandwich Island. See *Journals*, II, 472–3. George wrote: 'We all agreed that this island was one of the finest we had hitherto seen in the new group, and seemed to be well situated for the purpose of an European settlement', *Voyage*, II, 243. This was not a bad prediction, since Efate later became the headquarters for trade in the New Hebrides Group, which it still is.

[2] I.e. Nguna.

[3] Undine Bay.

[4] The whole of the north coast of Efate is fronted by a shallow fringing reef. The eastern entry into Undine Bay is blocked by Rinali Reef, which is easily visible some distance off. The largest of the 'small Isles' referred to is Kakula, a low coralline sand bank just south of Pele.

[5] North Peak or Mt. Williams in the Sovu range on Erromanga rises to 2500 feet and is normally visible from a considerable distance, but appears detached.

[6] Cook was now determined to 'get to the South in order to find the Southern extremity of the Archipeloga' i.e. the New Hebrides. See *Journals*, II, 473.

[7] George records that some victims were crawling about the deck 'emaciated to mere shadows [and] we had not one lieutenant able to do duty; and as one of the mates, and several of the midshipmen were likewise ill, the watches were commanded by the gunner and other mates', *Voyage*, II, 244.

that those Dogs, who had eaten the raw Entrails or garbage of the fish, were the worst affected, & had more severe symptoms than those, who had eaten only of the boiled fish, or its skin, which was very though & thick. The dog, which had been stung for experiment's sake with a poisoned arrow, ate 28 hours afterward, of the garbage of the fish & was when he ate of it not yet in the least sick or anyways affected by the poisoned arrow, however it must be allowed, that the poison, which the Natives lay on very thick in the substance of a gum or Extract of some plant was nearly all gone off from the arrow employed in the Experiment, & we were very desirous of making the Experiment as soon as possible, therefore was the first arrow of the kind employed we got, & the next day we got enough better armed & covered with the thick Substance; but then the disease broke out among the Dogs, who had eaten the Entrails of the Fish, & we therefore have postponed all Experiments till all Dogs are better. The arrows are of reed, have an Ebony point, to which another point of bone is tied by coire in a very curious manner, this coire is painted red & green, & the bony-point is smeared to the thickness of the back of a knife with this substance. I cannot omit to mention, that the Shark we caught the same day, with the poisoned Fish, when examined, had a bony poisoned point sticking in his head, shot through his very skull.[1] The wound was quite healed & not the least mark on the outside left: to the bony point stuck still a part of the wooden point & the stuff with which they had been tied together, but both coire & wood were rotten; which in my opinion proves, that the fish are not affected by this poison, & that a Shark may be wounded in the very brains & however live & thrive well. This Shark was 9½ feet long.

The circumstance that the dogs, which had eaten the Garbage, were more violently affected by the poison, than those who had eaten the boiled meat, proved, if I am not mistaken, that the poison consists in the food or plants or fruits that had been eaten by the fish, & therefore this poison being still in the *primae viae* of the fish operated stronger than their flesh or meat; where the poisonous particles had been conducted by the chyle[2] & blood only. At about 6 the new Isle bears from S26°N to S3°E., the angle

[1] The Malekulans commonly fished with bows and arrows and were deadly shots. It was, however, normal to noose sharks from canoes rather than shoot them.

[2] The white milky fluid formed by the action of pancreatic juice and bile on chyme. The poison is alkaloid in nature. Cf. George, *Voyage*, II, 244–5.

being in all 29°. All night we had little wind, & in the morning neither very much; we stand now at 10 o'clock for it, but we lay to leeward of them. There is still another long tract of land seen more to windward:[1] which shows this cluster of Isles or Land to be considerable enough. The Thermometer at 71, in my Cabin 72½. Saw a whitish large bird at a distance, perhaps a Booby. Allmost a dead calm.

*July ye 29th* ♀ The calm continues. We are tossed about without steering. In the beforenoon a breeze comes on. The Thermometer at 71°, in my Cabin 72½.

*July ye 30th* ♄ Our patients are something better, but not quite, for now & then the pain returns & the weakness remains. The Dogs are all recovered. This afternoon at 3 o'clock a young Dog was taken & a wound was made in his thigh & some of the Stuff from the Arrow & likewise the green Substance were scraped off & put into the wound & then covered with a sticking plaster, in order to keep the supposed poison in the wound; at six o'clock the Dog was still well. We had been driven from the new Land[2] during the calm & being obliged to keep to windward. Since this morning we stood for it; at twelve o'clock at noon we were distant from it at least 12 leagues; at 6 o'clock in the Evening about 6 leagues. What had appeared as several Islands seemed not to join into one Isle:- The wind is fallen during the night & we drive again off from the Shore. The Thermometer at 71½, in my Cabin 73°.

*July ye 31st* ☉ The Dog who was operated yesterday with the pretended poison is as well as possible, eats & plays with the other dogs, & limps only a little on account of the wound. Another Dog, who had eaten of the poisoned fish & had been almost quite well, except a little weakness in the limbs, lay in a boat, which they filled with water in order to draw the chinks of it together, where the Cutter leaks, got wet & cold & lay in it several hours, which made him quite contracted & lame. The Gentlemen likewise complain, that their pains & stiffness of limbs return, when they get cold. Upon the whole, every evening the Symptoms of uneasiness, restlessness, pain & numbness or heaviness in the limbs return. Yesterday night & this morning another land was seen due South

[1] Apparently Traitors' Head, which consists of three remarkable hills, on the eastern side of Erromanga, separating Portenia and the so-called Cook's Bay. On the following day, as Forster notes, 'What had appeared as several Islands seemed now to join into one Isle'.

[2] Erromanga.

at a distance, which seemed to be of some extent.[1] The Land before us seems at this distance barren & has but few trees. We saw this morning a great smoke, which proves it to be inhabited. It seems to be an inchanted Isle, for we cannot come near it, hindered by calms & contrary wind. Calm all night & the most tantalizing Situation is ours; to be in Sight of Land & not be able to approach it in any shape; & though perhaps this land would not afford us any refreshments, no more than *Mallicollo* did, it is however agreable to have intercourse with human Creatures, & to see their manners, habitations, plantations, the plants & animals of the country & to hear & examine their language. The Thermometer at 74°, in my cabin 74½°.

Aug. ye 1st ☽ Still a calm, caught two Sharks, which were surrounded by Pilotfish & Suckingfish. The one had four Turtles of about 18 Inches length in his belly, as was therefore as much an Epicur as any of our Aldermen, & will be therefore highfed, which his rank smell sufficiently anounced; but the very moment he came on deck, not a bit of him was left; the Sailors being very desirous of having as much as possible of his flesh. Besides the Turtles the latter Shark had 2 large Cuttle-fish & the Feathers & Skeleton of a Booby in his belly: & though so well fed, he disdained not a piece of Saltpork, which sufficiently proves the insatiable voracity of this Animal. When he was hooked, we were afraid of loosing him & sent therefore some bullets from a Musket into his belly. The first caused him violently to bleed, & he plunged immediately into the depths, but came soon again up; the last killed him downright: & we hauled a noose over his fins & hoisted him by a tackle into the Ship. During all this calm a current has set us several leagues to the NW.[2] All night & towards morning we had a little gentle breeze, which set our Ship forwards towards the new Isle, we tacked once & then returned to our old course: We saw a rock lying off the peaked Saddle,[3] which had appeared so

[1] The island of Tanna, 25 miles to the south. There has been much error and confusion over the name and its spelling. Cf. J. Inglis, *In the New Hebrides*... (London, 1887), pp. 21–2 for the following very salutary remarks on this matter, and on the mistaken use of Ipare: inland. 'By the way, some people spell this word, Tana. This spelling would be correct if it were a Malay (i.e. a Polynesian word), where every syllable ends in a vowel. But in this case it is incorrect. It is a Papuan word, and as you hear it pronounced, the first syllable ends in a consonant; it is not pronounced Ta-na but Tan-na'. All modern Hebridean maps show Tanna. See p. 586, n. 4 below.

[2] There is often a strong westerly set with rough seas between all these islands, particularly during the SE trades season.

[3] The reference is to Goat Island, a precipitous islet, 200 feet high, covered with trees, lying five miles northeast of Traitors' Head. The peaked saddle or Traitors' Head

remarkable from far off & hope to see & examine this Land somewhat nearer, for as it is so far to the South, from the other Isles towards New-Zeeland, we shall perhaps find the Inhabitants to be of the same kind as those in N.Z: though, I must confess, it is in my opinion more probable, that they are of the same race, with those we have hitherto seen in *Mallicollo* & the adjacent Isles.[1]

(I have had the misfortune to hurt myself in the Marquesas by getting into a boat, this caused me the bowels when they were inflated with a flatulent stuff, which I had eaten, to make a rising in the groin: when I fell on the hill in *Otahaitee* on April ye 29th I felt in the same place more pain. A few days ago I had the misfortune to run with that weak part, in the dark, against the key of the door to the Master's cabin, which was open: but before yesterday I had the ill-luck to slip on the deck, when it had been washed, & though I did not fall, I got however a hurt by it, & since that time I feel a kind of uneasiness in the Groin, & the bowel stands a bit out, but may be shoved back at the least touch. I am afraid this will end with a rupture.)

We were this morning alarmed by a fire in the Stewarts-room, where near the Lamp a piece of *Otahaitee*-Cloth was left, which took fire, & raised a great Smoke. Every body was afraid, that the fire might be in the Sailroom under the Gunroom, but it was soon found & put out.[2] The Dog who was operated or inoculated with the pretended poison is still well, the wound is not inflamed & discharges fine pus & is in a fair way to be soon healed again. The Thermometer at 72° in my Cabin 74°.

Yesterday night 4 boobies were seen about the ship.

*Aug. ye 2^d^* ♂ The Land before us is high, wooded, but has glades, & even some plantations on the slope of the hills could be observed. The Coconut-Trees we can see look poor & are decaying & small, so that it seems the Climate is too cold for this plant;[3] for really the air is a good deal cooler in these western

constitutes the extreme end of the peninsula dividing Portenia from Cook's Bay. The penninsula itself decreases in height inland. See also p. 579 below.

[1] The reference to possible kinship between the Erromangans and Maori of New Zealand, i.e. to the possibility of a sharp boundary between the 'Melanesians' and 'Polynesians' is an interesting speculation, apparently based on climatic considerations. Erromanga in 19° S is perceptibly cooler than the northern islands, especially in the 'winter' season.

[2] Cook makes no mention of this fire but George (*Voyage*, II, 247–8) records their dreadful alarm, 'confusion and horror' and Sparrman, too, adds a similar note.

[3] The real problem probably was not so much coolness as a lack of water, this being the dry side of the island. See p. 560, n. 2 above. Whether the southern New Hebrides are really 'cooler' than islands in a similar latitude in Polynesia may be doubted.

climates, than in the more easterly Isles, though under the same parallel. However I wish to have an opportunity to search these new climates, for I am sure they must have new productions & different in many respects from those we have seen before: but these are *pia desideria!* We are to float on the water for ever, to have very few relaxation a shore & it is as if envy would have it so, that lands should be discovered, but none of its productions, because people think that if any man but they themselves makes discoveries, their reputation & fame would decrease in the same proportion, as that of others gets a little addition.

In the Afternoon saw a kind of harbour[1] on the W. side of the Isle, we went a little way in, & found 22 fathom fine Sand, afterwards 35 fathom no ground, then 24 coralrock & 27 fine Sand. There were small beaches in various places, & here & there plantations, chiefly of bananas, & several houses & inclosures made of reeds were observed. We saw about 30 natives running up & down a shore. They seemed black & armed with bows & arrows, & one man had two spears, their women had a kind of long petticoats made of leaves & straw hanging down to the half of the leg & deeper. They had much the appearance of the people in *Mallicollo*, the Men had the Genitals just so wrapped in, as the former. We soon saw another point & afterwards another bay,[2] for which we stood, but we were a breast of it, when it grew dark. A marine who was drawing water for the washing of the deck, leaned too hard upon the rail, which gave way & he fell over board; he could not swim, but the ship was brought to in an instant, several ropes were thrown over board, of one of which he got hold & the Sternladder was thrown over whereon a Man descended & helped him up, which was for the poor fellow a lucky escape.[3] In the Evening we saw a great many Smokes & fires

[1] Port Elizabeth on the north-west side of Erromanga. As a result of subsequent earth movements, the corresponding depth is now 14 fathoms, sand and coral, less than a cable off-shore. *P. I. Pilot*, II, 151.

[2] Dillons Bay, on the west side of the island, six miles south of Elizabeth Bay, named by the Irish adventurer Peter Dillon who discovered sandalwood here in 1825. The place is readily distinguishable by a deep gap in the hills and a wide river, Williams river, and was from 1845–1865 a major centre of the New Hebrides sandalwood trade. See J. W. Davidson, *Peter Dillon of Vanikoro: Chevalier of the South Seas* (Melbourne, 1975).

[3] George (*Voyage*, II, 250) records how the marine's 'comrades' conducted him immediately below, changed him and revived him with brandy. All this 'particular tenderness', we are told, was 'the result of an *esprit de corps*, to which sailors are at present utter strangers'. The unfortunate marine was William Wedgeborough, who had a propensity for drink and for falling overboard. He finally drowned at Christmas Sound, Tierra del Fuego on 22 December 1774.

ashore. The wind is fallen, & it would be unlucky for us, if the tide or current should set us in shore during night, as we are so near land. We stood with the head out, & had a calm during night & in the beforenoon. We are about 2 leagues off the land. We might as well have been all this time at an anchor & try to get wood & water in, of which we are in want: especially as the water got at *Anamocka* is all briny & not drinkable. The anchor was yesterday ordered to be held ready, but as soon as some officers shewed a wish to stay in the harbour, & said it seemed there might water & wood be gotten & perhaps the natives would exchange some yams & hogs, that very moment orders were given to stand out. The Thermometer at 77°, in my Cabin 79°.

Aug. ye 3d ☿ The calm continues, some few light airs set us gently into the yesterday's harbour. We hoist boats out, man & arm them. They were sent to sound, they found no ground but close in shore: & further on they found 20 fathom, 3 cables length from Shore, which might have given further off good anchorage, but the Capt was impatient,[1] ordered the Signal to be hoisted & a gun to be fired; so the pinnace came, & a faint breeze springing up, we stood out again at Sea, & shall perhaps drive in shore again, in a new calm. During night we went round the NW. point of the Isle & were near a rocky Isle, which lies off the Saddle-Peak. We observed some wood on [it] & as we seemed near it & as we were in want of wood the Capt ordered ye boats to be hoisted out, & sent one in shore, to look for a landing place, but the distance which we had thought to be trifling, was very great & then the Capt sent the other boat after in order to see whether there was any landing on it,[2] but we found such a surf & so dangerous rocks, that we were afraid of staving the boats & returned onboard. We saw a large bat flying among the trees on the Rocky-Isle. We observed fish on the rocky bottom & wanted to fish them with a line & hook, but they refused biting. When we were returning, we saw a Water-Snake on the top of the water, & took her up. We found it was the same which we found so plentifull last year in *Amsterdam* on the little Isle in *Maria Bay*: it is Dr *Linnæus's Anguis*

[1] The impatience was Forster's more than Cook's, who despatched Gilbert to sound for an anchorage in Elizabeth Bay but the ship drove past the northern point of the bay thus necessitating the pinnace's recall to assist with towing. See *Journals*, II, 476.

[2] 'The hopes of making some botanical acquisitions, engaged us to embark in one of these boats', *Voyage*, II, 251. The 'Isle' was Goat Island, a small, uninhabited, rocky, precipitous pinnacle 200 feet high. The 'Saddle-Peak' was the summit behind Traitors' Head seen on 1 August. See p. 576, n. 3 above.

laticaudatus, which upon examination had a loose Fang in its Jaw, & is therefore probably poisonous. When *M. de Bougainville* was in *New-Brittain* & Snakes were caught in a Seyne, one of which bit a Sailor, but by remedies the man was preserved, though some Symptoms of the poison did appear; perhaps it is this kind, which over all the South-Sea is very common: however I must confess the people in the Society-Isles did handle them freely, & said they could not hurt. The Specimen we found had 232 *Scuta abdominalia*, 2 Squamas before the Anus & 32 behind, which is somewhat different from Dr *Linnæus's* Specimen, which had 200 *Scuta abdominalia* & 50 *Squamas subcaudales.*[1]

*Aug. ye 4th* ♃ We stand in to a kind of bay, to leeward of the Saddle-Peak, & if there is any Anchorage, we shall probably drop our Anchor, for we want both wood & Water very much. We found a place sheltered from the wind, that is here most prevailing *viz.* SE.[2] The bottom black Sand, gradually decreasing from 35 to 20. 18. to 16 fathoms. The bay is very wide & capacious, more than 6 or 8 miles wide & about 4 or 5 miles deep.[3] On the East Side at its entrance is the steep remarkable Saddle-Peak; towards the bottom the hills are more sloping: Every part of it is cultivated between the bushes, with plantains & other things & we observed such partitions of reeds as we found at *Amsterdam* between the plantations. The shore was full of Natives, several came off swimming, for the people on this Isle seem not to have any boats,[4] but none did chuse to come near the Ship, but returned ashore, they cried & screamed aloud to us. The people seemed of the same kind as those in *Mallicollo*,[5] but one of the Men that came off swimming had red hair[6] & was fairer than the rest. Nothing is now more to be wished, but that we may get wood & water, that

[1] Forster drawing no. 170 as *Coluber laticaudatus*. See also p. 385, n. 1 above for a note on the nomenclature. Beaglehole (*Journals*, II, 477, n. 2) cites George's reference in *Voyage*, II, 251 and mentions that 'Linnaeus *Coluber laticaudatus* was a composite of two species, *Laticauda laticaudata* and *Laticauda colubrina* (Schneider); the specimen figured by Forster was the latter'. See also *Journals*, II, 558, n. 7 and 560, n. 2. New Hebrideans tend to give sea snakes a wide birth.

[2] A good observation. The misnamed Cook's Bay to the south is by contrast exposed to the SE and is in consequence unsuitable as an anchorage.

[3] The sand is brown rather than black. Portinia Bay – said by H. A. Robertson in *Erromanga the Martyr Isle* (London, 1902), p. 19, to be a corruption of a local name Potnuma but more likely of the name of an early sandalwood ship *Portenia* – is in fact 8 miles wide but only 2–3 miles deep. See *P. I. Pilot*, II, 152.

[4] Canoes here are in fact rare.

[5] I.e. they are markedly negroid in both appearance and culture, much more so than the Tannese or Efatese.

[6] Presumably bleached with burnt lime; the man may well have been a visitor from Tanna.

the Natives may be quiet & peaceable & be prevailed upon to sell us their hogs, plantains & Yams. I likewise wish to be able to get a good many new & curious plants. The Gentlemen who had been poisoned by eating the red Fish at *Mallicollo* are not yet free from new returns of Symptoms, several are still weak in their limbs, others have all their teeth lose & the Skin of their Gums & Palate is coming off.

The Dogs that were poisoned by eating of the Fish are all well except one, who lay in the boat sick, when it was wetted & lay half a day in water, is quite contracted & will eat nothing but is decaying.

The Dog which was inoculated for to try the poisoned arrows is as well as can be wished, eats, walks about, plays & the wound seems to heal: but however he eats little.

Two boats & the Captain in one of them went this morning in shore, in order to look for a good wooding & watering-place. They came near the shore under the Saddle-Peak, where there was no landing-place.[1] A great Number of Natives stood on the beach, & some came into the water & got some trifling presents of Medals, Otahaitee cloth etc. They followed the boats as they rowed along shore. There was a little projecting point, behind which there was a good landing place,[2] there the Captain went with the boats. He landed, gave some presents, & asked for water, which they brought in a Bamboo, & got a few Coconuts & one Yam, but when he went again into the boat, they took an oar away, but a Native took it from the Man who had it & threw it towards the boat in the water; then they got hold of the gangboard, & of two other oars & would not let them go. The Capt then wanted to shoot the Fellows with small Shot, that held the Gangboard, but the Flint was so bad on his & two other Muskets, that none would go off, at last two other Muskets went off & two men were killed,[3] they hove Spears, one of which wounded a Sailor[4] in the Cheek & wrist, they likewise flung stones and shot some arrows but none was wounded by them, the people in the Cutter had the same misfortune that several of their Muskets

[1] Apparently Port Narevin (Portnarevin) or Walter Bay, which lies northward of Traitors' Head in the SW part of Portina Bay. The outer edges of the reefs here are steep-to but there is a small boat cove in the SE corner of the bay, marked by a shoal rock.

[2] The actual landing place is a narrow, stony and steeply shelving, hence no doubt the press of the crowd on the boat.

[3] According to Sparrman (p. 149) *four*, and one European. Several people were wounded but only one man, a chief named Narom, was killed. Cf. Robertson, 1902, pp. 18–19 and *Journals*, II, 479, n. 7.

[4] Solomon Reading. See *Journals*, II, 878.

would not go off, but some however went off. The Natives began to run off, but came again on the point & threw Stones & fired Arrows, but several of them were wounded, that crawled off through the bushes on all four. At the first noise of the guns, we hoisted another boat out, & sent it armed to the Cap^{ts} assistance. We fired a Swivel over the heads of the natives & another large Gun to frighten those opposite the Ship.[1] The Capt came immediately off & the other boats having sounded & found regular soundings towards the Ship came likewise on board. Their Spears, of which we had three, were miserable blunt sticks. The arrow was bearded on one side, but had not hurt *Mr Gilbert*, though it struck his naked breast.[2] We hove the Anchor after breakfast, in order to go deeper into the bay to protect the watering-place, but the Capt was persuaded by the 1st Lieut. & the Master to go round the Saddle Peak into the other harbour, to eastward of it.[3] We tacked for that purpose all the morning, in order to clear the point but could not bring it about. The Thermometer 73½, in my Cabin 76.

Aug. ye 5th ♀ There was a strong current against us between the Isle

[1] It is related that a woman working in her garden lost a finger, shot clean off by a cannon ball. See Robertson, 1902, p. 19. Sparrman, however, records only one such missile, a four-pound ball, which fell short of the beach.

[2] This account of the 'affray' at Erromanga since it was gleaned mostly from Cook – the Forsters both remaining on board the *Resolution* – is close to the Captain's report (*Journals*, II, 477–9). The trouble came when George's account was published (*Voyage*, II, 253–8) and Wales (*Remarks*, pp. 71–9) took to it, reproducing it alongside the official narrative as one prime example of 'the Doctor's sole aim to misrepresent and depreciate and he is so eager to do both, that he is continually laying himself open to detection'. Concerning the actual landing, negotiations, attack and counter-attack there is in fact little material difference between Cook and George Forster. The latter included, however, some pertinent remarks on the unreliability of the flints for naval muskets; a sentence on the 'people' amusing themselves by firing at the Erromangans 'as often as their heads appeared' and George could not 'persuade' himself 'that these people had any hostile intentions in detaining our boat'. The 'levelling of a musket...provoked them to attack our crew' thus producing in turn an 'equally necessary....manoeuvre' and response from the Europeans. George answered Wales (*Reply*, p. 34), making the bold assertion that even Cook 'might suppress in writing the mention of such facts as were unfavourable to his own character, even tho' they could at most be construed into effects of unguarded heat'. Cook certainly played down unfavourable circumstances, including those involving his officers, people and 'gentlemen'. Had he not been so taciturn we might have more on 'Mr F's' behaviour! However Forster may well have been right in thinking that the Erromangans were anxious only to be rid of their 'ghostly guests'. The real source of the difficulty, however, appears to have been the convergence upon the scene of a great concourse of people not normally resident in the bay and of a natural anxiety on the part of the competing clans to monopolise the attentions of these strange newcomers. The resulting scuffle was inevitably interpreted as evidence of hostility and responded to accordingly.

[3] This is the only authority we have that Cook was influenced to leave Portinia (Potinia or Polenia) Bay by Cooper and Gilbert. Cook records that he found the anchorage 'indifferent' and seemingly incapable of supplying 'all our wants', *Journals*, II, 480.

& the rocky Islet, where we went yesterday for, till we were quite round the point, & discovered about 3 o'clock, the whole bay[1] clearly open before us, it was deep & seemed to have several creeks or coves, the Land surrounding it looked charmingly fertile & to the South of it, the hills had the most gentle slope for an immense extent, & were cultivated; in fine it was a most promissing Spot. When at once we discovered to the South opening beyond the S. point of the Isle, a Land which we had seen July ye 27th more than 8 days ago.[2] The sight of this new Isle makes us again forget, that we want water & wood, & we stand directly for it. At about 7 o'clock we had the S. point[3] of the Isle we left just a breast of us, & are probably 10 or 12 leagues off from the New Isle; & shall be near it by daybreak, if the breeze stands; or perhaps sooner. At 10 o'clock we saw a light or Fire[4] on our beam & another under the Studding-Sail-leach: which shews that the Land is nearer than we expect & that it has more extent, than we at first were aware of. The next morning perhaps will disclose more. We tacked in the night, & at daybreak we saw Land in several places, we had passed one low Isle,[5] which lay to the N. another was at 7 o'clock about East,[6] another NEb.E[7] & the Isle we stood for is a very large one, lies NW & SE. & has on its SE. side a Volcano at the end of a low range of hills: the Volcano itself is not very high;[8] we saw the Smoke coming out in columns of reddish Smoke, rising often like a Tree, just so as Pliny describes the same of the *Vesuvius;* we soon heard at each new quantity of Smoke a rolling in the Volcano like that of Thunder, & these Explosions often followed one another very closely. The Smoke is not allways like, sometimes whitish, sometimes of a reddish dirty grey, which latter circumstance happened, either when the hot ignited Ashes were thrown

[1] Cook's Bay, a broad, deep bight on the south side of Traitors' Head. The land here is low-lying and fertile and clothed in thick forest but is excessively malarious. Cook's river which empties into the bay is navigable for several miles.

[2] I.e. Tanna.

[3] Pilbarra point.

[4] The distant glow of the volcano on Tanna. See n. 8 below.

[5] Aniwa, a small, low island, 120–150 feet high in 19° 18′ S, 169° 35′ E, 13 miles ENE of the NE end of Tanna.

[6] Futuna, a precipitous, table-topped, non-malarious volcanic peak, 1931 feet high in 19° 31′ S, 170° 11′ E, inhabited, like Mele and Fila on Efate, by people of Polynesian extraction.

[7] This sighting is unidentifiable unless, perhaps, the reference is to Loanapakel, the elevated north-eastern promontory of Tanna, or the southern end of Erromanga which rises to 3500 feet. George omits it.

[8] Mount Yasur, a low volcanic peak, 600 feet high, which fairly dominates this side of the island. It lies about 2¼ miles westwards from the eastern extremity of the island, has two distinct craters and is constantly active.

up, or when the Ashes & Smoke were illuminated from the Crater by the Fire.[1] The whole Isle looks to be apparently limestone, which I judged from the whitish Cliffs towards the Sea.[2] The Volcano itself is of a reddish grey, & quite barren, as if it were formed by the Ashes & Pumice-Stones.[3] The rest of the Isle is well wooded, & fine Coconut-Trees[4] were observed on it, & so did we see a Canoe sailing along Shore, which shews, that the Isle is inhabited. Boats are now hoisted out to look for a harbour under this Volcano.[5] Two boats with Natives followed our boats. When our people had found a good Anchorage, black Sand for 4 to 7 fathom, they made the Signal for it, & the Ship stood in for the harbour.[6] We let go the Anchor in about 4 fathom water. A number of natives in boats came near us. A few of them gave us Coconuts & Yams, & got some presents for it. The number of their Canoes increased considerably & I counted one time 17 of them; about 3 of them were so large, that 20, 21 & 22 people were in them, the least Canoes had 2 & the larger 5 or 7 & even 10.[7] All had Spears, Clubs & Bows & Arrows. One old Fellow wanted to take the Meat out of the Net, which was towing a stern, but he desisted immediately when told not to do it; however one fellow shook his dart at us, & still another prepared his bow & arrows & pointed them at every one in the Ship. We a little after desired them to stand back & fired a large Gun towards the Shore, & all of them jumped overboard into the water, but we made Signs to them & they all immediately returned, however they kept off.[8]

[1] A good description. The peak is still as active as it was in Cook's time, erupting every few minutes from one or other of its several vents. The resultant ash is carried on the back of the SE trade wind as much as 10 miles from the crater and often smothers and weighs down all the vegetation in its path.

[2] Much of the coast at this point is elevated coral and steep-to, and generally devoid of suitable landings. See also the geological note p. 614 below.

[3] The peak is indeed built entirely of its own scoria and is prone to alterations in shape by accretion and erosion by wind and water. The crater itself is a quite awe-inspiring sight, several hundred feet deep and several hundred yards across and extremely precipitous right to the bottom, without a vestige of vegetation. See also p. 599, n. 7 below.

[4] This side of the island, the west side, is indeed well wooded and there are impressive stands of coconuts, particularly at Sulphur Bay.

[5] The entrance to Port Resolution is almost indistinguishable from the sea.

[6] '. . . a small snug bason' (*Voyage*, II, 261) called by Cook Port Resolution and by the Tannese Uea.

[7] The canoes of this district are larger than most New Hebridean canoes. The largest of those described here would nonetheless seem to have belonged to nearby Aniwa or Futuna or been used in voyaging to them.

[8] According to George (II, 263) 200 people leaped out of their canoes, except one friendly young man who remained standing in his canoe, conversed very loudly, and seemed to laugh at their fears.

A little while after a Canoe, wherein there sat an old baldpated Fellow, paddled towards the Buoy & began to tow it off; when that would not succeed, he returned & wanted to untie the rope from it, & would have done it, if not hindered. We haled & cried to him not to do it, but he was not at all disturbed & got a charge of small Shot,[1] he threw the buoy over board, but soon after returned to the task & a gun was fired with a ball just short of him, which thus terrified him, that he let it all go & brought a Coconut. We thought not to be deep enough in the bay. The boats sounded, & said there was a Channel from 3 to 7 fathom water.[2] We sent a boat with a hawser & an anchor in, but scarce had the boats left the buoy, when a Man in a Canoe[3] was tempted by the buoy & came to it: We saw plainly he was afraid of taking it up, but the temptation seemed to be irresistible, he went 3 or 4 times on & off; at last he resolved to take it, when a wall-piece or Musketoon was fired, whose ball fell close to the boat, & after being thrice reflected from the water, it fell ashore, where a good many people stood, who immediately ran away. The Man had left the buoy, but seeing himself safe, he returned to it; another ball-piece, a swivel & lastly a great gun was fired, which terrified all the people & cleared the beach of them. We then went to dinner.[4] The Thermometer at 73½, in my Cabin 78°.

*Aug. ye 6th* ♄ We brought the Ship nearer in, but drove out of the Channel & she struck twice, & soon after several times more;[5] however she came soon in deeper water, & all was well. We then went a shore in order to look for water; there were two boats & the longboat well armed & besides all the Marines. As soon as we landed,[6] some few people sitting not far off on the beach ran off. We beckoned them & they all returned. On the left hand[7] there came a great body of people, armed with clubs, Spears, bows & arrows, about 150 in all, & they offered us green bows of young Coconuts in Sign of peace, & we gave them Medals & pieces of

[1] According to George (II, 264) Cook fired with small shot and 'hit him with some'.

[2] The floor of the harbour was upraised in 1878 by some 20 feet. A second earthquake a month later raised it another 12 feet. A further movement in 1888 lifted it again by 30 feet. The harbour is now entirely silted up and unusable. See W. Gunn, *The Gospel in Futuna* (London, 1914), p. 178.

[3] According to George (II, 264) this was another man.

[4] Cf. *Journals*, II, 482–3 and *Voyage*, II, 262–3.

[5] '...in warping her in she struck several times.' (*Voyage*, II, 265). According to George they went to dinner *after* the groundings. Cook omits any reference to the subject.

[6] In the SE corner, *Journals*, II, 483, n. 1.

[7] 'On our left, or to the westward', *Voyage*, II, 265 i.e. the Enekahi side of the bay.

Otahaitee-cloth & they brought a good many Coconuts. We told them to sit down & drew a line, which they should not transgress. I found first the Watering place[1] & very good fresh Water; we drew the Marines up & filled two small Casks of Water. I saw all common plants, except a peculiar Grass & the *Mimosa simplex*.[2] I began to inquire for the Names of things & got several Words, which shew the language of this people different from any we have hitherto heard of. A few words seem to be the same with those at *Amsterdam* & the neighbouring Isles: but the greater part are quite different.[3] They said the Name of their Isle was *Tānnā*.[4] Several of them had their bows strung & arrows ready on it. We made Signs they should lay them by, & they did. We found the least motion of our Marines terrified them, that they all ran off: only a few old fellows remained then standing. I am afraid, they will one time or other before we leave the place, be troublesome to us, & force us to kill some of them in our defence, which I would be sorry to see. They are a stout well limbed race of people, better & stronger than those at *Mallicollo*, have black hair, some are woolly, some not. Several have plaited their hair in innumerable thin strings,[5] & even the beard of some is knit below the Chin into a knot or kind of tail. They are naked, have a string round the belly[6] & a case of a Mat or something like it round their Genitals,[7] so as those at *Mallicollo*. Their women are not so ugly & deformed as those at *Mallicollo;* they wore a kind of petticoat down to the knees round the waist & a chain of mother of pearl

[1] A pond (*Voyage*, II, 266). '...a Pool of excellent water not above Twinty yards from the shore...', *Journals*, II, 483, n. 2.

[2] *Acacia simplicifolia* Schinz et Guillaum.

[3] According to George (II, 267) 'sometimes they expressed the same idea by two words one of which was new and the other corresponded with the language of the Friendly Isles'. One may suspect the presence of visitors from nearby Aniwa or Futuna but the Polynesian influence on the eastern side of Tanna is nonetheless very marked.

[4] 'This...we looked upon as a great acquisition; for the indigenous name of a country is always permanent, *Voyage*, II, 267. Forster is, of course, mistaken. George himself notes (II, 267) that the word Tanna signifies *earth* in the Malay language. It is in fact the word for *ground* in the Weasisi dialect. An alternative, Ipari or Ipare, which has been suggested from time to time as the true native name, signifies merely *inland*. C. B. Humphreys, *The Southern New Hebrides* (Cambridge, 1926), p. xv and Beaglehole after him (*Journals*, II, 489, n. 4) are in error on this point. The Tannese had no single name for their island. Cook's name has been adopted out of convenience, following missionary and official example.

[5] According to G. Turner, *Nineteen Years in Polynesia* (London, 1861), p. 77 some six or seven hundred, the resulting collection, some 12 to 18 inches long, thrown back off the forehead, and hanging down behind. The style was especially affected by a community of disease makers, so-called 'priests', at Kasurumene near the volcano.

[6] But not nearly so tautly drawn as at Malekula, *Voyage*, II, 266.

[7] I.e. the universal New Hebridean penis wrapper.

round their necks. I saw two young tolerable Girls, with a Spear each in their hands. Their Youths commonly have bows & arrows, the Men & old Men have Clubs & Darts.[1] Having watered, we all reimbarked & went on board.[2] The Volcano has constantly been heard thundering, & the Smoke coming into the harbour in the Afternoon fell as Ashes down & was biting in the Eyes. The Volcano seems to be 4 or 5 miles distant, if not more. The shore is black sand & pieces of pumice stone, but very small.

During all the Evening the Volcano[3] has continued his thundering, allmost every 4 or 5 minutes, & there were some Explosions that lasted about half a minute. Now & then only the Smoke is illuminated from the bottom of the Crater, & becomes visible. The whole deck is covered with Ashes & cinders, & the Falling of them things is hurtfull to the Eyes.

We saw today 2 or 3 large Owls[4] flying; one the Natives frightened so with their Shouts; as she flew along the Shore they flung so many stones at her, that she attempted to fly towards the Ship, but settled on the Sea. A Canoe came off & took the Owl up & brought it us on board. We saw then that it is of the same kind with that at *Tonga-Tabu*, which is called at *Zeylan Bakkamuna*.

In the morning several preparations were made with the Anchors, in order to bring us nearer in shore.[5] We saw now & then a Canoe come to the Ship with a couple of Coconuts or Plantains, & then go & return with a new Cargoe of 2 plantains.[6] There was a fellow who wanted to sell the Captain a Club, when the things agreed for,[7] were sent down, he took them without sending the Club up. The Capt[t] told him to give it, he would not

[1] An interesting observation which suggests either the inadequacy of the local bow or some differentiation of function in war. The Tannese also used slings, spears, thrown with the aid of a becket, and a specialized throwing stone the *kawas*, shaped like a scythe stone. Cf. G. Turner, 1861, p. 81.

[2] Both sides were naturally very cautious and on edge at the first meeting. Cf. *Journals*, II, 483 and 851–2 for Cook's and Wales's accounts.

[3] Mount Yasur or Yahuwey.

[4] Barn Owl, *Tyto alba* sp. Forster recorded this bird from Tanna in *Descr. Anim.*, p. 256 under the name *Strix Bakkamuna*. See Amadon, *American Museum Novitates*, no. 1176 (1942) p. 13 and E. Mayr, *Birds of the Southwest Pacific* (New York, 1945), p. 184. It is called *himir* locally.

[5] 'I now found it was practical to lay the ship nearer to the landing place, and as we wanted to take in a large quantity of both wood and Water it would greatly facilitate the work as well as over-awe the Natives...', *Journals*, II, 483. As Cook goes on to say, the ship was now moored by four anchors broadside to the landing place. George (*Voyage*, II, 268) sets the scene of the anchorage in much more detail.

[6] According to George (II, 268) '...natives appeared at sun-rise coming out of their groves and consulting together on the beach'.

[7] I.e. some Tahitian *tapa* (*Voyage*, II, 269).

& got a load of shot into his face; he paddled off & was pursued by a ball from the Musketoon & several more were sent after him, some of which struck very near him, then the 3 people left the boat & swam a shore. Immediately after a little man[1] came off in a Canoe with Sugarcane, Coconuts & a couple of Yams; he seemed to be a Man of some consequence, & had been yesterday a peacemaker; he got a red Otahaitee Ahòu, & as they never come off unarmed, the Capt. got hold of a couple of Clubs, that lay in the Canoe, & hove them overboard, & pointed to the people ashore to lay aside their Arms. We saw a vast Number of people assembling from all parts of the Isle, especially over the hill from the W. side of the bay;[2] we desired them, when we came ashore to go back & to lay aside their Arms, but they did not stir in the least; we kept off from the Shore & rowed nearer to that Side & beckoned again to go away & lay the Arms aside[3] but they refused & were quite ready for engagement in a compact body of more than 600 men.[4] Then the Capt ordered to fire a Musket-ball over their heads; which had a good effect, for they all began to run, or at least a great Number of them, for several stood their ground.

[1] A little old man (*Voyage*, II, 270). It was Cook's Paowang, Sparrman's Pavjangom, the Forsters' Pawyangom. Sparrman has an amusing account of his antics on the previous day with a mirror Cook had given him. Such was his preoccupation with his image – which he had no doubt never seen before – that he was gradually carried out to sea by the ebbing tide and had considerable difficulty in getting back. Sparrman, *Voyage round the World*, pp. 151–2.

[2] Viz. the Enekahi side of the bay, towards the volcano.

[3] Cook apparently approached within twenty yards of the beach and called and made signs: 'The little old man [Paowang] and two others stood between them [i.e. the two parties] in the middle unarmed', *Voyage*, II, 271.

[4] Estimates vary. Cook (*Journals*, II, 483) speaks of 'not less than a thousand', and 'some Thousands'; Wales of 'some thousands'; George Forster (II, 271), more reasonably of seven hundred on the west side and two hundred on the east side, 'also armed but more peaceable', and Sparrman (*Voyage*, p. 153) of 'several thousands on both sides of the swamp'. The difficulty is readily enough explained. There are on a recent count some 200 villages on Tanna and some 115 tribes, divided into two major confederacies, Numrukwen and Koyometa, the former now generally occupying the east side of the island, the latter the west. The division between 'salt-water' and 'bush' – 'shipee' and 'man-war' or Kwotexen and Mwanahnepwe – each with their own private paths – would seem to be more recent and to some extent derivative. Cf. J. Guiart, *Un siècle et demi de contacts culturels à Tanna (Nouvelles-Hébrides)* (Paris, 1956), pp. 11–14, 90–2. At the time of Cook's visit and for several generations to come there was considerable discord between the Karumene and their Neraymene allies on the eastern side of Port Resolution and the more numerous Enekahi on the western side, backed by the powerful Kasurumene near the volcano – all Numrukwen tribes – hence the hostility of the people to the west towards Cook as the supposed partisan of those to the east, and the refusal of both parties to allow Cook and his men to range about freely on the west side of the harbour or visit the volcano. The Karumene and another harbour tribe, the Warumene, were eventually driven out in 1845 by the Neraymene, with Enekahi and Kasurumene help, and thereafter took up residence in the bush behind Port Resolution.

There was a Man close to the water side, who shewed his backside & clapt his hands to it, which is the usual way of challenging among the Nations of the South-Sea. The Capt ordered another ball to be fired, & immediately after it was done, the whole artillery on the one Side on board the ship ie 5 large Guns, 2 Swivels & 4 Musketoons were fired, which terrified them in such a Manner, that they all fled.[1] The little old Man beforementioned had erected ashore a pile of plantains & he stood unconcerned near it, nor did he run away, & when we came ashore, he came up to us, offered his plantains & desired us not to shoot any more. We stretched ropes, to make a partition between our people & the Natives,[2] which they never came near, & desired them to be unarmed, which those on one side complied with, the other party did not attend to; but all behaved well, & at the least motion they ran away; so that we were sure of having nothing to fear: We collected just a couple of plants. I collected likewise a good many words into my Vocabulary. At noon we returned on board, having got a good Quantity of water.

Aug. ye 7th ☉ In the Afternoon we went ashore & got some plants, for as there were no Natives on the beach, they being all returned home, we could make some excursions up into the woods, where we saw a plantation in the hills & below I went a good way up & collected plants. The Ships-crew hawled three or four times the Seyne & got upwards of 310 pounds of Fish, chiefly Mullet, Tenpounders & Angelfish: the second kind in great Quantities.[3] The little old Peacemaker[4] came & brought me a hog, for which I gave him a large Nail, & a piece of Otahaitee-Cloth. We gave him several Fish & he was very glad. The people with him were all unarmed & we were good Friends. This night we had some rain & the Volcano did no more thunder, but at 4 o'clock in the morning I saw him blaze now & then up, & the clouds of smoke

[1] According to Sparrman (p. 154), 'This, producing a tremendous crashing among the shot-away branches, hastily dispersed the whole army of Indians who had not made one shot, or thrown a single stone'. It may nonetheless be doubted whether the peace could have been preserved much longer.

[2] '...to guard the waterers', *Voyage*, II, 273.

[3] According to Sparrman, 282 pounds, most of them a species of *Mullus*, among which was a large *Esox argenteus* (of 10 pounds). Sparrman adds: 'During the night we managed to catch many covalls, albacores, and other fish with hook and line from the ship; we also caught the red paragas, poisonous in Mallicolo, but eaten here without harmful results', *Voyage round the World*, p. 154.

[4] I.e. Paowang or Pawyangon. Hodge's engraving of the landing at Tanna (Cook, *Voyage*, II, pl. LIX) was praised by George as 'interesting...composed...with great ingenuity'.

had all the various hues from yellow to orange, red & dark purple dying away into a reddish grey & into dark, where night had spread its veil over. The Stars shining through in the lucid spots. In short it afforded a new & quite singular view. When the smoke came out a fresh, the clouds of it were illuminated from the bottom of the Crater, & formed a head divided into various parts, more so than smoke from common fire does. All the Objects were gilt or tinged with yellow, orange, red or purple on the edges exposed to this light. All this caused a peculiar effect, but the hill itself & the mouth of the Volcano, were concealed a good way beyond the first neighbouring hills.

The next morning we saw great Numbers of people ashore,[1] coming from the right-hand-side Hills, & in a little time the beach was covered with them. We went ashore for to cut wood, & we found it necessary to make again a partition with the rope. The natives would not part with their Arms, though offered a handsome price: a couple of spears & arrows were however bought.[2] I gave the old Peacemaker a hatchet,[3] & shewed him the Use of it. He was as happy as can be imagined. There were others, who wanted likewise the hatchet, but I told them, they should have for each hog a hatchet, for a large race of plantains a knife, but they brought none off. A Marquise was erected for the Astronomer on shore. Wood was cut & guards disposed; they were often wanton & saucy & frisked & threatened with their arrows & spears, slings etc but till I was gone on board to dinner nothing happened.

*Aug. ye 8th* ☽ During we were on board,[4] a fellow a shore was very saucy & shewed the Lieut. of the Marines his naked backside, & was otherwise threatning & making disturbances, for which impudence the Lieut, shot & wounded him in the Thigh, & then the Fellow made off & the others ran away, but the old & steady people soon pacified all, & remained quiet, & all came off about 3 o'clock. After every body had dined, we hawled again the Seyne a shore, & got about 48 pounds of Mullet & Brasil-Pike. There were a few Natives when we came, but in an instant they increased to great crowds,[5] but the greatest part they were unarmed, having

[1] '...not near so numerous as the day before', *Voyage*, II, 282.

[2] 'Some were not so strict and parted with both darts and spears', *Voyage*, II, 283.

[3] '...for a pig which [he] had brought the day before', *Voyage*, II, 283.

[4] An obvious Germanism.

[5] 'Possibly, out of curiosity, many of them had come from the interior of the island on a visit for the first time, and some of the youths could not properly control their

left their arms in the bushes. It seems the Natives dread to be exposed to the cold & moisture of the Evening-air[1] & therefore begged leave to go to sleep, which we readily granted. We see therefore plainly, they are ashore only for making the honours of their Country. The next morning after breakfast we went ashore on the right hand side of the harbour.[2] We were obliged to wade through the Surf among the lose large stones, which was troublesome enough, because we had to take care of our Arms. We climbed up the steep Sides of the hills,[3] where we got two new plants. We came down again sliding on our backsides these precipices, which the nimble Inhabitants walk with the greatest ease. We found the Stones ashore various; the large & Chief Strata are of a Clay-Marle; very soft & crumbling in the open air to pieces, especially when growing wet. We found a kind of black Sandstone, besides that there was something similar to *Rotten-Stone*,[4] & lastly did we also find some pieces of Chalk, either quite pure or mixed with a yellow or reddish Substance, perhaps Irony. Coral Rocks were likewise in great Quantities there of the *Madrepora Astroites* & others. We marched a good way along this Shore, & examined plants. We were just willing to march up the Country in a gently sloping Path, when *Mr Sparman* saw a Native with a Club; he came directly down & we made ready for to receive them in case of an attack; but they came all down with Coconuts; we would have let them come nearer, but they were all armed & in great Numbers: so we told them to leave their Arms behind & we retired gradually towards our people ashore.[5] We gave them some trifles, but we soon found they were afraid of touching the things they got from us, & if they did they took them between two leaves, as if it were some dirty, poisonous thing.[6] We got Coconuts & Sugar Canes, & a kind of leaves of

arrogance and mischief, especially as there were not the least trace of leaders, commanders, or discipline among them', Sparrman, *Voyage round the World*, p. 155.

[1] Not out of decency as George (II, 284) suggests, but out of fear of ghosts and supposed ghostly influences, and above all of the nocturnal anopheline mosquito and malaria which was rampant here.

[2] I.e. facing south, or, as George puts it, 'the steep mountain on the west side' – Enekahi (*Voyage*, II, 284) an 'enemy' country. Sparrman and the two Forsters made up this shore party.

[3] The 'hills' in question rise about 500 feet and were in Cook's day well populated.

[4] A decomposed siliceous limestone.

[5] The party's withdrawal on this occasion was no more than prudent. They were trespassing on 'enemy' territory.

[6] A local *tapu*. Women were forbidden to touch men's food. Similarly, men were forbidden to pick up food with their bare hands on pain of dropsy, i.e. elephantiasis. It was also believed that if a sacred man burnt a man's 'rubbish' – anything he had touched

a Fig,[1] I suppose (as far as I could judge by the Fruit) which they had wrapped in leaves & dressed in the Oven, which were very well tasted. They gave me likewise 2 ripe Horse plantains.[2] We talked very much together by Signs, I collected several words of their language & they were quite familiar & friendly:[3] their women & Children came down, & brought us something to eat; but could not bear to be looked at, which allways alarmed them in such a manner, that they ran away. They have caps of a large plantain leaf wrapt round their head, the grown Women have a kind of petticoat round their waist made of leaves of a grass or read growing longer in proportion as the women grow older, & some have Mats of the same stuff about their Shoulders:[4] the young girls have a string around the waist, & a little bunch of grass & leaves is tucked up between their legs, another bunch of the same leaves hangs down the back. Some have Earrings of Coconut Shell or another Sea Shell, & of the latter Substance they often have Neck laces; a great part wear a white stone in the *Septum narium* which is perforated.[5] The Volcano is now quite pacified, smokes & in the night; the smoke is firy & illuminated from the Crater, but the thundering Noise is quite ceased.

*Aug. ye 9th* ♂ In the Afternoon I went ashore, where they hauled the Seyne, but there were too many people of the Natives, that I durst not venture to go into the bushes; & collect there plants. I confined myself to the Skirts of the woods & collected a few words of their language. We got hardly 2 dozen of fish; chiefly

or discarded – (*nahak*) that man would fall ill and die if the priest were not at once propitiated. In this case, picking up an object with a leaf served to protect the recipient from malign, foreign influences and disease. Cf. also *Journals*, II, 487, n. 4.

[1] Locally called *nihm*, i.e. *Ficus* spp.

[2] *Musa* sp., locally called *nipin*.

[3] George tells us more about this expedition, especially of his father's special friendship with Oomb-yégan (Umbjegan of *Reise*) with whom he made 'a reciprocal exchange of names'. Hereafter the Forsters were 'adopted among the natives [and] continued upon the best terms imaginable, and collected great supplements to the vocabulary', *Voyage*, II, 284–5.

[4] 'The women are pretty well covered with their long girdles hanging down below the knee. They wear them occasionally also over the shoulders. They are made from the rolled and dried fibre of the banana stalk, are very soft, and at first sight look like hemp', G. Turner, *Nineteen Years in Polynesia* (London, 1861), pp. 79–80.

[5] One such item is listed in the Oxford 'Catalogue of Curiosities' (item 149) although it is now apparently missing. According to an early missionary: 'Their ears are dreadfully disfigured by earrings. Some have holes in their ears through which a child's hand might pass. They also pierce holes in their noses in which they wear a little piece of reed horizontally...All wear some ornaments of beads – whales teeth &c &c round the neck. On the arm above the elbow joint they wear rings made from the cocoa nut, and from these the men suspend their spear thrower and sling', G. Turner, 'South Seas Journals', London Missionary Society, New Hebrides (Tanna). P.R.O., L.M.S. Box 9, 134, 19 December 1842.

Mullet & Tenpounders. There was one *Echeneis Neucrates*[1] or *Indian Sucking Fish*, which is very well represented in *Seba*. The under Snout ends in a point & is longer than the upper Jaw, a black band runs along the sides & has a whitish Edge, growing darker of an Iron colour towards the back: it has 24 carvings for Sucking on its head & the pectoral Fins are pointed, which character sufficiently distinguish this fish from the common *Sucking-Fish*.

On the next morning we went again ashore, where a party was sent out to fetch some ballast on the right hand side of the harbour.[2] I went with Mr *Sparman*, Mr *Patton*, my Son, my Servant & a Marine, who was to convoy us. We climbed about the hills & discovered one new plant: but we saw that it is difficult to walk with safety in a place where one ought to be continually on one's guard on account of the Natives, whom we can by no means trust. When we came to the place, where the party took the ballast, we saw there a hot well, whose water had such a heat, that we could not hold a finger above a second in it.[3] I shall before we leave the Isle take the opportunity to assay the Water & examine with a Thermometer its heat: we can perhaps give a bathing to some of our rheumatic people, for the water seems to be medicinal, at least its taste was not quite fresh.

*Aug ye 10th* ☿ The Captain brought a Native[4] off with him from the watering-place. He dined with us, & seemed easy & was perfectly happy. Capt Cook told me, he had the Name of the Sky in the Language of *Tànnā*, & as I had the Name for the same, we compared them; they were different. We appealed to our Guest, & he with a great deal of ingenuity put one hand out, & pointed to us, that this were *Ne-ǎy*[5] the Sky; & then he moved the other

[1] A species of Remora (Echeneidae). The reference is to A. Seba, *Thesaurus* (Amsterdam, 1758), III, 103, pl. 33 (2). See also p. 570, n. 1 above.

[2] The western or Enekahi side, as the sequel shows. The eastern side is referred to as Samoa Point.

[3] 'The interior of this mountain is a vast furnace, and in some places the crust is so thin, that in passing over it, it is like walking on a hot iron plate...The greater part of the mountain, however, is covered with vegetation, and is inhabited by a population of some five hundred people, scattered about in several villages...Around the base of this mountain, and among the rocks on the west side of the harbour, there are several hot springs, which are of great service to the natives. Their degrees of heat vary. Some form a pleasant tepid bath, and to these the sick resort, especially those suffering from ulcerous sores. Some rise to 190°, and others bubble up about the boiling point. Every day you may see the women there cooking their yams, and other vegetables, in hollow places dug out, and which form a series of never-failing boiling pots', Turner, *Nineteen Years in Polynesia*, pp. 71–2.

[4] Cook's Whaago or Forster's Fannòkko, according to George, *Voyage*, II, 287.

[5] *Neai* in modern Tannese orthography.

hand under it & showed this were *Nābòòă*,[1] the Clouds; in short he showed himself a sensible, intelligent Man. He gave us the Names of several Isles, which are hereabouts: *Irro-măngā*[2] is the Isle with the Peaked-Saddle, where we came from & had been one night at anchor. *Immèr* is a low Islet, just opposite the Mouth of this Harbour. *Irronăm* is an Isle to the East of *Tànnā*, which we saw when we came into this harbour: & he pointed to the Eastward of South & said there was the Isle of *Annătom*, which we knew nothing of.[3] Our Guest saw the Dogs we had on board, & he called them *Boògā*, Hogs,[4] which proves, that the Natives of these Isles know not any Dogs. He was very desirous of having one, & the Capt gave him a Dog & a bitch, & made him a present of a hatchet, a large piece of Otahaitee-Cloth & several other trifles. He went with us, as happy as a Prince. He ate before his going off dinner with us: he tasted Salt-Pork, but not above a Morsel & gave away the rest. Yams, boiled, roasted & fried in Hogs-Lard, were his food & a little Apple-Pye. He drank a little Wine, but wanted no more: & as soon as he reached the Shore he went off to his home. I went a good way along Shore,[5] but the Natives were alarmed & desired us not to go further:[6] therefore we returned. I then went in the woods back of the watering place, where we had been before towards the plantation on the hill; but we met some Natives who wanted to persuade us not to go on:

[1] *Napua*, as Forster says cloud.

[2] A Tannese, not an Erromangan name. The Erromangans have no single name for their island. The original would seem to have been *yeruman* or *yermama* = a man in the Kwamera dialect or perhaps *yerumanu*, a chief, or Irmwanga, a bush village behind Port Resolution.

[3] Immer (apparently another Tannese name) is Aniwa; Irroman (Cook's Erronan) is Futuna, Erronan being perhaps a Tannese version of the name of a district on Futuna, Iraro. The Aneityumese called it simply *Anhas*, the Bad Land, where food is scarce. Annatom is Aneityum, from Aneityo, a district on the island, borrowed by the Tannese and then borrowed back by the Aneityumese post-European and applied to the island as a whole.

[4] *Booga* (= *pukas*), as Forster rightly notes from the Polynesian word *puaka*. The Tannese have similarly adopted a Polynesian name for the dog, viz. *kuri*. According to Turner, one of Cook's dogs died soon after and the other howled so pitifully after its mate that the people killed it. The animal was successfully reintroduced about 1840. Turner, *Nineteen Years in Polynesia*, p. 87. Cf. also *Voyage*, II, 289 and *Journals*, II, 488. It is also instructive to examine Forster's Tannese words in his chart of South Sea languages in *Observations*. See also fig. 5.

[5] According to George Forster (II, 289) his father went 'to the eastward along the shore of the bay', i.e. on the Samoa Point side, amongst the otherwise friendly Karumene and Nataymene people.

[6] 'A great number of natives' (*Voyage*, II, 289). Cook with his new young friend 'Whaago' (Fannokko) had already been halted. 'I was desired to sit down and wait which I accordingly did, during which time several of the Gentlemen pass'd us, at which they shewed great uneasiness and importuned me so much to order them back that I was obliged to comply, they were jealous at our making the least excursions inland or even along the harbour', *Journals*, II, 488. The object of their solicitude on this occasion seems to have been the sacred place at Ile Pou at the end of the point. See p. 598, n. 11 below.

however seeing us determined, they went with us. We heard the Sea roaring beyond the Harbour on its S. side & we told the Natives we wanted to see the Sea: They carried us up to the top of the hill, having sent away one of their brethren. When we came to the highest part of the hill we saw the Sea,[1] & an Isle at 8 or 10 leagues distance, which the Natives called *Ānnătom;*[2] it was situated about SEb.S., is high & pretty large. Having got this sight we returned, though the Indians were as willing we should go further on, as they had been before, we should not go on, circumstances which together with the sending away one of their brethren, looked rather suspicious.[3] We hastened down the hill & came safely down, having got one new Plant.[4]

It seems the Islanders eat the people, whom they kill in battle, for they pointed to ye Arms, Legs, Thighs etc & shewed how they roasted & devoured the Meat of them. They showed us all this by signs.[5] We retired soon after on board, where we saw some fish that had been hawled up by the Seyne. One was a kind of *Sting-ray* with two Rings on the back of the tail, but they were both large, & they seem not to be the product of another years growth, both being pretty equal in Size. The Ray was the *Raja Pastinaca* of *Linn* & that variety of it called *Altavela* β.[6]

[1] According to Turner (1861, p. 70), it was a 'neck of low land which they crossed, but it is quite elevated (200 feet) and there is quite an expansive area of flat, habitable land on top. The party did not, of course, cross the island, as is sometimes stated, but merely Samoa Point.

[2] Aneityum, 50 miles distant, of which there is a direct view here, the rest of the SE coast of Tanna trending SSW.

[3] It would seem that Forster's companions (? Karumene) had at last steered him safely into their own district and away from Ile Pou in Neraymene territory. Having identified themselves with the Karumene at the beginning Cook and his men were not free to go where they chose even on this side of the bay.

[4] For this excursion see also *Voyage*, II, 289–91.

[5] Cook, unbidden, got a hint of the same practice, which he was cautious about accepting, *Journals*, II, 489. The following day George (*Voyage*, II, 300) reported positively on indications of cannibalism after, as they understood it, they were threatened with being 'killed and eaten...However, at present we could no longer be mistaken; for, having pretended to misunderstand them, and making them believe that we thought they offered us some provisions, we began to move forward, and expressed that we should be glad to eat something. They were very eager to undeceive us, and showed, by signs, how they killed a man, cut his limbs asunder, and separated the flesh from the bones. Lastly, they bit their own arms, to express more clearly how they eat human flesh'. Turner (1861, p. 83) observes that 'They delight in human flesh, and distribute it in little bits far and near among their friends'. The habit was nonetheless occasional rather than habitual and practised only in times of war and then often only by certain tribes. In such cases the flesh of the sacrificial victim, normally a member of the opposing confederacy, Koyometa or Numrukwen, male or female, was carried in great style along ceremonial paths from one *imeum* or *marum* (dancing ground) to another and consumed by a select few, generally men of some standing.

[6] *Raja pastinaca* var β *altavela* of *Descr. Anim.*, p. 256 (name only). There is no drawing. See p. 611, n. 4 below. Locally it is called *verau*.

The next morning we went after breakfast ashore. Some of our people saw before breakfast, when they were fetching water ashore, that great numbers of Natives went off with all their moveables, removing more inland. Seeing perhaps that these Foreigners are intruding, inquisitive beings, rumaging over all the Isle without their leave, they thought best to leave us this part of the Isle to ourselves, & to go out of mischiefs reach, with all their families, for fear of being hurt by their murdering weapons, which some of them had allready experienced. We found therefore but few Natives ashore.[1] We tried therefore to push on in the plain[2] behind the watering place: We found water here & there, & some plantations of Eddies or Tarro. All the plain has Coconut Trees, Rattatrees, *Hibiscus tiliaceus* & various kind of Bindweed (*convolvulus*), & very few other plants. We saw the *Tonga-Tabu* Pigeon[3] with the great Nob on the bill, but I would not shoot, for fear of alarming the Natives & the Ship. I found today out, that they speak in this Isle two if not three different Languages.[4] A Man

[1] In reviewing this passage later George offers the alternative opinion that these people were merely returning 'to their own dwellings, seeing that no further mischief was to be apprehended from the strangers, who had arrived among them', *Voyage*, II, 292. In general Port Resolution is a sickly place, thinly inhabited. The great majority of those who turned up obviously came from a distance, some from inland villages, others from shore villages as far away as Ipekel (Sulphur Bay) in the north and Kwamera in the south. It is evident that there was also a sizeable contingent of disease makers from the Kasurumene district. Having satisfied their curiosity and no doubt exhausted their food supplies, all these now went home.

[2] A vale rather than a valley, extending beyond a wide, sandy beach, and giving on to an extensive sterile ash plain, utterly devoid of vegetation. The area referred to here is, as Forster says, extremely fertile and covered with trees, among them huge banyans.

[3] Pacific Pigeon, *Ducula pacifica pacifica* (Gmelin, 1789). In the local dialect it is called *mak*.

[4] The subject is complex. There were in Cook's time and indeed until quite recently numerous local dialects and some six mutually unintelligible 'languages' on Tanna. Cf. the numerals of three Numrukwen dialects recorded by Turner in 1842–3.

1. Riti	Kaiti	Kaliki
2. Karu	Kaiu	Kalalu
3. Kahar	Kesel	Kisisel
4. Kefa	Kuet	Kuas
5. Grirum	Katilum	Kulkulup

A more famous example is *nahak* = rubbish or rubbish burning. Nahak, Narak, Netik, Nuruk. As Turner (1861, p. 84) remarks: 'It was...a grievous affair to find that, on going to a place four miles from our door, we needed an interpreter to communicate with the people'. A chance visitor like Cook might also expect to pick up Aniwan or Futunan or Erromangan or Aneityumese words. Cf. Beaglehole's comment: 'There was, in the language heard at some of the islands, evidence of Tongan influence; but to all intents and purposes Cook had sailed clean out of Polynesia into a new world – the world of Melanesia, marked by a multiplicity of tongues, a multiplicity of clans, a social structure, a system of beliefs and observances of which he could in six weeks obviously form no notion at all', *Journals*, II, xcvi. See also *Voyage*, II, 293–4. On Tanna Forster made a noble attempt at anthropology. See *Tactless Philosopher*, pp. 116–20.

who had seen Mr *Clarck*, the Lieu^{t}, shoot 2 Pigeons told me plainly, *mātte roòā Tàròope*, which is in a dialect of Tonga-Tabu, *killed 2 Pigeons*, & then he said *mārkom Kārroo-kee-èrree*, which likewise signifies *killed 2 Pigeons* in another Dialect & I had these words put down before.[1] The Numerals I had learned from them most certainly in two Languages.[2] It is therefore highly probable that these people are a mixed breed, between those that have peopled the South Sea Isles & some other tribe, which either drove part of the old Inhabitants out, or mixed with them. These Islanders have large heads of hair, which they divide into small parcels hardly of the thickness of a Pigeons feathers & wrap it in the bark of a *Convolvulus* so as we would do in making a *queue* but the difference is, one of their shocky heads contains some hundred such *queues*, which gives them a very droll appearance.[3]

Aug. ye 11th ♃ In the Afternoon we walked more than 2 or 3 miles up in the Country; we met several people, but when we told them we were shooting birds, they desired us to go on, & never troubled their heads about us; we killed several small birds[4] but lost them all in the thick grass & herbage. The natives will never part with their clubs & bows: Arrows & Darts they sell but sparingly.

It rained allmost all night. In the morning after breakfast we went up the hill on the right hand side of the harbour;[5] we went an easy path up. When we came to a spot clear of wood & reeds,

[1] *Mate* = dead, *rua* = two, *ka u'upa* or *urupa* = pigeon, all of which is certainly Polynesian, most probably Futunese or Tongan, as Forster says. The meaning of *markom Karroo- kee-erree* is clear enough but the words are rather more difficult to decipher. *Mak* or *mak apahm* hence *markom* = pigeon, *karu* = two and *kieri* no doubt means dead. J. R. Forster gives *marookee* = dead but concedes *carroo* = two. Cf. his Comparative Table, fig. 5.

[2] According to George (II, 293–4) their informant 'added at the same time, that the former language was spoken at the island of Irronan, which lies seven or eight leagues to the east of Tanna.* (*He likewise acquainted us, that Irronan was sometimes called Footoona)'. This leads George to suggest: 'Perhaps a colony of the same race, who inhabit the Friendly Islands, and all the easterly islands of the South Pacific Ocean, may have settled on the island; or perhaps the natives of Irronan keep up a communication with the Friendly Islands, by means of some Islands unknown to us lying between them' J. R. Forster is certainly correct is supposing that the southern New Hebrideans are a 'mixed breed', in fact of Papuans or 'Melanesians' and Polynesians, the latter comparatively recent migrants from Samoa and Tonga.

[3] Cf. p. 586, n. 5 above. Turner in 'South Seas Journal' (19 December 1842) adds that the Tannese also cut the hair off the upper lip but allowed the lower part of the beard to grow long 'and this they divide into a good many little tresses'.

[4] *Rallus tannensis* of *Descr. Anim.*, p. 275 was described under 12 August 1774 and George's folio 131 bore the same date. See Lysaght, p. 303. It is now the White-browed Rail, *Poliolimnas cinereus tannensis* (Forster, 1844). Type locality Tanna Island. George records: 'We shot indeed a number of small birds, but the grass was so thick that we lost almost all of them', *Voyage*, II, 294.

[5] George (II, 295) makes clear that this was the 'westermost corner' of the bay.

we saw there a smoke, & found the smell to be sulphureous, & the Earth so hot that we could hardly stand on it. We found two more such *Solfataras* on the hill, which we climbed up.[1] We reached even its summit, but found us still at least 2 leagues off from the Volcano, who made today several Eruptions & threw Stones up of an immense Size for they were seen even from the Ship:[2] as often as the Volcano rolled & thundered we saw new clouds of smoke come up from our *Solfataras*, which proves that they have a Connexion with the Volcano. The Earth seemed to be a Chalk or Marle impregnated with Sulphur steams into a *Hepar Sulphuris.*[3] In another place the Earth was a red ochre, which the Natives use to paint their Faces with.[4] We found several Species of Figs, which loved so much the warm Spot, that they throve well within a yard of the Sulphureous steam. The Solfataras are allways places free of bushes & Trees, though Grass, was seen on the clear Spots with the *Dolichos ensiformis*,[5] Ischaemum aristatum,[6] Paspalum disrectum,[7] the *Hedysarum heterocarpon*,[8] together with a small new *Oldenlandia.*[9] The smoking places were quite free of Vegetables, covered with a white or sometimes green coating. The Soil in them places is allways moist of the hot Steams, that rise therefrom, & from thence the hot Water it seems comes, we met with Aug. ye 7th near the sea at the foot of this very hill, they being only about 60 or 80 yards different in height.[10]

*Aug. ye 12th* ♀ In the Afternoon I went on the left hand side of the harbour[11] & found some *Yamboos*, *Arecca's* or *Cabbage Trees*[12] & several other things in the Plantations of the Natives, which are all on the hills, where likewise their habitations are, of which I saw about three. They are curiously thatched, but so low that they

[1] Cf. p. 593, n. 3 above.

[2] These are great lumps of molten lava which cool very rapidly on falling back.

[3] See p. 515, n. 2 above.

[4] According to Turner (p. 77) red was the favourite colour of face paint, the red earth being got principally from Aneityum. 'They first oil the face, and then daub on the dry powder with the thumb'. Black was also popular amongst certain tribes.

[5] *Canavalia ensiformis* (L.) D.C.

[6] *Ischaemum murinum* Forst? or *I. muticum* L?

[7] *Paspalum distichum?* Forster's hand here is very poor.

[8] *Desmodium heterocarpum* (L.) D.C.

[9] *Hedyotis foetida* (Forst.) J. E. Smith.

[10] For a more detailed account of this excursion see *Voyage*, II, 294–9.

[11] The eastern side, i.e. Samoa Point, 'where the natives had prevented our going on two days before' *Voyage*, II, 299. Cf. also Cook, *Journals*, II, 490.

[12] I.e. *Eugenia* sp, *nikiowa* locally, 'a cool watery fruit of the size of pears' (*Voyage*, II, 302); *Areca catechu*, the betel palm, *napuak*, the nut of which was not chewed here; and the common cabbage tree (*nuhwa* or *nipilig*), *Areca oleracea* or *Oredoxa oleracea*.

come down to the very Ground with their roofs;[1] they are pretty long & smoky for they have fires therein. I saw their plantations fenced in neatly with reeds of the *Saccharum spontaneum*.[2] The Natives are very jealous to let their habitations, wives & Children be seen, & allways desired us not [to] go on, & in order to frighten us, they told if we went on, we should be killed & eaten:[3] where I found they were too uneasy, I did not go further on, but when I saw an old Man of my acquaintance[4] I went on with him & passing through various plantations, I at last came to a fine clear Spot[5] where I saw the abovementioned three habitations; I passed unmolested, when they found I did not touch any thing belonging to them; on the contrary I gave them several presents; & we parted good friends.[6] In the Evening we heard severally the Noise in the Volcano & saw a blazing fire rise from it. Today the Volcano was very noisy & threw up a prodigious quantity of Ashes, which are nothing else but minute particles of Pumice Stone & some particles like points of Salts, long, pliant, transparent or rather like Asbest-particles. I went up again[7] the Hill to the *Solfatara* or *Avernus* in order to try its heat with a small portable Thermometer of Mr *Ramsden's* construction. When we came to the first, we saw the Natives on the higher Solfatara, we therefore did not stop at the first, but went immediately on to the higher *Avernus*, & there

[1] Cf. *Journals*, II, 494 and *Voyage*, II, 303.

[2] *Saccharum officinalum* L?

[3] See p. 594, n. 6 above. George (II, 300–1) notes 'Every morning, at day-break, we heard a slow solemn song or dirge sung on this point which lasted more than a quarter of an hour. It seemed to be a religious act and gave us great reason to suspect that some place of worship was concealed in these groves, and the constant endeavours of the natives to keep us from this place greatly confirmed us in this supposition'. This was perhaps either an invocation by fishermen to their 'deity' or, more likely, the daily practice of the ritual leading to the grand ceremonial of the competitive feast, *nekowiar*, or reciprocal exchange of pigs. On cannibalism on Tanna see p. 595, n. 5 above.

[4] Paowang. George, as usual, gives a much more detailed account of this day's encounters and doings. See *Voyage*, II, 294–306.

[5] '...on a fine open area of not less than an hundred yards square, on the skirts of which we saw three habitations of the natives...we noticed an immense wild fig-tree in one corner of the green...' *Voyage*, II, 302. It was a typical *imeum* or *marum*, a dancing square.

[6] Cf. *Voyage*, II, 302.

[7] On the western side of the bay, 'The singular nature of the solfatarra on the western hill much attracted our attention', notes George (II, 306), 'that we hastened thither again the next morning, and Mr Hodges was of the party'. So, too, was Wales, who borrowed Forster's Ramsden thermometer to test the temperatures around the solfataras. There was, it seems, some considerable 'philosophical' jealousy and a certain difference of opinion over these experiments between the astronomer and natural historian. A solfatara is strictly speaking a volcanic orifice in a dormant or decadent stage and from which gases (especially sulphur dioxide) and volatile substances are emitted. Avernus (lit. the birdless lake) was applied to that lake in Campania, the poisonous effluvium of which was said to poison the birds flying over it. See also *Observations*, pp. 141–2.

we found the Natives waiting for us, & they soon brought us some Coconuts. We examined some plants thereabouts, Mr *Hodges* drew something, & I hung my portable Thermometer in the Shade on a Tree. Before I left the Ship, half an hour past 8 o'clock A.M. my Thermometer was in my Cabin at 78°; having carried it in a case, in my pocket close to my body up the hill, it was at 87°: having hung for about 5 minutes in the open Air, in the Shade, on the hill about 20 yards from the smoking place I found it at 80°. I had with a stick made a hole deep enough to contain the Thermometer in its whole length. I put a small stick & put it through the Ribbon on the top of the Thermometer & then hung it into the hole, where in a few seconds, or in about half a minute's time it rose to 170°; we left it there for about 3 or 4 minutes[1] & got the Thermometer out at a Minute's interval at 3 different times & we found it allways at 170°, when it was taken out of the hole, but in the very instant, it fell to 160° & more. It is also clear that it is one of the hottest Steams, that can be found. The Natives desired us not to stir much in the *Avernus*, for it would take fire: we found higher up on the left hand of this second *Solfatara* several more, all smoking, & all of the same Nature with the above described. We walked higher up, in order to get to the top of a hill, from whence we might get a sight of the Volcano, but when we came nearer to some habitations of the Natives, they pointed us another road out as leading to the Volcano, but having carried us through several windings, we found ourselves near the seashore; & saw that the Natives had been artfull enough to bring us a great way from their habitations, where they dislike the Sight of Strangers.[2] We found one of our Natives, who came with us, seemed to be an intelligent Man, & gave us the Names of several

[1] Wales (*Journals*, II, 858–9) borrowed the thermometer, dug a hole and buried the bulb of the instrument 'for some depth with the Earth I dug out'. In one minute he got a reading of 210° F: 'It remained in 2½' but did not rise higher; and I could have wished it might have stood longer; but as the Thermometer was the property of another Person who did not chuse it should, & having none of my own which go high enough I was obliged to be content with this Experiment, which I do not think quite satisfactory, because I know by experience, that a Thermometer carried into a greater degree of heat will at first rise higher than its natural State and after some time fall to it, and it may be, that in such extream degrees of Heat as this was, the Aberration I am speaking of may be considerable'. Cook wrote down Forster's results and not Wales's (*Journals*, II, 491) but Wales got his way in the end. See p. 603 below, and Sparrman, *Voyage*, p. 156.

[2] The party had obviously strayed on to a Kwotexen path and were in consequence at once directed back along the appropriate Mwanahnepwe path to safer ground. See p. 588, n. 4 above.

Isles in the neighbourhood. First he gave the Names of those Capt Cook had heard several days ago, but he added to them 6 more. viz. To the South of *Tānnā*, *Màrren*, a little to SW. he pointed for *Togossùmmerā*, then WSW was *Reppihinnooèr*; WbN he pointed for *Towāreebàng* & behind it is *Noòā.*[1] Capt *Cook* enquiring for Names of Countries got about 80 of them; but he soon found out that all these *Whennooas* were on this Isle, for they had put *Assùr*[2] at the head of them all, which we knew to be the Name of the Volcano. I knew this circumstance & asked therefore, whether the Names of the Lands I had gotten were not on this same Isle?; but the Man said, there was *Tassee*, (the Ocean) between them & *Tanna*: & when he saw me make circles on the paper for the Countries, he made signs, it was right; what is more in favour of this, is that not one of these Names I got, was on Capt Cooks list, of 80 *Hennooas* given him before.[3]

Aug. ye 13th ♄ The Volcano continued to make a rolling thunder, & to throw up ashes, which were thrown with the wind directly into the bay, the beach & on board the Ship, so the whole deck was covered by them: in the Night the Fire could be seen. I went a path up on the back of the wooding & watering places; I came through some plantation, met some Indians, who wanted to conduct me & my party to the place, where I had seen before the Sea[4] & the Isles on the SE. side: but I soon found that they wanted to cheat & bring me again to the beach, where the Ship lies.[5] I therefore left them, & went myself through the Country & Plantations, but an Indian soon came after me & fairly brought me to the beach on the other side of the Isle;[6] he showed me *Anàttom*, & more to the North the other Isles, especially one which

[1] In order, Mt Melen (3275 ft), and Mt Tukosmeru (3500 ft), the two highest mountains on the island. The next two, 'Reppehinooer' and 'Towareebang' bear little or no resemblance to any modern place name on Tanna. *Repin*, however, means a plain, and *whenua* land and Reppinhooer is thus perhaps a piece of flat land in the direction assigned. Similarly, *towar* means a hill or mountain and *nepag* a point and the reference may well be to Loonengenapen (Green Hill) or Loukaramangan in the same district. Nooa, on the other hand, may well be Eniu which is just 'behind' these two.

[2] Yasur, the volcano.

[3] Cf. George, *Voyage*, II, 309 and p. 603 below. *Tasse* = *tahi*, the sea or ocean and Yasur is in fact the name of a district on Futuna so that Forster would seem to have got at least some things right.

[4] I.e. on the seaward side of Samoa Point, facing Futuna and Aneityum.

[5] He seems to have run foul of some Ile Pou people who were clearly anxious throughout to keep Cook and his men well away from their *imeum* or dancing ground.

[6] I.e. on the other side of Samoa Point, not the *island*, as has so often been suggested.

he called *Eatònga*, so that we now have the names of 4 Isles besides *Tànnā*.[1] After having staid a little while there, I returned to the beach, where they hauled the Seyne & got more than 250 pound fish, & among others 3 Rays of the new kind, with 2 Stings each, but the Natives wanted the Fish & when they had got them, they cut the tails with the Stings, & kept them for themselves & returned the Fish, which they probably do not eat. I was also again disappointed in seeing the Stings of this Fish, for when I came, the tails were gone; the rest of the Fish were Mullet, Tenpounders, a Garfish, some Horse Mackrel & 2 new Fish.[2] It is very remarkable that this Isle has a good many East Indian plants. We had gotten to day 2 or 3 new plants. The next morning we went again ashore, & I took a second walk on the hill to the left hand of the harbour,[3] where I soon came among my old Acquaintance,[4] & I went with them to the Sea-shore, & there we found a new grass, & on the road a couple of other plants. It is amazing how many kinds of Figs this Isle contains.[5] The Natives were exceedingly fond of us, & gave us various Fruits, Coconuts, Sugarcanes, & a Yam.[6] Their huts are on both sides open, the Coconut-mats make the Thatch, & one a bed. Sometimes 3 or 4 Families live in one hut & each has a separate Fireplace. The Thatch goes down to the ground.[7] I came late on board.[8] I found that

[1] I.e. Aneityum and Futuna (*Natonga* means simply *East*). The other isles – or districts on other isles – were, of course, Aniwa and Erromanga. It would thus seem that the geographical knowledge of the Tannese was limited to the southern part of the New Hebrides from Erromanga south.

[2] *Zeus argentarius* of *Descr. Anim.*, p. 288 and Forster drawing no. 191 recto and *Perca grunniens* of *Descr. Anim.*, p. 294 and drawing no. 191 verso, from which a neater drawing was made, no. 214. George (*Voyage*, II, 311) notes two 'poisonous' fish such as those caught at Malekula, which were eaten at once but without bad effects – 'a farther proof that those which poisoned the officers had fed upon some noxious vegetables, and by that means acquired a bad quality, which is not natural to them'. See p. 569, n. 7 above.

[3] 'The flat hill to the East side' i.e. Samoa Point. See *Voyage*, II, 312.

[4] Paowang again.

[5] *Ficus* spp., locally *nihm*. B. Seeman, *Flora Vitiensis* (London, 1865–73), pp. 247–8, citing Forster's material, lists *Ficus religiosa* of Forster, F. *septica*, F. *St pulacea*, F. *Indica*, F. *granatum* ('from which the Tannese made their cloth [*tapa*] instead of the paper mulberry'). G. Bennett later described F. *habrophylla* and F. *Tanensis*.

[6] Georg (II, pp. 312–3) notes a man cutting down a tree with a stone adze from Aneityum, 'a very laborious undertaking'. He also describes a tridacna adze made from shell imported from Aniwa. George adds that local clubs with a lateral blade shaped like a fleam were also imported from Aniwa. (*Voyage*, II, 326). One may suspect that at this stage of the year the man was cutting timber for a new house.

[7] Wales (*Journals*, II, 855–6) and George (II, p. 508) have short useful descriptions of Tannese dwellings. See also pp. 598–9 above.

[8] This was the morning when George started 'to hum a song' and sparked off a 'great variety of different airs' in German, English and Swedish for the natives' benefit. In return they performed some New Hebridean songs upon which younger Forster made some observations concerning notes, metre and the local syrinx of reed pipes. One of these latter

the many Isles of which we got the Names & which they had said, that their Situation was to the South & SW & W. are no more than Districts on this Isle: but I heard likewise that there were two *Eetongas*, namely to the NE. *Eetonga-pārhā* & to the South *Eetongā-āfwìh*: but they likewise told beyond *Eetonga-pārha* of an Isle called *Mòrre-e-mòrre*; but however it is not yet clear to me, how far this may be depended upon.[1]

Aug ye 14th ☉ Afternoon I went ashore late, & saw the Seyne hauled, & we got 20 or 30 pound of Fish. I took two of them out, for to draw & describe them, & did this during night sitting still at one o'clock.[2] The next morning several Gentlemen & Capt *Cook* desired to come near the Volcano in order to see it.[3] We went up the hill to the Solfatara & made there again the Experiment with the Thermometer, with that difference only, that the Thermometer was fairly buried in the hole we had dug for it. In my Cabin the Thermometer was at 78: on the hill, having been carried in my pocket, it stood at 80°, but having been buried for a minute in the hole, it rose at once to 210° or the degree of boiling water, where it remained statarious for 5 minutes, & as soon as we took it out, it fell instantly to 95° & gradually to the old standard of 80°.[4] To day the weather was very heavy, foggy & sultry. We went on up the hill, & at last came to some habitations, saw some fowls & a spot of ground, which the Natives had laboriously cleared of the wood, for a new plantation.[5] We

(item 154) was deposited with the Oxford collection. George sorely felt the absence of James Burney, 'that sincere and obliging friend' when he came to comment on New Hebridean music. See p. 378, n. 2 above and *Voyage*, II, 318–20 and 322–3.

[1] It is certainly true that some of Forster's names, e.g. Marren and Togossummera (Melen and Tukosmeru) were Tannese place names and several others as well. See p. 601 n. 1 above. It may also be surmised that 'Erromanga' was a local name, i.e. Irmwanga, a village a few miles inland from Port Resolution. Similarly, there is indeed an *Itonga* in the north (north-east) of the island, in the Green Hill district. And it may well be that there was yet another Itonga in the south, though the word signifies merely the east wind. For the rest, *parha* (*baha*) means west and *Morre-e-morre* is perhaps merely *murh*, island. Forster is clearly in deep waters here, though with a little more time at his disposal light might well have broken through.

[2] We do not know, unfortunately, exactly how many drawings, botanical or zoological, Forster senior did himself.

[3] Cook, Wales, Patten and several other gentlemen with Sparrman, the two Forsters and two men were in the party. *Voyage*, II, 327.

[4] See p. 600, n. 1 above for Wales's experiment and Cook's results in *Journals*, II, 491–2. According to George (II, pp. 327–8) 'The experiment to measure the degree of heat was repeated as on the 12th, with this difference, that the thermometer was entirely buried in the white earth where the vapour came up. After it had remained one minute in this state, it rose to 210°...and remained stationary there as long as we kept it in the hole, which was for the space of five minutes. Sparrman (p. 156) concurs in this figure.

[5] 'The wretched tools of the natives, and the necessity of working very slowly with them, to which we had been witnesses on the other hill, convinced us that this piece of

went still on till we found a fellow in a path, who wanted to oppose us in going on, when he was told, we wanted to go to the Volcano; he said he would shew us the road. I told the Capt, that this was a device of the Natives to bring us to the beach; he should go on & not follow this cheating fellow; he however chuse to go after him, & soon found that I was in the right.[1] We therefore returned, but missed the road in the bushes & went too much on the left in a new path & were at last so far gone in the bushes, that we did not know where we were. The best therefore was to return to the Seashore; when the Natives saw us do this, they immediately brought us SugarCanes, Coconuts etc. & in a little time we found ourselves on the beach. The people had in our absence hawled the Seyne & got a few fish, among whom there was a little curious Fish belonging to the Genus of *Herrings*, with the Upper Jaws elongated on each side to half the Length of the body.[2] The pond where the Ship watered in seems to be a river which comes somewhere from the high hills to the South, & after having run through a good way & coming to the lose Sandy Soil it is lost in the Sands & here & there appears in the shape of ponds being drained through the Sands.[3] In this pond the people observed fish, & having tried the angle, they found them to be very fine *Mud-Eel*; among a good many Eels,[4] that were caught this morning, there was one fish of the Shape & size of a very large Dace.[5] It proved to be likewise one of the *Clupea* or *Herring-Genus*, whose last Rays in the Dorsal & Anal Fins were elongated & setaceous & had large Scales. This & the preceeding Fish were new.

ground, which comprehended near two acres, must have required a great deal of labour and a long space of time to clear', *Voyage*, II, 328. In fact, the technique of 'slash and burn' associated with shifting agriculture in Melanesia is surprisingly quick and is normally completed within a single month, June, *mouk mai*, cutting brush month for garden. The smaller twigs are then heaped up and fired, the stumps that survive being left *in situ*.

[1] Another incident in the saga of the paths. George adds: 'A little farther on we were met by two natives, who came out of an adjacent garden of bananas, and continued to walk with us. Coming to a place where the path divided, another man appeared in that part which led into the country, and with his uplifted dart prohibited our advancing that way. We told him we were desirous of going to the volcano, and he presently pointed out the other path to us, and went before to lead the way. As we advanced, we took notice that he continually counted over our number.' In the end, after several adventures, the party was forced to give up all hopes of approaching the volcano and return to the beach. See *Voyage*, II, 328–31. Cf. also Cook, *Journals*, II, 492–3. George omits his father's advice to Cook.

[2] *Clupea mystacina* of *Descr. Anim.*, p. 295, and Forster drawing no. 243.

[3] The Nimiraunu which takes its rise in a waterfall at Ifekal on the north-east slopes of Mt Tukosmeru and finally discharges into Lake Siwi at the foot of the volcano.

[4] Locally, *vin* or *puku*.

[5] Locally *mumus*, *Clupea cyprinoides* of *Descr. Anim.*, p. 296 and Forster drawing no. 242 (labelled *Clupea setipinna*).

Aug. ye 15th ☽ The Capt went in the Afternoon ashore.[1] I staid on board in order to draw & describe the new Fish; my Son & *Mr Sparman* did the same thing for the plants. The Natives we saw the day before eat the fruit of the *Terminalia Catappa*,[2] which has a Taste absolutely similar to Nutkernel, & is a very delicious Food. The next morning I went ashore in the back of the wooding & watering-place on the plain. We saw a green Parrokeet[3] & shot it, & likewise a Kingfisher[4] of the same kind, as we had gotten in New Zealand & a Pigeon[5] of the *Tongā-Tàbu* kind, which had in its craw two fruits involved in a red stuff perfectly similar to *Nutmeg* & *Mace*, but without smell; probably it is *Rumpf's*[6] wild Nutmeg. I desired an Indian to carry me to a Tree with the Fruit I shewed him, & as he was dubious I offerred him a Mother of Pearl-Shell.[7] He went with us a little in the bushes & at last stopped near a Tree, which he said bore *Gvānāttān*,[8] for they so called the Fruit. I plucked some leaves of it, & looked for the fruit, but he said they were eaten by the pigeons. We heard two large Muskets fired & therefore returned to the beach. The Natives told us, one of their Men was tied to a Tree & beaten: this circumstance made us go on still quicker; for we thought there might have happened some disturbance ashore, & they might revenge themselves upon

[1] With Wales to Samoa Point on the eastern side of the harbour on a rewarding excursion ethnologically. See *Journals*, II, 493–5.

[2] The so-called Indian almond, the fruit of a middle-sized tree, a staple in most of the islands of eastern Melanesia.

[3] *Psittacus palmarum* of *Descr. Anim.*, p. 259. This description is dated 5 August 1774 which appears to be in error for 15 August. George's folio 48 was of this specimen. See also Lysaght p. 284. It is now the Green Palm Lorikeet *Vini palmarum* (Gmelin, 1788); type locality Tanna Island.

[4] White-collared Kingfisher *Halcyon chloris tannensis* Sharpe. It was also recorded by Forster under the name *Alcedo collaris* in *Descr. Anim.*, p. 256. Locally known as *kavite*.

[5] The Pacific Pigeon, locally *mak* or *mak apahm*. Cf. p. 596, n. 3 above and n. 2 below. It was also recorded by Forster on Tanna as *Columba globicera* (*Descr. Anim.*, p. 256).

[6] The nut of the tall forest tree *Myristica castaneafolia* A. Gray. Both its 'mace' and 'nut' are said to be substitutes for those of the genuine Nutmeg (*Myristica moschata* Linn. = M. *fragrans* or *officianalis*) with which it has often been confused. It does not, however, figure in the local dietary. Cf. B. Seeman, *Flora Vitiensis* (London, 1865–73), p. 205. For G. E. Rumpf, see p. 170, n. 3 above.

[7] Cook makes the laconic entry: '...he [Forster] took pains to find the tree, but his endeavours were not attended with success', *Journals*, II, 495, n. 3.

[8] A most entertaining comedy of errors. According to George (*Voyage*, II, 332–3) 'He conducted us about half a mile up into the country to a young tree, which, as he affirmed, bore the nutmeg. We gathered its leaves, but saw no fruit, which the natives said had all been eaten by the pigeons'. The subsequent argument turned not on the name of the tree, as Forster mistakenly supposed, but on the proper name for the species of pigeon concerned – *mak*, the ordinary Pacific Pigeon *Ducula pacifica pacifica* (Gmelin, 1789) or the Green Pigeon, locally called *iouinetuen* or *yawinatuan* or, as Forster spells it, guanattan. Cf. Paowang's contribution to the debate p. 607, n. 6.

us. We heard of our people nothing had happened amiss. When I came to the crowd of Indians on the beach, I shewed them the leaves of the pretended Nutmeg-Tree, & was told another name than that given by the guiding Indian. The guide came & said likewise that same name, but when I told him it was *Guanattan*, & that he had cheated me: he made signs to the other people to say it was *Gvanattan*. I made signs to be angry & spit out as if it were a bad thing: than the other Indians rebuked him & he stept back: Lieut *Clarck* who came to it said *I was kicking up a Cabal*, as his Expression was, & desired me not to do it; I told, *it was no Cabal* to tell a Man, he had done wrong, when he did so; & that the Natives knew themselves the thing to be so, & therefore could I never think *this to be a Cabal*. He said he would make me do as he pleased. I said I never had been put under his or any bodies orders & were not responsible for my conduct to him, which was besides harmless. He said, if I did not obey his orders, he would give orders to the Sentry to shoot me. I said, I would acquaint the Captain, that he assumed an authority, which never was given to him. We both went, told our Case the Captain, & though he seemed not to believe neither the one nor the other, he however said, I must be under regulations. I said this was not the dispute, but whether I should be responsible to *Lieu*^t^ *Clarck* for my harmless conduct or not, & he then said, he had no orders to give me; well, said I, then I beg You, for the Lieut was then gone, to give Y^r^ officers directions, not to meddle with me, in things which are not relative to them: he said he could do no such thing: then said I, I must be afraid to go ashore because every petty Chap in the Ship, even a coxswain, would pretend to give me orders; & so said he, *you must be under their orders*. I desired to give me this declaration under his handwriting, but he refused. I told him, He durst not be ashamed to write what he was not ashamed to say, & I believed he was afraid it would serve against him: he said he was not. Why then will you not do it, replied I. At last we gave up our dispute; but this Specimen only shall serve to shew, what a hard thing it is, to be on board a Man of war, where every petty Officer or boy pretends to command Men, that never were intended to be controuled by such inconsiderable beings: the greater part of these people are so used to command & to bashaw it over other people, that no Man of honour will for the future venture to go on any Errand on board His Majesties Ship, for fear to be ill treated by these imperious people, who cringe ashore for preferment, & are often thought to be civil, nay polite; but as soon as they return to their Element the Sea, they are as rough & boisterous as it. There may be a few Exceptions to it, but I have reason to believe, but few.[1]

*Aug. ye 16th* ♂ In the Afternoon a party[2] of us with Capt *Cook* went to the Sea-Shore beyond the plantations on the brow to the right hand Side of the harbour, but we saw very little of the Isles, because it was too hazy.[3] We shot a new *Certhia*,[4] black with a ponçeau head & a long stroke along the back. We came to the habitations of our friends, & there George got a present of plantains, Sugar-Canes, & Coconuts, & so we returned on board.

The next morning I went ashore, we shot a new *Pigeon*[5] & got a few plants & the fruit of the wild Nutmeg, to which the Mace was still sticking, which Fruit the old Peacemaker called *Nāmmerằmmer*,[6] & said it was different from the fruit *Gvānnatằn*. We had been on the west side of the plain a good way up in the Country, & returned on the beach having got no more any new plant. We found on the beach an old grey headed Man & a younger one, whom we had not seen before; all the people said

[1] This tirade of that familiar brand of righteous indignation peculiar to the writer found no echo in Cook's journal entries and George (*Voyage*, II, 333) merely records that they 'expressed strong marks of indignation at his behaviour, and the other natives likewise rebuked him' i.e. the erring Tannese nutmeg-tree namer. All was revealed, however, by that British sailors' conscience of this voyage, the redoubtable Wales (*Remarks*, pp. 97–8) who reported publicly that Forster was confined by Clerke for '*spurning with his foot, and spitting in the face*' of the native. George produced another version of the incident in his *Reply*, pp. 36–8. Here we learn more: not only did Forster question Clerke's authority to order him about, but he also, threatened with being shot, drew a pistol which 'put an end to these extravagant heroics'. 'That good humoured man', Clerke, may have been 'extremely waspish at the time', thought George. Both Clerke and his father 'have since laughed at the violent heat, to which they suffered such trifles to mislead them'. 'Where', asked George, 'is the man that is not sometimes run away with by passion?' Did George write that tongue-in-cheek? Certainly it was – or would have been over one hundred years later – what we might call a Gilbertian situation, with no disrespect to the master! It was one which the genial light-hearted Clerke later might have well laughed over.

[2] The party comprised Cook, Cooper, Pickersgill, Patten, Hodges and Sparrman and the two Forsters (*Voyage*, II, 333).

[3] They went 'on the flat hill to the Eastward this time', since Cook was particularly desirous to see Aneityum which however 'was in haze', *Voyage*, II, 333.

[4] The *kouiametameta, koyametameta* or *kauyameramera*, the bird of the Koyometa 'tribe'; *Certhia cardinalis* of *Descr. Anim.*, p. 262; George's folio 63 (Lysaght, p. 288) was of this specimen. Now the Cardinal Honey-Eater *Myzomela cardinalis cardinalis* (Gmelin, 1788). Type locality, Tanna Island.

[5] Probably the now-extinct Tanna Ground Dove *Gallicolumba ferruginea* (Wagler, 1829). See 19 August 1774 p. 610 below.

[6] See p. 605, n. 8 above. The confusion persists but at least yields the local name (not elsewhere recorded) of the bird in question, i.e. *nammerammer* or, perhaps more correctly, *inamerama*.

us his name was *Yeögăi* & that he was *Arèekee* of *Tànnā*, his Son's Name was *Yàttā* & his title or Dignity was called *koù-vosh*, which signifies either Heir, Successor or Viceroy, or something like it, as I understood.[1] But he would not come on board, to dine with us.[2] Yesterday our people had began to saw the large Clubwood-Tree which stood on the brow beyond the watering-place; the Natives did dislike this, & told us not to cut the tree; the Capt promissed it should not be done, but when he heard how far it was cut, he thought best to buy the Tree & he gave this morning to the little Peacemaker a Dog, Cloth & other things which satisfied him & so it was cut down.[3]

Aug. ye 17th ☿ We went ashore but could hardly get any thing in the plant way & the birds are very shy, so that we went away again having got nothing. The Natives are very fond of New-Zeeland green stones,[4] of Mother of Pearl-Shells & chiefly of Turtle-Shell, which they hang in round Rings in their Ears & have several of them. The next morning we went into the woods at the back of the watering place[5] among the Swamps & saw several black Parrokeets[6] with red heads & breasts, but they are amazingly shy & we therefore could shoot none, though we stood 2 hours on the same spot & were most miserably bitten by the *Mosquitos*.[7]

[1] '...a very decrepit old man', *Voyage*, II, 337 His name is more correctly rendered Iokai, and that of his son Iata. He would have been styled *ieremera* rather than *ariki* which is, of course, the Polynesian word for a chief. Kou-vosh (*kova*) signifies simply a child, a son. George adds that the son was a tall man, well proportioned, and remarkably well featured for a native of Tanna. The two wore not a string but a bark belt. 'The sashes of the common people were of a uniform cinnamon or brownish-yellow colour; but these two chiefs wore them printed with black lines, and chequered with compartments of black and red'. No deference was paid to them and they issued no command. From all this it appears that Iokai was a *yani lao*, a man of considerable standing amongst the Kasurumene beyond the volcano, whose role it was to take the auguries in time of war and otherwise protect the interests of the tribe. The post seems to have been hereditary. Cf. J. Guiart, *Un siècle et demi de contacts culturels à Tanna* (*Nouvelles-Hébrides*) (Paris, 1956), pp. 86–7.

[2] But they came on board next day with a boy of 14, Narrep, and sat down on the floor of Cook's cabin and accepted presents. They ate some yams but would eat nothing else. George adds that they all left the beach very soon for their own homes which they pointed out as far distant from the bay (*Voyage*, II, 340–2).

[3] Cf. *Journals*, II, 496 and *Voyage*, II, 337–40. Cook needed the wood for repairs to the tiller.

[4] Nephrite, imported along with quantities of gabbro, serpentine and garnierite, from New Caledonia. Cf. Aubert de la Rue, 'La géologie des Nouvelles-Hébrides', *Journal de la Société des Océanistes*, XII (December 1956), 69.

[5] '...in hopes of meeting by accident with the nutmeg tree', *Voyage*, II, 340. The same author gives a good description of the swamp with its massive banyans and endless troublesome mosquitoes. Ibid., II, 334–5.

[6] The Coconut Lory *Trichoglossus haematodus massena* Bonaparte, not described or illustrated by the Forsters.

[7] Apparently *Aedes* (*Stegomyia*) *hebrideus* Edwards, a persistent diurnal biter and a semi-domestic pest. Cf. J. N. Belkin, *The Mosquitoes of the South Pacific* (*Diptera and Culicidae*) (Berkeley, 1962), I, 457–61. *Anopheles* (*Cellia*) *farauti Laveran* which must also

I found a new plant, & saw three Ducks,[1] but my piece unhappily snapping twice, they all flew away; they seemed to me to be of the little purpleheaded black N.Z. Duck.[2]

Aug. ye 18th ♃ In the Afternoon we went to the place where we took our ballast in & tried the Thermometer in the hot wells. The Thermometer was in my Cabin 78°; when I came there, the same was at 83°, having been carried close to my body in my pocket, & in the Well it rose in 5 minutes to 191° & after it was taken out & the well cleared & made deeper, it stood again 10 minutes in it, & remained all the time at 191°.[3] We saw several small 2 Inch-Fish of the Blenny or Goby kind. They jump on the wet Rocks like Lizards, helping themselves with their little Fins as with Feet & are so nimble that with great difficulty but one was caught; they hunt for little Insects. Their Eyes stand on the top of the head, to guard them against all their Ennemies when out of the water; they are very prominent, that they may see better on every side & have Eyelids to cover them when they jump against the hard Rocks. I drew & described this minute nimble Animal.[4]

The next morning we went again to the same hot well, where we had been the day before & took the Thermometer with us; in my Cabin it was 78° & in the same well, where it had been the day before in, it rose to 187° after a 1½ minute staying in it, but it never rose higher. It was then low water & about 9 o'clock A.M: but yesterday the experiments were made at about 4½ o'clock P.M. at high water. From thence we went in the boat to the end of the beach, where the high rock begins & we came there in about half an hours time & put the Thermometer just in the place, where the water bubbles up, & it rose there in about a minutes time to 202½° & remained there so for several more minutes, without rising higher.[5] After that we went into the

have been present is ruled out not merely as a night-biter but by the simple fact that no one seems to have been infected here with malaria.

[1] Locally *gare*, probably the Australian Grey Duck *Anas superciliosa pelewensis* Hartlaub and Finsch, the only common duck in the New Hebrides. George (II, 336) notes a prodigious number of birds in a massive *Ficus religiosa* Linn.

[2] On their return from this expedition the party attempted to exchange axes for pigs and were refused despite the astonishment of those involved at the 'extreme utility of this tool' (*Voyage*, II, 336). The demands of the forthcoming pig exchange were obviously not so lightly to be set aside.

[3] Cf. *Journals*, II, 497 and 860–1.

[4] 'The same or a similar species of fish had been observed on the coast of New Holland by captain Cook in the Endeavour', *Voyage*, II, 343. It was *Blennius gobioides* of *Descr. Anim.*, p. 283 and Forster drawing no. 183.

[5] This experiment was tried specifically at Wales's suggestion, (*Journals*, II, 861).

woods, shot at a new Dove,[1] but it went off, though feathers & blood came off from it. We found a new plant, on a high Tree were Fruit & Flowers. The tree was inaccessible & we contrived to get the Fruit by throwing Stones & Sticks & by shooting at them: at last we cut a young high Tree, & by this we knocked branches with Fruit & Flowerbuds down & then returned for dinner.

*Aug. ye 19th* ♀ It seems either the Sea comes at high water by some subterraneous passages to the Volcano & causes & new ebullition & therefore a greater heat, & boils therefore the Water better, or the Volcano is not allways equally hot but cools gradually, till a new Eruption is caused & a new supply of hot Water is procured. There ought a series of Experiments to be made to ascertain this, which is impossible in a Ship, that wants hands for wooding, watering & new rigging the Ship, & can spare no hands for boats. The Volcano has been silent these two days, but two days ago he was continually thundering.[2] We went ashore & up into the Valley behind the Watering-place, & got a new plant. They hawled the Seyne & got about 200 weight of fish & among them 2 new Mullets,[3] & a new Whip-Ray,[4] but the first Lieu^t^, being desired to preserve the Stings of the new Ray, because I had begg'd the Capt some days ago to preserve them for me, on purpose cut them off & cut likewise the Fins of a new Mullet, which had been caught, that I might have no opportunity to describe it[5] We are all ready for sailing, but the wind is contrary.

The next morning went ashore in order to get some plants & birds,[6] but it seems the new plants are exhausted for we have

[1] Forster's description of *Columba xanthura* was undated in *Descr. Anim.*, p. 264. His son's folio 138 (Lysaght, p. 304) is the type of the species and the type locality is Tanna. Now the Tanna Fruit Dove *Ptilinopus tannensis* (Latham, 1790). See fig. 36a.

[2] Cf. *Voyage*, II, 344–5. Today the volcano still exhibits very irregular intervals between the emissions and explosions of incandescent scoria from one of several vents in the crater. The quiescent time been periods of intense activity, when explosions may occur every few minutes for two or three days, may last for two to three days as well. See also p. 617, n. 1 below.

[3] *Mugil salmoneus* of *Descr. Anim.*, p. 299 and drawing no. 237..

[4] Difficult to identify but possibly *Raja edulenta.* See p. 508, n. 2 above.

[5] If relations had deteriorated thus far then there was, indeed, some cause for Forster's later angers.

[6] Two species were described between 5–19 August 1774. They were (a) *Muscicapa heteroclita* of *Descr. Anim.*, p. 271; G. Forster's folio 158, dated 7 August 1774, is the type of the species (Lysaght, p. 308). Now the Yellow White-eye *Zosterops flavifrons flavifrons* (Gmelin, 1789). Type locality Tanna Island. (b) *Collumba ferruginea* of *Descr. Anim.*, p. 265; George's folio 142 was probably based upon the 'new Pigeon' shot on 16 August 1774. Type locality for this Tanna Ground Dove is this island. See p. 607 above.

Figure 35. Natural History of the New Hebrides.
(a) The Tanna Fruit Dove *Ptilinopus tannensis* (Latham).
Drawing by George Forster in B.M. (N.H.) – 'Zoological Drawings', f. 138.

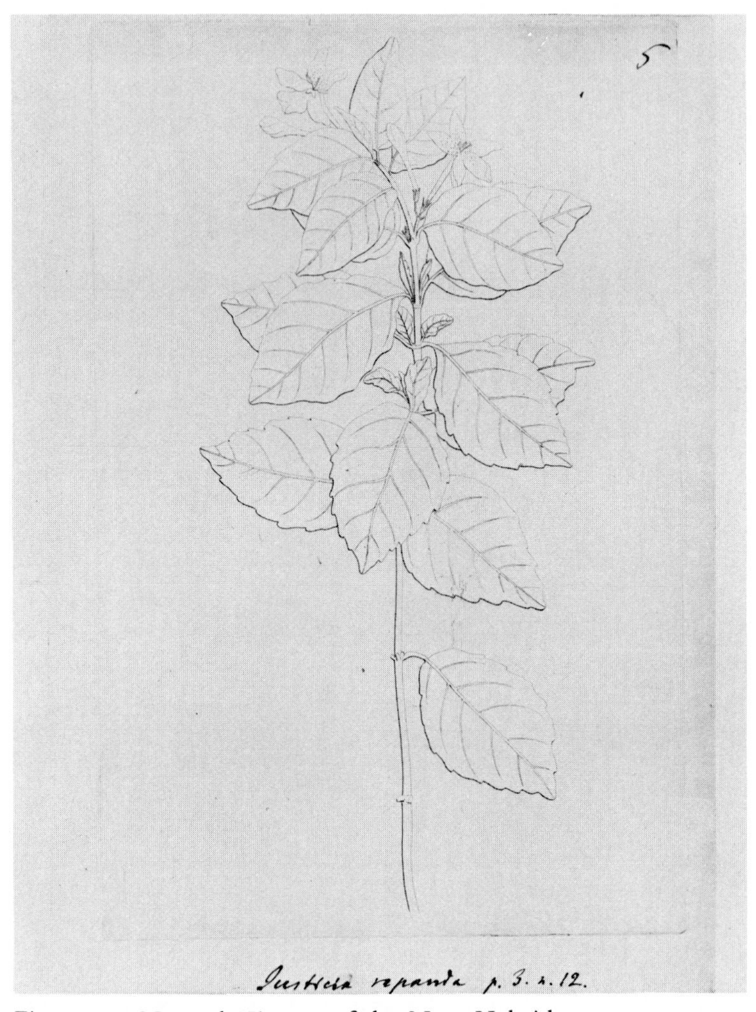

Figure 35. Natural History of the New Hebrides.
(b) *Justicia repanda*, now *Anthacanthus repandus* Nees in D.C. Drawing by George Forster in B.M. (N.H.) – 'Botanical Drawings', I, f. 7.

gotten about 20 allready, & the birds are vastly shy, & now more so than before, after all our Gentlemen have been firing at them for a long while. Today an Indian transgressing with several others the limits set them by the Guards at the Watering & wooding place, was gently drove back by the Sentry, but the Indian immediately took an Arrow & made ready to let fly at the Sentry; the Sentry cocked his piece & when he took aim at the Sentry,[1] he fired at the Indian & shot him through the Arm & through the Side, of which he died in a few moments. The Natives were in the Country very kind to us; though they met me far up in the Country, they were allways civil to us, & gave us Sugar-cane & Coconuts, & I can not say of seeing them once rude, they allways go from the Path & let us go by: they name or ask our Names & do us all the kindness possible. But on the watering-place they had behaved, *as is said*, very rudely for these 3 or 4 days; & this same Man had the day before pointed his Arrow at another Sentry in the Captains presence. The Capt[t] disapproved of this rash action, & sent the Marine, after having him relieved, prisoner on board; for he was that very moment arrived on shore.[2]

Aug. y[e] 20th ♄ Went in the Afternoon ashore, the Seyne was hawled & but few fish caught; two *Trigla asiatica*[3] were caught; an *Altavela* Skaite,[4] several Mullets, a speckled South Sea Mackrel,[5] some new Pearches & a Sea Horse,[6] which is the 4th caught in this Harbour. I made Remarks on these Fish.

The Natives seemed quite unconcerned at the death of their Brother,[7] whom they carried away; & brought as before Yams,

[1] This was an unusual incident. George notes that there were now rarely as many as a hundred natives on the beach, including woman and children, and these commonly sat down under the shade of the bushes. 'The civility of the natives on the whole, was very conspicuous towards us'. (*Voyage*, II, 341). One can only suppose that this fellow was a visitor from up country who did not take kindly to the limits imposed upon his freedom, or perhaps a local hot-head who had found something in the behaviour of the Europeans to irritate him.

[2] See *Journals*, II, 489–9. Cook was on hand at least to see the incident. The elder Forster was off botanising and George and Sparrman were away separately. Sparrman adds: '. . . the Lieutenant of Marines. . . contended that the man was entitled to believe he was not posted there merely to provide a target for arrows, without the right to defend himself. The Naval Lieutenant agreed with this. . .' The miscreant was William Wedgeborough, marine. See p. 578, n. 3 above.

[3] *Trigla asiatica* of *Descr. Anim.*, p. 236 (the Tahiti description) and p. 247 (Raiatea – name only) and George Forster drawing no. 241 (from Tahiti).

[4] *Raja pastinaca* var β *altavela*. See p. 595, n. 6 above.

[5] *Scomber trachurus* of *Descr. Anim.*, pp. 155 (Dusky Bay – name only), 257 (Tanna – name only) and 413 (diagnosis) and Forster drawing no. 223 (Dusky Bay).

[6] *Syngnathus hippocampus* of *Descr. Anim.*, p. 257. There is no drawing.

[7] Cook (*Journals*, II, 499) makes much more of this episode. According to him '. . . most

Sugarcanes & Coconuts. It is no wonder, that the Sentry took this liberty to shoot a poor innocent Man, since Lieu[t] *Clarck*, in the hearing of all the Sentries, & of the Cap[t] declared, he would shoot & would order the Sentry to shoot me, if I *would not obey his orders*, though I never was put under his orders, nor will ever obey them; it is the imperious, haughty behaviour of these Young Gentlemen, that has caused the poor Mans death; for when the Marines hear, that they may shoot a Man, whom the king & Government sent on purpose out in the South-Seas, how much more right must it be to shoot a poor, harmless, & contemptible wretch of an Indian: besides this, it plainly appears, that the order was given by Lieu[t] *Clarck* to the Marines & Sentries, never to put up with any insult but to fire immediately: which is right & just in people who are informed of the Superiority we have over them by our Fire-arms, but not by poor wretches, who do not yet know, how far these instruments may be deadly or not. Lieu[t] *Clarck* in order to save the Marine from flogging, went to the Cap[t] & told he had given the orders, & defended the Justice of this Action, but how far the Arguments will hold, is another Question.[1] We come here to take water & wood from these people, they do not know what we want, they appear & do us all kindness that lies in their power, but however not knowing our intentions, they allways carry arms

of the people fled, it was only a few I could prevail upon to remain; as they ran off I observed one man to fall and was immidiately taken up by two others who led him into the water, washed his wound and then led him off. Presently after some came and described to us the nature of his wound, which I now sent for the surgeon to dress, as I found the man was not carried far. As soon as the Surgeon came I went with him to the man, which we found expiring'. George (*Voyage*, II, 351) makes a bystander say 'Markom', i.e. dead like the pigeon shot by Clerke on 10 August. See p. 597 n. 1 above. Cook adds: 'This unhappy affair threw the Natives into the utmost consternation the few that were prevailed on to stay ran to the plantations and brought Cocoa nutts &[a] came and laid [them] down at our feet, so soon were these daring people humbled...', *Journals*, II, 499–500.

[1] This is an interesting new piece of information concerning an incident to which Beaglehole devotes (*Journals*, II, 499–500) a very long note. Briefly it has been assumed hitherto that Edgecumbe, the lieutenant of marines, may have given general orders to shoot if molested, directly contrary to Cook's instructions – which says Beaglehole, 'reads like nonsense'. Here Forster tells us the order was given by Clerke. Wales took strong exception to George Forster's long version of this incident (*Voyage*, II, 350–3) wherein he attacked the 'officer who commanded on shore' (i.e. Clerke) for intervening to stop 'the rascal', Wedgeborough, getting the flogging Cook was determined to give him. Wales (*Reply*, pp. 83–8), carefully sifting the evidence of the only reliable witness, Whitehouse, waded in boldly against Forster on Wedgeborough's and the unnamed officer's behalf. It was, wrote the indignant astronomer, 'one of the most malignant pieces of misrepresentation' in the Forster *Voyage*. George countered briefly (*Reply*, pp. 34–5), stressing that it was 'the officer's *orders*' which appeared unjust *not* the marine's actions. He also revealed that it was a matter of considerable contention between Cook and his officers who insisted upon Wedgeborough not being punished. Cook as usual certainly cast no opprobrium by name on Clerke, Edgecumbe or anyone else among his officers.

with them & seeing themselves driven away on their own ground & bottom by a set of armed Europeans, they think it no more but Justice to threaten to put the Arrow on the bow in their own defence, & we for that act order them to be shot. The first Mate Mr *Whitehouse*, who was within sight & saw the whole transaction, said to the Capt that not the Man with the bow & Arrows, but another poor innocent Man was shot, which makes the circumstance still worse.[1] Acts of violence have been allways the beginning of settling & establishing the power of Europeans among new discovered Nations; & if we justly detest the cruelty of the Spaniards in America, we must not give a handle to other Nations to tax our conduct in the same manner: & though perhaps this is less to kill a single Man than to exterminate a whole Nation & to make the poor remainders slaves, it is nevertheless a cruelty. The Spaniards were cruel in a less refined age; we should, with more light & principles, endeavour to avoid the reproach of following their footsteps. The blind Zeal for their religion, conducted by bigotted ignorant Friars, often inspired them with cruelty & inhumanity against the poor victims of their false zeal: but Protestants, who boast the principles of reformation, should shew them by their humanity & reformed conduct. But principles of religion are not to be looked for among Men of no principles. The Capt disadvowed this act to the last, but could not punish the Soldier without involving the officer in the same guilt, & therefore the Murder remained unnoticed.[2] Nay the Capt had ordered never to fire, unless the Natives were really the first aggressors, but Lieut *Clarck*, who commanded on shore, had given orders, that as soon as the Natives would threaten to fire an Arrow or throw a Dart, then Sentry should fire upon them.[3]

The next morning we unmoored, hove the Anchor, slipt the

[1] This was also Cook's belief (*Journals*, II, 499, n. 1) although, according to Wales (*Remarks*, p. 85), Whitehouse, the master's mate, 'an insinuating litigious mischief making fellow' in Elliot's opinion, later went back on his evidence.

[2] According to Sparrman (*Voyage*, p. 159) he finally got off with 'a couple of months' confinement', which one would have thought severe enough.

[3] This last sentence is carried over as a marginal entry on v, f. 131 and looks like a later addition. Why does Forster hound privately the capable, whimsical, light-hearted Clerke? Perhaps because he was a particular friend of Banks and would have much to tell that gentleman about the parvenu naturalist? George Forster's last sentence on the incident must have caused him some pain to write: 'The soldier was therefore immediately cleared, and the officer's right to dispose of the lives of the natives remained uncontroverted', *Voyage*, II, 353. Clerke never saw the condemnation since he went off in the *Discovery* on the third voyage and died off Kamchatka on 22 August 1779.

last cable, set sail, & left the launch behind to heave the Anchor.[1] When we were clear of the land, we brought to & waited the return of the launch, & then hoisted her & all the other boats in, & set sail again; the Course E.bS. The Thermometer at 74°, in my Cabin 75°.

Aug. yᵉ 21ˢᵗ ☉ The Island of *Tanna* is about 6 or 8 leagues long from NW to SE; its breadth I can as yet, say nothing of.[2] The hills of it, as far as appears from its cliffs towards the Sea, are a clay-Marle with Marle- & Chalk-Stones mixed. This lies in Strata of 6 Inches more or less, pretty horizontal or very little deviating. In a few places I found a soft black Sandstone, composed of the Ashes spread by the Volcano & a kind of Clay; here & there appeared the Substance called *Rottenstone*, which is a brown *clayey Tripoly*. This Rottenstone, I believe, is mixed with the above *Sandstone*, for I found where one Stratum left off, there the other gradually began ie the Rotten Stone was first quite pure, & more & more mixed with Sand. This Sand is as beforementioned, a Slag ejected by the Volcano; it is black & contains small glossy, shining particles, just as if the black Pumice-Stone were broken into Atomes.[3] This Sand covers all the beaches & I may say all the Surface of the Island, being only mixed with some Mould, & in this Soil all the plants vegetate & thrive exceedingly well, for we found here all kinds of plants as big as in other places: the only difference is that the Trees & plants stand not so fast rooted as in other

[1] Whether they left on account of the aforegoing affair is unclear. Cf. *Journals*, II, 498.

[2] Approximately 22 miles long by 15 miles at its widest point, seven or eight at its narrowest. George gives the position of the island as lat. 19° 30′ S, long. 169° 38′ E (Cook, Port Resolution 19° 33′ S, 169° 44′ 33″) and adds: '...I believe it does not exceed twenty-four leagues in circuit'.

[3] George (*Voyage*, II, 355–6) gives a shorter account of the geology of Tanna. Little work has so far been done on the geology of Tanna, although preliminary reconnaissance surveys have revealed some findings but Yasur (also known as Yasour) has been studied sporadically in the geological literature by occasional visitors and missionaries since the 1880s. Tanna appears to consist of andesitic and basaltic pyroclastics. The rocks of the centre are blanketed by ash produced from the periodic activity of Yasur and consist of crystalline, pumiceous, cindery tuffs, agglomerates, sometimes containing flow-banded cindery fragments of vitreous lava, breccias and some conglomerates which are possibly lahars. Faulted foraminiferal and coral limestones also occur along the edge of the plateau. Most islands in the Central Chain of the New Hebrides, in which Tanna lies, consist of primary or reworked volcanic rocks, commonly surrounded or clapped by raised reef limestone. For more details see the annual reports of the Geological Survey of the New Hebrides Condominium and François Dugas, 'A Bibliography of the Geology and Geophysics of the New Hebrides', *Technical Bulletin* (Committee for Co-ordination of Joint Prospecting for Mineral Resources in South Pacific Offshore Areas), I (1975), 54–73, where, the published Forster work is cited. See also De la Roue, 'La géologie des Nouvelles-Hébrides', pp. 77–9.

places, which accounts for the many broken down trees we found across the footways, & numbers of dead or half dead Coconut Trees which were seen among the bushes on the ground; nay some recovered after being overturned by Storms, & I have seen Coco-Trees, laying on the ground, & their tops took a new turn & began to grow upwards.[1] The Pumice Stones here are commonly black, but few are bleached & white. They are of various Textures, some were so entirely burnt out & light that they would swim on the top of the Water; others on the contrary had still so much Specific gravity, that they sunk at the bottom of the Sea. In several Pumice-Stones appear white fibrous particles, shining & sharp like Asbest. Higher up on the hills we found smoking & hot places, where we found commonly a white soft kind of Earth, exactly smelling like wet Chalk; it was often incrustated with a green or yellow Substance, which I believe to be Sulphur, so that this Chalk penetrated by aqueous & Sulphureous steams formed a kind of *Hepar Sulpharis*; its taste was styptic, & if I am not mistaken aluminous. In the same smoking hot places I saw a red kind of Ochre, just as moist & penetrated by the moist Sulphureous hot Steams, as the white Substance. The whole adjacent part had neither Trees nor Shrubs growing on; except the Figtrees, which sometimes grew within a few yards of this new *Solfatara*, which the Natives call *Ergoo-âs.*[2] At the foot of this *Solfatara*, about 60 or 80 yards lower, & almost level to the Sea at high water, are in several places hot wells. I tried the heat of the *Solfatara* on the hill twice, once I only opened a hole big enough to receive one of Mr *Ramsden's* Thermometers, with an Ivory Scale plate, & hung it in this hole up for several minutes & it rose to 170°; a second time I buried it entirely in the hole with the Stuff dug out of it, & it then mounted in a minutes time to 210°, or next to the heat of boiling water, & it remained thus for more than 5 minutes. I likewise went to the last mentioned hot wells, which no doubt communicate with the *Solfatara* & that with the *Volcano* on this Isle; for the wells are immediately under the *Solfatara* & one can trace a stroke of hot places down the hill, a great way very near to the wells: The communication of the

[1] The island is prone to devastating hurricanes, sometimes as many as three or four a year in the hurricane season (November–April).

[2] I.e. *kuas* or *kual*, an aperture. As Forster notes, these fumaroles are connected with Yasur. There are also several hot springs at Sulphur Bay to the north.

Solfatara with the Volcano appeared from the Smoke coming out in greater Quantities at each rolling thunder & new Eruption of Smoke from the *Crater*. The heat at the wells, where we took ballast in under a steep bank of the abovementioned black Stone, was tried twice, once at high water, when the Thermometer rose in less than a minutes time to 191° & remained thus for 5 minutes; we cleared the hole of pebbles & made it deeper for the reception of the Thermometer; it stood again more than 10 minutes in the hot water & rose not higher than 191°. But on the beach is another hot well, under a steep cliff of the above black Stone, where the Thermometer rose to 202½° in about a minutes time, & stood at the same degree for several minutes; it was then low water, & at the same time we tried again the well we had tried the day before & found it rose only to 187°, after staying only 1½ minute in it, nor did it rise higher, though left therein for several more minutes. This water is clear, has a taste somewhat adstringent, but it did not affect a piece of bright Silver laid in it, nor was any change caused by the addition of salt of Tartar; however the Experiments being made upon the Spot, in a very inconvenient place, & in a great hurry, I cannot quote them as decisive & therefore filled a glass-bottle with this water & corked & pitched it, in order to repeat the Experiments at leasure. The *Volcano* is on a hill about 4 miles distant from the Sea & about 8 from the harbour, where the Ship lay in, on a ridge of hills not above 120 or 150 yards elevated above the Surface of the Sea.[1] There is to the South of it another ridge at least as high again, divided from it by a Valley; the Volcano itself appeared to us by our glasses to be barren & formed of the Ashes & pumice-Stones thrown up by the *Volcano*, there was likewise a appearance of *Lava* here & there, & we saw certainly a smoking ridge, when we left the place, which was not observed before when we came in. For several days at the first beginning of our Stay, the Volcano made allmost every 4 or 5 minutes an Explosion of dense Smoke, which was gradually carried off by the winds, & wherever this Smoke was spread, there

[1] The peak is entirely made up of loose grey 'cinders' and is in consequence subject to notable changes in shape and height from erosion and occasional volcanic outbursts. According to a recent estimate, however, it rises some 980 ft to 1264 ft above sea-level. The crater itself plunges vertically down some 600 ft and is some 500 yards across. The several vents at the bottom are almost constantly active and throw up large quantities of siliceous, scoria bombs every three or four minutes. On the westward (landward) side there is a lake (Siwi) and beyond that an extensive bare ash plain. The scene even on a fine day is desolate and awe-inspiring.

the above Sandy or gritty Ashes fell down as a rain & were composed, as I observed through a Microscope, of small pieces of pumice Stone; of shining, irregular-shaped pieces of a black glassy Slag, which looked brownish & semitransparent when the light was reflected on them by the Mirror of the Microscope, of white transparent irregular-shaped pieces of Glass or Quartz; of fibrous shining, acerose particles like Asbest & of some black irregular opaque black particles; in short as particles of a substance which had undergone a violent change in the Fire. These Ashes lay on all the plants & Vegetables of the Isle, & one day our Ship was covered by them, when the Wind was standing from the Volcano; & the whole Surface of the Isle consists of these Ashes.[1] When M[r] *de Buffon* in his *Theory of the Earth*[2] speaks of the *Volcanos*, he says, *they are in the high mountains*. This Expression is for a philosopher too vague, too indeterminate. Which mountains does he call high ones? Those that are capt by Clouds, or such as are below that mark? and if below the heighth of the clouds, (which by the bye is likewise an indeterminate heighth) which heighth is convenient for Volcanos; or does he understand by high mountains, such as have none higher near them; if this is to be understood, there is an instance to the contrary to be met with in this Volcano of *Tānnā* because the ridge of Mountains to the South of the Volcano is certainly more than twice the heighth of the Volcano, if not 3 times. If he means 150 yards to be a *high hill*, I allow our Volcano is on a *high hill*: but I believe, there are but few, who would take the word *high hill* in that Sense: & the Volcano or Volcanos in the Isle of Ambrrÿm were by no means on high hills,[3] nor on the

[1] The ash is carried NW on the back of the SE trade wind as much as 10 miles away. Sparrman adds that all the plants and foliage were covered and weighed down with volcanic ash and in one night the deck of the ship was quite covered with it. The soil was in consequence provided with the greatest fertility for root vegetables (i.e. yams). He notes, however, one seeming drawback: 'This ash, getting into the eyes seemed to cause a dropping of the upper eyelid (*Ptosis palpebrae* or *Blepharoptosis*), the only malady we discovered among the people: since it also affected quite young people, it may have been sometimes an hereditary complaint'. See Sparrman, *Voyage round the World*, pp. 156–7 and p. 632, n. 5. One thing is certain. The general absence of surface water arising from superior drainage renders this area comparatively malaria free, hence the concentration of the population at this point.

[2] Forster had long been a close and critical student of Buffon since, indeed, he had first turned to the study of natural history in Nassenhuben. He used Buffon freely in his Warrington lectures on geology and mineralogy and later reviewed his *Époques de la Nature* (1779). I have dealt with their relationship and Buffon's influence on Forster in *Tactless Philosopher*. See also *Observations*, pp. 137–45 where Forster has more on volcanoes and discusses Buffon's ideas.

[3] Either his memory plays him false or his eyes deceived him. Mt Marum is 4380 feet, though usually covered with clouds. See p. 562, n. 3 above.

highest of that Isle. It is enough Volcanos are formed on elevations; hills, on dry land, or even in the Sea, under Water, of which there are instances.[1]

After it had rained allmost all night Aug. ye 11th the Volcano, which had been pretty quiet for several days, began again to rage & to cause a rolling thunder, & to throw up large Stones, as big at least as our longboat, else would they not have been conspicuous from the Ship at 6 or 8 miles distance. The corresponding *Spiracula* at the *Solfataras*, emitted at the same time new quantities of steams, after each new Eruption & rolling Thunder of the Volcano. I am therefore pretty certain, the Volcano has a Connexion with the Solfataras: & it is equally proved that the new accession of rain water, which entered the bowels of the Earth by some crevices or subterraneous conducts caused a new Fermentation & Ebullition in the interior parts of the Volcano.[2] The great size of the Stones that were thrown prove incontestibly the immense force of the expanded Air, which can lift up Masses with Velocity to a great heighth, that all mankind would have left untouched, though Assisted by Engines & powder & other Implements of our arts.

I cannot dwell any longer on this Subject of the Volcano, & of the various Mineral bodies of this Island of *Tanna*, as it would become too tedious. The fresh Water seems to be but sparingly divided over the Island.[3] The Valley at the bottom of the harbour is a marshy place, where the Water stagnates. Near the Seashore is a small pond where we watered at, & this is exposed to the open Air, but the rest stinks most intolerably like Bilgewater, being overshaded by Trees & bushes; this Marsh contains Millions of Gnats & Mosquitos, who incommoded our Sportsmen very much,

[1] And, if only he had known it, in the New Hebrides. Submarine eruptions are recorded between Goat Island and Traitors' Head on Erromanga (1881), between Epi and Tongoa (1889), and between Lopevi and Epi (1920). There have been intermittent wellings-up off Tongoa in much more recent times. Forster's observations mark a further important stage in his thinking on vulcanicity. Cook must have discussed the origin and location of volcanoes with Forster – and we can imagine Wales being party to the discussions – since he summarises this argument (*Journals*, II, 497–8) and sides with Forster in opposing the 'Opinion of Philosophers, which is that all Volcanoes must be at the summits of the highest hills'. Cook's observations on the volcanic activity of Ambrym were very close to those here put down by Forster.

[2] It is more likely that the vents had been occluded by the slumping of the sides of the crater so that the volcano was in consequence in the process of 'clearing its throat', as local residents say. It is nonetheless true that Yasur is subject to periods of heightened activity of an explosive nature which may indeed last some months at a time.

[3] Streams are indeed comparatively rare all over the island but there are nonetheless several notable streams and waterfalls, particularly in the south of the island.

one young Gentleman especially looked as if he had had the Small-pox, on face, hands & feet: & they are the cause, I believe, that this fine fertile Valley is not inhabited by the Natives;[1] they content themselves to plant here & there some Eddies, & on higher places a few plantains. The Trees & plants we saw here are allmost the same with those we met with at *Anamocka* & *Eetonga Tȁbu*, a few were new ones, & they did not exceed 18. We saw among others in the Craw of a large Pigeon we shot, two nuts, which I immediately took for a wild Nutmeg, which the Natives call by various Names; some said it was *Gvānnetȁn* or *Gvānnerȁn*, others *Gva-nòhee* & still others named the same *Nāmmerȁmmer* & the Tree it grew on *Neerȁsh* with long leaves & curiously vẹined on their underside.[2] I got afterwards from one of the Natives three wild Nutmegs, still wrapt in their coating of Mace; they have, it seems, nothing of that aromatic smell, peculiar to this precious drug, known under the Name of the *true Nutmeg*. They were at this time allmost all eaten up by the Pigeons, nor had they then any Flowers: they are however similar to a kind of Drug lately introduced into the *Materia Medica*, under the Name of *Faba Pacuris* or *Faba Sti Ignatii*, which the Chinese make use of in their Pharmacopies against the Flux, but having lately been tried in *Sweden* it did not allways answer: however if Experiments were repeated & attention paid to the peculiar habit of body it might prove a useful medicine. As *Quiros* in his memorial[3] mentions Nutmegs as the produce of *Mallicollo*, he probably means this peculiar species. If I ever return to that Country, I will attempt to get more of this Fruit, in order to make experiments with them in England. For having masticated both the Mace & Nut I found them both to be bitter in an eminent degree.[4]

The Natives cultivate *Cocos nucifera*, *Musa paradisiaca* & its various varieties, *Arum macrorhizon* & *esculentum*, *Dioscorea oppositifolia* & *alata*,[5] *Sacharum officinarum*,[6] for their food. They eat

[1] See p. 608, n. 7 above. It may nonetheless be suggested that the real difficulty was malaria which the Tannese well know how to avoid.

[2] See p. 605, n. 8 above. Neerȁsh is possibly *nesey* (of Guiart) or the English *neres*.

[3] Dalrymple, *Historical Collection*, I, 167. See also Kelly, I, 226, n. 3 and 230 and II, 286 and also p. 605, n. 6 above.

[4] The reputation of these islands as a source of nutmegs issued in a number of abortive commercial ventures to the New Hebrides in the nineteenth century.

[5] The smaller and the greater yam, the latter of which grows here upwards of 6–10 feet in length and 150–200 lbs in weight.

[6] The sugar-cane.

likewise the *Inocarpus edulis,*[1] the *Artocarpus communis* or *Breadfruit,* the *Eugenia malaccensis,* & *Jambos;*[2] the *Terminalia Catappa,*[3] a Fig with a purple pulp – *Ficus Granatum,* a small Fig which grows in large Clusters from the Stem of the Tree & is a Species of *Ficus Indica.* They eat likewise the young leaves of another Fig which is woolly like a Peach & which we call *Ficus tomentosa.* They cultivate the Hibiscus *esculentus* or *Okra* & dress the leaves. They have several Indian plants & such as grow in the Society-Isles viz. *Casuarina equisetifolia, Calophyllum Inophyllum,*[4] *Piper methysticum,*[5] *Dracæna terminalis, Hibiscus tiliaceus, Dalibarda,*[6] *Crinum asiaticum, Convolvulus peltatus*[7] & *Pes Caprae, Euphorbia Atoto, Anthemis Proteus, Dioscorea bulbifera, Lycopodium Phlegmaria, Sterculia foetida* & *Balanghas,*[8] *Hedysarum heterocarpon, Dolichos ensiformis, Melochia scandens,*[9] *Erythrina corallodendrum, Arecca cathechu,*[10] *Brunnichia acris* & *edulis.*[11] *Convolvulus Turpethum,*[12] *coelestis*[13] & *acuminatus, Commelina virginica,*[14] *Ageratum conyzoides, Croton variegatum, Ricinus Mappa, Ischaemum aristatum, muticum* & *Coelorachis, Acanthus ilicifolius, Citrus Aurantium* & several more.[15] We found but few Shills in the Seas surrounding this Isle; the Natives were fond of Mother of Pearl Shells & coveted them in a manner, which made me believe they were scarce.[16] They had various *Madrepores, Astroites* & others & some Natives used pieces of Coralrock about 18 Inches long & 2 Inches Diameter to throw at their Ennemy & to knock him in the head with.[17] We got fine Fish & in abundance

[1] *Inocarpus fagifer* (Parkinson ex Z) Fosb., the Tahitian chestnut.

[2] The so-called Malay apple, and the so-called 'rose-apple' – *Eugenia Jambos* (*Jambosa vulgaris*).

[3] The so-called Indian almond.

[4] *Calophyllum* sp., the local kauri, the gum which was used for caulking canoes.

[5] *Piper methysticum* Forst., kava, one of the most valued of the domestic plants of Tanna, intimately associated with numerous rituals.

[6] *Dalbergia.*

[7] *Merremia peltata* (L.) Merr.

[8] *Sterculia forsteri* Seem.

[9] *Melochia odorata* L.

[10] *Areca catechu* L., the betel nut palm, but apparently not *Piper betle* L., the betel vine, an essential ingredient in the preparation of betel. The New Hebrideans are, of course, *kava* drinkers; betel chewing reaches no further east than Santa Cruz and the Duff Islands.

[11] *B. edulis* = *Antigonon leptopus* Hook. Arn?

[12] *Operculina turpethum* (L.) S. Manso.

[13] *Merremia hederacea* (Burm f.) Hallier f.

[14] *Commelina diffusa* Burm. f.

[15] Cf. George Forster's brief botanical summary of Tanna, *Voyage,* II, 357 and Cook (*Journals,* II, 502), who noted: 'Here are likewise a greater variety of Trees and Plants than at any isle we have touched at that our botanists have had time to examine.'

[16] 'Shells indeed are scarce upon the coast, and the natives go in quest of them to other islands', *Voyage,* II, 357. The problem is the lack of suitable reefs and the general steepness of the coast all round the island.

[17] The *kawas* or throwing stone (12 inches long), shaped like a scythe stone or old fashioned office rule, peculiar to Tanna.

by the Seyne viz. *Mullet*, *South-Sea-Pike* or 10 pounders, *Brasilian Pike* or *Pipers*, *Cavallas*, *Garfish*, *Dolphin-Parrot*, *Sting* & *Whiptail-Rays*, *South Sea Mackrel*, *South-Sea Mullet*, *Angelfish*, *Sharks*, & *Sucking-Fish*; in a pond we watered at were fine *Mud Eel*. I observed a *Turtle* floating on the Water in the Harbour the day we departed. We found 3 kinds of *Pigeons*[1] viz. the knobbed *Pigeon*, a new green *Dove* with white specked Shoulders & a rusty headed *Dove*, two kinds of *Parrokeets*,[2] a green one & another black with a red head, breast & back: the Ceylanese-*Owl*,[3] a fine new black *Certhia*[4] with a vermillion-head & such a stroke along the back, a yellow *Flycatcher*[5] with white Eyebrows, the N Zeeland *Fantail Flycatcher*,[6] the purple *Duck* of N. Zeeland,[7] the blue red-bald *Coot*,[8] & several more birds, which all are very shy.[9] The *bats* which are small, caused every night a very great Noise like the Chirping of Locusts & Crickets, & were innumerable: There were rats in the Isle & the Natives made deep holes[10] in the ground about their Sugarplantations for to catch the Rats in, who besides eat the fruit of the *Sterculia foetida*, & many more. The Natives breed Fowls & Hogs[11] as the only domestic animals & we gave them besides some Dogs of both Sexes,[12] which we hope will propagate the breed there.

This fine & fertile Isle is well peopled by a race of Men, who have chiefly woolly crisp hair & beards & are very dark or allmost black, though there are some among them, who have the tips their hair of a brand yellow, & are fairer than the Rest.[13] They are all

[1] Respectively the Pacific Pigeon, Tanna Fruit Dove and Tanna Ground Dove, described above on the days they were first dealt with, as are some of the other species listed here.

[2] The Green Palm Lorikeet and Coconut Lory.

[3] Barn Owl.

[4] Cardinal Honey-Eater.

[5] Yellow White-eye.

[6] Collared Flycatcher *Rhipidura fuliginosa brenchleyi* Sharpe.

[7] Probably the only duck common to the New Hebrides, the Australian Grey Duck.

[8] The Purple Swamphen *Porphyrio porphyrio aneiteumensis* Tristram.

[9] And not surprisingly. The Tannese are particularly hard on their birds.

[10] According to Sparrman (p. 158) these were 'deep ditches'. In former times, at least, rats formed part of the local dietary. On the east side of the island they were merely trapped. In the open 'white grass' country to the north-west large numbers were caught with the aid of encircling fires.

[11] The islanders bred incredible numbers of pigs but these were strictly reserved for reciprocal ceremonial feasts.

[12] They did not in fact survive. See p. 594, n. 4 above.

[13] The Polynesian influence on the east coast of Tanna is very marked and many individuals have a Polynesian cast about them, no doubt from intermarriage with Aniwa and Futuna. The general absence of malaria as well as the great productivity of the soil have also played their part in moulding the superior physique of the people.

well made, the greater part of them tall & stout, but none of them is corpulent & fat. The features of several Men are very agreable, manly & very few are ill-looking. Their women are generally illfavoured by Nature and very ugly. I saw but one that had a smile upon her countenance & something agreable in her mien.[1] The Men are quite naked, have a string round the waist about the Navel, to which they ty the case of leaves by the Stalks, in which their genital parts are wrapt. I believe they are circumcised,[2] though I saw none; & only very small boys were quite naked; as soon as they are 5 or 6 years old they get ready the case for their genitals. The hair of these Men are dressed in a very peculiar manner. They take the Stalk of one of the *Convolvuli*, & peal its tough rind off, in which they afterwards *queue* a small part of their hair, hardly to the size of a pigeons-quill, & of these *queues* they have several hundred; in some they are very short & stand on End like Porcupine-Quils, in others they are about 5 or 6 Inches long & are laid on the crown of the head to both Sides, still others are 12 & more Inches long & hang backwards down.[3] By far the greater part of the Nation have the hair dressed in the above manner, but few wear them in the natural way. Now & then they ty the hair with a leaf & the greater part wear a small stick or read sticking in the hair to scratch the Lice with, & the same stick they made use of to eat Yams & meat, when they came to dine with us.[4] Now & then they have a reed with white Cocks feathers or those of a Hawk sticking in their hairs.[5] Their faces are commonly

[1] The lowly place of females on Tanna and indeed the New Hebrides generally is a recurrent theme in the literature, especially the missionary literature. Tannese women were certainly called upon to do a great deal of tedious work in the gardens, and in pre-Christian times at least, they were also obliged to endure the uncertain joys of polygamous union with older men. Added to that, in this exogamous society, they were essentially 'strangers' in their husbands' villages and putative enemies – a fact hardly calculated to improve their tempers. They nonetheless had a very considerable influence in local politics which they did not scruple to exploit. On this subject see George, *Voyage*, II, 324 and *Journals*, II, 504–5. J. R. Forster's long account of the customs and manners of the Tannese and the New Hebrideans should be read in conjunction with Cook (*Journals*, II, 503–8) and George's shorter summary (*Voyage*, II, 358–64).

[2] Superincised only, an operation referred to locally as *asigipen*. Cf. Humphreys, 1926, pp. 75–9.

[3] See p. 586, n. 5 above. The style never really went out on Tanna and on the general adoption in 1943 of the John Frum 'cargo cult' it was again widely taken up. In former times, it was also universal on Aniwa, Futuna and Aneityum. On Tanna it was chiefly affected by the Kasurumene priesthood amongst whom it was a sort of badge of office.

[4] To a people accustomed to picking and eating lice from each other's hair, this would not have seemed strange.

[5] The reference is to the *nayo* or *kayo*, a plume worn by chiefs and occasionally their wives as a mark of distinction at ceremonial feasts or exchanges of foot (*nekowiar*). These might give place at special festivals to much more ambitious headdresses, *kweriya*.

painted either black with soot, or a black Substance they get from *Irromanga*, looking somewhat like black-lead; or they employ a red ochre from the *Solfataras* for that purpose; both Colours are mixed with Coconut-oil & so laid on the whole Face; often one half is red & the other black, or only a red stroke or blotch is applied on the black face.[1] Seldom have I seen white strokes a cross the Face over the black & red, & that nothing may be wanting to beautify them, they have perforated the Cartilage of the *Septum narium* & wear a reed or a white cylindrical Stone in it. The Ears have very large holes, allmost like those at *Easter Island*, & they wear in them several Rings of Turtle-Shell, ¾ of an Inch broad & 1 Inch in Diameter; from them Rings often other Rings hang down; not seldom there is a white Ring among them, made of some Shell.[2] On the left Upper-Arm they commonly wear a bracelet made of Coconut-Shell, in which they stick a plant *viz.* one of the varieties of *Euodia longifolia*, or a *Croton variegatum*, or a *Lycopodium Phlegmaria.* Besides these plants I saw an unknown beautiful pale purple coloured *Epidendrum*, & another plant with roundish tomentose leaves, smelling like *Sage*. Their Genitals are wrapt in a case of roundish-oblong leaves of a plant smelling like *Ginger*,[3] & belonging certainly to that class, which is spirally tied on the outside by some tough Bindweed, & then attached to the string tied about the Navel round the waist. They wear now & then a plantain leaf, or a Matbasket in lieu of a Cap on their heads, but for the greatest part they have no coverings on them. They seldom walk unarmed, which seems to me to imply, that they have feuds & wars among themselves.[4] The upper arms & the belly are cut with a bamboo or Shell, & a plant is applied which raises a Scar elevated above the rest of the Skin.[5] These Scars on the belly

[1] According to Turner, 1861, p. 77, black was a sign of mourning. It was also a colour largely adopted by the Numrukwen. The 'red ochre', the colour of the Koyometa, came chiefly from Aneityum. Face painting was often a mark of distinction but it was most common in times of war.

[2] Of tridacna. The combined weight of half a dozen of these rings was, of course, very considerable, hence the enormous enlargement of the aperture in the ear lobe, frequently enough to admit a child's hand.

[3] Usually of banana leaves; otherwise the description is accurate.

[4] Turner, 1861, p. 82, remarks that during his stay on the island war was the rule, peace the exception. 'They were fighting during five of the seven months we lived among them'. On the other hand there were few casualties since they rarely engaged in 'close hand-to-hand fighting'.

[5] The Tannese in common with most New Hebrideans cicatrized the skin, either by burning or by cutting. In general, tattooing in Melanesia is confined to those islands more largely exposed to Micronesian or Polynesian influence. A notable exception is Erromanga where the women were all tattooed on each cheek and on the chin.

represent flowers & various whimsical figures. Their arms are first *bows & arrows*; the first of which are made of the best Clubwood,[1] & are very strong; the arrows are of a reed headed with a black wood, which is often jagged & bearded, nay some have several beards; others are only simply pointed, & now & then they have 3 points fixed to it, chiefly for to shoot birds & fish with. The *Sling*[2] is another weapon made of Coconut-Coire & commonly worn in the String round the waist or in the bracelet, & they use round Stones, which they pick for that purpose & carry in a leaf with them. The *Dart & Javelin*[3] is the third kind of missile Weapons employed by the Natives. They are made of a kind of pretty strait, but strong hard & knotty stick, pointed at the thickest end; they seldom excede half an inch in diameter, & are about 6, 7 or 8 feet long: the better sort of these Darts are at the end triangular & with a range of 6, 8 or 10 beards for the space of 6 or 8 Inches.[4] They throw these Darts at a short Distance, with an amazing force & velocity, by the help of a *Becket* made of a kind of Grass ie. a short piece of plaited rope, with an eye at one end, which they put on the Forefinger & a knot at the other, which is slung round the dart, & managed so, that the becket lies backward, the dart is held between the thumb & forefinger & rests forewards upon the other fingers of the same hand. At 8 or 10 yards distance, I have seen the Natives throw the dart thus that it not only hit a wooden stake of about 4 Inches diameter, but went cross through it. At a greater distance the chance of hitting & the force were both less. The same may be said of their arrows; at 8 or 10 yards distance, they hit a mark well & so strongly that they pierce a stake of the above dimension, but at a distance, which is double of the abovementioned or more, they have but little effect & seldom hit the mark,[5] for they seldom fire an arrow with all the elastic power of the bow.

[1] *Casuarina* sp. but in fact *Acacia*, the string being made of the inner bark of the hibiscus. The use of the bow in war is another Melanesian peculiarity. It is not so employed in Massim (New Guinea), Fiji, Micronesia or Polynesia. Even so it figured rather less on Tanna in intra-tribal war at any rate than the club and the spear.

[2] A Polynesian weapon, obviously borrowed.

[3] Properly so-called. A spear is essentially a thrusting weapon, retained in the hand. Here the preferred weapon was the javelin, thrown, as Forster says, with a becket, attached to the forefinger. The presence of the becket on Tanna is yet another evidence of earlier contact with New Caledonia, where it was also much used.

[4] The 'better sort of these Darts' would seem to have been spears of the kind commonly used on Aneityum, where the thrust was usually aimed at the knee so as to incapacitate the enemy.

[5] It would scarcely seem that the Tannese bow was any more effective in war than the Erromangan of which Cook's men had some slight experience. See p. 582, n. 2 above.

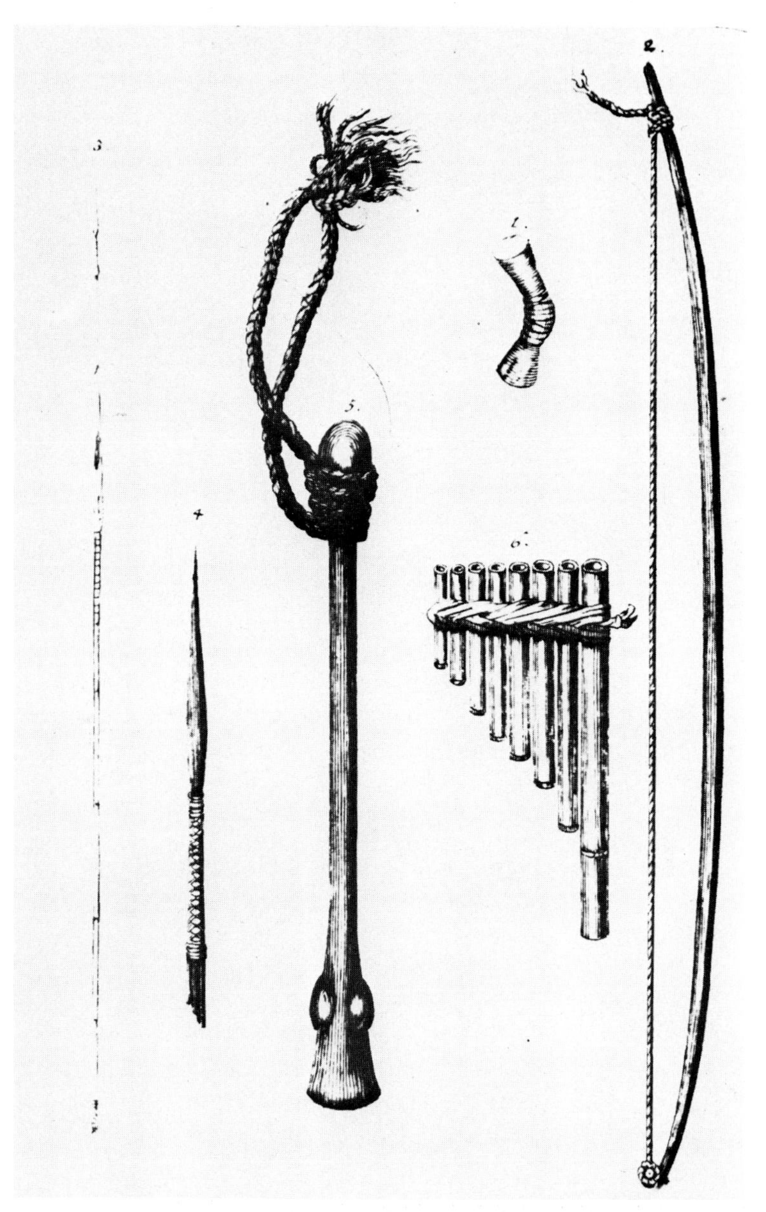

Figure 36. Artefacts and weapons of the New Hebrides. From G. Forster, *Reise*, II, tab. X after Cook, *Voyage*, II, pl. LXXXII.

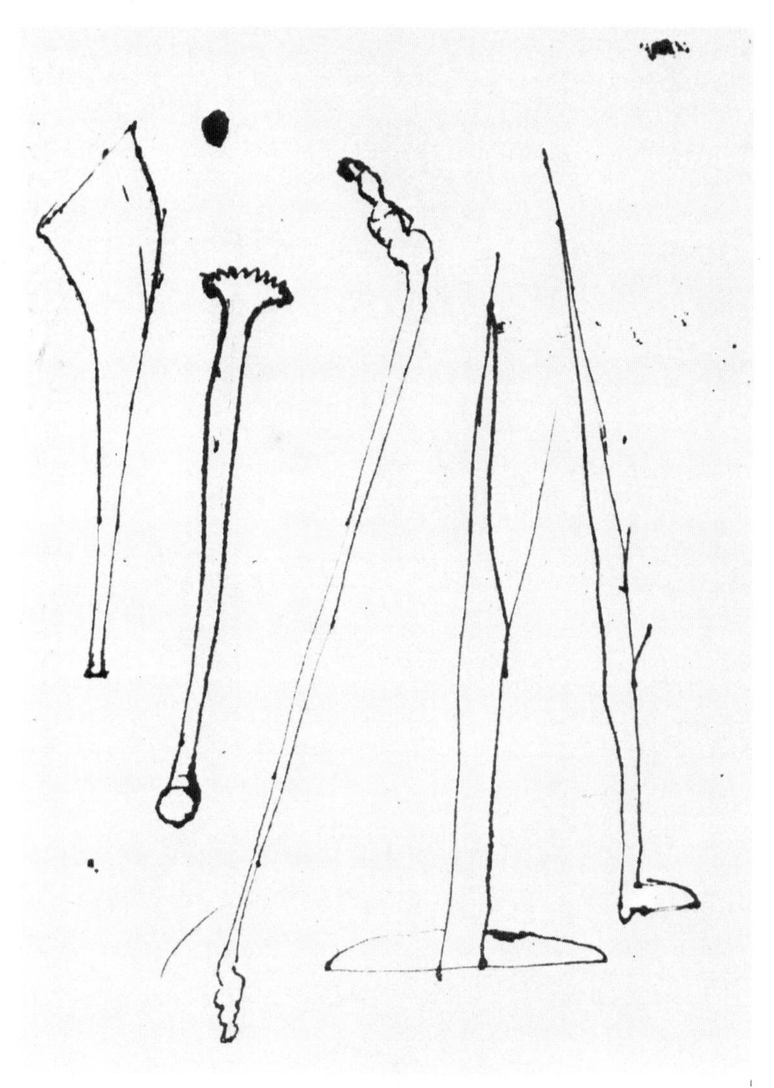

Figure 37. Sketches of five clubs of Tanna.
Ms germ. quart. 226, opp. f. 142, 21 August 1774.

If therefore the Europeans keep them at a distance, their arms are not much to be dreaded. For close engagement, they reserve the club, which every one commonly wears besides one of the before-mentioned missile-weapons.[1] The clubs are of a hardwood & made in 4 or 5 different Shapes. Those they value most are of the *Irromanga-Clubwood* & in the fashion of that Country; for there grows very little of this kind of wood on this Isle, whereas *Irromanga* has much of it. These valuable Clubs are strait, cylindrical pieces of wood about 4 foot long, on both sides knobbed; the end near the hand is round, but the end they strike with is commonly cut in the figure of a star, with prominent points.[2] Another kind of Club is made of a hard knotty wood growing on their own Isle, between 5 & 6 feet long & has a lateral natural knob of a root on its extremity; they said this to be the club of their Country.[3] The Club of the Isle of *Immer* is much of the same length with that of the Tanna-club, but instead of a knobby head, the root or a branch is so managed, that they cut out of it a lateral sharp part in the shape of a fleam, with which they strike. Sometimes this club has a fleam on each side. Still another kind has much the shape of a gun stock but with a sharp edge on one side. They are very expert to pary an arrow or dart sent by the ennemy with these clubs. Lastly have I seen pieces of Coralrock 18 Inches long & 2 Inches Diameter used by them as a weapon both to throw at a short Distance & to knock in the head in close Engagement. Thus far of their Arms.[4]

[1] In brief, an exchange of missile weapons was immediately followed by a close encounter with clubs in which phase of the battle most damage was done.

[2] Evidently a throwing club, based on the Erromangan *telughomti*, made only on the south or south-east side of that island. The head was cut in the shape of a star of eight points. According to H. A. Robertson, 1902, p. 371, it was less used as a weapon than as a 'money medium' at feasts. The Tannese 'star-club' was much larger than the Erromangan.

[3] The preferred weapons of the Tannese, normally very heavy, and wielded with both hands. In general Tannese clubs were much weightier than those of New Caledonia and would seem to have been based rather on Fijian exemplars.

[4] Opp. v, f. 142 are five illustrations of the clubs of Tanna. See fig. 38, George (*Voyage*, II, 278–80 and 326) transposes part of this excellent description of Tannese weaponry to an earlier stage in his account. Cook's descriptions (*Journals*, II, 506–7) draw heavily on Wales's journal, that 'gentleman' having been 'continually a shore among them [with] a better opportunity to see the feats which they performed than any of us...'. Wales (*Remarks*, pp. 79–81), it seems, thought himself a more qualified observer on Tanna's ethnology than Forster, particular over the question of cannibalism and music. He wrote (*Remarks*, p. 80): 'I believe there were very few unless I except Dr Forster and his retinue, who went more amongst the people than myself', and commented contemptously on many of Forster's other observations and experiments. Knowing Wales to be wrong in many particulars George countered bitterly and with some irony: 'The man who does

I have seen but one Man with a figure punctured on his breast.[1] Some twist the hair of the beard into a kind of rope.[2] The generality are smooth-skinned; however did I see some, who had a kind of crisp wooly hair of their whole body. Few of them wear a white poached Eggshell or a piece of Mother of pearl or a large Operculum of a shell on their breasts.[3] Their women are illfavoured & generally ugly. They wear nothing but a short kind of pettycoat made of leaves, which increases in length[4] in proportion with the Age of the Women. Young girls have only one bunch of grass before & another behind hanging down from the string round their waist. The Women have all the same ornaments as Men, Nose-Stones, Earrings, Shells on the Breast & Bracelets:[5] but Men wear now & then a piece of cloth of a coarse texture, made of the Bark of a Tree, round the waist as a Belt; the common kind is died of a Cinnomon or brown-yellow colour. The Chiefs have the same painted with lines of black, or even with lines & compartments of black & red.[6] The women have all their heads covered with a kind of cap made of a Plantain leaf or a Mat-Basket. Few are uncovered, & even very young Girls have these Caps. The women carry their young Children on their backs in a kind of bag made of a piece of cloth of the abovementioned kind. Their small Chickens they likewise wear in a Mat-basket, wherever they go to.[7] Besides this, it seems, they are the drudges & Pack horses of the Nation; we saw them allways loaded with Yams, Bananas etc., weeding their plantations, & working something or other.[8] The Men however clear the ground & cut

not believe the existence of what he has not perceived by his own senses, must greatly confine his knowledge as well as his belief...If it were not for the pleasure of finding fault, Mr Wales would never have published his pamphlet...he is resolved at all events to attack my father' (*Reply*, p. 49). The evidence in both Cook and Wales prompts the conclusion that here on Tanna the latter took every opportunity to diminish Forster in Cook's estimation as a 'philosopher'.

[1] Obviously a Polynesian visitor from Futuna or Aniwa. See p. 623, n. 5 above.

[2] Cf. Turner, 1861, p. 78. Those 'twisted beads...hanging down in lots of little curls, two or three inches below the chin, which are to be seen in engravings from the Assyrian sculptures, are precisely what is to be seen at the present day at Tanna, and especially among the priesthood at Kasurumene, near the Volcano Valley'. This particular affectation at least has died out long since.

[3] A 'gorget', a widespread ornament in Polynesia.

[4] And in bulk, one petticoat on another.

[5] A bracelet, nose-stone and a greenstone necklace were among the items deposited by Forster in Oxford.

[6] A mark of distinction. See p. 608, n. 1 above.

[7] An interesting observation which perhaps underlines the ceremonial importance of the fowl on Tanna. The practice would now seem to have disappeared.

[8] See p. 622, n. 1 above. Women are still the chief burden bearers on Tanna.

down the woods with their bone Shell or Stone Hatchets & afterwards they set them a fire, & in that ground they plant the slits of Yams much after the manner mentioned by *Rumpfius* in his History of Amboina plants Vol. 7.[1]

The women here exercise here the Art of Cooking,[2] they gave me once a Pye made of Bananas & in its middle were leaves with Coconut Kernel; these Leaves I suppose to be the *Okras* or *Hibiscus esculentus*; at another time, I got the young leaves of a Fig-Tree, whose Fruit is woolly like a Peach & which they call *Gombaba*,[3] dressed in a Banana-leaf & we found it a very fine leaf, & I often tasted them with the Natives raw. Their way of eating is cleanly for they never touched the Victuals with their Fingers, but took allways fresh green leaves to hold them in. And as the Ashes of the Volcano make all the leaves & trees, under which they must walk, very dirty, they find that it is impossible to keep any thing clean between their Fingers. When they got anything from us, they took them likewise between two leaves; whether they use these leaves out of a principle of cleanliness or out of Superstition, thinking everything coming from us either enchanted or morally unclean, I cannot decide. They did however use allways leaves.[4]

The Natives exercise hospitality in a high degree. In the beginning they were very averse to let us go higher up into the Country & near to their habitations, especially did we find the Inhabitants of the hill[5] towards the Volcano more mistrustfull than all the rest, nay they were determined to hinder us from going on rather by cheat: ie showing us a wrong way, leading to the Seaside, instead of landwards in; or they prepared to hinder us from going on by main force; twice did I see a man stand in the

[1] The old men then sieved the soil through their fingers and the seed yam was finally planted in a large mound six feet high and 30 feet in circumference. The resulting yams often measured ten feet in length and weighed upwards of 200 pounds. For G. E. Rumphius see p. 170, n. 3 above. Rumphius in J. Burman (ed.) *Herbarium Amboinense* (Amsterdam etc, 1747), v, 346, 350–1, 353, 355–6, pls 120–3 and 125 describes six separate kinds of yam. All are today considered to be varieties or forms of *Dioscorea alata* Linn, to which Forster is probably referring. There were only six volumes of *Herbarium Amboinense* (1741–50).

[2] Any vegetable food is first wrapped in banana leaves and then placed in a traditional earth oven, lined with stones. Pigs were generally cooked whole.

[3] The word seems not to have survived.

[4] See p. 591, n. 6 above. Another custom which has only recently died out. George, however, adds: '. . .as this was not a general custom, and almost entirely neglected as soon as we became better acquainted, I cannot lay any stress upon it', *Voyage*, II, 363. It may thus be supposed that this was very much a ritual matter and probably confined to particular classes of persons, i.e. priests, and practised only when they were present as a means of limiting their power to injure.

[5] Enekahi.

path, once with a Sling & a stone in it, ready to let it fly at us; & another time a Man with Darts wanted to hinder our progress.[1] The Natives on the Seaside[2] were more hospitable, friendly & tractable, seeing me determined to go land inward, they at last went with me, & brought me to their plantations & houses, invited me to sit down, fetched Coconuts to refresh me, & gave me Sugar-Cane, Yams & Bananas to take: afterwards as often as I came to this little Town,[3] they repeated allways the present, & all the Men, Women & Children surrounded my Company as their common Friends. They danced, gave us a song, & shewed every mark of kindness & friendship. They were repeating a kind of solemn Song in the Town on the brow to the East of the Harbour, every morning very early; & we could never make out whether it was of the religious kind or not.[4] For upon the whole it is difficult to make any remarks upon their religion, as we did not know anything of their language & learned it but gradually & as we stood there but a few days. The N.E. point of the harbour seemed to me to contain some sacred place; for though I had been everywhere on that side, they never would let me go on further on towards the point, & one day, when I really would have gone further, several of their Men told me, the people there would kill & eat me.[5] Besides this I frequently heard of them & understood

[1] See p. 588, n. 4 above. It may be doubted whether Cook could have done anything to mollify these people, even if he had chosen to favour them on his first landing.

[2] I.e. the eastern side of the harbour, or Samoa Point. As has been suggested these people were concerned to prevent their visitors from straying into enemy territory.

[3] I.e. Samoa. As George notes, Cook and his people were much less welcome in the other town, Ile Pou.

[4] See p. 599, n. 3 above. It may be added here that the various rehearsals of the ritual of the *nekowiar* had each their allotted time, the men of the host tribe the early morning. Whatever the case, the place was very *tapu* to every one else, including casual visitors from abroad. Samoa itself was the centre of various sorts of magic, including the catching of turtles and sharks and the manipulation of the sun and the rain.

[5] They were perhaps not altogether jesting. It was one of the prerogatives of the local chiefly line to eat any visitor whom they had a mind to, as well as the bodies of men killed in war. Cf. Guiart, 1956, p. 401, n. 5 and p. 595, n. 5 above. Wales, of course, 'was never threatened with being eaten' (*Remarks*, p. 50) but he did, it seems, consider with Cook Forster's futile attempts to find out something about New Hebridean 'religion', a complex subject. Cook cites 'Mr F' and his 'opinion' that 'at the East point of the harbour... were some thing or a nother, sacred to Religion...'. He remained, however, sceptical, thinking it merely a Tannese natural desire to fix 'bounds to our excursions'. To be fair we must note that both Forsters realised their own limitations in dealing with this complex issue, even though in the interests of anthropology, they did strive hard to find out more. 'It cannot be expected', wrote George Forster (II, 363) 'that during the little stay which we made at Tanna, and in the confined situation to which the distrust of the natives reduced us at first, we should have been able to collect more certain and instructive observations, or an exact detail of the whole extent of knowledge among the natives'. Beaglehole (*Journals*, II, 501, n. 2) cites the solemn song passage from the *Voyage* and then himself gives flight to fancy about J. R. Forster's 'rather romantic imagination, which had fed on Druids

by signs, that they eat those of their Ennemies, whom they kill in battle: for they shewed the manner of killing the Man with the Club, & how they cut the arms & legs off, & how they bit & ate the flesh with their teeth.

It is remarkable that these people of *Tanna* speak most certainly two if no more languages among themselves. They often said us the names of things in the Language of *Annatom*[1] & *Irronan* or *Footoona* which is nearly related to the Language spoken in the Friendly Isles of *Eaoowe*, *Tonga-Tabu* & *Anamocka*, & allways said me it was thus called at *Irronan* or *Footoona*, but often they gave us likewise the names in the *Tanna*-Language & said it was thus called in *Tanna*. Whenever I had an opportunity of hearing both Vocables & the Language to which each belonged I never failed

4 5 1 2 3

to observe it in my Vocabulary. The Numerals they gave me[2] in 3 languages. One is similar to the way of counting in all the South Sea Isles, & goes to 10. The other two kinds of counting go no farther than five; from whence they set out again, & repeat the same numerals in case they want to count more than 5.[3] If I am

and certain ingredients of the forested Tuetonic past'. No one would have been more surprised at that remark than the hard-headed theologian from Halle, J. R. Forster, trained in the rationalist determinist theology and philosophy of the German Enlightenment – in the traditions of G. W. Leibniz, Christian Wolff, S. J. Baumgarten and J. D. Michaelis and so on.

[1] There was a close connection between the people of Port Resolution and those of Anelgauhat on the south side of Aneityum and another between those of Lenakel on the west side of Tanna and Aname on the north side of Aneityum. There was similarly a close connexion between the shore people of Port Resolution and the Futunese who, it may be suspected, were chiefly responsible for maintaining contact between the various islands of the southern New Hebrides.

[2] Since he was discussing language Forster seems to have thought it prudent to remind himself with this superior numbering system that even English had a preferred order in sentence structures! See also his list of 41 Tannese words in 'Comparative Table of Various Languages', *Observations*, opp. p. 254. In this same connection the work of a long-time student of Melanesian languages S. H. Ray, *A comparative study of the Melanesian island languages* (Cambridge, 1926) can be consulted with profit.

[3] Cf. Aniwa: Tasi, Rua, Toru, Fa, Rima, Ono, Fitu, Varu, Iva, Tonga furu and Port Resolution (as recorded by G. Turner) Riti, Karu, Kahar, Kafa, Krirum, then Krirum riti, Krirum karu etc. Eleven on this system is krirum krirum riti. The system is the same throughout Tanna, with the usual dialectal differences. See also the remarks in S. H. Ray, *A comparative study of the Melanesian island languages* and relevant notes in Rev. D. MacDonald's *South Sea Languages* (Melbourne, 1891), vol. II, especially those of Rev. Gray (pp. 108–62). 'Cook may be forgiven for the paucity of his linguistic observations', notes Beaglehole (*Journals*, II, 504). But in Forster senior, one of the acknowledged masters of language of his period, we can be less forgiving; indeed there is little to forgive. Even Wales (*Reply*, p. 80) conceded that in the matter of New Hebridian language affinities Forster senior made some good points but elsewhere he denigrated his linguistic abilities roundly. George (*Reply*, p. 47) put that record straight, although in the *Voyage* (II, 359–60), he only briefly summarised their linguistic researches and the three 'distinct...tongues' they found on Tanna.

not mistaken, the Inhabitants of the brow on the E. Side of the harbour, seem me to be a colony from the above Isles, or have some Natives of the above Isles among themselves, or have at least some intercourse with them.[1] I saw an *Irromăngā*-Man, & he gave us a song different from those of this Country.[2] The other people told me of him, that he came from *Irromăngā*. This & that they go to *Irromăngā* to fetch Clubwood, to *Immer* & *Annatom* to fetch Shells & Stones for Hatchets, proves that the Tanna-men navigate; for we saw no boats in *Irromăngā*, even not one.[3] We saw about 20 boats in the first days of our Stay at *Tanna*, which are built partly in the same manner as in the other South Sea Isles viz. the keel is an excavated piece of wood, to which they fix the Sides by ropes of Coconut-coire; the only difference is, in the *Society Isles* they sow the planks together by holes pierced through the boards, & here they fix cleats to the boards & then haul the Ropes through the cleats.[4] In the *friendly Isles, Anomocka, Tonga Tabu* etc they sow the planks on the inside together, through holes pierced through a ledge left standing on each side of the plank. Short they all sow their boats together: & this seems to be the most ancient manner of constructing embarkations & Vessels, before they used nails & Iron to fix the planks to the knees & timbers they sowed them with flax together. Pliny sais 1.24. i.40 *Cum sutiles fierent navės*,

[1] As has been suggested, the Polynesian influence in south-east Tanna is very strong. One may thus find endless traits in the local culture reminiscent of Polynesia. A Polynesian 'god' Mauitikitiki shares Mt Melen with the local culture hero, Karaperamum. It may nonetheless be suspected that the preservation at least of the peculiar character of the culture of Samoa Point owes a good deal to the frequent residence of Aniwans and Futunese in the village. The early history of this settlement is, of course, lost in the mists of time.

[2] One hesitates to spoil a pleasant story, but the man concerned almost certainly came from Irmwanga, an inland village in the Port Resolution district. That Erromangans ever actually visited Port Resolution, whether in their own or Tannese canoes, is highly dubious. Forster's deduction concerning the navigational ability of the Tannese is also open to doubt. They undoubtedly often went as far as Aniwa (15 miles) or Futuna, steering by the light of the volcano but, as has already been suggested, the true navigators in the southern New Hebrides were the Aniwans and the Futunese.

[3] The Erromangans nonetheless have canoes, though these are usually not more than 12 feet long and carry only 5–6 men.

[4] The *negau* or *niko* of Tanna is no more than a dugout made from the trunk of a breadfuit tree and fitted with a single wash-strake and an outrigger. Cook notes that the joints were covered on the outside by a thin batten chamfered off at the edges, 'over which the bandages [i.e. lashings] pass'. See *Journals*, II, 503 and 863 for Wales's description. It is perhaps relevant to add here that the Tannese canoe was not plank-built. Plank building or carvel building in the Pacific is a late, post-Arab, introduction, restricted to certain of the Solomon Islands, to Micronesia, and to Fiji–Tonga–Samoa and to Ra'iatea, Tahiti and the Tuamotus. Forster's reference is to the ancient Mediterranean carvel system in which the thwarts were inserted after the planks had been sewn together. In the newer system, as he says, the framing was put together first and the planks nailed on later. See also p. 634 below.

lino tamen, non sparto unquam sutas.[1] In the 9th & 10th Century after Christ, when all the Vessels in the Mediterranean were nailed together, a Vessel was thrown upon some part of the coast of Syria, whose planks were all sowed together, this the Author of the Voyages of some Mahammedans to China, published by Renaudot,[2] p. 53, declared to be an *Arabian Vessel from Siraf, whose construction is such that the planks are not nailed, but joined together in a peculiar manner, as if they had been sowed* etc.[3] When the more civilized nations nailed the planks, those that were less acquainted with the Arts & mechanicks sewed them. The whole East nails now the planks & the *naves sutiles* are left only in the Isles of the South Sea. Upon the whole, all the customs & manners of the Inhabitants of the South-Seas are not entirely new but have been observed somewhere or other before. The better Sort of the people in the *Society Isles* wear sometimes very *long nails*; & the *Collection of Voyages of the Dutch East India Company* Amst. 1702. tom 1. p. 392[4] mentions that the Inhabitants of *Java* wear long hair & *long nails.*[5]

We observed in the *Society Isles* the greater part of the Chiefs to be of a *large Size, an athletic habit of body* & some *very strong*;[6] & *Father Gobien*[7] in his history of the Ladrones or *Marian Isles*, 1700., as well as Dr *Gemelli Carreri*[8] found the Inhabitants of them Isles of a *great size*, well *proportioned limbs, very corpulent & strong.*

We found that the Inhabitants of *Tanna, Irromanga,* & *Mallicollo wore large Rings in their Ears,* & *had likewise a stick or stone in the*

[1] 'Although ships were sown together, they were sown with flax, never with esparto grass rope.'

[2] Eusebius Renaudot (trans.) *Ancient Accounts of India and China by two Mohammedan Travellers...* (London, 1733). The original French edition, was published in Paris in 1718.

[3] The reference is no doubt to the use of dowels, a widespread practice amongst Arab ship-builders which reached Indonesia but not the Pacific proper.

[4] French edition by R. A. C. de Renneville, *Recueil des Voyages...* (5 vols), which was an adaptation of Issak Commelin's original 1646 Dutch collection. A London edition appeared in 1703. Forster used Renneville.

[5] An odd juxtaposition. The thesis has, of course, often been embroidered upon. Cf. E. S. Craighill Handy, 'The Problem of Polynesian Origins'. *Bernice P. Bishop Museum Occasional Paper*, IX, No. 8 (1930), 1–27, who speaks of the conquest of the original settlers of Tahiti by the seafaring *hui ari'i*, the chiefly Tangaroans from Indonesia, who thereupon subjected the *manahune* to their rule. It need hardly be added that there is no real evidence for the hypothesis. The aristocracy of Tahiti were in every respect Tahitian.

[6] On this see also *Journals*, I, 123. The disparity may well have been the result of better nutrition and some degree of inbreeding or sexual selection within the *ari'i* class.

[7] Charles Le Gobien (1653–1708), French historian and Jesuit secretary and procurator of Chinese missions in Paris. Published *Histoire des Isles Marianes* (Paris, 1700).

[8] J. F. Gamelli Carreri, Italian traveller of the second half of seventeenth century, who in 1693 left Europe to travel in Egypt, Palestine, Persia, the Indies, China, Philippines and Mexico. He returned to Europe in 1699 and published *Giro del Mondo* (Naples 1699–1700) which went through many editions.

perforated Septum of the Nose. We observed *they had bracelets of Coconuts, Shells & small plaited Shellwork on their Arms.* We found they employed *a kind of Lime in Anamocka & the friendly Isles to powder their hair with, nay some used a yellow or Orange coloured powder of Turmeric for that purpose.*[1] All this has been observed by other Navigators in other parts. viz. *Jaques le Maire* in the Collection of Voyages of the Dutch East India company tome 4, p. 648,[2] found the *Papooas to wear Rings in the Ears, in both Nostrils & the perforated Septum of the Nose,* he *saw they used Bracelets on their Arms above the Elbow & wrist: he observed their hair were powdered with Lime.* Nay Dampier speaking of the Inhabitants of the Isle of Garret Dennys in New Guinea,[3] *observes that they wear a stick of 4 Inches long & of the thickness of a Finger in the perforated Nostrils; & other Sticks in the Ears, just so as we saw at the Friendly Isles* & that they strew *their hair read, white & yellow.*[4]

I saw several Men in *Tanna,* who had so long & great Eyelids,[5] that they were obliged to lift their heads up, in order to see objects that were upon a horizontal line with their Eyes. *Dampier* found the people of New Holland open'd their Eyes but half, because they use themselves from their Infancy to shut their Eyes against the Moskitos, & that they lifted allways the head up, when they wanted to look at a distant object. *Dampiers* reason may be true, but I may add another, namely the Smoke in which the people commonly live in their huts, obliges them to keep the Eyes shut, & perhaps causes a relaxation in the Muscles of the Eyelid, so that they cannot lift them up & after a couple of Generations whole families are naturally born with so long & great Eyelids, for I

[1] See *Voyage,* II, 277 and *Journals,* II, 505. It was in fact to bleach their hair.

[2] Le Maire's account appeared in Renneville, *Recueil des Voyages* (1754), IV, pt. 2.

[3] The bibliography of William Dampier's published voyages is extremely complicated. Forster probably used the best available 1729 edition of his works. Here he refers to Dampier, *A Continuation of a Voyage to New Holland...* (London, 1729), III, pt. 2, 202–3, originally published in 1709. Dampier described the inhabitants of '*Garret Dennis* Isle' on 3 March 1699: Forster however does not quote verbatim, as his italicising implies.

[4] *In margin:* The Inhabitants of *Mallicollo* made Friendship with us by putting the Seawater with one hand on their heads and *Dampier* found the same custom among the Inhabitants of *New Guinea,* vol. 3, p. 186 – v f. 147. See Dampier, *Continuation of a Voyage* (London, 1729), II, 186.

[5] Cf. p. 617, n. 1 above. Apparently ocular myopathy or progressive external ophthalmoplegia, a disorder marked by pigmentation of the retina, retinal degeneration, and impaired vision as well as relaxation of the muscles of the eye-lid. As Forster suggests the condition appears to be at least partly inherited. Cf. J. N. Walton (ed.), *Disorders of Voluntary Muscles* (London & Edinburgh, 1974), pp. 583–6. Myasthenia gravis may, it seems, be ruled out.

observed this inconvenience in several little boys of 5 or 6 years old.

We saw the Inhabitants of *Tanna* had their bodies cut with figures & flowers that left elevated scars; & *Thevenot* observed in *Decan* several women with flowers cut into their flesh.[1]

It is very common in the *Society Isles* to rub the hair & anoint the body with Coconut-oil perfumed by the Perfumewood, & other Ingredients. *Pyrard*[2] found that the people in the *Maldive Islands* rubbed their body & hair with perfumed oils.

In the *Society Isles* the people puncture their body with a black made of Charcoal & water, which formes blue,indelible figures on the skin; and *Pietro della Valle*[3] observed the same Custom among the Arabians. We saw the same custom at the Marquesas, the friendly Isles, New Zeeland & Easter Island. The women of the New Zeelanders puncture chiefly their Lips; & *d'Arvieux*[4] & *de la Rogue* observed the same custom among the Arabian women, so as *Boullaye le Gouz*[5] found this punctuation of the Lips among the Bedouins of the Desarts about *Tunis* & *Tremessen*.

We saw several people in the *Society Isles* who had a thick, hard

[1] Cf. *Voyage*, II, 277–8. Jean de Thévenot (1633–67). nephew of Melchisedec Thévenot (1620–92), the voyage chronicler, linguist and geographer, was himself a remarkably exact observer, a good mathematician, botanist and geographer, and an avid traveller. In 1655 he left Europe for seven years of travel in the Near East and then in 1664 went via the Levant, Tigris, Ispahan and Persia to India where he travelled widely. His *Relation d'un Voyage au Levant* appeared in three parts (Paris, 1664–84) and the three-in-one *Voyage* in Paris in 1789. D. Lovell's English folio edition *The Travels of Monsieur de Thevenot* appeared in London in 1687. See also Surendranath Sen (ed.) *India Travels of Thévenot and Careri*... (New Delhi, 1949). See also p. 623, n. 1 above.

[2] François Pyrard (1570–1621), French adventurer and traveller, left St Malo in May 1601 and visited Madagascar, the Comoro Islands and was shipwrecked in the Maldive Islands in July 1602, where he was enslaved until 1607. Pyrard then resumed his travels to India, Ceylon, Malacca, Java and Sumatra and returned to Europe in 1611. The enlarged edition of his *Voyage de François Pyrard aux Indes Orientales, Maldives* etc. was published in two volumes in Paris in 1615, following other editions in 1611 and 1613. His voyage was also edited for the Hakluyt Society in 1887–9.

[3] The reference is, of course, to tattooing. Pietro della Valle (1586–1652) was an aristocrat in the service of the pope. In 1614 he travelled to the Holy Land and Persia where he led an adventurous life before going to India. In 1626 he returned to Rome. His lively useful epistolary *Viaggi* appeared in Rome in four parts (1650–58) and an English trans. by G. Havers was published in London in 1665.

[4] Laurent D'Arvieux (1635–1702), a native of Marseilles, was a greatly respected Turkish scholar, traveller and consul throughout the Arab and Mohammedan lands surrounding the Mediterranean. His fellow townsman Jean de La Roque (1661–1745) took notes from D'Arvieux on his travels for *Voyage dans l'Arabie heureuse* (Paris, 1716); English edit., London, 1718. La Roque, a Marseilles merchant, himself travelled to Syria and other parts in 1689 and published his own *Voyage* in 1722 (English edit., London, 1742).

[5] Sieur François de Laboullaye le Gouz (*c.* 1610–69) travelled widely in Europe, Persia, India and the Near East. His *Voyages et Observations* first appeared in Paris in 1653.

Leg, or Elephants-foot;[1] & *Francis Pyrard* saw the same disease among the *Naïrs of Calicut* in *Ceylan*.

I observed some people at *Tanna*, who were infinitely more hairy over the body than I ever saw an European & the same author found the Natives of the Maldives to be in general more hairy over all the body than the Europeans.[2]

These few instances will sufficiently prove that the customs, manners, diseases, peculiar to one country, are often found at a great distance in another Nation; & that nevertheless this Argument of similarity of Manners, will not allways prove that one Nation is descended from the other. If allmost all the customs are the same or nearly so; if the language corresponds; if there is a probability of their Migration to the more remote parts, these arguments together have some weight is proving a relation between these Nations, but never one single Custom, or a few words may be used as Arguments in favour of it.[3]

The Canoes of these people at *Tanna* have outriggers, & those which are large contain about 20 people. Their sails are low & triangular, the broad Side being uppermost & the Angle below.[4] Their oars are illshaped & clumsy.[5] The huts of these people are commonly long thatched roofs coming down to the very ground & open on both Ends. The roof is made of Mats of Coconutleaves tied to some stakes disposed here & there in the ground & tied on top together.[6] They lie pele-mêle on mats of Coconut leaves & have a fireplace for each Family, for several of them live together in one hut. Their fences inclose part of the plantations & sometimes

[1] The reference is to filariasis and in particular to its sequel, elephantiasis, a disease caused by a microfilarial worm, *Wuchereria bancrofti*, carried by mosquitoes, in Polynesia by *Aedes polynesiensis*. It would seem that the condition was rare enough in Cook's Tahiti but much more common in the early nineteenth century as a result of ecological change. As Forster suggests, filariasis originated in the west and was carried eastwards into the Pacific.

[2] A sound observation. The preceding six paragraphs (v, ff. 147–9) are lightly deleted. George did not make use of this scholarship in his *Voyage;* it represents J. R. Forster's developing thinking as a comparative and clearly well-read anthropologist.

[3] Forster returns to this fascinating theme more fully in *Observations*, esp. pp. 252–84.

[4] It may be added that the Tannese canoe had no mast, the triangular sail being guyed to the sides of the vessel by a couple of vangs. It was in consequence able to sail only before the wind. Any change of wind direction in the course of the voyage thus obliged the navigator to resort to his paddles once more. The fore and aft rig, i.e. the original ocean 'kite' sail hoisted to a mast so that the vessel took the wind on the beam, was, like carvel building or plank building, a late development in Micronesia and Polynesia which by-passed Melanesia. See p. 630, n. 4 above.

[5] The Tannese paddle was about two feet long and spade-shaped.

[6] On Tannese dwellings cf. *Journals*, II, 494–5 and 855–6. George (*Voyage*, II, 360) was less impressed: '. . .their houses are mere sheds, which barely cover them from the inclemency of the weather'.

small spots of ground near their houses, but these fences go seldom every where round the planted ground, as if it were enough to mark out, that it is a plantation.[1] Besides Sugarcanes, Plantains, Yams, & Eddies, other plants are cultivated, especially is the *Euodia*, a strong smelling plant, one of these they cultivate: & what is remarkable, Culture has produced 3 or 4 varieties of this plant; the *Croton variegatum* has likewise a place in their plantations, they have no other use of all these plants than to wear them in the bracelet of the left Arm. Their government seems to be patriarchal. Each Family having the oldest Man at their head, but he is not obeyed or respected like a Sovereign. The Chiefs seem to have very little Authority over the people & they are perhaps more heads of Families of a certain rank, who perpetuate the Name of *Areekee* or *Aree* in their Family without any authority; perhaps they are only the Counsels of the Nation, whom they occasionally consult, & who lead the rest in their Wars.[2] The little time we stood among these good people gave me, who was besides occupied in collecting plants, birds & fish & describing them, & who made collections of words of their Language, & observations on the Volcano, Solfatara & hot Wells & had long Excursions among the thickest bushes; only the Opportunity to make these few incoherent Observations on this Isle, its Soil, products & Inhabitants.

We return again to our wonted Element the Sea.

. . . . *natat uncta curina*

. . . . *vocat jam carbasus auras.* Virg. AEn. 398. 417[3]

In the Evening a Booby was seen about the Ship, & we were very near a high Table hill, which forms the Isle of *Irronan.* We tacked several times during night & saw in the morning the Isles of *Tanna, Irronan, Anattom* & *Irromanga. Immer* being too low & too small to be seen at such a distance from it, which was about 12 or 14 leagues.[4] We observed that the Volcano on *Tanna*

[1] It was the custom to tether or enclose the pigs rather than allow them to forage.

[2] Cf. *Journals*, II, 507–8. The subject is complex. It may, however, be said here that there is an almost extreme division of authority on Tanna. Perhaps two out of every three men on the island can lay claim to some sort of 'chiefly' privilege or authority, whether as magicians or functionaries in the various dances or festivals or as custodians of the impedimenta of particular rites and ceremonies. There are perhaps 600 true 'chiefs' (*ieremera*-or *ieremwanag*- or *yani niko* etc.) on the island, one for every ten or eleven people, so that there are often several chiefs in any one village, half a dozen for each of the 115 tribal groups. In brief, few societies are more 'democratic' than the Tannese or, as Forster found, more difficult to penetrate. On all this see Guiart, 1956, pp. 9–12 and 107.

[3] '. . . the freshly tarred (caulked ship floats) . . . already the sail invites the wind'.

[4] About 40 miles.

excretated[1] vast columns of smoke. The Thermometer at 72°, in my Cabin 72°.

Aug. ye 22^{d} ☽ We passed in the Afternoon & Evening the S. & SW. side of *Tanna*, which appears very much to advantage on that side forming very gentle slopes from the range of high hills. The breeze fresh during day & also during night & was very favourable.

Neptunus ventis implevit vela secundis Virg. AEn. VII. 23.[2]

The next morning we found ourselves on the leeside of *Irromanga*, & we saw at a distance the large New Isle[3] we had passed July ye 27th P.M. The Therm. 74°, in my Cabin 73°.

Aug. ye 23^{d} ♂ We saw several kinds of Boobies; & on the South Side of the great new Isle we observed about 4 smaller Isles forming a very fine harbour.[4] The fine breeze set us forward.

Iamque Dies coelo concesserat, almaque curru
Noctivago Phoebe medium pulsabat Olympum Virg. AEn. X. 215[5]

We made all the speed possible, & returned to the place where we had been about a month ago, with amazing velocity & we can say with the poët of our Ship:

. . . . fugit illa per undas
Ocior & jaculo & ventos aequante sagitta
Virg. AEn. X. 247.[6]

For we were next morning on the South Side of *Mallicollo*. We had the Isles of *Ambrrym* with it Volcano, *Paoom* & the high Peak at the East of it,[7] together with the large Isle of *Apèe* in sight.

[1] Not completely legible. Cf. *Journals*, II, 508–9.

[2] 'Neptune filled the sails with favourable winds'.

[3] Efate. They were steering 'NNW. . . in order to finish the Survey of it and the other Isles to the NW', *Journals*, II, 509. See also *Voyage*, II, 365–6. Wales thought Efate one of the 'most beautiful & desirable Islands we have yet seen in the South Seas'.

[4] '. . . near the middle of the SW side and close to the shore lay three or four small islands within which seem'd to be safe Anchorage', *Journals*, II, 510. There are several small reef islets at this point, clearly visible from the sea. There are also several more substantial islets, viz. Eratapu, Erakor – a sand bank – Fila – a coral outcrop off Pango Point guarding the entrance to Vila harbour – and Iririki just behind it. There is also the artificial islet of Mele in Mele Bay. The very fine harbour was not the modern Vila which Cook would very likely have missed but either the indentation between South Bay and Pango Point or, more probably, Mele Bay. Cook naturally also missed Havannah Harbour, a deep water port on the west side of the island fronted by Leleppa and Moso islands.

[5] 'And now day had withdrawn from the sky, and kindly Phoebe [i.e. the moon] was pounding half-Heaven with her night-wandering chariot'.

[6] 'She sped over the waves faster than a javelin, or an arrow that rivals the wind'.

[7] See p. 564, n. 5 and 6 and p. 569, n. 1 above. The name is now attached to the island to the west, the modern Paama, and Lopevi is separated from it. See also *Journals*, II, 510: '. . . the land comprehended under the name of Paoom appeared to us now to be two Islands, some thing like a Seperation was seen between the Hill and the land to the West'.

Mallicollo had a very rich appearance, & all Vegetation seemed to be luxuriant on it. We observed in a bay about 2 small Isles.[1] The Therm. 76°, in my Cabin 75°.

Aug. yᵉ 24ᵗʰ ☿ We observed a great many people in passing by, two Canoes attempted to come to us off, but the Ship was going too quick for them. Beyond the point which formed the very great & deep bay[2] we now opened, the Country has no more that rich & luxuriant appearance, & though we saw habitations to the very tops of the hills, the Country had nevertheless some barren spots. We observed several Boobies in the Evening. In the Night we passed the N. point of *Mallicollo*[3] & were in the morning a good way in *Bougainville's* Passage;[4] for we had to the North & N.W. a large & high Land[5] in Sight which had on its S. & SE. & E. side a good many Isles.[6] We could see the *Isle of Lepers* at a great distance. The Thermometer at 76°, in my Cabin at 77°.

Aug. yᵉ 25ᵗʰ ♃ We saw a good many more Isles on the East Side of the great Isle, than Mʳ *de Bougainville* had seen,[7] & the further we go on the more Land we see. We stood on & off during night. In the morning we found ourselves a breast of the last Isle,[8] we turned to the West & saw that in the great Isle a large bay full 5 leagues wide was opening, which we began to suspect to be *Quiros's Bay of Sᵗ Philip & James.*[9] All the Isles we passed were bluff & ended in a flatt low point, running out chiefly to Northward.[10] We observed not one Coconut on these Isles, which had here & there the appearance to consist of Chalk-Cliffs.[11] There was plenty

[1] Or *one* that Cook was certain of, viz. Tomman, off Milip Point. Cf. *Journals*, II, 510–11 and 511, n. 1.

[2] Rock Point and Ten Stick Island off it. The 'great & deep bay' is obviously South West Bay. The coastline lying beyond it from Hook Point to Pacey Point has apparently always been uninhabited. See Deacon, *Malekula* (1934), p. 6.

[3] Matanavat or perhaps rather North Cape, thus missing the great indentation of Lambumbu Bay in the night.

[4] Bougainville Strait between North Cape, Malekula and Malo.

[5] Espíritu Santo.

[6] They were Araki, Venue, Tangoa, Ulelapa, Tu Bana, Maloku on the south side and Aore and Tutuba on the south-east side, off Palekula Point, and, of course, Malo, the largest of them all, Cook's St Bartholemew. George applied the name St Bartholemew Isles to all 'the small islands which lie' before Espíritu Santo to the south. Behind them, he incorrectly speculated, might lie Quiros' anchorage in the Bay of St Philip and St James (*Voyage*, II, 368).

[7] Aesi, Mavea, Malila, Pilotin, Ladhu and Thion Islands.

[8] Lathi-hi (Sakau) island.

[9] Cf. *Journals*, II, 513 and Kelly, I, 203, n. 1. See also p. 639, n. 4 below.

[10] The reference is to the various islands lying off the east coast of Espíritu Santo. See n. 7 above.

[11] See *Journals*, II, 513, n. 1. In fact of up-raised coral, which, as Forster indicates, shows through the scattered clumps of casuarina covering them.

of Clubwood growing on all of them. Therm. 76½, in my Cabin 79½.

Aug. ye 26th ♀ Entered gradually the bay, had calms; saw many Natives on its W. Shore, & a boat, similar to those in *Mallicollo* came off, but the people kept at a distance & would never come near, though we invited them. We tacked all night. Sounded several times & had with 130 & 140 fathom no bottom. Next morning we stood in again but were becalmed.[1] Therm. 75½, in my Cabin 78½.

Aug. ye 27th ♄ Went a little in Shore, but had very little or no wind; three Canoes came off, with 3 angular Sails.[2] The people had Feathers on their heads in great bunches.[3] Some had a white Shell tied to the Forehead. Some had just such bracelets, as the people in *Mallicollo* & belts, to which a piece of mat was fixed, a palm broad, which hung down before above the knees, & another such piece was behind. They had some darts in their boats. One had a curious airy cap made of a small leaf of the Sagoe-Tree. They looked black, had woolly, crisp hair, but were stouter & better shaped than the *Mallicollo*-men.[4] They got medals, Nails, Otahaitee cloth, red bays & other Presents;[5] but they returned nothing, except a branch of the pepper-plant. They called the low country at the bottom of the bay *Attālāòne* or *Tālàòne*[6] & had names for the Country on the other sides of the bay, but we could not get the Name of the whole Isle.[7] Two boats had been sent in shore, they found the people shy & running away, but they left them presents, close in shore were Soundings but deepened immediately

[1] Forster is uncharacteristically laconic here. Cook writes: 'We were no sooner tacked than it fell calm and left us to the mercy of the swell, which continued to hurtle us towards the shore...', *Journals*, II, 513, n. 8. George reflects the alarm and notes that they even thought of hoisting out the boats to tow them off. (*Voyage*, II, 369–70).

[2] The triangular sail is the oceanic sprit sail, without a supporting mast. See p. 634, n. 4 above.

[3] Figured in F. Speiser, *Ethnographische Materialien aus den Neuen Hebriden und den Banks-Inseln* (Berlin, 1923), Taf 36 (30).

[4] The people of the district of Sakau of Espíritu Santo (Cape Quiros) are, or were, quite distinct in both language and culture from those of the head of the bay whom Quiros describes. Forster's brief account would suggest that they were late migrants from the south-east Solomons. Cf. F. Speiser, *Two Years with the Natives in the Western Pacific* (London, 1913), pp. 137–8.

[5] Cf. *Voyage*, II, 371.

[6] George (II, pp. 371–2) has *Talla one*. The valley is now almost depopulated and the name does not survive unless perhaps the reference is to Mt Takar (Turi) or to the modern anchorage at Talomako.

[7] One early suggestion is Minaru but there is in fact no name for the whole island. On this see Parsonson in Kelly, II, 377.

& they saw a large river with fresh water.[1] When the natives in the Canoes saw the boats returning, they went away.[2] The Natives understood the word *Fennòoă*,[3] Land, but none else of the various Languages we knew a little of. We hoisted the boats in, & stood out of the harbour again. Next morning we were at the W. point of this bay,[4] which is about 6 leagues deep in all. Calm. The Therm. 74½, in my Cabin 76.

Aug. ye 28th ☉ We stood on alongshore, as well as the calm would permit. Saw in the Evening the W. most points of the Isle. A Shark was caught with a new *Monoculus* sticking to its back, which we drew.[5] This day looking for some passage in a book in my Cabin, I got a small Scorpion with the book out, & it run over my hand into my Sleeve from whence it was dislodged & killed. These creatures commonly sit between the Bananas, & thus are brought into the Ship. A Booby[6] was caught in the main Yard & we found it to be a *Pelecanus Fiber*, but it had a blue not red Membrane on the Face, nor was the Rump white but dusky grey; perhaps it was a young bird or a difference of Sex. The rest corresponded well with the Description. Therm. 81, but it had been exposed to the Sun, in my Cabin 77.

Aug. ye 29th ☽ Calm, Several Sharks, Dolphins, Bonnitos & Boobies were observed about the Ship. In the night the Natives kept great fires to clear the ground for plantations.[7] The W. Side of the Isle is very high.[8] Therm. 76½°, in my Cabin 75½°. A Dolphin was struck & caught.

Aug. ye 30 ♂ The breeze freshened. We caught 2 large Albecores. Saw many boobies, some grey, some speckled white & grey: tacked for to get into the Straights[9] between the N. Isle & *Mallicollo*. Therm. 74½°, in my Cabin 76°.

[1] Several streams discharge into the bay at this point but the river in question is clearly Quiros' Jordan, the Yora. See Kelly, I, 209, n. 2.

[2] See *Voyage*, II, 372 for George's more detailed account of Pickersgill's boat expedition ashore. George (II, 373 note) has some unusual praise here for Dalrymple's 'useful and judicious Collection of Voyages'.

[3] *Fenua* or *whenua*, the Polynesian word.

[4] Cape Cumberland. There was still some doubt amongst the officers whether the Bay was in fact Quiros' St Philip and St James. See *Journals*, II, 515–18 and *Voyage*, II, 368. There is, of course, now no question that it was Quiros' discovery.

[5] As *Monoculus squali* in George Forster drawing no. 253.

[6] Probably a Brown Booby *Sula leucogaster plotus*.

[7] In preparation for the planting of the taro, the staple here, in October and November.

[8] Between 3,500 and 4,600 feet. See Kelly, I, 207, n. 2.

[9] Bougainville Strait.

*Aug. ye 31st* ☿ Tacked still on & off, the breeze fresh. Saw several Fish & several Boobies. Therm. 74½°, in my Cabin 76°.

*Sept. ye 1st* ♃ Tack still on & off & at last about noon began to enter the Passage of M. de *Bougainville*. We saw a bay to the North, but by far not so deep as represented by M^r^ de *Bougainville*. About 6 in the Evening put the Ship about & stood on SSW. in order to go to the South again.

Tendunt vela noti : fugimus spumantibus undis
Qua cursum ventusque gubernatorque vocabant
Virg. AEn. III. 268.[1]

We left now again off to search these Seas[2] for further discoveries, & return to colder climates, & hope this last Expedition to the South will be crowned with Success, & that we at last shall be restored to the embraces of our Friends & Families, from whom we have been long enough separated.

Vertitur interea caelum & ruit Oceano nox,
Involvens umbra magna terramque polumque.[3]
Virg. AEn. II. 251.

Our Course SSW then SbW & at last South, so as the wind would permit us to stand on.

In the morning

Postquam altum tenuere rates, nec jam amplius ullae
Apparint terrae, coelum undique & undique pontus.[4]
Virg. AEn. III. 192.

We saw a Tropicbird, & several flying Fish. The Thermometer at 74°, in my Cabin 75½°.

[1] 'The south winds stretch our sails: we flee over the foaming waves where the wind and the helmsmen called the course'. We miss here, as Forster retreats to his Latin books, his usual lengthy summary of an important survey finished, of important new discoveries made. As soon as they leave the Bay of St Philip and St James Forster retreats into himself temporarily. He was a brooding disappointed man at leaving such a magnificent opportunity as Espíritu Santo without a closer scientific investigation. The bitter anger, unusually repressed here, came out fully in George's *Voyage* (II, p. 373). There was one more reason for Forster's withdrawal and surly silence. He had no idea where Cook was going next. He had, in short, lost the Captain's confidence. The stage was set for deeper controversy yet.

[2] Cf. *Journals*, II, 519 and *Voyage*, II, 376.

[3] 'Meanwhile the heavens revolved and night swept over the sea, embracing in deep darkness both earth and sky.'

[4] 'After that our ships reached the deep sea; no longer could any land be seen – just sea and sky on every side.'

Sept. ye 2^d ♀ The breeze fresh, a head Sea. Course South & SbE. Saw several Boobies & flying Fish. Therm. 75°, in my Cabin 76½°.

Sept. ye 3^d ♄ The breeze fresh. Saw several Boobies, & flying Fish. Variable winds & rain in the morning. Therm. 71°, in my Cabin 74½°.

Sept. ye 4th ☉ Little Wind. Saw a Booby, & several Dolphins of a great Size attending the Ship. In the morning at 7 o'clock *Mr Colinet*[1] saw Land a head & a great way to leeward, which appeared very high, & seemes to stretch away to the SE & on the other side quite to the West. When Capt *Cook* went in the *Endeavour* along the Coast of New Holland off the *Sandy Cape*, he saw in the morning more than hundred Boobies coming from the East, passing the Ship & going directly to the Low marshy places of the Main for Food, & he then supposed that they came from some Rocks or Islands to the East, where they had passed the Night. This *Cape Sandy* is in 24° S. Latitude, but the Land we see, is in about 20°; but this Isle, or some others at the back of it, may extend so far South.[2] When M. de *Bougainville* was sailing from *Mallicollo*, he found himself somewhere in a smooth Sea, which made him suppose that there was some Land to the South, which intercepted the Swell;[3] for we find now & Capt *Cook* found in the *Endeavour* before a great Swell from the SE. The Population of New *Zeeland* being most certainly made from the North; because the Language of the New-Zeelanders has so great an Affinity with the Dialects spoken in the South-Sea-Isles, made me allways suspect, that there was a string of Isles, which made this population possible; for if in all the Interval between *Amsterdam* on one side & *Tanna* on the other, there is no other Land, it is difficult to say, how the people came to New-Zeeland: for the embarkations of these people are so slight, the winds so strong, & the Swell so common from the South & S.E. that it might be looked upon next to impossible, that these people could come to this Land. How far this suspicion may be true, time must show.[4]

[1] James Colnett. [2] See *Journals*, I, 321–2.

[3] See Bougainville, *Voyage* (London, 1772), p. 305.

[4] This is, at least, an interesting embryonic theory and proof again of Forster's emerging thinking on Pacific anthropology. George (*Voyage*, II, p. 378) wrote the final word on it. 'As we had found the inhabitants of the New Hebrides not only entirely distinct from the New Zeelanders, but also different amongst themselves, this new country offered itself to our eyes very opportunely in order to account for the population of New Zeeland; but the sequel convinced us that our ideas were very premature on this subject, and that the history of the human species in the South Seas cannot yet be unravelled with any degree of precision'. See also *Observations*, pp. 252–84.

The Land seems to be very extensive; at noon we were at 6 Leagues distant, the Extremes bearing from S.30.E. to S.69.W. Lat. 19° 53′ South. Therm. 74½, in my Cabin 74°.

Sept. ye 5th ☽ We got a calm, & advance very little, if at all. Before 4 o'clock P.M. several Smokes were seen on the Land, & a gentleman, who had been at the Masthead, pretends to have seen the Smoke burst out from a Volcano, which however none could observe as yet. The Westermost point is somewhat lower than the rest of the Isle, & there seems a great Inlet or bay to run in before it; to the North of it one or two small Islets are seen, & further on North a pretty large Isle, with another small one still more to the North. We saw 3 Sailing Canoes coming off, who supposed our Ship perhaps to be of the Size of their Canoes, & judged by that of the distance & therefore came off; but as they found the distance so great, & the Size of the Ship so large, they returned in land. This their coming off, either shows the people to be very friendly & goodnatured, or very bold & warlike, or perhaps both.

There is Land to be seen at a great distance to the East, & some at a great distance to the W. between the Isle & the great Land:[1] but we are becalmed, & have the Ships head to the North: for tho' we are still more than 3 or 4 leagues off the land, there are however breakers seen nearer, which supposes it seems a reef. There were large black birds seen, like Boobies, with long yellow or whitish bills.[2]

In the morning we went in shore & found that this Island is surrounded by a great Reef on its Northside; we saw several Canoes with two Sails each, coming on the reef & there they were fishing. Soon after several more Canoes put off, they passed the Reef & came towards the Ship. We saw an opening in the Reef more to the West, we therefore stood for it: & hoisted the boats out, who soon made the Signal of good Anchoring within the Reef. One of the Canoes came close in with them, & the people pointed to one of them that he was the *Areekee*, & when our people gave them Medals & other presents, the Natives gave them all to the *Areekee* who gave our people about 5 fish, but they were all rotten & stinky.[3] The Ship stood in, but we found, there was still

[1] 'The whole land, appearing to be very extensive, was honoured with the appellation of *Nova Caledonia*', *Voyage*, II, 378.

[2] Probably *Sula* sp.

[3] Cf. *Journals*, II, 527–8. Pickersgill, George tells us, was one of the officers out with the boats. They had, therefore, a useful informant.

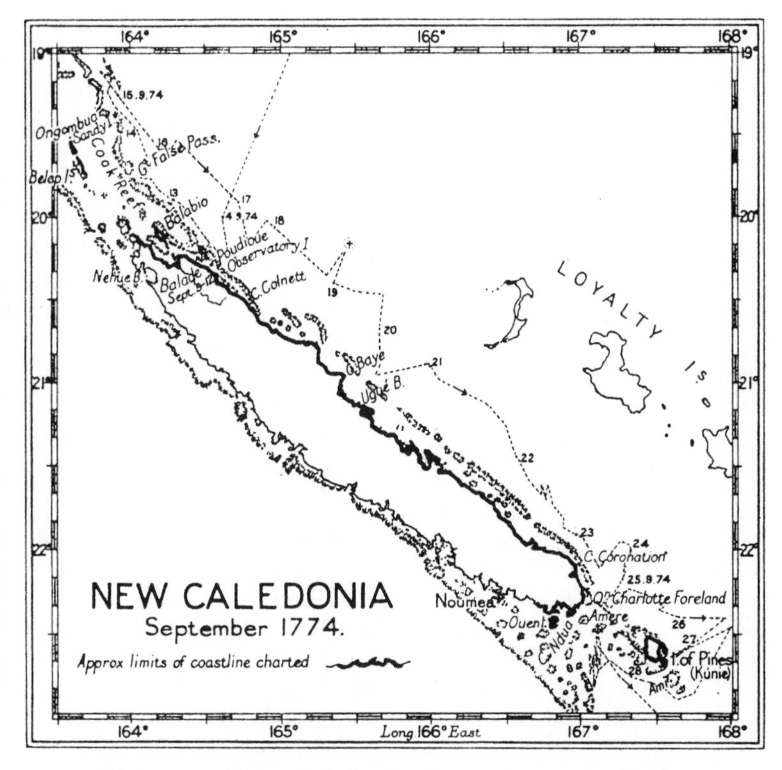

Figure 38. New Caledonia, September 1774 *(68).

more than 4 or 5 mile to the Shore & there we saw close in shore another reef. The Inhabitants are very swarthy, & pretty much alike to the people at *Tanna*, they were naked, their Canoes have a kind of rail on the outside, for to lay the oars in paddling behind & to fasten the rigging of their Masts & Sails to it. The Country has wood, but no underwood & the Trees are very sparingly scattered over the country. They have a few Coconuts, Bananas & other plantations. Their houses look pretty much like those drawn in *Le Maire* & *Schoutens* Voyage in *Cocos* Island. *viz.* they are round Beehives, with a low hole to creep in.[1] The Natives had

[1] The reference is probably to Dalrymple, *Historical Collection*, II, 'View of Cocos Island...', opp. p. 24.

no arms, except a few Darts like those in *Tānnā*, & they were very friendly & good natured. If they have pigs in plenty & greens to assist us with, we shall be happy in finding this Island.

We found a small Islet in the harbour surrounded with Reefs, & we came very near it, but found some Shoals so that we dropt from it & let go the Anchor;[1] we were soon surrounded by a great many Canoes: all of which are sailing & double, have a kind of plattform between the two boats, & some soil & Ashes where they keep a fire on. They had Spears & Beckets as in *Tànnā* & clubs with stars; & likewise a Weapon in the shape of a Scithe but with a short handle, or like a Pick-ax. Their slings are singular, with oblong heavy Stones, pointed on both sides, made I believe on purpose.[1] The Genitals of these people are wrapped in a piece of cloth & some tie the case to the String round the waist, others let it hang down, some have so long a piece of cloth of bark, that it goes under the Chin & is there tucked under a Rope, which many wear round the Neck. After we came to an Anchor, we went to *7br y. 6th* ♂ dinner & a great many of these people came on board, & saw us dine & were very desirous of eating Yams, but Pork or wine they would not taste. They admired every thing red, but gave scarce any thing in return for red cloth or beads. After dinner we went a shore, with two boats & about 12 marines. When we landed we found a great number of people ashore, some armed, some not. Some wore high Caps of black Stuff with a red piece of birds-feathers & some other feathers of Cocks on top. I observed a curious Spear, whereon a curious face was carved in the grotesque manner. We asked for water & they pointed round the East-point a good way.[3] We therefore took leave of them & went in the boats accompanied by two Natives towards the watering place. We went over a deal of Shoal ground along a shore lined with Mangroves, of more than one kind. We saw there several Inlets & went up an Arm & observed a good many Ducks[4] of which two were shot, which our Indians greatly admired: but they were less frightened than I imagined they would be. We came after

[1] Beaglehole (*Journals*, II, 529, n. 5) has a note on their exact anchorage at Balade off Observatory Isle, now Pudiu or Poudioué.

[2] Cf. Harvey's note on the weaponry, *Journals*, II, 529, n. 7 and also *Voyage*, II, 385–6.

[3] George (*Voyage*, II, 382) and Cook (*Journals*, II, 530) give more detail here on their landing and reception.

[4] Probably the Australian Grey Duck *Anas superciliosa pelewensis* Hartlaub and Finsch, the only common duck in New Caledonia. See also *Journals*, II, 531, n. 4.

several windings to several of their houses & plantations. These houses are round, with a low Entrance, full of Smoke & hot on account of the Fire they have in, to keep out, as I believe, the Mosquitos, which are plentifull in these Marshy places, though to day but few were observed, on account of the cool weather. The houses are made of reeds & other leaves. Their women & all Females wear a kind of round pettycoat, sometimes black, sometimes white, sometimes black below & white above it, consisting of a kind of leaves or filaments, on a string round the waist, about the length of a Span. Shells & other Ornaments of small pieces of green Stone are wore by both Sexes. Close to the houses were low Coconut Trees, *Arum Macrorhizum* & *esculentum* & Sugarcanes planted, which they water by little rivulets of fresh water carried there on purpose in elevated trenches. There were spots of Eddies set under water. We stood a few Minutes a shore & I got a new plant, & saw several which I had seen before, & hastened away, because it grew late. We saw a great many Ducks, Herons,[1] Owls,[2] Gulls[3] & other birds, & heard some pretty birds singing, perhaps we may get tomorrow some more. The people in general seem Goodnatured, some old fellows are bold & surly; but generally we find them very good. When we first came ashore, the Chief *Natiăbooma*[4] held a Speach, & before he began, a Man cried out aloud & immediately a Silence ensued & he then began to speak & sometimes in an interrogatory manner, when some old Men allways answered & then he continued to speak; this happened likewise a little while after, when another Chief came & began to speak with the same Circumstances. I observed among the people several with very thick Elephants-Legs, some with two, some with one, & one Man had just such an arm. It is hard, swelled but it seems without any continued pain. I saw a few with ulcers & sores on their feet & hands. We examined the Genitals of one of the Natives & found they had undergone a kind of operation somewhat similar to the circumcision viz: they split the Foreskin, & then tie the part, which gradually decays & falls off. This is the practice at *Otahaitee* & the Society Isles, & I believe here, for the

[1] Probably, mostly, the White-faced Heron *Notophoyx novaehollandiae nana* Amadon, 1942.

[2] Probably the Barn Owl *Tyto alba lifuensis* Brasil, 1916.

[3] Not specifically identifiable.

[4] Teabooma of *Journals*, II, 530 and Teà-booma of *Voyage*, II, 382. See also *Journals*, II, 544, n. 3.

Man next to me shewed me, that the Foreskin was slit & then stripped backward over the *glans*.

When we were near the huts of the Inhabitants we saw on the Embers of their Fireplace a large Pot, of about 4 or 5 gallons capacity. It was made clumsily, roundish, thick & of a reddish clay.[1]

At the place where we first landed we saw a Man well limbed & at least 6 Foot 6 Inches high. Upon the whole, tho' the Natives are black, & have woolly hair, there are however the greater part, well shaped & featured by far better than those at *Mallicollo*. The Earlap is so dilated that they can fold the lower part over the Ears, as in Easter Island, though it is not customary here: but they put however often a Sugar-cane-leaf scrolled up into the Ear.

The next morning we went ashore to find water & we collected a good many plants & shot several birds.[2] Yesterday night late a Man, who was our Butcher, a laborious, indefatigable Man, had the Misfortune to fall down the Main hatchway & grew very ill over night, & at last died probably from a fractured skull & extravasated blood in the head.[3]

We found Water in a small river. The whole Country has no underwood, & the Tree growing chiefly here is the *Cayputi* or Linnaei *Melaleuca Leucadendnum*.[4] Rumph calls it *arbor alba* & so it is; the bark being white & going easily off & concealing behind it, ants, beetles, Lizards & Scorpions. Capt *Cook* says the Country looks much like N. Holland. The Inhabitants are very peaceable & goodnatured, absolutely harmless. Having found Water, we all returned on board.[5]

*Sept. ye 7th* ☿ The Capt prepared to go to a little Isle, where the Astronomer was gone this morning, in order to observe there the

[1] Opp. VI, f. 6 is a very crude outline of this pot. See also *Journals*, II, 531 & n. 3 and *Voyage*, II, 389. George gives the fuller account of their excursion to find a watering place.

[2] Several species were described under this date by Forster. They were: (a) *Certhia fasciata* of *Descr. Anim.*, p. 263. It is *Certhia undulata* of Sparrman's *Mus. Carls.*, 1787, No. XXXIV. Now the Barred Honey-eater *Guadalcanaria undulata* (Sparrman, 1787). There is no Forster drawing; (b) *Muscicapa xanthetraea* of *Descr. Anim.*, p. 268, now the Rufous-bellied Whistler *Pachycephala rufiventris xanthetraea* (Forster, 1844). No illustration; (c) *Loxia melaleuca* of *Descr. Anim.*, p. 272; folio 40 and Lysaght, p. 282. Now the White-breasted Wood Swallow *Artamus leucorhynchus melanoleucus* Wagler; (d) George's folio 124 of the Pacific Golden Plover *Pluvialis dominica fulva* (Gmelin, 1789) was dated this day. See also *Descr. Anim.*, p. 258.

[3] This is the best account of Simon Monk's death. See *Journals*, II, 533, n. 3.

[4] *M. leucadendnum*. George (II, p. 391) extends this note and cites Rumphius's description from *Herbarium Amboinense*, II, 72.

[5] Cf. George's longer account of this morning's excursion, including his rudimentary remarks on soil and geology (*Voyage*, II, 390–1). Cook was not on this ramble.

Ecclipse. I desired the Capt to go ashore in the Afternoon, to collect more new things. We dined at one o'clock & when we just sat to our dinner the Officer sent & let me know the boats were going, because the Capt was absent.[1] This was premeditated. They did not acquaint me they would go so early, nor could I go without dinner. In short the first Lieu^t wanted to disappoint me. He is a weak Man, & acts very inconsistent with himself & all principles of reason, & thought to do me a deal of harm by doing so, & after dinner he refused me a boat to let me go ashore, though there were hands enough to give me a cast to the very nigh shore, & many people were just then standing & laughing to divert the Indians: one traded before every bodies Eyes, another scratched a Sow to divert the Indians, but the Lieut said, he would break none off from their business: in short, the whole of the Affair is this, the greater part of the Men in the Ship have begun to calculate their pay & find that it will not amount to 4000£ Sterl., which government allows me, & therefore I am the object of their Envy & they hinder me in the pursuit of Natural History, where they can, from base & mean, dirty principles, beneath any Man of Sense. I get my Money if I had not the opportunity to get one plant or bird described the whole Voyage. If I am disappointed the fault is not mine, but the public looses by it, who pays & whose chief views are thus defeated, by Men who are Servants to the public, & ought to promote, not hinder the common cause. But it cannot be otherwise expected from the people who have not sense enough to think reasonably & beyond the Sphere of their mean grovelling Passions.[2]

Capt Cook arrived. I acquainted him with the whole, he could not approve of it: but things were over; & the lost time could not be redressed. He went tho' late ashore & I went with him & got another plant. We are indefatigable, but cannot prosper if every step is taken by envious persons to cross & hinder me.

The next morning Capt. Cook went with me, my Son, Mr Sparman, Mr Gilbert, & 2 Midshipmen & 3 Sailors up the hill; we found the whole consisted of a *Saxum quarzosum & mica aurea*

[1] He was taking part in observations of an eclipse of the sun on Observatory Isle which 'came on' about one p.m., just as Forster apparently was sitting down to dinner. See *Journals*, II, 532–3.

[2] This confrontation, the first of the New Caledonian series, is mentioned nowhere else. In the *Reply* (p. 9) George openly suggested that much of the antagonism towards them stemmed from their shipmates' 'envy' over J. R. Forster's apparently generous allowances.

& corneo fissili mixtum.[1] These particles were mixed in various proportions. We saw the *Cayputi* Tree growing on these barren hills to the very top, but thinly; it was more & more degenerated & shrubby on top. We passed several rivulets of Water even near the top, & found several new plants. The Capt. made such a haste, in the very heat of the day, that my Son & myself & one Midshipman were knocked up. A little way from the Summit, under a hill where they bury their dead as they told me, I saw at a distance stakes stuck in the ground with branches on top & some dry grass on it. We came another way down, & joined the brooming & watering party.[2] When we went up the hill we met great numbers of people about 200 coming from beyond the hill, to see us & the Ship, who all went back up the hill, & again down with us.[3]

*Sept. ye 8th* ♃ After dinner we went again ashore to the W. of the watering place, where I found a kind of Hornstone full of Garnets,[4] & several new plants, & a few birds;[5] among the plants was a *Protea*, & a *Passiflora* which two genera grow, the one only in Africa & no where else & the second in America only; this Isle therefore connects the 3 Continents Asia, Africa & America, for we find a good many Indian plants here.[6] The Cap^ts.^ Clerck saw at the Mouth of the River a fine large Fish struck with a Spear

[1] *Lit:* Quartzose rock mixed with golden mica and with fissile horn (stone). It is the Mt Panié mica schist of modern geological maps. George calls it 'quartz and glimmer' (mica).

[2] This expedition in which Cook and Gilbert got high enough – without the Forsters – to see the sea on the further side of New Caledonia and for a considerable distance along the northern and eastern coastlines is best read from Cook (*Journals*, II, 533–4), who was struck with many similarities between New Caledonia and New Holland. George (*Voyage*, II, 395–7) gives us more geology and mineralogy.

[3] *Corvus cinereus* of *Descr. Anim.*, p. 260 was described on this date. See also folio 53 (the type of the species) and Lysaght, p. 285. Now the Melanesian Graybird *Coracina caledonica caledonica* (Gmelin, 1788).

[4] This is garnet schist of the Mt Panié schist complex. See *Voyage*, II, 399, for more details of this evening excursion.

[5] Two species were described under this date viz: *Coracias pacifica* of *Descr. Anim.*, p. 261; Forster folio 54 and Lysaght, p. 285. Now the Glossy Starling *Aplonis striatus striatus* (Gmelin, 1788) and *Muscicapa olivacea* of *Descr. Anim.*, p. 271, now the New Caledonian Whistler *Pachycephala caledonica* (Gmelin, 1789). There was no illustration of this bird.

[6] *Protea* is now considered to be a wholly African genus but some fifty species of the family Proteaceae are now recognised in New Caledonia. The genus *Passiflora*, though chiefly American, is currently recognised also in Australia and New Zealand, as well as in New Caledonia and other places. Forster's comments here foreshadow the conclusions of modern plant geographers that New Caledonia has strong affinities with Australia, Malaysia and the Pacific i.e. in all directions. I am grateful to Dr Lucy Moore for this note.

Figure 39. Natural History of New Caledonia.
Melanesian Graybird *Coracina caledonica* (Gm.)
Drawing by George Forster in B.M. (N.H.) – 'Zoological Drawings', f. 53.

by an Indian, he bought it for the Capt. & sent it on board. We saw, it was a kind of *Tetrodon*,[1] next kin to the Sunfish, it had a very large head & a Skin like the Dogfish of a rough Surface & some small speckles, its colour was a dull lead-colour. My Son drew it, but there was no time to describe the same, for it was to be dressed & therefore skinned. However it was too late to dress it for Supper so it was preserved for ye next dinner. When we were at Supper, one of the Servants came in, & shewed the Liver, which was large, & the Capt thought it might be fried & eaten, & this was consequently done, but as we had already eaten something & were rather more dry than hungry, we ate each but a little of it. The Capt ate about the Size of a Crownpiece, I about double the Quantity & my Son about half a Crown's size. Mr *Sparman* ate none, for he never eats any Liver of any Animal. An hour after Supper the Servant came in & told that having set the Dish down in the birth for their Supper, & having gone out for some business, their Dogs in the mean time jumped up & ate all the rest of the Liver & of the Row, but half an hour after they both grew sick & threw up the whole: we all laughed at this circumstance & had no suspicion about the badness of the Fish & went therefore to bed in hopes to go next morning early ashore.

I awoke about 4 o'clock in the morning & felt myself very giddy in the head & my hands & Feet were benumbed & my Stomach so heavy as if I had gotten a Surfeit. I got up, but I reeled like a drunken Man & could neither walk nor stand. I called for my Servant. I went to the necessary, had a Stool & was obliged at the same time to throw up the little liver I had eaten which burnt & excoriated my throat in coming up. When I came back to my Cabin, I asked my Son, how he was & he then said, that he had the same Symptoms, & when I told of it to Mr *Sparman* in the Steerage, where he sleeps, the Capt. heard it, & tho' he had long had the same Symptoms, he did not however think, that this was caused by the Fish-Liver; but my complaint alarmed him, he tried to get up & found he could neither stand nor walk. He then sent

[1] The Toadfish *Lagocephalus scleratus* (Gm). It was *Tetrodon sceleratus* of *Descr. Anim.*, p. 282 and George's drawing No. 244. Despite Forster's claim there was no time to describe the fish Cook wrote that 'luckaly for us the opperation of describeing and drawing took up so much time till it was too late so that only the Liver and Roe was dressed..... ', *Journals*, II, 535. The poisonous effects of the liver and gonads of pufferfishes are well-known; Forster gives a graphic account in *Descr. Anim.*, p. 254.

immediately for the Surgeon, who ordered us all warm water to cause a vomiting. We drank plentifully of it, & it had the desired effect. The Capt. threw very little up, I a great deal & my Son less than I, but a great deal more than the Capt. Than he ordered us a *Sangrey* of wine, acid of Lemons, Sugar & boiling water, that we might perspire after it. I got up at 7 o'clock, having plentifully perspired. The Capt lay till noon, my Son got up about 8 o'clock. We breakfasted, & I wanted to take a dose of Physic, which the Doctor had ordered for us all, but I had scarce swallowed it, when it came up again, with great violence. I drank one dish Tea more & went to bed; however I took a Spoon full of sweet oil of Olives, because I felt my throat quite excoriated. We were all drowsy, our Legs & Hands benumbed, could neither stand nor walk & but ill support our heads. My Son was up & fell a drawing. Mr *Sparman* went ashore to collect more plants & I went to bed, slept well & perspired all the time, till about noon, which did me a deal of good. The Capt. was about dinner something better, after some *Sedes*; & so was my Son.

Sept. ye 9th ♀ At dinner we ate but little, my Son grew sick, & threw up all the portable Soup he had eaten. Mr *Sparman* went again ashore & I again to bed, my head being giddy & my Limbs benumbed, & thus we continued all the afternoon; we drank some Tea & I had two Stools that night & felt a good appetite & had some Sago for Supper. There came several Indians on board that made Signs, on seeing the Fish, that it was bad for the Stomach & caused Sleep & Death; but we thought they wanted the Fish & I ordered the same to be offerred to them, but they refused it with evident Signs of aversion, which proved they knew the Fish to be poisonous & noxious. A little pig, I had gotten at *Tànā* & which had eaten all the garbage of the Fish, when it was cleaned in the Evening before, was found dead this morning & the Dogs who had eaten the Liver, were likewise not well. We took another Dose of *Sangrey* this night & went to bed. We all perspired & slept well. The Capt. found himself much better, but had already felt some pain in the wrist & ankles. I was drowsy & giddy, but my Son was it much more than I. I had been twice to Stool in the morning. My Son threw up his Breakfast, & took a powder of Jesuit's bark & went to bed. I began to write something, but I could hardly recollect, what I was writing & made several faults; however I brought something in my Vocabulary in order; & then growing something more easy, I described a bird & a Fish, which my Son drew.[1]

The Capt. sent this morning the Longboat & Cutter to the West, to see whether there is a passage out of the reef, & how the Isle looks there & whether there is any more Land to be seen; with orders not to stay without necessity, & to be cautious in landing.[2]

Sept. ye 10th ♄ The Natives came off as before, in boats & several came swimming, they began to grow fond of Iron, Nails, knives, hatchets & Gimlets. The Chief got yesterday a Hatchet of the Capt with a Gimlet & a Dog & a bitch; for he had sent Sugar-Cane, & some Yams, & I gave him two Days before, when the Ecclipse was, a very large Hatchet. At Dinner George parted again with his Pease-Soup: but the Capt & I were somewhat better. Mr *Sparman* was all this day employed in describing plants, & my Son drew a few in the Afternoon. I find that the pains will likewise attack me, & my weakness in the Limbs & the giddiness of the head is not yet over. If we find ourselves better to morrow, we intend to go ashore; & see what plants we can collect.

The next morning I went ashore & collected several new plants, for we found ourselves entirely better only a little weaker. The Natives are the most harmless & goodnatured Set of people, that we have as yet met with. They are poor on account of the barrenness of their Soil, which does not afford them many cultivated plants, & this makes, that they cannot give any away to us. Their houses are constructed over a skeleton of sticks in the Shape of a beehive; on the inside they fix to it a coating of Coconut mats & quite on the Inside another coating of the bark of *Cayputi*-Tree; on the outside is a thick thatch of a kind of grass;[3] but as we were so little ashore on account of our illness, & had enough to do with collecting plants, & did not understand much of their language, we could not learn which grass they employ for this purpose & for manufacturing their ropes & the petticoats of their women. They have but a few Coconuts & I saw no more

[1] This is the most detailed account we have of the fish poisoning and its effects. George (II, pp. 403–6) omits some of the symptoms and treatment here recorded and Cook, as usual, is brief and stoical (*Journals*, II, 535). Worst of all for the Forsters 'it prevented us making those researches, which from the nature of the country before us, would doubtless have teemed with a variety of interesting discoveries in every branch of natural history'.

[2] See *Journals*, II, 535–7.

[3] Cf. Cook's and Wales's much more adequate description of New Caledonian dwellings, *Journals*, II, 541–2 and 866. George (*Voyage*, II, 407–9) also inserts additional details of this morning excursion.

than 3 breadfruit-Trees. Sugarcanes, Eddies of both Kinds, Yams & Bananas are the plants, which they chiefly cultivate. They eat some Leaves & dress a bark which they dress & wrench, by which operation a thin Skin goes off & a kind of pulp is set free from the outer thick Rind. The pulp is eaten & the stringy sweet Rind they suck. I could never make them understand what plant it was they used in that manner. They eat a great many Shelfish which they constantly collect in their reefs. They have no other animal food, but what the sea affords them, & as I believe but sparingly tho' they are very expert at striking Fish with their Spears. We left them a Dog & a bitch, & if nothing intervenes a little Boar & a Sow are intended to be left here as a present; & if the breeds of these 2 kinds of Animals succeed, it must give them an easier animal food & a greater Variety of it. Our goat has kidded a few days ago, but both kids died. Had these kids lived long enough & had learnt to eat grass, we might have a chance to set them somewhere in the South-Sea ashore & to raise there a bread of Goats: but we have been infortunate in that respect. One of the Goats we bought at S[t] *Yago* died of the Scurvy, so did the Goat belonging to the Gentlemen in the Gunroom. A Goat & He-Goat we set ashore in N. Zeeland was killed by the Natives, a young He-Goat we had, fell over board & was drowned, & the old He-Goat we had, ate something in N.-Zeeland, which made him so mad, that he ran in the Sea & perished therein. This Goat we had covered at Otahaitee by the He-Goat Capt *Furneaux* left to *Otòo*, & she kidded within a few days of her time, but as she has miscarried twice in bad weather before this time, it was difficult for her to bring forth perfect young ones in due time. Had all these Animals lived & had all their progeny been preserved, we might have had enough goats to give away in several places in the South-Seas. It would be a real benefit both for future Navigators & likewise for the Natives of Otahaitee & New Zeeland to procure the first more Goats & Bulls & Cows, & the latter more Boars & Sows with some Goats; nay at Otahaitee Sheep would succeed very well & in several other places Goats might do extremely well. In *Easter Island*, Seeds of various plants as Yams, & Coconuts, with Breadfruit, & all kinds of Trees that Love a hilly country would do exceedingly well, & cause more moisture by their Shade & procure rivulets, to this now poor, parched up Island. In the *Marquesas*, Goats would thrive well & even Bulls & Cows, with

Sheep. In *Otahaitee* & the Society Isles, besides the enumerated Animals, it would be a fine refreshment for Navigators to find there sweet Oranges, Shaddocks, Pine-Apples & Water Melons.

In the *friendly Islands* sweet Oranges, Pine Apples & Water Melons with some of our Domestic Animals viz. Goats, black Cattle, & Sheep, would be a useful acquisition. In *Mallicollo* & the adjacent Isles, up to *Tànnā* Goats would be very usefull: with the above enumerated Fruit. Humanity would advise these things, were the distance & Expence not so great.

The people here will certainly be happy in acquiring some new domestic Animals as Dogs & Hogs, & in case they could get some more Tropical plants.

They use for several Ornaments a kind of ropes twisted with hair of bats, which they call birds; but we could shoot none of them, for they seem here scarcer than anywhere else in the Isles. In the *friendly Isles* for Instance they are hanging in day time from the Casuarina Trees by hundreds. We saw to day an inclosure of sticks, round a hummock of about 4 feet high, on which several sticks with large *Turbines* were put, & the Natives told us, that this was the burying place of the Chief of the District.[1] We got again from a Man the Names of several Lands & their bearings, the greater part of which seem to be on this Isle; except about 5 which seem to be distinct Lands. The Names I got amount to about 24 in all. If those which they pointed to ly SEbS are Isles & not Districts there are about 16 or 17 Isles more in that Direction: a very great *Archipelago* indeed![2] When it grows late & the Natives want to go ashore without having a boat, they all swim off. I saw 45 swimming off at once, though it is above a mile to the Shore. To day a Man was on board, who had 18 large Turtle Shell Earrings, all in one Ear.

7br yᵉ 11ᵗʰ ☉ We went ashore in the Afternoon & collected several plants. We observed that the birds live chiefly in the bushes & trees near the Seaside & higher up, we seldom saw a single bird. The Natives dress their Shells in large Earthern pots they put on the fire. They have a kind of Hatchet, different from those in the South Sea Isles, or N. Zeeland in regard to the helvit & fixing the stone in it; namely they cut into a piece of crooked wood a deep hole,

[1] Cf. Cook in *Journals*, II, 544, where some of this information seems to have come from the Forsters. See also *Voyage*, II, 410.

[2] The direction indicated is that in which the Loyalty Islands lie. Cf. *Journals*, II, 544 and 867–8.

just fitting the Stone; & have a short handle, the whole being naturally grown bent in that manner. The Stone is black, & some have the green N. Zeeland Stone, which they probably find here, for several wear it in small pieces on a rope going round the Neck, either in a globular or in an oblong Shape.[1]

Next morning we went ashore, we shot a couple of birds,[2] I collected some plants & some words of the Language of the Natives; & returned on board to dinner. All these days it blew fresh. Ever since we habe been here, every day several boats with Natives came on board: This was the first day that none came off.[3]

Sept. ye 12th ☽ In the Afternoon we returned on shore, for as to day the boats were expected back, we supposed the Ship would next day go under sail & we therefore went to collect whatever might fall to our hands. Today we shot two fine green Parrots,[4] with long tails & red on the Crown & Forehead, Wings & tail blue; the Neck yellow, Irides gold coloured, Feet & bill black, some had the tip of the bill yellow: on the crown were two narrow uprightstanding black Feathers, with red tips, of the length of the whole head. In short a quite new & beautifull bird. A yellowish Heron[5] was shot with a black head, 3 white black tip'd long Feathers, Neck & breast pale rusty colour; Back, wings & tail red-chocolate colour, bill black, Feet greenish yellow, *Lora* naked greenish yellow. Irides yellow: but the bird stunk most immoderately. We returned on board likewise with a couple of new plants. This Evening the Longboat & Cutter returned; they had had the misfortune to spring a leak in the Cutter, when they were 4 miles from any land: they found themselves obliged to heave a Cask with water & several other things over board to lighten

[1] In *Voyage*, II, 409 George, with a description, records that they purchased this hatchet, 'it being the first instrument relating to agriculture which we had seen in this country'. The Forsters also acquired clubs, slings and spears from New Caledonia, some of which items were passed to the Oxford collection ('Catalogue of Curiosities', 155–64.) The fate of the hatchet seems uncertain. Cook had some interesting remarks (*Journals*, II, 531–2) about the 'prevailing Passion for curiosities' at New Caledonia.

[2] Forster's description of *Certhia chlorophaea* was undated in *Descr. Anim.*, p. 264 and the species was not illustrated by George. It was the Silver-eared Honey-eater *Lichmera incana incana* (Latham, 1790). His description of *Turdus xanthopus* was dated 5–12 September (*Descr. Anim.*, p. 266). See folio 151 and Lysaght, p. 307. This is now the Island Thrush *Turdus poliocephalus xanthopus* Forster, 1844.

[3] See *Voyage*, II, 411–15 for details of this excursion.

[4] *Psittacus bisetis* of *Descr. Anim.*, p. 258; Forster folio 43 and Lysaght p. 283. Now the Crested Parakeet *Eunymphicus cornutus cornutus* (Gmelin, 1788).

[5] *Ardea ferruginea* of *Descr. Anim.*, p. 274, Forster folio 111 and Lysaght, p. 298. Now the New Caledonian Night Heron *Nycticorax caledonicus caledonicus* (Gmelin, 1789).

her & the water however gained very much, so that they could hardly keep her a float. They made with difficulty the next land & rowed her along shore, having somehow stopt up the leak & they themselves, the Rowers excepted, walked along shore from 6 o'clock in the morning, till about 5 o'clock in the Afternoon. The Longboat came still later on board. They had met with a heavy cockling sea all this day & a strong tide or Current. They had been to the Isle of *Ballabeeya*,[1] where they found friendly Inhabitants, who assisted them in every respect, as far as lay in their power. They saw no End to the Reef nor any passage in it. The Natives talked much of a great Land to the North or N.W. called *Mìngha* or *Minda* or something like that: & that its Inhabitants were warlike & their Ennemies. Their showed a Sepulcral Tumulus of one of their Chiefs, killed in battle in Defense of his own Country, by a Spear of the Natives of *Mìngha* or *Mìndā*.[2]

Next morning the Capt went ashore in order to give his Friend *Heebâi*[3] a little Boar & a little Sow: we went up the river where we had been the first time of our landing. I saw there on a hill a house of a Chief & behind it a row of wooden Pillars about 10 or 12 Inches square, 8 or 9 Feet high, with a carved head on Top. The old Man signified me by Signs, that it was his Burying-place. I shot that day a very small *Loxia*;[4] all green, the Forehead, Cheeks & Throat fine bright red; The Vent, coverts of the Tail & Tail itself likewise red. It is not bigger than a humming bird, for which I took it; but the black thick bill at first made me believe that it was a small Parrokeet, till after a more minute Inspection, when I got the bird into my hands, I found it to be a *Loxia* or *Grossbeak*. It is I believe the smallest bird of that *Genus*.

[1] Balabio.

[2] This expedition was led by Gilbert and Pickersgill. See *Journals*, II, 536–7. Forster got his detailed information on the expedition from Pickersgill that 'intelligent officer' (*Voyage*, II, 416–20). It was the frustration and disappointment at not going on this expedition – because of the still deleterious effects of the fish poisoning – coupled with the refusal of surgeon's mate William Anderson to give the Forsters any information on the ample new plant species, shells and other materials he had collected which led to the bitterest public outburst in the *Voyage* (II, p. 420, note) on 'the obstacles in all our researches' which the elder Forster imagined – and certainly not without good reason – were put in their way. Wales (*Remarks*, pp. 89–90) and Beaglehole (*Journals*, II, xlv–xlvi) have something to say on this passage, to which similar obstruction and incidents throughout the voyage had undoubtedly been leading.

[3] This was presumably Cook's 'friend' whose name is wanting in *Journals*, II, 537; he was one of the 'principal' natives whom they had met on the day of their first landing on New Caledonia. See *Voyage*, II, 389 and 421.

[4] *Fringilla pulchella* of *Descr. Anim.*, p. 273; Forster folio 153 and Lysaght, p. 307. The drawing is the type of the species; now the Red-throated Parrot-finch *Erythrura psittacea* (Gmelin, 1789).

We shot besides this, two other new birds, of the *Flycatcher-kind.*[1] We then returned on board for our dinner, where we found all boats hoisted in, the only Pinnace excepted & the small Anchor taken up.

*Sept. ye 13th* ♂ In the Afternoon the Capt went again ashore, & I went with him. He ordered in a large Tree near the Watering-place on the beach the following Inscription to be cut.

His Britannick Majesties Ship Resolution Sept. 1774

I found 2 or 3 new plants & got Specimens of such we had found before & which we wanted to habe in greater Quantity: & then took leave of this Isle.[2]

.... *Interea revoluta ruebat*
Matura jam luce dies, noctemque fugarat. Virg. Æn. x. 256
Nauticus exoritur vario certamine clamor, Æn. II, 128
Provehimur portu, terraeque (collesque) *recedunt* Æn. II. 72
Prosequitur surgens a puppi ventus euntes. Æn. II. 130[3]

We soon cleared the reef, & stood out in order to get round the reef, which surrounds the Isle of *Ballabeea* & joins it to *Pöë-mânghee,*[4] but we were soon sensible that this reef extended a great way to the North. We therefore hauled our wind again. The Thermometer at 8 o'clock in the morning at 73, in my Cabin 76.[5]

*Sept. ye 14th* ☿ In the Afternoon sailing along the reef, we saw a good many Boobies,[6] for I counted once about 17. Several Tropicbirds

[1] Probably *Muscicapa naevia* of *Descr. Anim.*, p. 269; Forster folio 159 and Lysaght, p. 308. Now the Long-tailed Triller, *Lalage leucopyga montrosieri* Verreaux and des Murs, 1860.

[2] Cf. *Voyage*, II, 323 and *Journals*, II, 539.

[3] Taking the last three lines of this mixed quotation first we should note that they are from Aeneid III not II. The translation offered for the whole is: 'Meanwhile daylight, rolling round, was hurrying in quite clear now, and had driven the night away / The shouting of the sailors rose as they worked in rivalry at their various tasks / We sailed from the harbour; the land and its hills receded from view [here Forster substitutes *collesque* (hills) for Vergil's "cities"] A wind, rising from astern, saw us off on our journey.'

[4] This name Forster uses as a running heading in his Journal from 7 to 19 September (VI, ff. 9–22).

[5] 'On leaving this place, we were far from being recovered, but had daily acute head-aches, and spasmodic pains over the body, together with an eruption on our lips. We also felt ourselves much weakened, and unfit to go through our usual occupations; whilst the want of fresh food greatly contributed to keep us in a lingering state, and retarded our recovery', *Voyage*, II, 323–4. This low state may have accounted for Forster's failure to give his usual summary of findings at a new landfall. This neither George (II, pp. 324–33) nor Cook, (*Journals*, II, 539–46) neglected.

[3] Probably the Australian Brown Gannet or Booby *Sula leucogaster plotus* (Forster, 1844). See also 16 September p. 657 below.

were observed. But soon after, we saw beyond the Reef an extensive Isle, & the Reef went still further North, so that we were obliged to hawl still more the wind. In the Night we tacked, next morning we came nearer the Reef; saw the Land again but the Wind fell allmost to a calm. Saw a Tropicbird. Therm. 74½, in my Cabin 77°.[1]

Sept. ye 15th ♃ We see the Land, & another divided from it still more to the North, & the more North we go the Reef continues. We saw at 6 o'clock the point of the Reef, but we tack'd at 8 o'clock & continued to do so all night. In the morning we bore away, but were stopt again by the reef & obliged to put about Ship: at 10 o'clock saw the Land again, 2 points before the beam to Leeward.[2] Saw a Tropicbird. The Thermometer at 8 o'clock 76°, in my Cabin 77°.

Sept. ye 16th ♀ Very little wind, & at last calm; we were within 4 miles of the reef, & a strong Swell set the Ship gradually towards it. The Cutter & pinnace were hoisted out, to tow the Ship off. In the Evening we had a little breeze but after midnight we were obliged to tow again. In the morning the Lieuts & I went in a boat to shoot birds, & killed a new Booby[3] & a new Tern.[4] I shot a Booby, but the 1st Lieut ordered the boat on board & would not go to fetch the bird, because I had shot it. When we were going on board a little breeze sprung up & we set our sails again. The Thermometer at 77°, in my Cabin 79½. I had for several days a *head ache* the remainders of the poison, for my Son had the same Symptoms. To day our Lips began to set out some little pustules.

Sept. ye 17th ♄ In the Afternoon we were again becalmed; a Booby came close to the Ship, I shot it & it was picked up alongside by a boat-hook. Towards night a faint breeze sprung up & in the morning we saw *Poemânghee* and *Ballabeea* again. The Thermometer at 75⅔°, in my Cabin 78½°.

[1] Opp. VI, f. 20 are the following notes:
♂ 73 Therm. Cabin 76.
Boobies, Land, Tropicbird, Long Reef.
☿ 74½
Boobies, Tropicbird, little wind.

[2] Cf. *Journals*, II, 547–9, where Cook discusses his reasons for not prosecuting his explorations to the north of New Caledonia.

[3] *Pelecanus Plotus* of *Descr. Anim.*, p. 278; folio 108 and Lysaght, p. 298. Now the Australian Brown Gannet or Booby *Sula leucogaster plotus* (Forster, 1844). See *Journals*, II, 549, n. 3.

[4] *Sterna serrata* of *Descr. Anim.*, p. 276; folio 110 and Lysaght, p. 298. Now the Sooty Tern *Sterna fuscata serrata* Wagler, 1830. See also p. 467, n. 4 above.

Sept. ye 18th ☉ Very little wind. Caught a Shark. The Thermometer at 74⅔, in my Cabin 77½.

7br ye 19th ☽ The weather calm & hazy. In the night & morning we had several Showers of rain & foggy weather. Saw great Quantities of Man of war birds, at least 17 were at once in Sight & several Fish were skipping about. The Thermometer at 72¼, in my Cabin 74½.

7br ye 20th ♂ In the Afternoon still calm & rainy. In the Evening a fresh breeze sprung up. We tacked about & saw in the morning the same Isle, where we had been a sevennight before, & though we were at least 24 leagues from our anchoring place & more than 30 from *Bāllābeèā*, we saw however this Island a head & somewhat more on the Weatherbow to the Eastward, so that it will prove at least 40 or 50 leagues long, & is therefore the greatest new Tropical Island we have hitherto seen, for I do not reckon in *N. Zeeland*, which was discovered before & is no more within the Tropics. It lies NWbW & SEbE, but seems to be but narrow across, for Capt Cook saw on the hill the Sea on the other side of it. It deserves to be called *New-Caledonia*, as we do not know its true Name, for what we got from the Natives were only Names of Districts on the Isle. Saw several Man of war- & Tropic-birds. The breeze gentle & fresh. The Thermometer at 71¾°, in my Cabin 74°.

7br ye 21st ☿ In the Evening the breeze fell & we had all night & next morning a calm. Saw Man of warbirds. Therm. 73, in my Cabin 74.

7br ye 22d ♃ All the Afternoon calm. In the Evening after 10 o'clock a faint breeze sprung up. The Land extends still more SE ward, & by what we now see, it extends more than 60 nearly, 70 Leagues. The Thermometer at 72½°, in my Cabin 73.

7br ye 23d ♀ Very little wind. Saw in the Evening a bluff point of the Isle, & this being King George's Coronation-day it was called *Point Coronation.*[1] Next morning we discovered a place, wherefrom constantly a Smoke arose, & this continued until Sunset & dark night & the place where the Smoke came from was pretty extensive, perhaps about half a mile in length; by help of our Glasses we observed here & there on this Spot some upright-standing Pillars, & though they stood in some places as it were singly, there was however more to the East a spot where they appeared pretty-close. I supposed, from what I saw, that they were

[1] Identified on modern maps with Pt Pouaréti. See *Journals*, II, 551.

a kind of Basalt-pillar of a regular Figure, so as the Rocks on the *Giant's-Causeway* in the County of *Antrim* in Ireland, and at *Stolpen* in Saxony, which are a kind of crystallized Basaltes. Several people thought them Trees, & I offerred the Capt a wager of a dozen of bottles in favour of my opinion, against his, who thought them Trees, provided we should come near enough to examine it & thus decide the Question.[1] We saw the Land everywhere red, probably from the few clay-particles, which are between the *Daze* or *Glist* & the Quartz mixed.[2] In general I believe this Isle to contain Minerals & perhaps chiefly of the Tin-kind. The Thermometer at 73½°, in my Cabin 76°.

7br ye 24th ♄ In the Afternoon we discovered that at a good distance East from *Point Coronation* the Basalt-Pillars project into the Sea: some are higher, some lower. In the Evening we stood off, & probably shall come in the morning near enough to settle the disputed point. We saw a few *Man of war birds* & several Fish jumping out of the water about the Ship. The wind gradually fell & during night & all the next morning we had a calm & were more off the Land than before: & saw a Cape which terminates the Isle to the East.[3] The Thermometer at 73°, in my Cabin 73½°.

Sept. ye 25th ☉ The calm still obtains, & we cannot even come near this promontory & go to the South of the Isle, or push on towards New-Zeeland to prepare our Crew for a fresh Southern cruize, by a plentifull eating of Greens & fresh Fish. In the Evening, at 6 o'clock, from the Masthead Land was discovered bearing S.35° E. about 12 Leagues distance[4] & a small Isle at SbW.,[5] the Extremity of the great Isle we have hitherto coasted bore SEbS. The Stone pillars at the great Isle are probably polygonal-Basalt-Columns, such as are found in Upper-Egypt near *Syene* or *Assuan* & at *Hayar Silcily*, where the Nile is very Narrow. They are likewise to be met with on the left hand side of the lake of *Bolsena* in *Italy*: at *Hildesheim* in his Britannic Majesties German Dominions; at *Yauer* in Silesia; in Saxony a few miles East of Dresden at a town called *Stolpen*, there is a hill formed by this kind of Bazalt-pillars & the Castle of the town is built on it. Nay even

[1] See p. 661 below.

[2] Glist (Cornish) and presumably daze are old terms for mica, but Forster was guessing here about the red colour of the land. This was probably due to the lateritic weathering of ultrabasic rocks. Both the mineralised zones in the Mt Panié schists and the ultrabasic rocks are now the basis of rich mining industries.

[3] Cape Queen Charlotte.

[4] Isle of Pines or Kunie.

[5] Presumably the islet Nuare.

in the Britannic Dominions they are to be met with in several places besides the *Giant's-causeway* near *Coleraine* in the County of *Antrim* in *Ireland* viz: at *Dunbar* in Scotland & in *Cana*-Island, which is four English miles long & lies to the Southward of the Isle of *Skye*, near the Isle of *Rum*, where the rocks to the Southward above the harbour, are formed into polygon pillars; & some affirm, that even opposite the County of *Antrim* on the opposite Shores of *Scotland* these *Basalt*-columns are seen, & extend along the Seashores for several miles as on the Irish side, see Phil. Trans. vol. 52. p. 1. pag. 98 & 103.[1] The next morning 3 more Isles[2] were discovered so that, if we could get but a fresh breeze, we might make discoveries of new Lands, never seen by any European. The *Cape East* of the long Isle has on its very summit a Colonnade of Bazalt, & the little Isle, which was seen yesterday & seems to be connected to the large one by a reef, has likewise some Bazalt Pillars, but the scantiness of the wind will not allow us to come nearer the Land & examine it more minutely. The Thermometer at 73°, in my Cabin 74°.

7br yᵉ 26th ☽ The nearer we come, the more disputes arise about these Pillars: all the military Men think them to be Trees, whereas the Experimental-Men are of Opinion that they are Stone-pillars erected by Nature. We go by Analogy & judge from what we have seen & read before, but they think it impossible that such Rocks could be formed naturally. We tried the Current, but found none, we hove the Lead but found no bottom. We put the Ship about in order not to come too near the Reef in the night. The little Isles seen yesterday are insignificant small things, except one which has a small hill & low land about it & in the Reef small Spots with such columnar things. The Ship is now endeavouring to get to windward of all the Land & all the Reefs. The Thermometer at 72½°, in my Cabin 73°.

7br yᵉ 27th ♂ The same bad faint wind. In the Evening about Sunset we got at once a fresh breeze & we now endeavour to go round the Isle which is surrounded by these columnar things. After ten

[1] George introduced some of these notes on basalt columns into his *Voyage* (II, p. 435, note) arguing that 'having so lately seen several volcanoes in the neighbourhood, and one so near as Tanna' they 'were greatly strengthened in this opinion' that what they could see were basalts. Beaglehole (*Journals*, II, 552, n. 4) has a long note on the philosophical dispute between Wales and Forster over this issue. The pertinacity with which each side held to its views was symptomatic of the low ebb to which scientific relations and confidences had sunk.

[2] See *Journals*, II, 553.

o'clock we had a smart Shower: & we tacked several times during night & the next morning but we cannot much gain by all our trips, Wind, Sea & Tide or Current being in all appearance against us. It is pretty cool. The Thermometer at 68°, in my Cabin 69°.

*Sept. ye 28th* ☿ We saw by our Glasses again these strange columnar things, they seem to be Trees; some say that such Trees had been observed in N. Zeeland about the River *Thames*, others again pretend they are *Bamboos*. I cannot but allow, that they have all the appearance of Trees, being thinly covered with some greens from top to bottom, but the Stem seems to be much too thick, & out of proportion for such Trees, & though it blows very fresh & we can observe the loose greens move to leeward, we however never see the Stems bent. These things look much like a Hop-plantation, only the poles are too thick & at least as a main yard or Fore-top-Mast. In short, though I may be wrong in my first opinion, that they are Stone-pillars, I am not yet clear what strange kind of Tree they can be.[1] In the night we made a long trip & put about at midnight; towards daylight we saw we had weathered the point of the Reef & we bore away along the weatherside of the Isle. Thermometer at 68°, in my Cabin 68½°.

*7br ye 29th* ♃ We saw the South-side of the large Island[2] a head & on the starboard-bow, & advanced gradually towards it; when we came to examine our Situation, we found we bore away too early, & we were in a *cul de Sac* between the Great-Island & the small & some Reefs connecting all the little interjacent small Islets. We tacked all night,[3] in the morning we were near a small Islet, full of such pyramidal things; we tacked inorder to get to leeward of it & the reef & after a couple of trips we came to an anchor. The boats were hoisted out & we went to the small Islet.[4] We saw there great many Gulls[5] of the same kind as at New Zeeland in

[1] With characteristic determination, goaded no doubt by Wales's irony, Forster held to his opinion when all others had fled it. Even Cook could not resist some comment on Forster's obstinacy. See *Journals*, II, 554 and 559. The 'strange kind of Tree' was the conifer *Araucaria columnaris* or *Araucaria cookii*, the Cookpine or *pin colonnaire*. At a distance Forster's mistake was, to be charitable, somewhat understandable.

[2] I.e. the New Caledonian mainland. See *Journals*, II, 555.

[3] For once neither Forster nor his son make any great play of – using Cook's own rare heightened language – their 'terrible apprehensions of every moment falling on some of the many dangers which surrounded us'. Cook's superb seamanship brought them safely out of this shoaly predicament into which his persistence and determination not to leave this coast 'till I was satisfied what sort of trees those were which had been the subject of our speculation' had got them. See *Journals*, II, 556–7.

[4] Améré or Botany Isle.

[5] *Larus scopulinus* of *Descr. Anim.*, pp. 106 and 257. The Silver Gull *Larus novaehollandiae forsteri* was the New Caledonian bird. See also p. 662, n. 7 below.

Dusky-Bay, of which several were shot, but all fell into the Sea, & drove away, & only one was gotten in the Afternoon; we saw several New plants & likewise the *Lepidium Piscidium* & *Tetragonia oleracea*.[1] A large Hawk[2] was observed, & a couple of Pigeons[3] & the curious Thing was at last found to be a Spruce or fir-Tree (a *Cypress ratheo*)[4] of a new kind: & we cut one of them by way of Essay & returned on board. We found fire-places on the Islet, but no Inhabitants. Thermometer at 69½, in my Cabin 78°.

Sept. ye 30th ♀ In the Afternoon we returned to the Islet, found some more plants, the *Anguis platura*[5] & several Shells. One Hawk which proved to be *Osprey*[6] was shot, but all the other birds were gone. We cut some more of the Spruce Tree for Masts to boats & Studding-Sail-Yards: & returned on board in the Evening. Next morning early we hove the Anchor & stood out of this Reef as far as the little breeze would permit, but it soon failed: however about 9 o'clock a gentle breeze sprung up again & helped us towards the Mouth of the Reef. The Thermometer at 71°, in my Cabin 72½°.

Octobr ye 1st ♄ We have however found the N. Zeeland-Gull, which we drew,[7] besides the Osprey & a small Flycatcher,[8] on this small Islet which you might walk round in a few minutes, and more than 20 or 30 different Species of Plants, of which several are absolutely new ones.[9] We are now quite becalmed, & as we are here still between the Reefs & must depend upon the Tide & Currents, our Situation is not very agreable, especially as the Bottom increased at 2 o'clock 75 fathom, at 5 o'clock 130 fathom, & at 6 o'clock no ground with 150 fathom. At half an hour past 7 o'clock there appeared to the Northward a phænomenon in size

[1] *Tetragonia tetragoniodes* (Pallas) Ktze.

[2] Mentioned in *Descr. Anim.*, p. 257 as *Falconem haliaetum*. The Osprey *Pandion haliaetus*. But see also *Voyage*, II, 438 and note.

[3] Several species of pigeons and doves occur in the New Caledonian area. See also Beaglehole's note on the Giant Pigeon of New Caledonia, *Ducula goliath* Gray, *Journals*, II, 558, n. 8.

[4] Certainly *Araucaria columnaris*.

[5] See p. 508, n. 4 above.

[6] See n. 2 above.

[7] Silver Gull *Larus novaehollandiae forsteri*. When Forster described *Larus scopulinus* (*Descr. Anim.*, p. 106) he attributed the painting to Hodges. In view of his comment here that they drew the New Caledonian bird it is possible that folio 109 (Lysaght, p. 298) in fact represents it and not the New Zealand bird *Larus novaehollandiae scopulinus*.

[8] Forster referred to this bird as *Turdum minutum* (*Descr. Anim.*, p. 257). He had earlier described the New Zealand Yellow-breasted Tit *Petroica macrocephala macrocephala* (Gmelin, 1789) as *Turdus minutus* (*Descr. Anim.*, p. 83). The bird met with here was probably the Yellow-bellied Robin *Eopsaltria flaviventris* Sharpe.

[9] Forster's account of Botany Isle, its possibilities and natural history, is best read in conjunction with Cook (*Journals*, II, 557–60) and George (*Voyage*, II, 438–9).

& brightness as the Sun, but paler; it soon burst & several bright sparks came from it, the lowermost in form of a pear left a blueish light trace behind & it was heard to make a hissing noise, as if some Oakum were set a Fire. I have observed that such Phænomena are commonly the Forerunners of a stout Gale, whether we shall meet with one, time will show.[1]

In the Night a fresh breeze sprung up & we passed happily the Entrance of this Reef; when on a sudden the wind settled in South & increased into a fresh Gale; we steered ESE & EbS & went on charmingly. It rained a good Shower at 4 o'clock in the morning. We saw Tropicbirds, some Boobies & a black & white Tern. The Thermometer at 69°, in my Cabin 70°.

Octobr ye 2d ☉ The Gale fresh, the weather airy. Saw a white & black Booby & some Tropicbirds. The Observation I made yesterday about the Gale following the fiery Meteor is confirmed. Saw a great many Man of war birds. Caught a large Shark & a great many more were seen about the Ship, but none was caught. In the beforenoon the Wind fell, but not the Sea. The Thermometer at 66½, in my Cabin 68°.

Octobr. ye 3d ☽ Allmost calm; Saw a white Booby,[2] Tropicbirds & Man of war birds. At Midnight the wind freshened & we could make Sail. Passed the Tropic again. I got a cold from the wet, which rushed into my bed through the Decks, for the working of the Ship has opened all the Seams & we have no pitch to caulk & pitch them. The Thermometer 65°, in my Cabin 67°. We had Squalls & a Shower of rain in the morning.[3]

Octobr ye 4th ♂ The Gale still continues & sets us towards N. Zeeland, where we hope to be in a fortnight or thereabouts, if the wind stands good. We had today at dinner part of the Shark caught last Sunday. As it is fresh meet, every body is very eager to eat of it & if properly prepared & dressed it is commonly very good. It ought to be cut into slices, after it is skinned, then it should be sprinkled with Salt & hung up, so that the pieces do not touch one another for 24 hours or less, squeezed & washed, & then

[1] Forster elaborates on this in *Observations*, pp. 119–20.

[2] Blue-faced Booby *Sula dactylatra personata* Gould, 1846.

[3] We miss here, perhaps because of Forster's oncoming depression and renewed dissatisfaction with his lot, the usual bringing together of his findings as we have noted above, p. 656 n. 5. Here again, when they finally leave New Caledonian waters, Cook (*Journals*, II, 561–3) and George (II, pp. 441–2) give a brief resumé of the discoveries. As George concluded, New Caledonia still offered the explorer much scope and 'an ample field to the naturalist'.

parboiled, fried & stewed with vinaiger or vine, which is by far the best method. The Shark we had for dinner had not been sprinkled with Salt, nor well squeezed & washed, for by these methods the oily fat particles should be disengaged, which make the meat strong & heavy. I ate too much of it & had an Indigestion & was very sick in the Evening, which I ascribed at first to the rolling of the Ship, but I found soon the Fish to be the cause. This detail might seem to be in a wrong place, but as many people detest Shark, & might at Sea especially in such Voyages as ours is, be very glad to eat some fresh meat, I thought a little Digression on this Fish necessary, as it affords a good, well tasted, & salutary food if not eaten in too great Quantities; and it has been frequently eaten by Seafaring people; & only some, who cannot get the better of the prejudices of Education, might by this account be tempted to eat this Fish. The wind less, but a great Sea. The Thermometer at 64°, in my Cabin 69°.

*Octobr. ye 5th* ☿ Fresh breeze, but too near WbS & WSW, so that we cannot go more Westerly; for as we are now near the Longitude of *Cape North*, the Captain wishes to keep on the Westside of the Northern Isle of New Zeeland, in order to have a better chance of running into *Queen-Charlotte's Sound*, than last year, when we were obliged to beat the windward for more than a week;[1] & as we have no time to lose for to reach *America* & to go on the last part of our Southern cruize we ought to be carefull in avoiding every thing that could disappoint & detain us longer than ordinary: but the Wind sets us much to Eastward, unless it becomes more favourable, & in that case we must keep on the East Side of the Isle & perhaps go to *Mercury-Bay*[2] in about 36° 50′ S. Lat. which is the most likely to afford us Fish, Crayfish, Oysters, Shags, Wood & Water & some Sellery for to refresh & prepare us against the great Cruize: for upon the whole, this Voyage is, according to all those who have been in the *Endeavour*, far more severe & hard upon our Crew, who get less fresh provisions than those in the Years 1769 & 1770.[3] The Thermometer at 65½, in my Cabin 72°.

[1] Cook, at this juncture, is silent in his journals about his exact intentions. Forster is correctly conveying, however, cabin gossip. See *Voyage*, II, 443.

[2] Where the *Endeavour* had anchored in November 1769.

[3] 'All our officers,' notes George (II, p. 440), 'who had made several voyages round the world, and experienced a multiplicity of hardships, acknowledged at present, that all their former sufferings were not to be compared to those of the present voyage, and that they had never before so thoroughly loathed a salt diet.'

Octobr ye 6th ♃ We saw two Albatrosses, a Sight we little expected in these low Latitudes, which makes me believe, that the Winter has been very severe towards the South.

The first Lieut. caught ye 29th Sept. A.M. when the Capt was ashore on the little Island, a fish of the identical kind, which had poisoned the Capt, my Son & myself Sept. ye 8th. He heard from everybody the fish was poisonous; but he obstinately refused to give ear to these good advices; he ordered the fish to be cleaned & skinned, & wanted the same to have dressed, & accordingly it was dressed; but his Messmates fairly laughed him out of his mad design to eat the fish, when they saw that a friendly & serious advice would not persuade his mulish temper.[1] However a little Dog given by the Capt to Mr *Clerck* had eaten some of the guts & garbage, & this poor Creature has ever since been in a most miserable condition, growning, howling, & having lost entirely the use of all its Limbs, that its sight must move the heart of the most hardened & indolent, but in him who procured this fine mess & his equals, there is

> At last extinct each social feeling, fell
> And joyless inhumanity pervades
> And petrifies the heart... *Thompson's Spring*, 304.[2]

These 3 days I have not been able to enjoy my Cabin. The Decks are now by the rolling & working of the Ship quite opened at all her Seams; we have no pitch to mend them, by each washing of the Deck my & my Sons Cabins were drowned in a Deluge of Salt-Water & at each rain in one of fresh. I begg'd the Capt. to give me the Floor-Cloth of his Cabin, but he only choose to grant me that of the Steerage which was quite worn away: in order to cover the Cieling with it & to carry off the water chiefly from

[1] George inserts this story in its proper chronological place but omits the more vindictive asides (*Voyage*, II, 339–40).

[2] The Scot James Thomson (1700–48), with his blank verse rich in natural description and reflective digressions and his interest in the scientific and philosophical thinking of his day, was also a favourite poet of William Wales. See *Journals*, II, xli and 782–3. Here we see – using Beaglehole's approving words on Wales – that Forster also 'carried poetry in his mind', and not only that of the ancients! Forster's rendering of the lines from Thomson's *Spring* are also accurate: Wales was not so fastidious with his quoting from memory. One suspects that Forster, true to form, had the 1744 London edition of Thomson's *Seasons* to hand wherein these lines (305–7) appear as part of a revision of former versions. The textual provenance of Thomson's *Seasons* is intricate and difficult. I have relied upon Otto Zippel, *Thomson's Seasons: Critical Edition...* (Berlin, 1908). Needless to say Forster, strictly, is quoting out of context: his aversion was of men, not of nature.

my bed, for if I should be always wet in my bed I could expect nothing but death in the cold Climates. He gave strict orders to the Carpenter about it, but it was done in so slovenly a manner, that I still after several days work or bungling in my Cabin, am subject to the same Inconveniences.[1] The wind is entirely gone down, & a great Sea tosses us about: a boat was hoisted out in order to try whether an Albatross might be shot; we fired severally at them but the Shot is too small & though the Feathers came off none was killed. The Thermometer at 62½, in my Cabin 66°.

Octobr yᵉ 7ᵗʰ ♀ The weather is absolutely calm, our Officers went again in the Afternoon out & shot 2 Albatrosses, a Shearwater & a Petrel. The Calm continues. The Thermometer 63⅓°, in my Cabin 68°.

Octobr yᵉ 8ᵗʰ ♄ Still calm. In America the people who carry Horses & Cattle to the W. Indies call the Latitudes where the Trade winds end & the variable ones begin, *Horse Latitudes* because they commonly lose there Numbers of Horses, being either becalmed, & having not Food enough they must kill them, or they lose them there by bad weather, for there it is, where they meet either with calms or great Gales.

In the Afternoon a gentle Breeze sprung up, which gradually increased & we could have the Course S.W. all the night & next beforenoon. No bird is seen. The Thermometer at 65⅓, in my Cabin 70½.

Octobr yᵉ 9ᵗʰ ☉ The Course at Noon SWbS. The Breeze still continues. About Sunset a great Shoal of Large Fish like Porpesses passed the Ship & frisked about it, one of which was struck with a Harpoon, & two boats being hoisted out, it was shot & killed by 5 Musket balls, & then brought on board, where I found after Examination that it was the *Dolphin* of the Ancients or *Delphinus Delphis* Linn. Willoughby's Drawing is upon the whole tolerable.[2] The Fish was 6 Foot long. Its shape is strait & conic; The Tail compressed on both Sides & inated[3] above & below. The Head goes down rounding & then runs out in a flattish pointed beak.

[1] George passes over this complaint in silence.

[2] F. Willoughby, *De historia piscium* (1686), p. 26, pl. A1, fig. 1. For Willoughby (or Willughby) see p. 170, n. 2 above. The following detailed notes and description of the dolphin are lightly crossed through (VI, f. 33) and represent Forster's first, necessarily hasty, efforts to describe the animal before it was cut up for broiling and frying. The prize was Cooper's and he may not have surrendered it willingly to Forster. The detailed description is in *Descr. Anim.*, p. 280 and George's drawing is No. 31.

[3] Illegible at the beginning of this word. Possibly 'marginated'.

The Eyes are small & lateral. The Airhole between the Eyes is semilunar. The subject was a Female, & had its Genitals in a slit before the Anus. The back is dark blueish grey or steel-grey, the belly white, a white band or stripe goes across the beak: a white spot is on the Dorsal Fin, which is high triangular & falcated behind. The Tail flat (*plagiura*) horizontal, lunated & in the middle emarginated. The Carina of the fleshy part of the Tail runs out to its very Extremity. Its teeth are sharp & numerous, in the Upper Jaw are 88 & in the lower-one 88, but they sit deep in the Jaws; the Breasts are on both Sides of the Slit conducting to the Genitals, each in a peculiar Cavity, with a Nipple of the Size of a large Pea, & when cut. the Breasts were full of Milk. Behind & a little above the Eye is a little hole, which probably leads to the Ear. The Heart had two Ventricles & two Auricles, but the Foramen ovale was shut. The Pectoral-Fins are lanceolated.[1]

The next morning the Fish was cut up, skinned & distributed among several Messes, as far as it would reach; & I must confess, though it was something dry, it was however very good. The Meat was rather black, but not in the least Fishy, for all the Fat part was cut off.[2] The Thermometer 63⅓°, in my Cabin 66½°.

Octobr ye 10th ☽ The breeze fresh, the Sea smooth. In the morning we had several Showers of Rain, & at daybreak we saw at SW a small Island, we came up with it at ½ an hour past 8. It is high, steep, bold & covered with the same Cypress-Trees, which we took in the other Isle for Stone-pillars.[3] Its breadth is about 2 miles. We had at a good distance off regular Soundings of 22 & 20 fathom Water, the bottom Sand & Shells. There were a good many Boobies & Petrels of the (*Procellaria Gavia*)[4] about it. We tack &

[1] *Opp.* VI, f. 33 are two very crude outlines of a dorsal fin and tail.

[2] '...indeed little art was required to make any kind of fresh meat sute our taste who had been living for so long on salt' (*Journals*, II, 564–5).

[3] The pines were, of course, not the same, although closely related, as Cook, Wales and the carpenter soon saw. Here it was the Norfolk Island Pine *Araucaria heterophylla* (= *excelsia*). See *Journals*, II, 565–6 and 869. Surprisingly neither Forster nor his son wrote much on this noble tree.

[4] In *Descr. Anim.*, p. 279 Forster noted 'Procellarias Gaviam, tridactylam et fuliginosam'. *Procellaria gavia* was the name he gave (*Descr. Anim.*, p. 148) to the Fluttering Shearwater *Puffinus gavia gavia* (Forster, 1844) described from Queen Charlotte Sound in 1773. *Procellaria tridactyla* (*Descr. Anim.*, p. 149) was the Northern Diving Petrel *Pelecanoides urinatrix urinatrix* (Gmelin, 1789) also from Queen Charlotte Sound, and *Procellaria fuliginosa* (*Descr. Anim.*, p. 23) was the Great-winged Petrel *Pterodroma macroptera macroptera* (Smith, 1840) from the Atlantic Ocean in 1772. The Providence Petrel *Pterodroma solandri* (Gould, 1844) and, probably, the Flesh-footed Shearwater *Puffinus carneipes hullianus* Mathews, 1912 formerly bred on Norfolk Island, and the Wedge-tailed Shearwater *Puffinus*

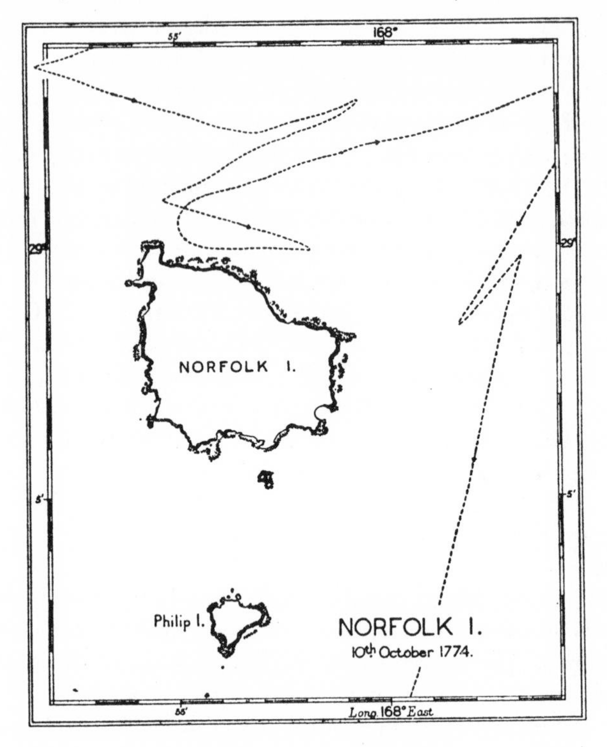

Figure 40. Norfolk Island, 10 October 1774 ★(70).

come nearer & nearer to it. The Thermometer at 62½°, in my Cabin 65°.

Octobr ye 11th ♂ We dined early & immediately after dinner we went in two boats ashore. The Isle is everywhere surrounded by large rocks, washed & surrounded by the Sea at high Water. The Shore with large Stones, & the beach barren, the ascent to the Isle immensely Steep & high, full of Bindweeds & other creeping plants, so that it costs immense labour to get up to its woody parts, which have very little Underwood, & where we could easily walk.[1] The plants are for the greatest part New Zeeland ones, viz.

pacificus pacificus (Gmelin, 1789) and the Norfolk Island Allied Shearwater *Puffinus assimilis assimilis* Gould, 1838 still do.

[1] They landed at the more sheltered eastern end of Duncombe Bay below where the Cook Monument now stands. A visit to the site with Merval Hoare in October 1976 convinced me of the 'immense labour' any aspiring naturalist would have to get from sea to plateau level. On this occasion many of the bird species mentioned by Forster were also seen.

the Flaxplant, (*Phormium tenax*), *Tetragonia oleracea*,[1] *Mesembrianthemum acinaciforme*,[2] *Oxalis corniculata*, *Coprosma lucida*, *Ripogonum scandens*.[3] But we saw besides the *Arecca oleracea*,[4] the *Cupressus*[5] we had found in *New-Caledonia* & others which are quite new:[6] but we found few or none in flowers. The rocks had several Nests with the *Pelecanus Piscator*,[7] of which we got an old & a young one. The *Parrots*[8] are nearly the same as in N. Zeeland, only something less in size & brighter in colours, the *Perrokeets*[9] are quite the same, the large *Pigeons*[10] are not in the least different. There were the same Fantails[11] & a fine *Small Turdus*,[12] red belly, black head, & back, Tail & wings, white Forehead & a part of the Upper Coverts of the wings; the Female is of a brownish green, has no white & very little red on the breast, the Legs without incisions, & yellowish; & several more very beautifull birds,[13] some of which were shot. Our people caught fine fish near & on the Rocks in

[1] *Tetragonia tetragoniodes* (Pallas) Ktze.

[2] *Carpobrotus acinaciform* L. Bolus.

[3] *Ripogonum scandens* Forst.

[4] *Roystonea oleracea* (Jacq.) O.F. Cook.

[5] *Araucaria columnaris* (Forst.) Hook.

[6] Presumably including the Norfolk Island Pine. For further plant identifications, especially the New Zealand nikau (cabbage palm) and annotations see *Journals*, II, 567–8 and 869 and Merval Hoare, *The Discovery of Norfolk Island* (Canberra, 1974), pp. 7–14, where the author reproduces the relevant portions from each of the journals and published accounts.

[7] Blue-faced Booby (or Masked Gannet) *Sula dactylatra personata* Gould 1846. See *Descr. Anim.*, p. 279, Forster folio 107 and Lysaght, p. 298.

[8] Norfolk Island (or Philip Island) Parrot *Nestor meridionalis productus* (Gould, 1836), now extinct. See *Descr. Anim.*, p. 279.

[9] Norfolk Island Red-crowned Parakeet *Cyanoramphus novaezelandiae cookii* (Gray, 1859). See *Descr. Anim.*, p. 279.

[10] Norfolk Island Pigeon *Hemiphaga novaeseelandiae spadicea* (Latham, 1790). See *Descr. Anim.*, p. 279. Now extinct.

[11] Norfolk Island Fantail *Rhipidura fuliginosa pelzelni* (Gray, 1862), See *Descr. Anim.*, p. 279.

[12] *Muscicapa dibapha* of *Descr. Anim.*, p. 267; Forster folio 150 and Lysaght, p. 307. Now the Scarlet-breasted (Norfolk Island) Robin *Petroica multicolor multicolor* (Gmelin, 1789). See also *Vögel der Südsee*, Taf 7, p. 72.

[13] No reference is made in *Descr. Anim.* to these 'several more very beautifull birds' and it is difficult to know the species to which he refers. Wales, collaborating closely with Cook on the island's natural history, saw e.g. Banded Rails (*Journals*, II, 869). George (II, p. 446) found 'The melody of the birds was very pleasing in this little deserted spot, which if it had been of a greater size, would have been unexceptionable for an European settlement'. For the 'exceptionability' of Norfolk as a European settlement see Merval Hoare, *Norfolk Island: An Outline of its History 1774–1968*) (Brisbane, 1969) and for an appeal for the Forsters' bird descriptions and their rightful place in the natural history of the island see T. Iredale, 'J. R. and G. Forster, Naturalists', *The Emu*, XXXVII (1937), 95–9. Forster senior later returned more critically to Norfolk Island natural history when working on the German translations of John White's *Journal of a Voyage to New South Wales* (London, 1790) and John Hunter's *Historical Account of the Transactions at Port Jackson and Norfolk Island* (London, 1793). See *Tactless Philosopher* pp. 288 and 317–8.

pools, some of which were new, & all well tasted. We got a good Quantity of fine Cabages of the Cabage Tree, & some other greens.[1] We got a fine Yard for a Top-gallant-Sail, of the Cypress-Tree: & had the Isle been but accessible & could we have carried the Wood off, there were Trees, that would afford Timber for large Masts. In short this is a pretty fine & useful Discovery, & had afforded us upon the whole more good things than the large Isle of *N. Caledonia*. Had the Captain thought of, he might have put 2 small pigs on the Isle, which would soon have grown into Herds of wild Hogs: for the Isle has greens & food enough for many 100 Hogs. There was likewise a little rill of water, but it was very small. It was called *Norfolk-Isle*, in honour of the Dutchess of Norfolk, who recommended it to Capt Cook to have one Isle named after her.[2] In the Evening we put off with regret from this unexpected & agreable Isle. We ate fish & cabage made into Sallad, & were as happy as possible. All the Night we tacked in order to come round the S. East end of the Isle & in the morning we saw another large rock to the South of it.[3] A good many Whales were seeing frisking & playing in the water. The Boobies & Shearwaters came in Flocks off in order to fish, for here is likewise a Bank with regular Soundings on this side the Isle. The Thermometer at 64½°, in my Cabin 67°.

Octobr ye 12th ☿ The Soundings still continue from 32 to 35 Fathom though we are 4 or 5 Leagues off. Perhaps this will make a fine *Fishing-bank* in the South Seas. I believe the Bank extended a good way on the North-Side of the Isle, for we had more than a days-Sail from it smooth water, & we have now allways smooth Water, which is in my opinion a good proof, that the Bank still continues:[4] & as we saw many Whales & great Numbers of Boobies fishing off the Isle, it is probably a good place for Fishing.

[1] See *Journals*, II, 567, n. 5.

[2] Forster is the only authority we have for the noble lady's importuning of Cook, 'an important link', notes Merval Hoare, 'in Norfolk history' (*Discovery of Norfolk Island*, p. 12).

[3] Perhaps the flat Nepean Island or, more probably, the larger higher Philip Island both of which lie south of Norfolk. But the latter (about one mile square in area) would surely be identified as more than 'a large rock'. Cook records (*Journals*, II, 568) 'some high Islots or rocks, which serve as roosting and breeding places for birds'. Today Philip Island, in contrast to Norfolk, is 'a textbook example of the waste and mismanagement of land . . . for the most part a man-made desert' (J. S. Turner and others, *Conservation of Norfolk Island*, Melbourne, 1975, p. 18).

[4] This is not a bad guess. The Norfolk Island Ridge extends southwards from the New Caledonia–Loyalty Islands area to the west of the Northland peninsula of New Zealand. See also *Voyage*, II, 447.

At one o'clock P.M. we were off the Bank,[1] & the wind continuing fresh, we make a good way towards N. Zeeland. Saw a Booby in the Evening. The Therm. 66½, in my Cabin 69°.

Octobr ye 13th ♃ The breeze still continues: & we go on finely. The Thermometer at 64 – in my Cabin 68°.

Octobr ye 14th ♀ Fine breeze; saw many Albatrosses. Had in the Night a heavy dew. Thermom. 62½, in my Cabin 67°.

Octobr ye 15th ♄ The breeze still mends. Saw Albatrosses, again a copious Dew fell during night. Thermomet. 61¼, in my Cabin 67°.

Octobr ye 16th ☉ The breeze fresh. Saw Albatrosses, Pintadas, N. Zeeland diving Petrels & black Shearwaters. A little Rain towards Night. Thermometer 61°, in my Cabin 67°.

Octobr ye 17th ☽ We expect now soon to see the steep Shores of New Zeeland, if the Wind continues.[2] In the Night we had Squalls & several Showers of rain: the Wind is become more northerly & at last is come more round to the West: & we had Thunder & Lightning. In the morning we saw *Mount Egmont*, one of the highest Hills, covered with eternal Snow & Ice allmost half way up.[3] Several diving Petrels & black Shearwaters attend the Ship. We sounded 70 fathom, Muddy bottom. The breeze freshened. The Thermometer at 58°, in my Cabin 61½°.

Octobr ye 18th ♂ The breeze turned into a fresh Gale; we go 8 Knots & think ourselves happy for not being on the other side of the Isle, where we might perhaps be a sevennight beating to windward before we might get into Harbour, whereas we now have hopes of coming in next morning. During night it blew fresh. In the morning we saw *Admiralty Bay* a breast of us, Cape *Stephens*, Point *Jackson*, Cape *Koamaroo* & *Terawittee* appeared, & just in the Entrance of Charlotte-Sound we found a strong rippling caused by the wind & tide. We found hard Squalls come over the hills in going in, varying every moment, & about 11 o'clock in the morning we anchored. The Thermometer at 57½ in my Cabin 60°.

[1] Cf. *Journals*, II, 568.

[2] '...we...advanced with a fresh breeze towards New Zeeland, where we could expect to meet with regular refreshments after our tropical cruize, which towards the latter end had greatly weakened the crew, by confining them to a putrid salt-diet, and which had proved particularly fatal to the officers and ourselves, by means of the poisonous fishes that unfortunately fell in our way', *Voyage*, II, 447. Cook is silent at this point about such conditions.

[3] Cf. George's description of Mount Egmont and environs in *Voyage*, II, 447–8.

petunt portus; & vela secundi
Intendunt Zephyri: fertur cita gurgite (*navis*)
Virg. AEn. V.32.[1]

Octobr ye 19th ☿ The weather squally & rainy. We went after dinner ashore, & hauled the Seine, but got no Fish. I shot 8 Shags, the Captain one & one Curlew, & 9 young ones were knocked down from the Nests. We found that the Natives had turned up the Root, under which we had buried a bottle, with a letter for the Adventure. We suspected the Natives, because we found no bottel & letter replaced, & the large root of a Tree turned thus, that the Inscription was the reverse way.[2] A few Fish were caught along side especially Dogfish, one large Bream weighing 11¼lb, & several Colefish, & Nightwalkers.[3] We brought likewise a few Greens on board. Next morning at 4 o'clock we warped deeper into the bay & got a good birth about 9 o'clock, & when I went soon after ashore & collected some old plants, of which we had but few Specimens. I found likewise a new plant. We shot about 10 large Wattelbirds, a Curlew, Perrokeet, small Wattlebirds etc.[4] Capt Cook examined again every thing about the place where our Tent had been last time, & there we found several Trees cut down, that we left standing & especially was one Tree cut down with a crosscut-Saw, which we had left standing & to which our Tent-rope had been fixed last year: besides this, above the Fireplace of the people, who had been a year ago ashore, were all the large Trees cut down, & only the small branches were left on the shore, where we used to land. The Natives have no Saws, nor do they cut so large Trees down for burning, in such Quantity as we saw, it was done here: all these Arguments convinced us, that the *Adventure* had been here after us. I observed moreover, that we had left vast quantities of young Onions in the Garden: the Natives did not like our onions, & as we found at present not one left, & only a few Leeks were standing, it seemed to me to be a strong Argument, that an European Ship had been here. No

[1] 'They set off for the harbour and favourable (west) winds filled the sails; the ship was carried swiftly over the deep'. Forster substitutes *navis* (ship) for *classis* (fleet) from the original. He occasionally alters a word in these quotations, where the scansion is the same, so that it suits his narrative.

[2] See *Journals*, II, 570–1 and *Voyage*, II, 449.

[3] The New Zealand fish and birds are described in more detail for the two previous visits to Queen Charlotte Sound.

[4] Respectively the South Island Kokako, *Haematopus* sp; Red-crowned Parakeet and South Island Saddleback.

body but Cap[t] *Furneaux* & M[r] *Banks* knew something of the Situation of *Queen Charlotte's Sound*; it is therefore highly probable, that one of them had been here, & I am more inclined to believe the former was here, because he had taken away the bottle, which Mr *Banks* would not have done, finding it was a direction for the *Adventure*. If we now compare this circumstance, with the Rumor we heard at *Oriadèa* 2 days before we sailed, that there were 2 Ships arrived at *Huahaine* 3 days before,[1] it is still possible that one of the Ships was Capt. *Furneaux* in the *Adventure*, & that going along the Coast of America, he fell in with *Mr Banks's* Ship & came in Company with him to *Otāhāitee*, & *Huahaine*; & then however it remains difficult to Account, how it were possible for Capt. *Furneaux* not to come immediately to *Oriadea*, or supposing his Crew were too sickly to go away without refreshing first, why did he not send a Letter to *Cap[t] Cook* either by a boat or by some Natives & promissing them a valuable consideration to be given to them by *Cap[t] Cook* in case they delivered the Letter. Short this cannot be cleared up, before we reach England again, or at least the *Cape of good* Hope.[2]

8br y[e] 20th ♃ In the Afternoon we accompanied the Capt. to *Cannibal Cove*, where the Boatscrew collected a good many fine Greens for the Ship's Crew, & we shot 5 Shags with double Crests & several other birds. I found there on the Hill to the North a young Stock of a true *Cabbage-Tree* (*Arecca oleracea*),[3] which is the more remarkable as this place is so much to the South. But the Natives were not to be met with. We fired again a Gun in the Evening, that the Natives might hear it & come to see us, because they commonly provide us with fish for a trifle. The next morning we had bad weather, a cold southerly Wind, blowing from the bleak Snowy hills, & at last rain. As my Son & I had a cold & something was to be described & drawn we stood at home, & expected a good day again for fresh Excursions.

8br y[e] 21st ♀ All the Afternoon we had dreadfull weather; it blows

[1] See *Journals*, II, 425–7 and p. 527 above.

[2] Cook (*Journals*, II, 570) quickly deduced from the evidence that it was the *Adventure* which had preceded them for her second visit in December 1773. See Furneaux's narrative, *Journals*, II, 143–4. Forster was right in one respect however: the true story of the *Adventure's* fatal visit to Queen Charlotte Sound was not revealed conclusively until they reached the Cape in March 1775.

[3] Undoubtedly the nikau palm, *Rhopalostylis* (*Areca*) *sapida* which is the most southerly palm in the world but would be unexpected in Queen Charlotte Sound. It is now known to 44° S in the Chatham Islands. The casual name *Areca oleracea* was given to a plant, without flowers or fruits, which they saw growing in gardens in the New Hebrides. See G. Forster, *Prodromus* (1786), Appendix and *Voyage*, II, 451.

hard & in Squalls & it rains continually, which will make it disagreable to walk in these woody regions, on account of the wet from the Trees, & what is worse we cannot stir out of the Ship, for to fish, to shoot birds & to get Greens for us. And I am also disabled from getting some few plants or other things in the Natural History way. All the Night along rain. Next morning foggy & drizzling rain, but calm.

*8br. ye 22^d^* ♄ Still wet weather. In the Evening the Wind came N.W. & began to drive away the fog & Clouds lying on the Mountains. Next day we had fine weather, warm Sunshine & a gentle wind; all the birds were alive, & a good many were killed by the various Sportsmen, who went out to get some fresh provisions. After breakfast the Capt. went with me, my Son & Mr *Sparman* out towards *point Jackson* & we shot there about 18 two-crested Shags[1] & one Parrot:[2] & I got a few plants.

*8br ye 23^d^* ☉ In the Afternoon we went towards the *Hippa* & made a Fire as a Signal for the Natives if any are at the bottom of the bay. We collected again Specimens of such plants as we had not many of. We then embarked & went round *Motuaro* & shot on its Eastside about 13 Shags of the same kind as mentioned before, who allways sit & build their Nests on the rocks, so as the black & white kind[3] allways sit & build on Trees. We shot likewise a fine *Albatross*; & collected a few plants where our Cabbage Garden had been, which was run into Seeds.

The next morning my Son drew a new Fish of the *Cyclopterus*-kind[4] & I described the same. Mr *Sparman* went ashore & shot a few birds, which we put into Spirits. Though it was foggy in the morning, it cleared up, higher up the day.

*8br ye 24th* ☽ In the Afternoon Mr *Sparman* & I went ashore, & shot a few birds, collected some few Specimens of known plants, & picked some Shells up along shore. My Son drew two plants again & a bird, which he had drawn before, but he gave them a more picturesque twin; if the weather prove fine to morrow we shall go somewhere up the Sound on a shooting party & perhaps in Quest of the Indians; if they be not eaten up by some stronger party, that waged war against them. New plants are not more to be gotten in any plenty, especially at this season of the Year, &

[1] Spotted Shag. [2] South Island Kaka.

[3] Pied Shag.

[4] *Cyclopterus pinnulatus* of *Descr. Anim.*, p. 301 and G. Forster drawing No. 248. See p. 250, n. 1 above.

as it is the third time already, that we are here in this same harbour; nor can we expect many new plants, having searched for them very closely before. The next morning early a couple of Canoes were seen off the point towards Long-Island; they had their Sails up, but when they saw the Ship, down came the Sail & they paddled back as fast as possible. After breakfast the Capt went out with us to Shag Cove, where we shot five Curlews & eleven Shags. We heard the Natives shouting on the South Side of the Cove, & after our sport with birds was over we went to them: some of them were retired high up the hills, where we saw them at a distance, but others were below, on a small hill near their huts among the bushes. When we landed we called them down, & down they came; nosed us, & hugged us with their lousy, dirty rough Winter-dresses. There were not above 3 or 4, whom we knew among the whole, the rest were such, as we had either not seen, or at least not often; so that we should know them again. We gave them some Medals, a smallpiece of red bays, a Nail, & some bits of Otahaitee-cloth; & they gave us a great Quantity of very fine Fish; & as we had nothing more to give, nor they to exchange, they promised to come to morrow to the Ship. They told of some, for whom we enquired, that they had been knocked in the head, & of others that they were gone over to *Trāwhìttee.*[1]

8br ye 25th ♂ As it was late, we hasted to our dinner, & we stood in the Afternoon on board, where George drew a small Blenny, which was described in *Dusky-Bay*, but had not been drawn before.[2] Next morning early all the Indians came in 5 Canoes along side of the Ship & sold a good many Fish, of which one was a new Pearch[3] which we drew & described: then afterward they sold Curiosities of green Stones & various other things. After breakfast George, Mr Sparman & I went ashore, but we got only one bird & no plants except a couple of aquatic Mosses. About noon we returned on board.

8br ye 26th ☿ In the Afternoon I & my Son stood on board, & the Mosses were described & drawn. We had all the day fine weather.

[1] The Europeans' suspicions, George reports (II, p. 454) were aroused by this meeting. 'We suspected from this circumstance, that a fatal misunderstanding had happened between the natives and the crew of some European ship, and we naturally thought of our consort the Adventure'. He was, of course, writing this with hindsight knowledge. The 'principal man' of this 'small village', records George, was 'Peeterré' (Cook's 'Pedero'), possibly Pitirau.

[2] See p. 269, n. 5 above.

[3] *Perca prognathus* of *Descr. Anim.*, p. 309 and George Forster drawing No. 218.

Next morning the Indians brought us again vast Quantities of Fish, & we are entirely supplied by them. After breakfast I went to *Motuaro* & got there hardly any thing worth my while, & the great trouble I took to climb up to the very Summit of the hill. I found no vestiges on the post fixed there, of the *Adventure's* being there. I carved in the Post. *Resolution. 1774. Octob.* & climbed down a Valley on the other Side the Isle; but got no new things, except a few *Pohe birds.*[1] We returned late on board.

8br ye 27th ♃ We dined late & I stood on board. Mr *Sparmann* went ashore, & got nothing. Next morning the weather was misty & cold, & as the Natives came again with great Quantities of Fish on board, I got a few Vocables of their Language: & brought some things over side, which had been collected by us.

8br ye 28th ♀ The weather foggy. There circulates on board a Story, made up I believe on purpose, that the Natives told, that a Ship arrived on the Coast of the Northern Isle in a great Storm, & was there broke to pieces. The Men in her were safed on shore, & had an Engagement with the Natives, wherein they killed many Natives, but not being able·to keep up a Fire, the Natives came up & killed & devoured them all. This our people interpret to have been the fate of the *Adventure*, but the Natives are by no means constant in their Story, so that there is little to be depended upon this Tale.[2] In the Afternoon the fog & mist increased, & the weather grew cold, the wind coming over the snowy Hills of the Northern Isle. The Thermometer was in the Evening at 58°. The next morning we had a fine day & went with the Capt to Westbay,

[1] The Tui.

[2] Cook, too, adopted the same cautious sceptical attitude towards this rumour (*Journals*, II, 572–3). George, however, reports in more detail on the elaborate steps they took to confirm, through 'Peeterré' and a friend, that the *Adventure* had been in again at Queen Charlotte Sound. At this point in his *Voyage* narrative (II, pp. 456–67) the younger Forster summarises the 'massacre' at Grass Cove (Wharehunga Bay) on 17 December 1773 and its grim, grisly aftermath. This hearsay account contains some interesting comment on Furneaux's relative, John Rowe, master's mate, and in charge of the fated party. Although possessed of 'many liberal sentiments' Rowe had, too, 'the prejudices of a naval education, which induced him to look upon all the natives of the South Sea with contempt, and to assume the kind of right over them, with which the Spaniards, in more barbarous ages, disposed of the lives of the American Indians'. Burney, the 'judicious and humane', George tells, us had been a check on the impetuous Rowe. From here George, citing in detail the fatal encounters of Tasman and Marion du Fresne with Maoris, launches into a long and useful discussion on European and Polynesian contacts. Arguing that Europeans 'perhaps unwittingly' could commit affronts on 'natives' he comes very close to comprehending or at least discerning the concept of *tapu* and its breaching. We can certainly discern here the humane and liberal younger Forster, the revolutionary of later years. See *Journals*, II, lxxix–lxxxi and Burney's log of the Grass Cove incident, *Journals*, II, 749–52.

where we shot several Shags & Curlews & looked there for the pigs & Fowls we had landed there very near a year ago, but we could find no vestiges of them.

8br yᵉ 29ᵗʰ ♄ In the Afternoon we looked into the hindmost Cove of Westbay, which was fine verdant Shores covered with tall Trees, but found no Sport; we therefore hasted back to Ship Cove, where we saw a few Natives & got of them several Fish, & among them a quite new kind. We had besides gotten 2 new plants. We returned late & dined & supped together after 6 o'clock in the Evening. Next night we had a gale & rainy weather, & this continued all the morning & beforenoon. We described in the mean time our new Fish & two plants & all were drawn.

8br yᵉ 30ᵗʰ ☉ We find the weather cool tho' the Thermometer shews no more than 57°, which is a very moderate fine degree but our bodies, coming from between the Tropics, are so relaxed & so sensible to the least change of heat, that we think this cold, tho' we know we must expect worse & colder weather, when we come to the South again. In the Afternoon windy & now & then a small rain. The Natives have been fishing all the beforenoon in the rain, & brought Congers, & large Breams to sell. They are very fond of our large Fish-hooks. Next morning & all night very strong Gales & rain. The Natives came on board & sold a good many green Stones.

8br yᵉ 31ˢᵗ ☽ The weather continues stormy & rainy, & tho' it is disagreable for us we will nevertheless put up with it, provided the bad weather & Storms would rage out, & allow us a good passage to *Cape Horn*, for which we must soon put under way, if we shall end this Year our Expedition. The next morning the tempest was subsided & we had fair weather. The Indians all went together away from the place, where they had been living opposite the Ship. We breakfasted early & after breakfast the Capᵗ offerred me a boat to *Long Island* or *Tòngā-Òngā̀*. I also prepared & after being landed I walked the whole length of it, & collected some plants & one small mossy new plant. When I came to the End of the Isle, I set fire to the old dry Ferns, with which this Isle is overrun, in order to show the Indians at the bottom of the Sound this as a Signal, in case any live there. The Gentlemen that came with me saw, whilst I was on the hill, a black boar on the low flatt part of the beach; probably one, we or Capt. Furneaux left here, & which the Natives had brought over to this Island.[1] About dinner we returned on board.

9br yᵉ 1ˢᵗ ♂ In the Afternoon we stood on board & drew & described some plants & brought them overside. The fire I had kindled, burnt more & more southward & may perhaps burn all the dry Ferns on the Isle & make room for better plants.[2] The Capᵗ intends to try to get the boar & set him with a pregnant Sow, somewhere on the Mainland ashore, or if he cannot catch him, to leave him the same Sow for a Compagnion. Next morning it blew very hard, & several Canoes with Natives came into *Indian-Cove* & a little while after they came on board & brought Fish & Curiosities, of which great Quantities were bought. They had especially bone *Pate-Patoos*, green-Stone or *Jade* & some of their Cloth, & various other things. My Son had a swelled Cheek & could therefore not go ashore, & I had something to write & collected Words for my Vocabulary. Mʳ *Sparman* went alone ashore.

9br yᵉ 2ᵈ ☿ It blew hard & rained in the Afternoon & all the night along, so that we could not stir from the Ship. Next morning we had a fine day & the Capt. went with us to Grass Cove & we shot there 12 Pigeons, 3 Shags, 4 Wattle birds, 3 Pohebirds, 2 Perrokeets & 4 small Wattlebirds, with one Hawk, & a yellowhead,[3] 30 birds in all. We collected there some Plants & especially one which we had found at the Cape of *Good Hope* & sent to *London* for the Phil. Tr. under the Name of *Falckia.*[4] The other was a *Viscum*,[5] besides that a new *Sophora*[6] upon whose Fruit & Leaves the Pigeons feed & another plant: so that this Excursion has been usefull to us.[7] There came many Indians that

[1] Cf. *Journals*, II, 573.

[2] Not, perhaps, the best ecological argument for the *New Zealand* bush.

[3] Respectively the New Zealand Pigeon; shags not specifically identifiable; South Island Kokako; the Tui; Red-crowned Parakeet; South Island Saddleback; New Zealand Falcon and Yellowhead.

[4] This probably refers to the plant to which the Forsters later gave the name *Dichondra repens* in *Characteres Generum Plantarum* (1776). This convolvulaceous herb is superficially similar to *Falckia repens* of the same plant family, which grows in South Africa. Linnaeus and Thunberg, who described the genus *Falckia*, probably had access to the plant sent to London. Forster had enjoyed close relations with his 'particular friend' and botanical mentor, the former melancholy pupil of Linnaeus, Johan Peter Falk (1727–74), while in St Petersburg in 1765–6. See *Tactless Philosopher* pp. 33 and 38.

[5] *Tupeia antarctica* (Forst. f.) Cham & Schlecht.

[6] Not specifically identifiable.

[7] George (II, p. 467) records that they 'advanced far into the country' around Grass Cove on this day.

day on board, & traded for Curiosities & brought Whores on board, but brought no Fish, for which reason the Capt ordered that no body should be allowed to trade for Curiosities.[1]

9br ye 3^{d} ♃ We got a Shower of rain, & visited all the small coves there, & every one afforded something to us. We returned late on board & made a meal at 8 o'clock, serving both for Supper & dinner, & went to bed very much fatigued. Next morning we had rather cold weather. Several Indian Canoes came alongside in order to trade: but Capt *Cook* sent them away, because they had no Fish: for the Ship's-Crew are mad after Curiosities; & buy them preferably to fresh Fish; tho' the fish would be more palatable than the Salt-Provisions & more wholesome to them.

Nov: ye 4th ♀ In the Afternoon was still cold, windy Weather. Next morning not much better, all the Indians are gone off, except one wretchedly poor, & indolent Family in the Indian Cove. We went to them in order to buy Fish, but the poor Creatures had none,[2] nor any thing else, except several bundles dry Fern-root of the *Acrostichum bifurcatum* which they beat on a Stone & put on the Embers for a few moments & then it is eaten; but it is upon the whole only a miserable, insipid Food. We picked a few Ferns & Specimens of the Spruce-Tree & returned on board.

9br ye 5th ♄ In the Afternoon we are to go to *Long-Island* & set there a Sow, which is with Pigs on shore as a Companion for the Boar, we saw there last time. When we came there, we found that the pretended Boar was a Sow & therefore we brought our Sow back, in order to make a better Use of, & intend to go there another time to catch the Sow, & set the same somewhere else a shore with a Boar; if the Creature is not too wild & can be caught. Next morning was a fine day, & we went up the Sound to explore whether there is an outlet somewhere in the Sound. We came up & saw several Canoes a fishing; they paddled off when they saw us; we chased them, & soon overtook them, & inquired of them

[1] George reports in strongly deprecating terms here of 'the rage of collecting arms and utensils' among the crew, even to the extent, it seems, of robbing the Maoris (*Voyage*, II, 468–9).

[2] But they had, according to George (II, p. 469), something else to attract certain Europeans: 'Each of their huts contained a fire, of which the smoke entirely involved them; however, by lying down close to the ground, they were less incommoded by the smoke than if they had sat upright. Notwithstanding the inconvenience of this situation, there were not wanting several of our shipmates who readily took up with the same lodging, in order to receive the caresses of the filthy female inhabitants'. The 'groveling appetites' of the 'brutish sailors' and some of their superiors came in for a hard time from George's pen on this occasion.

whether there is any Outlet into the Sea; they were our old Friends, & sold us Fish, but as to the Question they seemed not to understand us: we pushed up to the SW. & saw a very long Arm before us, which seemed to take a turn to the West & another to the South. We saw another Canoe, coming up towards us, & we joined & asked them, whether there was in this Arm & outlet into the Sea; but they told us, there was none, but that there was one the other way to the East or thereabouts: we therefore returned a rowed towards a place, where the Fishing Canoes were gone to, when we came near, we saw great Numbers of Natives come together from both Sides along the Sea-shore, where we had landed & where we found a Chief whose Name was called Tringo-Boohee.[1] We landed & nosed the Chief & his Son, & bought Fish & other things, & enquired again about the Outlet; they seemed to intimate that there was one, up the Arm we were to go in. We took therefore leave of them & entered into that Arm of the Sound.

Nov. ye 6th ☉ The place where *Tringo-Boohee* lives is at least 5 leagues distant from *Ship-Cove*. We found the next Arm much narrower than the former, & not far from *Koheghe-nooee*,[2] the Settlement of *Tringo-Boohee*;[3] there is an Arm to the right, forming a deep Cove, whose bottom we could not see,[4] & we suspected there to be the Passage but some Natives there informed us, that it was still higher up: though we still doubted of this circumstance, we however began to suspect something, for we found a strong rippling of the tide, which we could hardly expect in an Arm so sheltered as a Mill-Pond, & so far distant from the Sea. We stood on; the Arm went more northerly & had various Coves. We found several more places where we observed a strong rippling of the tide. We saw likewise a good many *Shags of the*

[1] Beaglehole (*Journals*, II, 575, n. 5) suggests Te Ringapuhi or Te Ringaopuhi. There is also some slight discrepancy between the sources as to just how far they proceeded up Queen Charlotte Sound on this expedition before turning into Tory Channel – the easterly arm to the sea. Forster's account suggests that they may have proceeded well beyond the inland entrance to Tory Channel (perhaps as far as Blackwood Bay?) before turning back to tackle the eastern outlet to the sea. Cf. *Journals*, II, 575 and *Voyage*, II, 470–2.

[2] Ko Heke-nui. Cook's and Forster's spelling of Maori names agree closely here, suggesting, perhaps some co-operation. George (II, pp. 472–4) gives a longer account of their trading with the Maoris here.

[3] Who, George tells us, was 'a little elderly man, but very active, lively and friendly; his face was punctured all over in scrolls, by which he distinguished himself from every one of his countrymen present'.

[4] Perhaps that inlet on the southern shore of Tory Channel, leading to Opua Bay at its extremity. However there are several deep coves so located.

crested kind,[1] flying backwards & forwards, who seldom have their nests any where else, but on such rocks, as are near to the open Sea; this confirmed our Suspicion, tho' we saw as yet nothing & could not observe any heave of the Sea upon the rocky Shores. At last something further than 3 leagues from *Kohèghe-noòee*, we saw the Sea break along a rocky Shore & concluded from thence, that the outlet would be there. We saw a *Hippa* or strong hold of the Natives at a distance surrounded with high pickets, & after a long & tedious rowing, we fairly saw the Sea opening & observed the Northern Isle opposite the outlet of the Arm, & sounded not quite in the middle 13 fathoms Water. Having made this discovery, we returned at about 4 o'clock & came on board after 10 o'clock, fatigued with sitting & exhausted with fasting.[2] We supped hastily & went about 12 o'clock to bed. Next morning was cloudy & gloomy weather. *Capt Cook* took a Native & gave him a Shirt a pair of old Breaches, an old Coat & a pair of Stockings, which he had put on him, & so disguised this Fellow that many could hardly think him the same Person they had seen before: his Name was *Peetèrre*.[3] We went over to *Long-Island* in order to catch the Sow, but could not see it; so we returned & killed on the return a new Shag[4] described before in June 1773. It began to rain & grow bad weather. *Pittìre* had been with us to *Long-Island* & afterwards dined with us.

9br ye 7th ☽ It began to rain, & it continued so all the After-Noon. We got information from *Pittère*, that though in the SW Arm of the Sound, there was no passage for a large Ship to go out to Sea through, however a small boat like our Pinnace might go out to Sea.[5] He likewise related that about 10 months ago a Ship had been here, & was gone out to Sea again & had not been shipwrecked as other people told us.[6] It rained all the day & blew very hard.

[1] Spotted Shags.

[2] Forster's account of this long row is in some respects more detailed than Cook's (*Journals*, II, 575–6).

[3] Cf. *Journals*, II, 576–7. Cook used this opportunity to enquire further after the *Adventure*.

[4] Undoubtedly the King Shag *Leucocarbo carunculatus carunculatus* (Gmelin 1789), first collected by Forster on 21 May 1773. See p. 283, n. 7 above.

[5] This is, of course, not possible, unless one carries the boat.

[6] See *Journals*, II, 577. George was also fascinated by Pitirau's and his comrades' 'singing on shore'. He found the Maoris 'far superior in variety to that of the Society and Friendly Islands; and if any nation of the South Sea comes in competition with them in this respect, I should apprehend it to be that of Tanna'. Again George relied upon 'that same intelligent friend', James Burney, who had supplied him with tunes before, to give him some specimens of New Zealand music. These he reproduced, closely following Burney's notes, *Voyage*, II, 477–8. See also Burney, *Private Journal*, pp. 56–7 and pp. 378 and 602, n. 8 above.

9br ye 8th ♂ The Rain & blowing weather continues still. We have wooded & watered, & rigged the Ship a new: but the Carpenters have begun to caulk the Sides of the Ship, though we have nothing to pay her Seams with, except a little Putty made of Chalk & Slush,[1] which is bad enough; & as soon as this business is finished, we shall go to Sea; besides this the Astronomer, wants still to stay here in order to settle the Longitude of the place; though it must seem very strange, that a Man who has been 3 times here, & each time during 3 weeks at least, could not settle the Longitude in that time. *Mr Bailey* was 7 weeks before us here in 1773 in March: & Mr *Green* was I believe in the Endeavour 3 weeks, & nevertheless the Longitude of the place is not yet settled: which either proves that the pretended accuracy of the Astronomers is not so great, as they will make others believe, or that they do not attend to their business & are negligent; or that the weather is so bad that they cannot observe; though we had fine days enough during our stay here.[2]

It rained again all night & blew very hard, which hinders me from going out, & from getting new plants: though we got but few new plants upon the hole, viz. not above 9: nor can we do any other business, when the Ship is in harbour & in confusion: these rainy days are therefore very tedious to us; & more so as I & George have both got a Cold last Sunday.

Nov. ye 9th ☿ In the Afternoon we went out to the Shagrock towards *Point Jackson*, but it blew hard & rained, however we got 12 Shags old & Young. We took Greens in for Seastore, & returned besides with the Male Flowers of a new Plant. It rained hard all night, & blew very fresh. The next morning at 6 o'clock the weather changed, & the Natives brought us a good many Fish of which we bought a good many for Seaprovision, & salted them down for that purpose. If I can get ashore, I'll try, whether I can get after breakfast the Female Flowers to our new Plant. *Capt Cook* saw yesterday ashore near the rivulet the place, where *Mr Bailey's*

[1] See *Journals*, II, 577–8.

[2] If Forster was saying such vindictive things openly then there is small wonder that he and Wales were now at loggerheads. Cook, on the other hand, confirms that astronomy and longitude-taking were to the fore in ship-board talk and thinking. He, however, had nothing but praise for Wales's 'abilities [which] is equal to his assiduity'. The astronomer 'lost no one observation that could possibly be obtained', and of Queen Charlotte Sound and other ports of call on this voyage, Cook thought that 'few parts of the world are better assertained' (*Journals*, II, 580–1). George, the conciliator, passed over this passage entirely in silence.

Astronomical tent has been fixed last year, after our departure from this place, & it seems the Natives say, that after our going away an other Ship has been here.

I went after breakfast ashore, & saw likewise to the West of the Garden the place where Mr *Bailey's* Astronomical tent had been fixed. I observed the hole where the Clock had been standing; & the Pickets, where the ropes of the Tent had been fastened to. I went in quest of the Female Flowers of our new plant, & cut several Trees of the kind down, but all was in vain. We took also leave from the place: the Tent was struck, the Ship unmoored & hove near a peak, & every thing kept ready for to sail at a moments warning.

Nov. ye 10th ♃ In the Afternoon we hove the Anchor, & went a little out & dropt an other Anchor. We went ashore to the *Indian-Cove* for to look out a piece of timber for a Spar: & I went likewise there, & having cut 5 trees down I luckily found the Female flowers & large Berries to the Plant we found two days ago, & which smells remarkably sweet, something like an Auricula or Lily of the Valley: the Berries, Leaves & the Bark, have all something of the same Smell, but fainter: the whole Air is embalmed if you happen to stand under or near such a Tree in Flower.[1] The Berry contains a kernel or Nut tasting somewhat Resinous.[2] Our Wood-Cutters met not with the same Success, for having found & cut a fine tree, the Carpenter had fixed upon, they found the Tree could not come down, but leaned upon another, which was likewise cut, when both began to fall, but were intercepted by a third, so had there been time enough for doing it, they might have cut perhaps a whole range of Trees for to get one. We therefore left them, as it grew late, having shot 11 birds for a Pye. The Boats are all hoisted in & to morrow morning nothing is left but to heave the Anchor & to set the Sail & go away, provided the present favorable Wind stands. Now having every thing prepared, all hands turn to their Suppers, & soon will take a refreshing Sleep.

[1] Among the New Zealand species collected or described by the Forsters the only one with male and female flowers on separate trees and with berries enclosing a kernel seems to be *Hedycarya arborea* J. R. et G. Forst. The male flowers have a faint musky fragrance but berries, leaves and bark are not notably aromatic. The previous year's berries could be found along with fresh flowers in November.

[2] Withal the Forsters were quite content scientifically with this third visit to the Sound. 'We collected', notes George (II, p. 479) 'ten or twelve species of plants, and four or five sorts of birds, which we had not seen before'.

Nox ruit, & fuscis tellurem amplectitur alis.
Æn. VIII. 369.[1]

Next morning at 4 o'clock, the Anchor began to be hove.

Oceanum interea surgens Aurora reliquit. Æn. IV. 129.
Idem omnes simul ardor habet, rapiuntque, ruuntque:
Littora deseruere : Latet sub (nave) æquon Æn. IV. 581.[2]

We soon cleared *Cape Koāmăroo* & the *Brothers* & somewhat after saw the South Entrance to *Queen Charlotte's Sound*, for we went close in Shore, within 3 leagues or thereabouts. The bottom of this Arm, where the Indian *Hippa* is, lies opposite *Grass-Cove* on the other side of the ridge of hills. We see the high hills beyond *Cloudy Bay* covered with eternal Snow & Ice & approach Cape *Campbell* gradually, but being under the high land, we cannot profit so well of the fine breeze. The Thermometer on deck at 8 o'clock A.M. 58½, in my Cabin 62½.

*Nov. ye 11th* ♀ In the Afternoon, we saw *Cloudy Bay* for the first time not cloudy & observed it to be a very large spacious & deep Bay: on its South-side it is terminated by a bluff point:[3] but afterwards Clouds collected & shut up the whole from our Sight. Between 4 & 5 o'clock P.M. we were a breast of *Cape Campbell*, being a low Point, with hills that have here & there white chalky or marly Spots: beyond it within the Straights is a good tract of low Land.[4] We proceeded & saw the immensely high *Lookers on*, which were wrapt in clouds, & shewed their snowy Summits above the Clouds.[5] We observed Albatrosses, black Shearwaters, diving Petrels, & next morning a Port Egmont Hen (*Larus*

[1] 'Night rushed down and embraced the earth in her black wings'.

[2] Taking these two quotations together they translate: 'Meanwhile Dawn rose and left the ocean' and 'The same frenzy gripped them all at once. They seized the tackle and hurried off. They left the shore; the sea lay beneath the ship'. Forster again uses *nave* (ship) for Vergil's *classibus* (fleet). In Vergil's text the sense is: 'the sea could not be seen for ships'.

[3] Possibly White Bluffs, two miles north of the mouth of the Awatere River.

[4] He possibly means the plain at the mouth of the Wairau River whereon arose Blenheim and other settlements. If so the view must have been a good one. Possibly, too, he was looking into Clifford Bay.

[5] Despite what Beaglehole writes in *Journals*, I, 252, n. 4 it is clear that Forster (and presumably therefore those who sailed with him and had been here before in *Endeavour*) identified the 'Lookers on' not as the Kaikoura peninsula but as the high mountains behind it i.e. the Seaward Kaikouras.

catarractes).[1] The wind fell over night & became southerly, which hinders us to go to S.E. Thermometer 58½, in my Cabin 66.

Nov. ye 12th ♄ We were becalmed; towards night a gentle breeze sprung up. We saw *Cape Palliser* & the *Snowy Mountains* of the Southern Isle. In the night the breeze mended & in the morning we went at the rate of 5 Knots an hour. We saw Albatrosses, small blue Petrels, N. Holland[2] & black Shearwaters & before breakfast an animal of the Cetaceous kind about 10 or 12 yards long, a pointed head but blunt at the Extremity, with two deep longitudinal furrows & on each side two upstanding high ridges, all mottled over with white spots, small Eyes, two semilunar Spouting holes & two lateral fins but none on the back, the tail horizontal: All the Animal black with a few white spots: the body bellied out beyond the head.[3] The Thermometer at 59°, in my Cabin 65°.

Nov. ye 13th ☉ The greens we have brought off from N.Z. & which we eat cause to me & my Son a Looseness in the night, & I begin to feel rheumatic pains in my Legs. We had very little or no wind. During night the breeze sprung up. In the morning there was an appearance of land on our starboard bow, we hawled up for it, but found it to be a bank of clouds & fog. About 7 bells A.M. a Seal was seen, several Albatrosses, Port Egmont Hens, black & N. Holland[4] Shearwaters & small blue Petrels of all kinds were observed together with Pintadas. The Thermometer at 54½°, in my Cabin 62°.

Nov. ye 14th ☽ The bank of clouds was at last dissolved in a Fog, which grew very thick & fell very moist on cloths & every object exposed to it. Saw a Seal in the Evening along side of the Ship & several Pintadas[5] & other Petrels. During the Fog we had a great Swell of the Sea. The breeze mended during night & we had all the morning a fine wind, but now & then a few drops of moisture & rain. The Thermometer at 54½, in my Cabin 61°.

[1] These four birds respectively were (probably) the Wandering Albatross, White-chinned Petrel, Northern Diving Petrel and Southern Skua. Hereafter the many birds seen on this long run are only identified where possible on the first sighting.

[2] These birds were, respectively, probably the Wandering Albatross, *Pachyptila* spp. and the White-headed Petrel.

[3] George (II, p. 482) follows this description closely. Possibly, notes Dr Peter Whitehead, this is 'the Southern right whale, *Balaena australis*, which lacks a dorsal fin; the ridges would have been the prominent lower lips, and the white Spots parasitic excretions; the "bonnet" characteristic of the species is not mentioned, but the specimen was not full grown'. Beaglehole (*Journals*, II, 581, n. 2), drawing on Dr R. A. Falla, identifies it as 'an abnormal specimen, probably a sperm whale'. Opp. VI, f. 53 is a sketch of the creature.

[4] White-headed Petrel. [5] Cape Pigeon.

*Nov. ye 15th* ♂ The wind still continues: Pintadas & *black & white Shearwaters*[1] about the Ship (*Procellaria capensis & inexpectata*). My Looseness still continues & causes me even gripes. I shall begin today to drink Wort, as a preventative against the Scurvy. In the Evening we had rain, & in the night likewise. Saw many Albatrosses, Pintadas, large black yellowbilled Shearwaters,[2] blue-banded Petrels, whiterumped Petrels,[3] black & white[4] ones & a Port Egmont Hen (Larus catarractes). Seaweeds passed the Ship several times. Thermometer at 49½, in my Cabin 58½°. Yesterday in the Afternoon we found the Ship had sprung a leak on the Starboard-bow not far from the Stem, but in 8 hours it increased only 5 Inches in the Pumpwell, we cannot mend it, till we get calm weather, or come to an Anchor somewhere.[5]

*Nov. ye 16th* ☿ The wind still continues. In the Evening saw a Port Egmont-Hen & heard several Pinguins croaking. Saw common, sootcoloured[6] & yellowbilled[7] Albatrosses, whiterumped, blue, & black & white Petrels & Pintadas & several bundles of Seaweed were seen. In the night Rain. Thermometer at 48°, in my Cabin 55°.

*Nov. ye 17th* ♃ Saw a bundle of weed & heard Pinguins croaking, & saw the same birds as last day & more Seaweeds. Rain in the night. Gloomy weather & some rain. Therm. at 49°, in my Cabin 56½. The wind North.

*Nov. ye 18th* ♀ I got a cold in the small of my back, & the Capt got likewise one & his Feet chillblained, by sitting near a port, where the Wind blew through the Chinks. The same birds as before appeared & several Pinguins were seen, & bundles of Seaweed. The Thermometer at 48°, in my Cabin 56½°. Altered yesterday the Course to ESE.

*Nov ye 19th* ♄ Altered the Course to East. Yesterday P.M. before we altered the Course having the wind aft, the Ship rolled very violently: & as Mr *Harrison*, the Watchmaker has represented to the board of Longitude that a Ship's position in rolling weather deviated never beyond 20° from its perpendicular position, I am perfectly sure, that our Ship was more than 40° degrees deviating,

[1] Mottled Petrel.
[2] Probably the Giant Petrel.
[3] Probably Wilson's Storm Petrel.
[4] Again probably the Mottled Petrel.
[5] Cook is silent about this, although Clerke (*Journals*, II, 580, n. 3) records the leak, occasioned by the ship's plunging.
[6] Light-mantled Sooty Albatross.
[7] Grey-headed Mollymawk.

in some of the most violent rolls.[1] I saw the Chain plates fairly under water & some of it came even on the Quarterdeck. The Chests in the Gunroom broke lose from their lashings, & the Astronomical Quadrant rolled about from one side of the Ship to the other. The wind before the beam, Course E½S & EbS. & East. The weather foggy. Not many birds attend the Ship. Pinguins are heard & Seaweeds are seen. The Thermometer at 48°, in my Cabin 53½°.

*Nov. ye 20th* ☉ Weather foggy & at last rainy, all the Night continuing: next Morning a thick fog, resolved in a drizzling Rain. Very few birds appear. The Thermometer at 46°, in my Cabin 51°.

*Nov. ye 21st* ☽ The wind dying away, & foggy with rain. Very few birds in Sight. Thermometer at 44°, in my Cabin 50°.

*Nov. ye 22^d^* ♂ Fine breeze, but still foggy. Blue Petrels in Sight, & some Penguins heard. Thermometer at 43°, in my Cabin 52°. (This rise of the Thermometer caused by the Smoaking of the Ship & of my Cabin).

*Nov. ye 23^d^* ☿ The wind dying away into a calm: foggy. A great many Blue Petrels in Sight. Saw many Porpesses. Towards night a faint breeze springs up. Sounded with 150 Fathom – no Bottom. Tied a corked & sealed empty Bottle to the Lead & sent it down, came up, the Cork pressed into the Bottle & full of water. All night & next morning calm. Saw great numbers of blue Petrels & several yellowbilled Albatrosses. Thermometer at 41½°, in my Cabin 59°.

*Nov. ye 24th* ♃ Still a calm. The Ship rolls very much. Towards night a gentle breeze sprung up. Saw great numbers of blue Petrils, saw a few yellowbilled Albatrosses. Thermometer at 43¼°, in my Cabin 54°. Saw Pinguins early in the morning.

*Nov. ye 25th* ♀ The breeze freshened a little. Cloudy in the Afternoon. The breeze still mends, during night & next morning. Foggy in the night. Fine weather in the morning. Several black & white & blue Petrels & yellowbilled Albatrosses are seen about the Ship. The Thermometer at 42°, in my Cabin 51½°.

*Nov. ye 26th* ♄ If this weather stands, & the breeze continues, we shall in 4 or 5 days more, have navigated half of our way from N. Zeeland to Cape *Horn* & celebrate thereabout Christmas. The

[1] Even Clerke, the veteran mariner, is moved to record the 'heavy swell' and rolling for 24 November. See *Journals*, II, 582, n. 3. Wales set up his own apparatus to measure the angle and extent of the ship's rolling. See *Journals*, II, 587.

breeze continues all night & next morning. Saw several blue Petrels & a few yellowbilled Albatrosses. The Thermometer at 45°, in my Cabin 52½°.

Nov. ye 27th ☉ The breeze very fine, foggy weather. Course EbN. This 24 hours run is the best ever since we have been in the Ship; for she made 184 miles by the Log & as the wind has been rather aft the beam, the following Sea has set her more forward so as the Log, & she is certainly a head of the Log.[1] Thermometer at 45°, in my Cabin 51½°.

Nov. ye 28th ☽ We advance amazingly on the pinions of the swiftest gales; but however these Gales carried away our Main-Top-Gallant Mast, broke the Leech Rope of our Main Sail & Split our Main-Top Stay-Sail, & their roughness not contented with that carried a large Sea against our Rudder, which gave it so sudden a Jerk that the Tiller-rope broke; had the Tiller not been the moment secured, we ran the risque of carrying away our Top-Masts.[2] We saw several white & black Porpesses & several blue Petrels, with some yellow billed Albatrosses. Weather foggy. Thermometer at 44°, in my Cabin 53°.

Nov. ye 29th ♂ The Gale still continues, it is foggy & the Sea washes the Sides & Decks of our Ship. A few birds attend the Ship. The Thermometer at 45½°, in my Cabin 53°.

Nov. ye 30th ☿ The wind falls, still foggy. All the day & night calm, foggy & a great Swell. The Therm. at 45¼°, in my Cabin 52°.

Dec. ye 1st ♃ A Gentle breeze springs up. Course NE: still foggy. Several blue Petrels & yellow billed Albatrosses about the Ship. About 8 o'clock put the Ship about. Course ESE, for she broke off before, even so high as sometimes to make the Course on the other tack N.bW. Foggy & drizzling all night & next morning. The Thermometer 45°, in my Cabin 52½°.

Dec. ye 2^d ♀ Rainy & foggy. First calm & a great Swell, then towards Evening a gentle breeze sprung up. Course ENE & more North. The Thermometer at 44½°, in my Cabin 49°.

Dec. ye 3^d ♄ Still foggy, a fresh breeze; many yellowbilled Alba-

[1] Cook now reached another crucial stage of decision-making. 'I now gave up all hopes of finding any more land in this Ocean and came to a Resolution to steer directly for the West entrance of the Straits of Magelhanes, with a view of coasting the out, or South side of Terra del Fuego round Cape Horn to Strait La Maire. As the World has but a very imperfect knowlidge of this Coast, I though the Coasting it would be of more advantage to both Navigation and Geography than any thing I could expect to find in a higher latitude, *Journals*, II, 583.

[2] Cf. Cook's and Clerke's entries for the same days, *Journals*, II, 583.

trosses about the Ship. The Thermometer at $43\frac{1}{4}$°, in my Cabin 49°.

Dec. y^{e} 4th ☉ The breeze fresh, a great Swell from N.W. Several yellowbilled Albatrosses attend the Ship. There blows a fresh Gale. Course EbN. The Thermometer at 41°, in my Cabin 48°.

Dec. y^{e} 5th ☽ The Gale still continues, the weather dry. The Ship pitches on account of a great Head Sea. Carried away the Flag Staff; the Course E$\frac{1}{2}$N, a strong Gale; a few sooty Albatrosses attend the Ship. The Thermometer at $42\frac{1}{2}$, in my Cabin $47\frac{1}{2}$.

Dec. y^{e} 6th ♂ The Breeze fresh. Two Showers of Hail. The Course E; several yellowbilled Albatrosses attend the Ship. The Thermometer at 40°, in my Cabin 45°.

Dec. y^{e} 7th ☿ Our Navigators agree, that we have more than 1000 Leagues to N.Z. & that we are therefore more than $\frac{2}{3}$ of the Passage to Cape *Horn* & that it is still possible to celebrate Christmas in some Harbour. A fine breeze: we go large: the Course ENE. Several Hailshowers came down in Squalls. Several yellowbilled Albatrosses are seen. The Thermometer at 44°, in my Cabin 48°.

Dec. y^{e} 8th ♃ The weather fine. The Captain has a return of swelled feet & Obstructions, my Son has likewise swelled Legs, all owing to the Scurvy. I find myself pretty well. The breeze abated, a few yellow-billed Albatrosses about the Ship. The Thermometer at $44\frac{1}{4}$°, in my Cabin $53\frac{1}{2}$°.

Dec. y^{e} 9th ♀ It is now 4 weeks past since we left Queen Charlotte's Sound & are about $\frac{2}{3}$ of the passage to Cape *Horn* & in a 14 night more we have a Chance to be at the latter place or its neighbourhood. The wind is no more favourable, but goes round. The Thermometer at $44\frac{1}{3}$°, in my Cabin $51\frac{1}{2}$°.

Dec. y^{e} 10th ♄ Rainy & foggy, the wind unfavourable, but changed, a great head Sea. Thermometer $43\frac{1}{2}$°, in my Cabin 50.

Dec. y^{e} 11th ☉ A very fine gale, very favourable. We go on at a great rate. Few yellowbilled Albatrosses about the Ship. Thermometer at 43, in my Cabin $49\frac{1}{2}$.

Dec. y^{e} 12th ☽ The breeze quite aft, we had run at noon 180 miles, but now the wind goes down: Few yellowbilled & sooty Albatrosses about the Ship. Thermometer at $43\frac{1}{2}$, in my Cabin $48\frac{1}{2}$.

Dec. y^{e} 13th ♂ At noon we had 145 miles on the board. The run seems to be most prosperous, & some of our Gentlemen expect to see Land in 5 days more, which would be certainly one of the most extraordinary Passages considering the Great Distance. The wind fell towards Evening & Part of the night calm. After midnight a gentle breeze sprung up. A few yellowbilled & sooty Albatrosses attend the Ship. The Thermometer at 44°, in my Cabin 50°.

*Dec. ye 14th* ☿ The breeze fresh & favourable, now & then a Squall comes on. We observe great numbers of blue Petrils about the Ship, with some sooty & yellowbilled Albatrosses. The blue Petrils have not been seen for a long space of time, ever since the first of December. The Thermometer at 44°, in my Cabin 49½°.

*Dec. ye 15th* ♃ Our Navigators estimate themselves hardly 100 Leagues off Cape *Deseado*,[1] so that we have hopes to see Land in a couple of days & to be at an Anchor before Christmas. Some Showers of a few drops only. Saw blue Petrils & a few sooty yellowbilled Albatrosses. In the Evening several 10 or 15 feet long Animals of the Cetaceous tribe passed the Ship. They were more 6 or 8 foot in Diameter, had a blunt head & on the middle part of the back a fin of about 8 or 9 Inches high pointed, elevated & falcated behind.[2] The Thermometer at 45°, in my Cabin 51½°.[3]

*Dec. ye 16th* ♀ The wind constantly favourable: the weather mild: a few Showers of Rain now & then. The birds are allmost all gone so that hardly a Petrel or Albatross appears. The Thermometer 46°, in my Cabin 51½°.

*Dec. ye 17th* ♄ Some Showers. Few birds. The wind gentle, the weather mild, & agreable. Saw in the morning many blue Petrils & some large common Albatrosses, & likewise early at 4 o'clock a Seal was seen. The Thermometer at 45°, in my Cabin 52°.

*Dec. ye 18th* ☉ Fresh wind. Several Squals & Hail Shower. Expect to see the Land, but at night nothing could be seen as yet. Shorten Sail. Ever since last morning we went more northerly. NEbE½E. the Course. Brought to for the night. Saw at Midnight the Land, supposed something to the Southward of *Cape Deseado* or *Desire*. Made Sail again at 3 o'clock in the morning. The appearance of the Land is none of the most favourable ones. For the hills tho'

[1] At the north western extremity of Desolation Island at the Pacific entrance to the Strait of Magellan. See *Journals*, II, 585, n. 4.

[2] The blunt head suggests the Pacific pilot whale, *Globicephala macrorhyncha*, an identification already made for Forster's 'Bottlenose' of 8 June 1773, p. 295, n. 1 above. See also p. 306 above. However some doubt must exist, for he would surely have recognised the same species again.

[3] For this same day Cook records 'some diving Peterels', identified by Beaglehole as possibly the Magellanic Diving Petrel, *Pelecanoides magellani* Mathews, *Journals*, II, 585, n. 2.

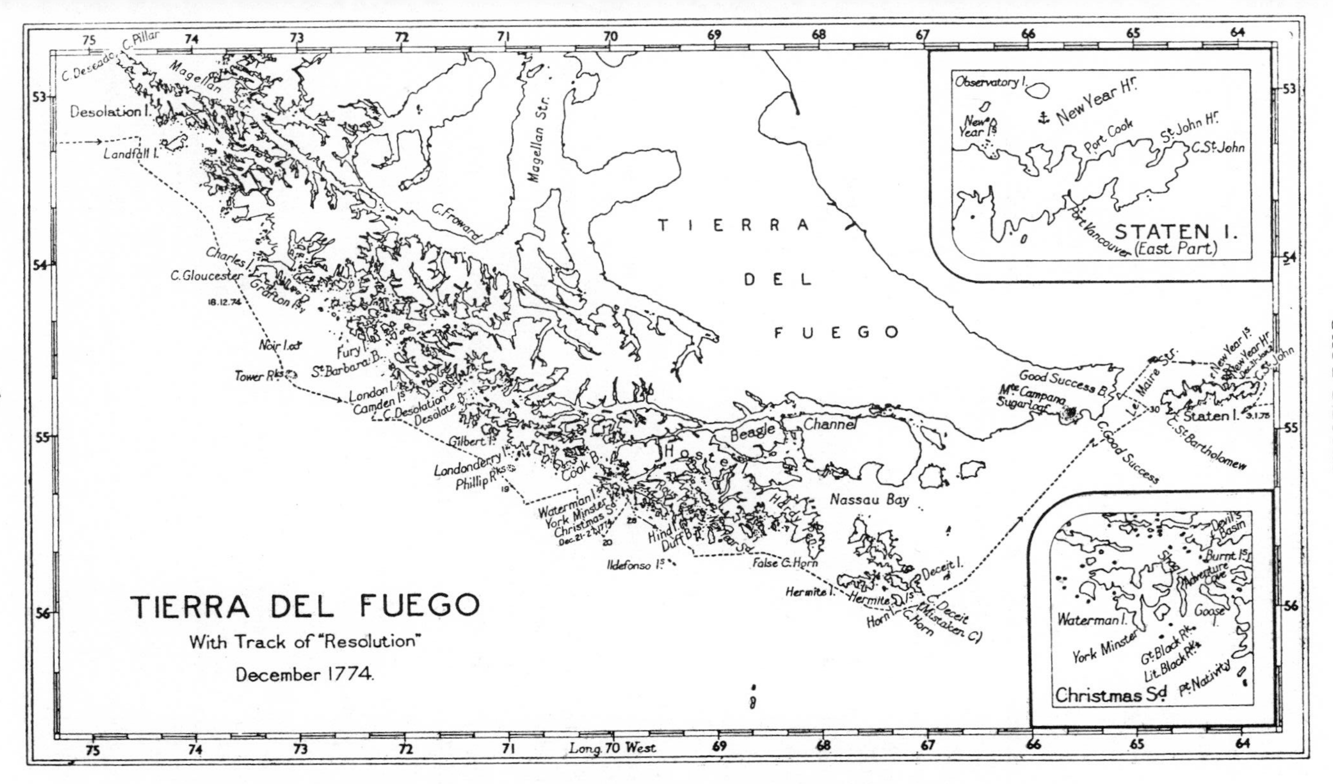

Figure 41. Tierra del Fuego, with track of the *Resolution*, December 1774 *(79).

not very steep nor ver[y] high, are however bleak & barren & all the inland ones are covered with Snow. If this is their appearance about the Summer-Solstice, what must this Land be in the depth of Winter, when they are deprived of the influence of the now more elevated Sun. I believe that the saying of Pliny Hist. nat. l.4 c.26. may then with more propriety be applied to it, than to the Country he was speaking of:

Pars mundi damnata a rerum natura, & densa mersa caligine.[1]

Besides this, the whole is broken Land; nothing but Breakers, Rocks & little Isles appear along the Land farther in, of which we see only now & then something, on account of the haze & the continual Squalls, that shower down upon it. We see great flocks of Shags,[2] black Shearwaters[3] & Port-Egmont-Hens,[4] flying along the Land, which is a Sight which takes off something of the harshness of the Scene; especially to people, who have scarce tasted any fresh meat, ever since we left N. Zeeland, & who are quite weaned of the taste of a good joint of meat.[5] The wind fine, the weather mild, sometimes squally. The Thermometer at $46\frac{3}{4}°$, in my Cabin $52\frac{1}{2}°$.

Dec. ye 19th ☽ We have an Isle in Sight; off it lies a Rock like a Cone or Sugarloaf, something like that lying off the Isle where *Cape Noir* or *Black* lies on, according to *Frezier's* Voyage to the South-Sea: we find this Towerrock of a singular appearance joins to the Isle by a low point of Land: At 3 o'clock we were due West of *Cape Noir*; we went at 6 miles & 3 fathoms & were at 4 o'clock about 4 Leagues distant, the Cape bearing N 6°E & three other little rocks bearing East, 2 miles distance.[6] We see no Land a head, nor any NE from us, where it seems the Canal of *Ste Barbe*

[1] 'A part of the world cursed by nature, and plunged in dense fog (mist).'

[2] Possibly the Rock or Magellanic Shag *Phalacrocorax magellanicus* (Gmelin, 1789). See p. 699, n. 3 below.

[3] White-chinned Petrel.

[4] Probably the Chilean Skua *Stercorarius skua chilensis* Bonaparte, 1857 which breeds in Tierra del Fuego and on the outlying islands.

[5] Cf. George's first description of the land and the run from New Zealand in *Voyage*, II, 483–5. The younger Forster expunged most of the routine daily entries from New Zealand to South America. Cook himself observed that 'I never was makeing a passage any where of such length, or even much shorter, where so few intresting circumstance[s] occrued', *Journals*, II, 587.

[6] We lack here Cook's precision in the identification of the islets, rocks and capes of this difficult coast. From Cook (*Journals*, II, 588–9), however, we can determine that Forster is describing Noir Island and the rocky islets which are off it, the Tower Rocks. For Frezier see p. 146, n. 2 above and *Journals*, II, 589, n. 3.

mentioned by *Frezier*[1] is: our Course is SE. We shortened Sail late in the Evening. The wind falls. A current sets us in shore. At 3 o clock in the morning bore away. Course East. The Land is here more uniform & as it seems compact. Now & then we see a rocky Isle lying before the Land, which is here throughout covered with Snow on the Summits of the hills, & in some places the Snow comes down to the very Water's-Edge.[2] The weather mild & warm, & changes into a calm. About noon a Current sets us off Shore. We see great many small birds at a good distance to the South, and several yellowbilled Albatrosses.[3] Saw likewise one Seal, & several Pinguins[4] something red about the Eyes & Bill. We sounded & had 50 & 45 fathom, bottom Gravel & Shells; at about 4 miles distance from the next Rocks & 2 or 3 Leagues from the Great Land.[5] The Thermometer at 8 o clock 46°, in my Cabin 54°.

Dec. yᵉ 20th ♂ In the Afternoon we had Eastwind, & were obliged to stand on & off the Land. Towards night the breeze died away & in the morning we were again becalmed: the Current setting us to the SE or something more towards East. We saw more than 30 Grampusses blowing & frisking about the Ship, chiefly in Couples. We were visited by Flocks of Seals, each of 3, or 4 up to seven & more: Pinguins[6] came likewise in Sight. We observed Port Egmont Hens, [7] & grey Gulls, yellowbilled Albatrosses,[8] Shags,[9] & black Shearwaters.[10] In the Sea were great Shoals of small Fish, & several long, red Filaments of the Blubberkind.[11] The Appearance of the Land is much the same: Rocks covered with Snow, & all the rest barren. All this confirms still Pliny's saying.[12] The Thermometer at 48°, in my Cabin 55°.

Dec. yᵉ 21st ☿ Who would or could believe it, that we should have reason to complain of calms in the neighbourhood of *Cape Horn*

[1] Clerke was reading the same source, ibid. The Barbara channel does run into Magellan Strait.

[2] They were now off Cook's Cape Desolation, at the entrance to Bahia Desolada or Desolate Bay. Cf. Cook (*Journals*, II, 589–90): 'it commenced the most desolate and barren Country I ever saw'.

[3] Grey-headed Mollymawk.

[4] Magellan Penguins *Spheniscus magellanicus* (Forster, 1781). See 1 January 1775, p. 706 below.

[5] Cf. *Journals*, II, 590.

[6] Probably Magellan Penguins.

[7] Chilean Skua.

[8] Grey-headed Mollymawk.

[9] Probably the Rock or Magellanic Shag.

[10] White-chinned Petrel.

[11] A pelagic colonial tunicate, probably a species of *Pyrosoma*.

[12] Pliny's saying: the one quoted on p. 692 above.

so famous for tempests & Hurricane's.[1] In the Afternoon we stood in shore having again an Easterly wind, & seeing an opening between some Isles & Rocks we stood in. The place looked very barren. We had all along the Coast regular Soundings, but when we came in the Mouth of a Bay we had at 150 fathom ground & in some places 70.[2] We stood however in. Three Lieu^ts^ & I went to some Rocks on our larboard Side, where we saw a great many Shags; but they were so shy, that we could get none of them. We saw some Geese[2] whereof the Gander is white & the Goose black & white, have yellow Legs: the Gander a black bill, the Goose one of the colour of a human Nail. We fired in rain at them & at some Port Egmont Hens.[4] I killed a *Que-branta Huessos,*[5] ie *Procellaria ossifragus* with a green bill, all sooty-dusky & as big as an Albatross. We came in a cove at an Anchor & next morning we went in a boat further into the Port where we found a Cove quite landlocked, some Wood & Water & good Anchorage with regular soundings.[6] We shot a couple of Geese[7] male & Female who had 7 Goslings, who betook themselves to the Rocks & climbed most excellently the most steep parts of them. We killed likewise several Shags, of the kind with a large granulated red Knob on the bill,[8] such as we had seen in N. Zeeland. We saw the same black Oystercatchers[9] as in N.Z. & some black & white ones.[10] We found several curious plants, several of which had Flowers; & a fine orange blossomed *Berberis*[11] with Holly-Leaves,

[1] George (II, pp. 485–6) took up this theme with an added note: 'The destruction of vulgar prejudices is of so much service to science, and to mankind in general, that it cannot fail of giving pleasure, to every one sensible of its benefits'.

[2] They were standing into Christmas Sound. Cf. *Journals*, II, 591 and fig. 42.

[3] Lesser Kelp Goose *Chloephaga hybrida hybrida* (Molina, 1782). See 2 January 1775, p. 707, n. 3 below.

[4] Chilean Skua.

[5] Giant Petrel, *Macronectes giganteus* (Gmelin, 1789). Forster's description of *Procellaria ossifraga* of *Descr. Anim.*, p. 343 is dated 28 December 1774. His son's folio 93a was probably the same bird. See Lysaght, p. 294.

[6] Adventure Cove on Shag Island. See *Journals*, II, 592. George (II, p. 487) tells us that he, his father and Sparrman accompanied Cook on the quest for a safer anchorage.

[7] Lesser Kelp Goose.

[8] King Cormorant *Phalacrocorax albiventer albiventer* Lesson, 1831.

[9] Black Oystercatcher *Haematopus ater* Vieillot and Oudart, 1825.

[10] Fuegian Oystercatcher *Haematopus leucopodus* Garnot, 1826.

[11] *Berberis ilicifolia* Forst. For the botany of this visit to South America the scientific world has George's 'Fasciculus plantarum magellanicarum...' in *Commentationes Societatis Scientiarum Gottingensis*, IX (1789), 13–45. This plant is described therein (p. 44). In a note to me Dr David Galloway, who has revised the Southern Hemisphere Strictaceae, suggests that the lichen *Stricta orygmaea* (collected by Menzies from New Years Harbour on Staten Island in 1787 and so known since 1803) should now be known as *Pseudocyphellaria berberina* (G. Forster) D. Gall & P. James. The Forster and Menzies plant specimens of *B. ilicifolia*

& saw some more & several Birds. Though the place has a gloomy look, it will afford us however some refreshments. Fish we got none. It is now our business to remove the Ship, to the new Cove: but costs much labour on account the want of wind, & all must be done by warping. The Thermometer in my Cabin $58\frac{1}{2}°$. The weather is fine, warm & very mild.

Dec. y^e 22^d ♃ In the Afternoon we brought our new Acquisitions of birds & Plants overside. We got some Fish of a new Cod Kind not above 4 or 5 Inches long, yellow & very delicate.[1] The next morning the Captain went deeper in the harbour towards the snowy Mountains, which we suppose to be part of the Main-Isle of *Terra del Fuego*;[2] we got on an Isle,[3] where we found a great part of the Moss & Plants lately burnt, so that the Natives must not be far off. We saw some Ducks, but could not come near them. When we drew in shore, we saw a large Bason[4] of half a mile Diameter perfectly sheltered, with good Anchorage, Wood & Water coming down in several fine Cascades. Here we found two old Birds, with some Young ones, shaped like Duck & very shy, running on the Water & beating it with their Wings, which gives them such a velocity as hardly a Bird has, when flying ever so swift. Former Navigators had called these Birds *Race-horses*.[5] I suppose them to belong to the Diver Class. We collected in these parts several curious little plants & one with a beautiful red Flower on a Shrub, growing very low, of a new Genus, we had before found in *New Caledonia*. We visited several Isles & shot some Shags,[6] Curlews[7] & one Duck,[8] which is of a greyish brown above, of a pale rusty colour below; the *Speculum* is coppercoloured & shining, below edged with green & the secundary Quillfeathers are white, the tail in the Duck short, but pointed; in the male

in the British Museum (Nat. Hist.) are, I am informed, the same. See D. J. Galloway and P. W. James, '*Pseudocyphellaria berberina* (G. Forster). D. Gall & P. James: Notes on its Discovery and Synonymy', *Lichenologist*, IX (1977).

[1] *Gadus magellanicus* of *Descr. Anim.*, p. 361 and drawing No. 178.

[2] They were, of course, strictly speaking off the coast of Hoste Island, separated from Tierra del Fuego by Beagle Channel. See *Journals*, II, 593, n. 5.

[3] George (II, pp. 487 and 489) gives us more detail on the geology of this low island and of Adventure Cove. Cook (*Journals*, II, 593) called it Burnt Island.

[4] Devil's Basin.

[5] Magellanic Flightless Steamer Duck, *Tachyeres pteneres* (Forster, 1844). See 2 January, p. 708, n. 1 below and *Voyage*, II, 492–3.

[6] Possibly the Rock or Magellanic Shag.

[7] *Haematopus* sp.

[8] Perhaps the South American Green-winged Teal *Anas flavirostris flavirostris* Vieillot, 1816.

somewhat longer & likewise pointed. We dined on a Rock upon fine large Muscles, & large Arbutus, some Biscuit & Salt Beef.

We found on an Isle several empty huts of the natives. Several were round, made of branches of Shrubs, stuck in the Ground, the leaves were still green on them. They cover these Skeletons with Seals Skins, for we saw still some pieces on them. One hut was made of strong Sticks & pointed.[1]

The day we were gone to the bottom of the bay, we found some Sellery & filled allmost the boat with. We found this kind infinitely superior to that found at N. Zeeland.[2]

*Dec. ye 23^d^* ♀ We shot likewise some birds like Wagtails[3] near the Sea shore, & living as I suppose upon Shrimps & other small marine Insects. Three small Plovers[4] were likewise shot. We got this day several Showers, & found it colder upon the whole; but when we were under the snowy hills, it was infinitely more so. We came late home & supped & went to bed quite tired.[5] Next morning, we went round the Isle under which our Ship lays.[6] We took to the Westside first, & returned on the Eastside. We met with two flocks of Goslings, each of five young & a white Gander and the Goose[7] black mottled with white, both have yellow legs. The one years young Ganders have black Quillfeathers in the Wings. We got a couple of fine plants.

*Dec. ye 24th* ♄ We went along the Isle & had good many shots at Shags, but they are very hard lived birds. At last coming on the EastSide of the Isle we saw several Geese on the Rocks & shot 2 of them of whom we might have gotten every one, had we taken the proper precaution of going on the Rock & thus approaching them. They are frightened at the boat, but let a single man come near. We brought home 9 old Shags & 5 young ones & 3 Geese.[8] We went the next morning to a place, where we heard of Lieut. *Pickersgill*, who had been sent out on purpose upon discovery &

[1] This note on the huts is added in the margin of VI, f. 62.

[2] This note is in the margin of VI, f. 63.

[3] Forster's *Motacilla gracula* of *Descr. Anim.*, p. 324 was based upon these birds as was George's folio 160. See also Lysaght, p. 309. It is now the Patagonian Cinclodes *Cinclodes patagonicus* (Gmelin, 1789).

[4] Not specifically identifiable.

[5] This day's expedition is best read in conjunction with George's account (II, pp. 489–94) and Cook (*Journals*, 593–4). Both supplement this account.

[6] Shag Island. See *Journals*, II, 595.

[7] Lesser Kelp Goose.

[8] Cook gives a fuller account of this expedition which took in Port Clerke on Waterman Island. See *Journals*, II, 595.

surveying, that a great Quantity of Geese were to be met with, but when we were going round an Island which lies between the Ship & the above mentioned Goose-Cove, we found on the Sides & slopes of the Rocks towards the open Sea, great Flocks of Geese. We landed, though the Surf was very great, & begun to engage the Geese, & as we fell in along Shore with more & more, & were fortunate enough to drive great numbers of them into precipices & hollows where the boat below could shut them in, when they flung themselves down the Rock into the Sea. We had very lucky Sport; some fell down into crevices of the Rocks & jammed themselves perfectly in, so that they could not stir, so that we shot & caught 62 in all, & with this rich Spoil we came late on board, having spent all day in procuring the Geese, landing in a high Surf & climbing slippy dangerous Rocks.[1] But all this was counter-balanced by the Satisfaction that we should now have to give to all our people on board fresh & good Provisions. Every three men got a goose: & several Shags were given besides to our Pinnace-crew.

*Dec. ye 25th* ☉ Mr Pickersgill went another way to the Goose-Cove, & collected before several Eggs of Terns[2] on an Island. When we came on board, we heard that 4 Canoes with Natives had been on board & that they were very good natured People & gave willingly away every thing they had; Spears & Sealskins & various other trifles. We were much fatigued, & prepared every thing for to treat as many Gentlemen as our Cabin & Table could hold. We were disturbed during night by our Ships-Crew, who allmost all got drunk[3] in honor of the Christmass-day. The Sailors had every thing good to eat & to drink in Plenty & could now, as their Expression is, celebrate the Feast & live *like Christians*, or as people of Sense would call it, *like Beasts*: for the little sense they have, was soon lost in Liquor: & clamour & fighting was all over the Ship seen & heard.[4]

It rained in the morning; but the Natives came however off in 4 Canoes. These Canoes are made of the Bark of a Tree; the Gunnel seems to be formed of the bark of the Boat bent round a stick &

[1] They had their sport on Goose Island. George writes that they brought home sixty-three geese. Cf. *Journals*, II, 596 and *Voyage*, II, 496–7.

[2] Not specifically identifiable.

[3] *Erased*: to celebrate.

[4] The sailors, observed George (II, p. 506) 'continued to carouse during two days without intermission'. Cook put most of them ashore in the open air 'to recover'.

sowed fast: the Inside is set out wit[h] small pliant Sticks of an Inch Diameter, which give the whole boat its stiffness & solidity. They have some Stones & Earth in the middle of the Canoe, whereon they keep a constant Fire, & by the help of small paddles they convey them away from one place to another, but in a very slow & indolent manner. Every boat holds from 5 to 8 people, Children reckoned in. The Natives are a short set of people, the upperparts stout, the Shoulders & Chest broad, belly strait & well filled, but the feet are by no means proportioned to the Upperparts. The Thighs are thin & lean, the Legs bent, knees large. The Scrotum long. The Men had nothing to cover their privities. Their Features are hard, the Face broad, the Cheekbones outstanding, Nose flat, the Nostrils & Mouth large. Hairs strait & black, hanging about the head in a shocking manner. Their beards are thin & cut short. They had only a small piece of Sealskin hanging round their Shoulders. They were painted red & sometimes white. And stunk immoderately after Thrane-oil. The women are much of the same make, their Breasts are hanging down, but not so much as in the Nations in the Isles. Their dress much the same as that of the Men, but they have a small piece of Skin about their Privities fixed to a string tied round the waist. Some wore caps of white Geese feathers standing down to the Face, which they sometimes changed & set upright. I saw only a small patch of Guanacoe-Skin sowed to a Cloak of Seal skin. They had often small strings of shells of the Helix kind round their Neck fixed to thongs & strings of Leather. Their Lances are long of a light brittle wood, died black, to which they fix by thongs points with jags on one side. Their bows are short & small, the Bowstring of Leather, the Arrows of wood, short, feathered on one End, & without points, which are of Stone & they carry them with them in bags, they would part only with one of the kind, which was a miserable piece of black Slate. They were very friendly, peaceable, & parted willingly with many things. Their Language seemed to us very unintelligible; & though I pointed to many things, in order to get the Names of them, they seemed to be too stupid for the signs. The only word which they often repeated was *Passerai*. They have all a kind of Lisp in their Language, many *r*'s & an *l* preceded by a *th*, something like the double *Ll* of the Welsh. They shivered all with cold, even in the mildest weather & seemed to be the most wretched & dirty of all human beings I ever saw in my Life. When they found that no body wanted to give them more trifles, they embarked again in their Canoes & paddled gradually away.[1]

*Dec. ye 26th* ☽ We sat down to our Dinner, which consisted chiefly of Dishes made of Geese in various ways. Our Soup was made of geese, we had Geese boiled, roasted, & in Pyes, & plenty of fine Sellery in the Soup & for Sallad. All went on with a great deal of mirth & Glee & we went to bed at 3 o'clock in the morning at broad daylight. We found that we could hardly shut our Eyes, or have the least comfortable nap, for the noise of the drunken Ships-Crew, who were continually fighting, *de gayeté de coeur*. The Captain sent all drunken noisy fellows a shore, to take there an airing & get sober again. The Natives paid us another Visit.

*Dec. ye 27th* ♂ We described various plants & birds. My Son, Mr Sparman & I fell sick at dinner from the Soup with Greens & could eat nothing. My Son had got a Rheumatism in his Leg. The next morning[2] we went again to our Goose Island in order to collect some Provisions for our Sea-Stock. We went in two boats & were lucky enough to get 18 Geese more, 2 Shags,[3] a Curlew & 4 young Goslings that were nearly fledged. This time we went round the Isle & saw on its Northern Side 2 fine & spacious Harbours, as safe & good as can be wished, with wood & Water close to it.

[1] These terse notes on their unprepossessing visitors – written, we must suppose, in the middle of Forster's own not insubstantial Christmas festivities – formed the basis for George's much longer description of these people and their culture (*Voyage*, II, 498–506). Cook's account (*Journals*, II, 597 & 600) was also short. George, who found these 'natives' 'too stupid, too indolent, or too wretchedly destitute of means' even to guard themselves against the 'inclemency of the weather', was, like Cook, unimpressed with them. Not only was 'their whole character...the strangest compound of stupidity, indifference and inactivity' but they also stank enough even, Cook noted, to threaten to spoil their Christmas appetites and, George reasoned, to deter 'our boldest and roughest sailors' from striking up the more usual 'intimate acquaintance with the women'. George used this opportunity to cast some shafts at the prevalent contemporary philosophies of 'noble savage', that 'ill-natured system of philosophy [which] is only copied from Seneca, who made light of the distresses of others, being himself in affluence'. 'Till', he wrote (II, p. 503), 'it can be proved, that a man in continual pain, from rigour of climate, is happy, I shall not give credit to the eloquence of philosophers, who have either had no opportunity of contemplating human nature under all its modifications, or who have not felt what they have seen'. Wales (*Remarks*, pp. 99–100) attacked the Forsters' foray into 'philosophy' here and received (*Reply*, p. 36) the usual spirited answer. Philosophy apart, George's descriptions of the 'Fuegian nation' here – 'probably', notes Beaglehole (*Journals*, II, 596, n. 3), 'a sub-tribe of the Yahgans, who spent a great deal of time in their canoes' – are the best. The Oxford 'Catalogue of Curiosities' (items 165–8) show that Forster at least acquired a sealskin coat, a spear, a piece of jagged bone and a shell necklace in this part of the world.

[2] '...some of the people being tolerably sober' – *Voyage*, II, 506.

[3] Possibly the Rock or Magellanic Shag *Phalacrocorax magellanicus* (Gmelin, 1789). Forster's description of *Pelecanus magellanicus* is dated 28 December 1774 (*Descr. Anim.*, p. 356). It was illustrated by George on folio 105. See also Lysaght, p. 297.

*Dec. ye 28th* ☿ The Natives had been again on board, & got off when they saw nothing could be gotten more. They eat Seals flesh, & presented pieces of it to our people. They stink therefore so strongly, that it is easy to find them out with shut Eyes at a Distance, especially if they are to windward of you: all their Apparel of Sealskins, their Arms & utensils are all strongly tainted with the smell of Thrane-oil. We came late on board. My Servant had been on shore, to collect plants, & had got a good many, but none new. We observed however that Dr Patrick *Brown* is wrong in calling the Jamaica white *Cinnamon-Tree*[1] the *Winters-Bark*:[2] for we found the latter belonging to a different Class & Genus. We unmoored next morning, having been well refreshed with greens & Fowls in this place & having gotten a good stock of water & wood. We hove the Anchor at 8 o'clock & set Sail, with a fair wind at West. We steered for some Islands, we had seen towards the SE quarter, when we came into this Harbour. They are probably those called in some Maps *Islands of St Ildephonso*,[3] though it is difficult to say, who first called them so. We had frequent Showers of Rain all this day.

*Dec. ye 29th* ♃ We passed them Isles in the Afternoon, & then altered our Course & went eastward & afterwards saw the coast of *Tierra del Fuego* in the intervals of the Squalls.

It blew fresh all night. We wore Ship during night. In the morning at about 5 or 6 o'clock we passed the famous *Cape Horn*. The Thermometer was at 50°, in my Cabin at 55°. We passed afterwards *Barnevelds Isles*[4] & saw on some Rocks that lie before them, such Flocks of Shags as I never saw before: the tops of them were all covered with 1000's of these Birds. We afterwards saw *Evouts Isle*[5] & steer now for the *Strait le Maire*.

*Dec. ye 30th* ♀ We have a fine breeze & a following Sea & some say that we shall come in *Success-Bay* at an Anchor, in order to see whether the *Adventure* is or has been there,[6] or to let her know, that we have been there; how far these Guesses will prove right, time will show.

[1] *Canella winterana* (L.) Gaertn. For Browne's work see p. 172, n. 3 above.

[2] *Drimys winteri* J. R. & G. Forst. See also p. 701 below and *Journals*, I, 51.

[3] Ildefenso Islands.

[4] Bernevelt Islands, lying beyond the southern entrance of the Strait of Le Maire, so named by Schouten and Le Maire in January 1616.

[5] Cf. *Journals*, I, 48.

[6] That was Cook's intention, as he himself makes clear in *Journals*, II, 603.

In the harbour we were in, was very little wood, & what we saw of it was small, crabbed & rooted in the Mosses on the Rocks. We found among the Vegetables of this place, the famous *Winter's-bark*, which has so often been confounded with the *Canella alba*,[1] growing at *Barbadoes*, *Jamaica* & in *China*; but Sir *Hans Sloane* in his Natural History of Jamaica, vol. 2. p. 165 remarks, that the true *Winter's bark* differs much from the Jamaica *Canella alba*, & however it has been allways thought to be the same: so much is it true that prejudices cannot easily be rooted out. I have formerly tasted the *Canella alba*, & think it tastes even different from this bark; this has a very high degree of pungency; & the color is brown, whereas the *Canella alba* is white: & I believe their Virtues to be widely different tho' I cannot yet decide upon that Subject without Experiments, which I may perhaps make, when I return to England & have time from my other avocations for doing it. I suspect this to be as adstringent as the *Jesuit's bark*,[2] but abounding with more aromatic, & volatile particles. It is however remarkable, that when we were at New-Zeeland we found a plant, whose Character of the Flowers & Fructification we described, & called it on account of its bitter, pungent, somewhat aromatic bark *Drimys*[3] (from δριμυς *acris*, *pungens*). The Characters of this Plant, we found coinciding with our *Winter's bark*,[4] which has the same Qualities & nearly the same taste. Captain *Winter*[5] found this bark very near 200 years ago in the year 1577 in the Magellanic Straits & used it as an antiscorbutic & stomachic for his crew. Sir *John Narborough*[6] brought some home, & the people in the *Dolphin* & *Endeavour* did the same, & some of our English most eminent Physicians have it since prescribed with good Success. It might grow & thrive well all over the northern parts of Europe: viz. Ireland, Wales, Scottland, Norway, Sweden & Russia, perhaps even in warmer Climates for ought we know. We found only buds upon it & no flowers &

[1] *Canella winterana* (L.) Gaertn. See p. 700 above.

[2] *Cinchona officinalis* L.

[3] *Drimys winteri* Forst.

[4] *Pseudowintera axillaris* (J. R. & G. Forst.) Dandy.

[5] William Winter who was with Drake in the Straits of Magellan in 1578. Cf. *Journals*, I, 51, n. 3 and *Voyage*, II, 488.

[6] d.1688. Narborough was an English naval commander who led an abortive expedition to the South Seas in 1669–71. He was in the Straits of Magellan in October 1670. A narrative of the expedition was contained in *An Account of several late voyages & discoveries to the south and north*.... (2 vols, London, 1694).

some imperfect Seeds. The leaves are fleshy, oval, smooth, pale green, below blueish; the bark is white on the outside & brown on its inside. The flowers have from 6–10 white Petals, more than 20 filaments inserted in the receptacle; & it belongs therefore to the Class of *Polyandria* in *Dr Linnaeus's* System; it has 4 or 5 germina & afterwards, ovated capsules with many Seeds in it. And thus we have at last determined the Generic Character of a plant, obscurely known even since 200 years.

We found upon the whole about 7 new birds, 3 fish, & 20 plants in the harbour we were in, tho' at first it was far from being promising; such a Collection, as we made during the Course of one week, 2 days of which we did not stir from the Ship on account of the drunkenness of our Crew, & all was, as it were gotten in 5 days.[1] If we anchor in *Success bay*, where the woods are more common, we may perhaps make a more ample collection. We saw in the Afternoon the Lands near *Straight le Maire* & *Staaten Land* & came nearer, tho' the breeze died away. We tacked all night & morning & were at noon in the midst of the Straights which are 7 or 8 leagues broad. The Thermometer at $53\frac{1}{2}°$, in my Cabin $56°$.

*Dec. y^e^ 31st* ♄ We stand in as it seems for *Success Bay*: after 2 o'clock a boat was sent in the Bay, with orders to look whether there are any Signs that the *Adventure* has been lately there, & to nail a Chart to a conspicuous Tree, whereon was written: *Resolution passed the Straights* Dec. ye 31st 1774.[2] We were scarce gone near the *Tierra del Fuego*-shore, when we found ourselves surrounded by at least 20 or 30 whales & hundreds of Seals. When the Whales blew to windward, we found the Effluvia of their breath stinking in a most infecting manner, & poisoning all the air with a cadaverous Smell for 2 or 3 Minutes. We likewise saw a very curious Sight: first

[1] This should be compared with Cook's summary of the natural history of Christmas Sound in *Journals*, II, 599–600. Undoubtedly there was close co-operation here. Among the new birds not mentioned in the previous pages of Forster's journal but which were described and drawn were the following: (a) *Vultur Plancus* of *Descr. Anim.*, p. 321, dated 26 December 1774; folio 33 and Lysaght, p. 281; the Southern Caracara *Polyborus plancus plancus* (Miller, 1777); the painting is the type of the species; (b) *Motacilla seticauda* of *Descr. Anim.*, p. 328, dated 26 December 1774; folios 161 and 162; Lysaght, p. 309. It is the Thorn-tailed Creeper *Aphrastura spinicauda spinicauda* (Gmelin, 1789) and (c) *Motacilla magellanica* of *Descr. Anim.*, p. 326, description dated 28 December 1774; folio 163 and Lysaght, p. 309; now the Magellanic Babbler *Scytalopus magellanicus* (Gmelin, 1789). The painting is the type of the species.

[2] Pickersgill went in the boat to look for the *Adventure* and made some observations on the natives at Success Bay. See *Journals*, II, 603 and *Voyage*, II, 510.

we observed at a distance the body of a Whale come up, & now & then a thing like a tail of a fish as it were beating the Whale; the general Run of Sailor said, it is a *Thrasher beating the Whale*: but unfortunately for these Naturalists, did the thing happen to come quite close to the Ship, & we saw plainly, that a Whale of about 30 or 40 foot long, turned on its back & kept the belly uppermost, & began to beat on both Sides the Sea with a terrible blow with his long Pectoral fins, which as well as the tail are black above & white below, the belly seemed to have longitudinal wrinkles.[1] Sometimes the Whale fairly jumped out of the Water with the whole body & fell again into it with a loud Explosion made by his Fins: nor is this Astonishing that a huge mass of about 40 or more feet long & 8 or 10 feet diameter should cause a great Explosion by its heavy fall into the Water. Sometimes there were two Whales frisking together in this manner, & certainly the greater part of the Whales we saw were all in couples, probably this is their time for Love, & this tumbling of these huge Masses are only the Preludes precedent to it; which appeared to us so awkward on account of the clumsy shape of the Animal & its slow motions; they seemed to have a flatt belly & a pyramidal 3 angular shape of the body. The Boat returned, had seen some Natives, with bracelets of platted Silverwire twisted round boma[2] Reeds, pointing at them & calling *Passerai*. No vestiges of the Adventure's having been there, were to be met with. We passed the Straights & stood on along the North-Coast of *Staaten Land*. It rained during night & part of the morning. It was foggy. We saw at the East Extremity of *Staaten-Land* several Isles, [3]one especially full of Seals, Shags & Birds. We shall come to an Anchor under the Lee of this Isle[4] & try to get some Seals & Birds. The Thermometer at $48\frac{3}{4}°$, in my Cabin 55°.

Interea magnum Sol circumvolvitur annum
Et glacialis hyems Aquilonibus asperat undas[5]

Virg. Æneid. III. 284

[1] The length and colour of the fins, as well as the animal's behaviour, suggest a Humpback whale, *Megaptera novaeangliae*. Cf. also *Voyage*, II, 509–10.

[2] The meaning is not clear: the word, indeed, is not fully legible.

[3] New Year Islands.

[4] Observatory Isle. See *Journals*, II, 604–5.

[5] 'Meanwhile the sun, in its long course round the year, rolled on, and the icy north winds of winter made the waves rough.'

1775.

Jan. ye 1st ☉ Having dropt our Anchor, Boats were hoisted out & we went ashore. It rained several Squalls. We found on the Rocks, all along the Shore of the Island, vast Numbers of a kind of Seal, which deserves to be called the *Sea-Lion* with far greater Justice, than that observed by *Lord Anson*[1] in his Voyage at *Juan Fernandez*, for the Males of this our Seal have all a shaggy long kind of Hair, from the head down to the Shoulder & fore-Fins; the Configuration of the head in the Females is somewhat related to that of a Lionness, & the tawny somewhat yellowish colour of their Hair all contribute to bring a Relation about this Seal & the Lion. The largest Males we saw were from 12 to 15 Feet long. The Lionnesses from 6 to 8. One of the middling Males after the Skin, Entrails & Blubber were taken away weighed 550lb weight; so that the largest of them certainly must have weighed 1000 or 1200 lb. They snort & roar, are polygamous, have one or two Cubs at a time; the Females bleat like Calves, & the Cubs like Lambs. They lie in Families together, with the young Cubs & such young ones as are not fit for propagation. The old Males lie separate, are very torpid & indolent but fierce, peevish & cruel. None of the others must approach their Resting-place, or else they must fight. I saw some with many gashes on their back; & when they fight they seize one another on the back & Sides with a rage & fury hardly to be described. The Females coax & fondle the Males with their Snouts about theirs, & when the old surly Bashaw groals & grumbles, or snaps at her, she prostrates herself at his Feet & endeavours to assuage his tempestuous temper. In their Amours I observed one couple, where the Female, after many blandishments, at last swam in the Cove of the beach they lay on, together with the Male; & having both frisked for many Minutes in the Sea, they both hasted on Shore, she laid herself close to the Waters-Edge on her back down & the Male immediately covered her, having everywhere many Bystanders of every Sex round them. The Copulation lasted about 8 to 10 minutes. Some Females that we killed had perfect Cubs in their Wombs, & one it is said, miscarried the Moment she was struck with a Club. We saw several Mothers carry their Cubs in their Mouths into the Water. Others were so frightened, that they ran off & left their young

[1] See p. 705, n. 4 below.

ones behind ashore. The Male & Female join muzzles, as if they were kissing one another. They now & then scratch their heads with their hind-Fins. It is highly probable that these Animals do not eat for a long time, when they are fat & highly fed; for several which were cut up on purpose, had nothing in their Stomachs; one Lion had about a cap full of Stones of the Size of a Fist & under in his Stomach, & a Sea-Lionness had a couple of Stones. These Animals are not quite new, for that able Naturalist *Steller* found, observed & described them in *Bering's Island*[1] when he & his Ship-Mates were cast away on it & he first called them Sea-Lions; and Dom *Pernetty*[2] in his Voyage to ye *Falkland Isles*, distinguishes them from the Sea-Lions of Lord *Anson* at *Juan Fernandez* & he can be so much the more be believed as Lord *Anson's* Sea-Lions & these maned one's were both in ye *Falkland islands*. Mr de *Bougainville* in his Voyage round the World, gives likewise an Account of the Animals at the *Falkland-Islands* & among them he mentions these *Sea-Lions* with Manes,[3] whom he thinks to be less in size than *Lord Anson's* kind, & whom he calls the *Sea-Elephants* on account of that Trunk they have on their Snouts, but he seems never to have seen *Lord Anson's* animal, for he mentions only 2 kinds of Seal tribe, at the *Falkland-Isles*; & as *Dr Linnaeus* has already taken in Ld Ansons Seal under the Name *Phoca leonina*, I called this *Phoca jubata*.[4] Mr *Pennant* in his *Synopsis of Quadrupeds* has certainly been misled by the name of Sea-Lion & therefore joined the Accounts of two different Animals together, which are certainly different. The Sea Lion of *Juan Fernandez* has a snout hanging down over the lower jaw & has no mane; our animal has a Mane & wants the Snout; the first has feet, & nails to it; our animal has only Fins before & behind, & the nails are

[1] See p. 706 below.

[2] Antoine-Joseph Pernety (1716–1801), chaplain on Bougainville's voyage to the Falklands in 1763. See Beaglehole's note *Journals*, II, 599, n. 5. He published *Journal historique d'un voyage fait aux îles Malouines...et deux voyages au détroit de Magellan* in 1769 and it appeared in English in 1771.

[3] L. Bougainville, *Voyage round the World* (London, 1772), p. 57. I have cited the English translation by Forster since it is that version to which Forster himself most often refers. In his translation of Chapter IV. 'Detail of the natural history of the Isles Malouines' (pp. 44–70), Forster added some useful and sometimes detailed notes, especially on the ornithology.

[4] See *Descr. Anim.*, pp. 313 (name) and 317 (description) and George's drawing No. 4 (pencil only). Forster wrongly assumed that his animal (*Phoca jubata*) was Steller's animal, which was the Northern sea lion *Eumetopias jubatus*. Forster's beast was the Southern sea lion, *Otaria byronia* Blainville, although he seems to exaggerate the size. Anson's animal was the Southern elephant seal *Mirounga leonina* (Linnaeus, 1758), as mentioned by Pernety and Bougainville.

mere small specks or indications where the Nails should be. As I make this Observation with Candour, I am conscious, this able Naturalist will as soon as he is better informed correct this trifling mistake in his useful & excellent work, for I know his Candour in acknowledging mistakes, & I am sure he will not be offended at my taking notice of it in my private Journal, for I have no intention to disoblige or to expose my Friend.[1] After having killed several Lions & Lionnesses, some few of us went up in the Isle.[2] We found there a new kind of Seal viz: the same which we found in Dusky-Bay & which *Steller* had called the *Sea-Bear* (*Phoca ursina* Linn.)[3] we killed some of them, they have a more hairy Skin, than the Lionnesses & of a blackish grey colour, are less & more attached to their Young ones, as we constantly found. We got a hard Rain-Shower. I went still higher up into the Country & at last saw some *Pinguins*[4] of which I shot one, which we drew & described; it is eatable, & pretty heavy. We shot several Hawks[5] & Turkey Buzzards,[6] which are a kind of Vulture, we likewise shot one Goose,[7] & came late on board.

Next morning[8] we found a strong wind & tide. The Capt sent the Cutter towards the Main of *Staaten Land*, for to explore there a Harbour, with orders not to land, but to sound only & to describe the port & to return immediately: this prevented me from going with them. After Breakfast the Capt went again ashore.[9] A good many young Shags were killed by our Pinnace-crew, &

[1] Forster correctly criticises Pennant here for confusing these species. In the second edition of *Synopsis of Quadrupeds* (1781) pp. 532 and 534 this was corrected. George (II, pp. 512–15) gives a long account of the Southern sea lion, supplementing his father's English description with some substantial taxonomic details and references to earlier voyage sightings.

[2] Observatory Island.

[3] *Phoca ursina* of *Descr. Anim.*, pp. 64 (New Zealand); 315 (name only) and George's drawing No. 2 (as *Phoca antarctica*, Dusky Bay, 31 March 1773). This is the Southern fur seal, *Arctocephalus australis* Zimmermann, See pp. 244 and 247 above. Cook (*Journals*, II, 605) appreciated the differences between the fur seal and the sea lion. See also *Voyage*, II, 516.

[4] Forster's description of *Aptenodytes magellanica* was dated 3 January 1775 (*Descr. Anim.*, p. 351). Drawing No. 83 is of this species (Lysaght, p. 292). See also 'Historia Aptenodytae', 1781, pp. 143–5, fig. 5 and *Vögel der Südsee*, Taf. 22, pp. 77–8. Now the Magellan Penguin *Spheniscus magellanicus* (Forster, 1781).

[5] One of these 'hawks' was described on 3 January as *Vultur Plancus* (*Descr. Anim.*, p. 323). See drawing No. 34 and Lysaght, p. 281. It was Forster's Caracara *Phalcoboenus australis* (Gmelin, 1788).

[6] No doubt the Chilean Turkey Vulture *Cathartes aura jota* (Molina).

[7] Lesser Kelp Goose.

[8] This was, of course, 1 January 1775 civilian time.

[9] i.e. to Observatory Island.

Figure 42. Birds of the South Atlantic.
(a) Upland Goose *Chloephaga picta picta* (Gm).
Drawing by George Forster in B.M. (N.H.) – 'Zoological Drawings', ff. 65 & 71.

Figure 42. Birds of the South Atlantic.
(b) South Georgia Teal *Anas georgica* Gm.
Drawing by George Forster in B.M. (N.H.) – 'Zoological Drawings', ff. 65 & 71.

half of them put in the Pinnace. We shot several Geese about 5, & several Gulls, Hawks & a kind of new Bird, white as Snow, sitting on the Rocks, with cloven feet, the external Toe however is somewhat joined to the middle one. The bill is strong, compressed on the Sides, arched above & below towards the point, & from the Forehead to the ovated Nostrils covered with a kind of plates of a corneous structure. The Face is partly naked & covered with white small Warts, the Eyes a reddish brown. In Short it is a quite new & ordinary bird, of a new Genus, which I called *Chionis lactea.*[1] We killed likewise several Pinguins & two *Quebranta-huissos.*[2]

*Jan. ye 2^d^* ☽ In the Afternoon we returned ashore, killed 4 Geese[3] & 2 new Ducks,[4] one of the Geese, which my Son shot was a new one.[5] A Crane[6] had been seen & a Curlew.[7] We found immense Quantities of young Shags & Pinguins & filled the Boat again. I shot 5 white Birds[8] more. All this day several Boats had been busy in killing Seals & taking their Blubber & several Skins & Harcelets in. We returned late on board, it blew a fresh Gale. The Tide & Current hindered our Cutter[9] from coming back & they came still later on board, having shot 5 *Racehorses* which we found to be a true large Duck, one of them weighing 16 lb. The males have a whitish head somewhat speckled with grey. White Eyebrows, Secondary Quillfeathers & belly; orange yellow bill, feet & two naked knobs on the Wing. The Rest is all of a greyish brown, the Female is of a darker hue & has no white head but for the rest

[1] Sheath-bill *Chionis alba* (Gmelin, 1789). See 2 January, see n. 8 below.

[2] Giant Petrel.

[3] Forster's description of *Anas ganta* was dated 2 January 1775 (*Descr. Anim.*, p.336). George's folio 66 is of this species (Lysaght, p. 288). It is the Lesser Kelp Goose *Chloephaga hybrida hybrida* (Molina, 1782). A female specimen, undoubtedly from the voyage, was described by Sparrman under the name *Anas magellanica* in *Mus. Carls*, 1787, No. XXXVII.

[4] Forster's description of *Anas lophyra* was based upon these birds (*Descr. Anim.*, p. 340) as was George's folio 78 (Lysaght, p. 290). It is now the Crested Duck *Anas specularioides specularioides* King, 1828.

[5] Forster's description of *Anas picta* was of this new goose (*Descr. Anim.*, p. 333). George's drawing No. 65 is the type of the species (Lysaght, p. 288). It is now the Upland Goose *Chloephaga picta picta* (Gmelin, 1788). See fig. 43 (a).

[6] Not specifically identifiable.

[7] Perhaps the Black-faced Ibis which was collected and described on 3 January 1775. See 708, n. 2 below.

[8] Sheath-bill *Chionis alba* (Gmelin, 1789). This was Forster's *Chionis lactea* of *Descr. Anim.*, p. 330. George's folio 125 was based on specimens taken this day (Lysaght, p. 301). See also *Vögel der Südsee*, Taf. 20, p. 77.

[9] Gilbert led this expedition. Cook called his harbour appropriately New Year's Harbour. See *Journals*, II, 606.

it corresponds with the Male. I called it *Anas Pteneres*[1] because it accelerates its motion by flapping the Wings on the Water like Oars. Next morning it blew fresh, but however a Couple of boats were sent a shore to take the Blubber of the Seals. I remained with my Son on board & described & drew the New animals. Mr Sparman went ashore, shot one Goose & got a new plant.

*Jan. ye 3^d^* ♂ The Officers got leave to go ashore & I went in the Pinnace & shot 4 Geese & a Duck. One Curlew of the kind Linnaeus calls *Tantalus*[2] was shot, which we drew & described next day. We returned very late on board.[3] All boats were hoisted in. Next morning at 3 o'clock the Anchor was hove. At 4 o'clock we set sail, & came to the NE Extremity of Staaten Land & found that these Isles we were at are yet a good way off from the *Cape of St John* & that *Father Feuilli's* Map is quite wrong;[4] his View of the South East side of *Staaten-Land* is tolerable. We met with sudden Gusts of Wind & Squalls & split some Sails. The Thermometer at 50°, in my Cabin 57°.

*Jan. ye 4th* ☿ We steered afterwards ESE & took our departure from the Land.[5] Saw several *Quebranta huessos* & yellow-billed Albatrosses & a few grey or blue Petrels. The Thermometer at 54½. The Sun shining upon it, in my Cabin 55°. We carried away in a sudden Squall our Main top Gallant Mast & the Starboard Maintop Studding Sail Boom. The same Squall carried 3 of my Shirts off, which were hung up for drying.

[1] Forster's description of *Anas pteneres* was based on these birds (*Descr. Anim.*, p. 338) as was George's folio 68 (Lysaght, p. 289). Now the Magellanic Flightless Steamer Duck *Tachyeres pteneres* (Forster, 1844).

[2] *Tantalus melanops* of *Descr. Anim.*, p. 332 and folio 117 (Lysaght, p. 300) were based upon this bird. Now the Black-faced Ibis *Theristicus caudatus melanopis* (Gmelin, 1789). See also *Vögel der Südsee*, Taf. 13, p. 74.

[3] Forster never got beyond Observatory Island which, wrote George (II, p. 521), 'notwithstanding its small size' abounded in birds. Forster was clearly chagrined at the lack of opportunity to go to the 'Main of Staaten Land', George (II, p. 517) also includes some geological notes on Observatory Island absent from the Journal.

[4] Louis Ecouches Feuillet (1660–1732), Franciscan botanist, astronomer and traveller, who published *Journal des observations physiques, mathématiques et botaniques, sur les côtes Orientales de l'Amérique Méridionale, et aux Indes Occidentales, et dans un autre, voiage fait... à la Nouvelle Espagne et aux Iles de l'Amérique* (Paris, 1725). He went round the Horn in 1707–11. George (II, p. 511) was rather critical of Feuillet's map of the New Year Islands. See also *Journals*, II, 609, n. 1.

[5] '...in order to pass our third summer season to the southward', *Voyage*, II, 522. Cook (*Journals*, II, 608–11) is much fuller on the difficulties of rounding and charting Staten Island and the adjacent islands. Both Forsters lack Cook's summary of scientific findings (*Journals*, II, 611–15) which was, however, clearly based upon their findings and a free exchange of information. It should be read (including Beaglehole's identifications) in conjunction with the Forsters' detailed day-to-day notes and observations above.

*Jan. ye 5th* ♃ The wind fresh, somewhat rainy. See the same Albatrosses & blue Petrils. The Thermometer at 44°, in my Cabin 53½°. The Ships Crew refuse to eat the Pinguins which have been boiled in the Copper, tho' the Captain, I & many Officers tasted & found them very good.[1]

*Jan. ye 6th* ♀ Changed the Course, run East. Gentle breeze. Few birds of the Above Kinds and a few storm finches[2] appear. In the beforenoon of the 5th a Halo was observed round the Sun 22° Semidiameter, dark in the middle, white in the circle, with some blue & other Colours of the Rainbow.[3] The weather mild. Breeze gentle. The Thermometer at 43°, in my Cabin 52½°.

*Jan. ye 7th* ♄ We expect to see Land in a few days, if there is such a thing as the *Gulf of St Sebastian.* I doubt of this Land; but believe there is some Isle or Isles, which form *La Roche's Straights* seen by the Navigator of that Name in 1675 & *D'Anville* puts down an *Isle de St Pierre* seen by the Ship *Lion* in 1756. *D'Anville* puts it in about 55° 35° W. Longitude from London but Mr *Dalrymple* in his Map of the Atlantic Ocean lays *la Roche's* Island, (which he declares to have been seen in 1756 by the Ship *Lion*) down in 45° W. Longit. from *London*, perhaps in order to bring it nearer to the Land about *St. Sebastian's Gulph.* Its Latitude is 54° South & some odd minutes.[4] But as this Isle is however East of *Falkland Isles* & Mr *Bougainville* affirms that yearly in Autumn a good Number of Geese arrived at the Isle and in *Accaron Bay* (which is most to the East) with an Easterly wind, I am apt to think that this may be considered as a collateral proof of the Existence of some Land to the East of *Falkland-Islands.*[5] We shall soon clear up this point at least. At 8 o'clock in the Evening we changed the Course to

[1] Cf. *Journals*, II, 615, n. 2.

[2] Storm Petrels, species unknown.

[3] Cf. Clerke in *Journals*, II, 617; *Voyage*, II, 522 and *Observations*, p. 117.

[4] Beaglehole, in that critical vein he reserves for Dalrymple, deals with the Gulf of St. Sebastian problem (*Journals*, II, ci and 615, n. 1) Forster here is simply echoing Cook's justifiable reservations about Dalrymple's geography, although George (II, p. 523) gives Dalrymple more credit for honest hard work than Beaglehole does. Antoine de la Roche, London merchant, was in these waters in 1675 and, rounding the Horn, was blown eastwards, probably discovering South Georgia. D'Anville the cartographer, we have already met (p. 481, n. 3 above) in connection with Forster's reading of Magellan's voyage while looking for the Marquesas. The Spanish merchant ship *Léon*, rounding the Horn in 1756, was also blown and carried eastwards, probably sighting South Georgia. D'Anville, whose caution Beaglehole admires, put the *Léon's* 'Ile de S. Pierre' into his hemispheric world map of 1761. Dalrymple collected all the known evidence into his *Collection of Voyages, chiefly in the South Atlantick Ocean* (1775). For these notes I have drawn heavily on Beaglehole (*Journals*, II, 616–17).

[5] Bougainville, *Voyage*, p. 60.

NW which with the Variation makes NNW & better; & with the leeway nearly North, so that being arrived in the Meridian of NW point of the Gulf *of St. Sebastian* as laid down by Mr *Dalrymple* & not finding any land, we haul up Northward[1] in Quest of the Land seen by the Ship *Lion* in 1756 as laid down by *D'Anville* in his *Mappe-monde*. We have a great Swell a head & our Ship pitches very disagreably. The Thermometer at $39\frac{2}{3}°$, in my Cabin 44°.

*Jan y^e^ 8th* ☉ The breeze continues & the disagreable pitching of the Ship likewise. We saw the black & whiterumped, the blue, & the large Sooty Petrels, with yellowbilled Albatrosses & some *Quebranta huessos.*[2] The weather mild, but the wind is gone more round & we are obliged to go NNE. The Thermometer at 44°, in my Cabin $49\frac{1}{2}°$.

*Jan. y^e^ 9th* ☽ Very fine & mild weather, little wind, & very little hopes of seeing Land: many dread to fall in with Land, for fear that this might retard our early arrival at the Cape: but as a new Land might perhaps have new plants, bird & fish, & as the little Store of Brandy will of course necessitate the Capt to return in time to the Cape, I am quite impartial, especially as the new Land might probably give us new Supplies of fresh Meat, & as hardly anybody is so sick on board, that a longer stay out at Sea, might be prejudicial to him. The hopes soon to put an End to all our Disagreable Situations, & wants, to hear agreable news from our Friends & Relations, to have soon the Opportunity of embracing all what is Dear to us, revive our Spirits, & rekindle in our breasts the social tender feelings of Father, Husband, Brother, Friend & Relation; which by a long disuse, among the Stern Aspect of the boisterous Sea, the dashing of the enraged Waves, & the Fury of the Winds, among the Sight of so various & strange Nations, the harsh Manners of rough, cursing, & often cruel Sailors, & the unnatural Life we lead after so long an Absence from any European Port have almost extinguished every Spark of humanity & the Softer feelings of social Life, & made us, as if it were, insensible to the Enjoyments & Comforts of Life: were it not for this sweet congenial hope, we should certainly feel the weight of our more than disagreable Situations, by far more. In the Evening

[1] See *Journals*, II, 617.

[2] Respectively the White-chinned Petrel; Wilson's Storm Petrel; *Pachyptila* spp; Great-winged Petrel; Grey-headed Mollymawk and Giant Petrel.

at 10 o'clock, the whole deck was moist, from a very heavy dew, which commonly has been reckoned as a certain mark of the Vicinity of some Land: how far this will prove true, time must show.[1] Fog in the morning. Saw some Seaweeds, a Seal & a few common Albatrosses, blue Petrils, & a few yellowbilled Albatrosses. The Thermometer at $43\frac{2}{3}$, in my Cabin 49°.

Jan. y^{e} 10th ♂ At 3 o clock in the Afternoon we went about, the Course NE; at 3 o clock in the Morning the Course was again altered & again at 8 o'clock to NE. Saw yellowbilled Albatrosses & Seaweeds. The Thermometer at 43°, in my Cabin 51°.

Jan. y^{e} 11th ☿ The Course at Noon EbN. We saw in the Afternoon several common, yellowbilled & sooty Albatrosses, some Quebranta huessos, one Pintada & several blue, whiterumped & some black Petrels. The Thermometer at 43°, in my Cabin 50°.

Jan. ye 12th ♃ We have now very little hopes of seeing any Land before we reach the Cape of Good Hope.[2] The Quantity & variety of the above Sea-Fowls is rather a Sign of being pretty far out at Sea & remote from any Land, contrary to what former Navigators had laid down. In the Afternoon a Pinguin & some Seaweeds were seen. Fogg & rain in the Afternoon & night & morning. The Thermometer at $40\frac{1}{4}$°, in my Cabin 49°.

Jan. y^{e} 13th ♀ Though we are to the South of *Halley's* track,[3] who in 1700 on Jan: y^{e} 30th & Febr. y^{e} 3^{d} *Saw abundance of Ice*; we find here however as yet no Ice. We sail East & are already passed the Land which is supposed to include the Gulf of St *Sebastian* & find no Land. Easy mild weather. Some yellowbilled Albatrosses & blue Petrels attend the Ship. In the night calm. In the Morning a Fogg, & the Wind East. At 6 o'clock in the Morning Course SSE. The Thermometer at 40°, in my Cabin 46°.

Jan. ye 14th ♄ We put about at noon, Course NNE. A good many blue Petrels & some yellowbilled Albatrosses appear. A fresh Gale, the weather very hazy; perhaps the wind blows over a Field of Ice, which brings us cold & foggy weather. About 6 o'clock in the Evening a white snowy Petrel[4] was seen, whom we never

[1] On fogs see *Observations*, pp. 108–09.

[2] Cf. Cook's *Journals*, II, 618.

[3] In part reproduced from Dalrymple's, 'Chart of the Ocean between South America and Africa . . .' (1769) as fig. 80 in *Journals*, II, 616. Dr Edmond Halley (1656–1742), eminent mathematician and astronomer, who voyaged scientifically in the *Paramour* pink (1698 and in 1699–1700) in the South Atlantic. See also *Voyage*, II, 523. Halley, as scientist in charge of a naval vessel, had experienced a number of problems with his naval officers.

[4] Snow Petrel *Pagodroma nivea* (Forster, 1777). Cf. *Journals*, II, 618.

observed, unless Great Quantity of Ice was near at hand. The same Bird was seen again in the morning & some Seaweeds floating. Saw two Quebranta huessos, several yellowbilled & sooty Albatrosses, blue, whiterumped, & black Petrels, Pintadas, & other aquatic Birds in great Abundance. At about 10 o'clock an Ice Island was seen a head or rather something to windward. The wind was abating. The Ice appeared like Land. The Thermometer at 35½°, in my Cabin 43°.

*Jan. ye 15th* ☉ The bets run high, whether it is Land or Ice. Some laid it was Ice ten to one. Others 5 to one that it is Land. It looks through the Glass like Land, covered on top by Snow; & some black Specks or Bushes appear below in the Snow. Before the Isle there are steep broken Rocks,[1] on both Sides the South & North appear broken Lands. We are quite becalmed. But hope soon to have a wind. If the Object before us be Land it must be a very high one, for we are at least 10 Leagues off, & the more we approach, the more it seems extended. It must likewise be colder than *Tierra del Fuego*, where we saw Snow in the latter End of December; but here even in the middle of January, all the tops of hills are covered with Snow,[2] and Pliny's Saying will still be better applicable to it, than to any other land:

Pars mundi damnata a rerum natura, & densa mersa caligine.[3]

However there may be some refreshments gotten, for though all the Appearances were against the barren Rocks of *Tierra del Fuego*, it gave us nevertheless Wood, Water, Greens & fine fresh Provisions, & a variety of New Plants & Birds. Many a thing to morrow will be cleared up.

La Roche saw in 1675 in 54° 20′ South Lat. an Isle & a passage between it, & another Land to the East, which makes *La Roche's Strait*: & it seems, that tho' we are much more to the East by 3 or 4 Degrees, the Latitude however is nearly the same, & makes it probable, that this is his Land, & perhaps part of the Gulph of *St Sebastian.*[4] The very pinching cold we feel in this place, the

[1] Possibly the Willis islands.

[2] South Georgia, as Beaglehole (*Journals*, II, cii) notes, is surrounded by extremely cold waters throughout the year. The submarine Scotia Arc on which S. Georgia lies, connecting it with South America and Graham Land, is broken between the Burdwood Bank and South Georgia allowing cold antarctic surface water to flow to the east and south of South Georgia where the Antarctic Convergence swings northwards. See also *Observations*, p. 30.

[3] See p. 692, n. 1 above. George (II, 525) preferred Shakespeare here.

[4] See Beaglehole's and James Burney's notes, *Journals*, II, 617, n. 2.

Snow we see on the tops of the Hills, & the Snow which has been falling all the morning & part of the Night, make it probable, that the Land before us extends a good way to the South, & that this Connexion of cold Regions, full of Snow & Ice causes this alteration in the climate, so much different from that of *Cape Horn* & *Tierra del Fuego*, tho' they be more to the South, than the place we are now in. It snows continually, blows fresh, & we have a great Sea, which makes the Ship pitch very disagreably.[1] The Thermometer at 34½°; in my Cabin 41°.

Jan. yᵉ 16ᵗʰ ☽ The gale freshens, the weather is still foggy & thick & good many blue Petrels attend even in bad weather. The Storm increases, the Sea runs high, the Snow makes the Air thick, we cannot see ten yards before us, happily the wind is off shore. If a Capᵗ, some Officers & a Crew were convicted of some heinous crimes, they ought to be sent by way of punishment to these inhospitable cursed Regions, for to explore & survey them. The very thought to live here a year fills the whole Soul with horror & despair. God! what miserable wretches must they be, that live here in these terrible Climates. Charity lets me hope, that human nature was never thought so low by his Maker, as to be doomed to lead or rather to languish out so miserable a life.

> ...*Aspera ponti*
> *Interclusit hyems, & terruit Auster euntes*
> ...*toto sonverunt aethere nimbi.*
>
> Virg. Æneid. II. 110. 111. 113.[2]

Yesterday at noon we saw several Birds surround the Ship, one kind attracted my Curiosity viz: a new *Pinguin*,[3] black above or rather blueish grey, white below, with a red bill, & white band going round the head just in the very *nucha*. I shot one which came close to the Ship, but the Capᵗ would not hoist a boat out to take it up. God knows, whether I shall ever see another bird of this kind! It snowed part of the night, & blew fresh. After 4 o'clock we set again Sails & saw the Land. We were to windward of the Isle we had seen on Saturday.[4] The Land was now all over covered with Snow, & extended a great way. Some of it was right a head.

[1] Wales (*Journals*, II, 619) took a reading of 42° during a 'Lee Lurch'.

[2] 'Rough stormy seas held them back and a south wind terrified them as they went...the storm clouds thundered throughout the air'.

[3] Gentoo Penguin *Pygoscelis papua* (Forster, 1781).

[4] Willis Islands. See *Journals*, II, 619, n. 3.

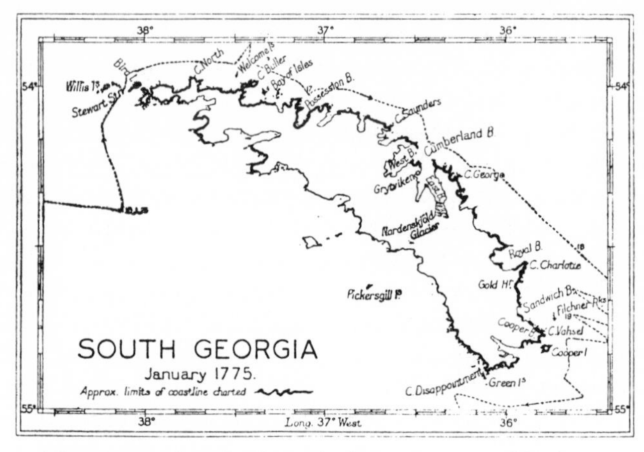

Figure 43. South Georgia January 1775 ★(81).

A vast number of the common, the yellowbilled & the sooty Albatrosses are seen, some Quebranta huessos, numbers of blue & whiterumped Petrils, black Shearwaters, & Port Egmont Hens. The Thermometer at 34°, in my Cabin 39½°.

Jan. ye 17th ♂ Bore away at 3 o'clock for the Straits between two small Islands off the great land. We were in the Straights[1] about 5 o'clock; on the Isle next to the Shore innumerable Numbers of Birds of various kinds were seen. We observed Seals, common, yellowbilled & Sooty Albatrosses, Shags, Port Egmont Hens & Quebranta-huessos, whiterumped & blue Petrels, Pintadas & black Shearwaters, small Divers,[2] & larger ones with a reddish brown streak along the both Sides of the Neck, Pinguins of two Kinds[3] & various other birds: the *Bird Isle*[4] was lower than that on the West Side; & it was green, except w[h]ere the steep rocks appeared nacked. Saw several Porpesses, with large white Spots or blotches. We sailed away along the Coast E.bS. & in the Night brought to. In the Morning half past 3 o'clock made Sail again, various Courses chiefly Easterly. Off the Coast there are soundings at about 2 or 3 miles, in the harbours is deep water. After breakfast the

[1] Stewart Strait.

[2] South Georgian Diving Petrel *Pelecanoides georgicus* Murphy and Harper, 1916.

[3] Both the King Penguin and the Gentoo Penguin breed on South Georgia.

[4] It was, in fact, so named by Cook (*Journals*, II, 620) 'on accou^t of the vast numbers that were upon it'.

Cutter was hoisted out & we went ashore with the Capt: we sounded here & there with 34 fathom but had no Ground: killed several ursine Seals, & a Sea Lion of Ld Ansons Kind, with Nails & Feet before & Fins behind but no Crest on the Nose, measured 13 Feet.[1] We killed several new Pinguins[2] blueish-black above, below silky white, bill red below, the point of the undermandible black: behind the Ears, two large ovated Gold-yellow Spots ending in a line under the throat running out & causing a yellow Spot, which is brightest under the throat & faints away into the white colour of the belly, all the yellow included in a black line; the back towards the tail black, head & throat black, feet black, tail pointed, wings white below, with a black oblong spot at the point. We killed a coupled of Ducks[3] with yellow bills & blackish green Legs; there are at the Cape such ones: killed a common Tern[4] (*Sterna hirundo*) & a new Lark.[5] The whole Bay[6] is included by high steep Rocks; wherever at the bottom of it a valley comes down, it is filled up with Snow changed into Ice, ending at the Water's Edge & breaking dayly off in pieces, with a great Noise. The Rocks a blueish, heavy Irone-Stone, or as they call it in Derbyshire *Dunstone*.[7] No other Vegetables but a grass which we found at New Years Isle, & a common Burnet, of both very little;[8] the rest either bare Rock or Snow & Ice. The Rock crumbles in Shingle. We saw Shags,[9] Guls,[10] Port Egmont-Hens,[11]

[1] See p. 705, n. 4 above. It was the Southern elephant seal. See also Cook's comment (*Journals*, II, 622). The 'ursine Seal' was the Southern fur seal.

[2] Forster's description of *Aptenodytes patagonica* was dated 18 January 1775 (*Descr. Anim.*, p. 347). George's drawing No. 81 was based upon one of these specimens (Lysaght, p. 291). See also 'Historia Aptenodytae', 1781, pp. 137–40, fig. 2. It is the King Penguin *Aptenodytes patagonicus* Miller, 1778. See also George's notes, *Voyage*, II, 528–9.

[3] Forster's description of *Anas xanthorhycha* was based on these birds (*Descr. Anim.*, p. 342) as was George's drawing no. 71, which is the type (Lysaght, p. 289). It is the South Georgia Teal *Anas georgica*, Gmelin, 1789. See fig. 42 (b).

[4] Probably a specimen of the Wreathed Tern *Sterna vittata georgiae*.

[5] The Antarctic Pipit *Anthus antarcticus* Cabanis. It was neither described nor illustrated by the Forsters. See also Beaglehole's identifications in *Journals*, II, 622, notes.

[6] Possession Bay.

[7] 'The rocks consisted of a bluish grey slate, in horizontal strata, of which many fragments every where covered the beaches. As far as we were able to examine them, they contained no other minerals of any kind; the whole country being useless, and frightfully barren in every respect', *Voyage*, II, 529–30.

[8] See Beaglehole's identifications (*Journals*, II, 622, n. 1) and *Voyage*, II, 529.

[9] Perhaps the South Georgian Blue-eyed Shag, *Phalacrocorax atriceps georgianus* Lönnberg.

[10] Perhaps the Southern Black-backed Gull *Larus dominicanus* Lichtenstein, 1823.

[11] Southern Skua.

Quackerbirds[1] or Sooty Albatrosses, whiterumped Petrels[2] & several other birds. The Capt took a view of the harbour & then took *Possession in his Britannick Majesties Name & His Heirs for ever*: hoisted a Flag on the Land, & fired 3 Volleys,[3] & then returned on board. The Thermometer at 36°, in my Cabin 42½°.

Jan. ye 18th ☿ We sail EbS along the Coast, with a moderate Breeze. The Coast is always similar to itself & varies not in appearance. The Rocks close to the Sea are barren & Steep; a few gentle sloping Spots have a little verdure, the tops are all Snowy & the bottom of harbours solid Masses of Snow & Ice. We brought to during Night; it was calm, & in the morning made Sail again. We see as is supposed the SE Extremity of this Land,[4] which therefore will prove to be an Isle of about 40 Leagues long, lying NW & SE. The appearance of it every where alike. But I must confess that the eternal Snow & Ice we see on this Land & its high Mountains rather imply either that this Land is connected to one of greater Extent or that in its vicinity is more Land of a very great Extent: how far this Conjecture will prove true time must show.[5] We see a head a thick Bank of Clouds & several Birds as before. The Thermometer at 38°, in my Cabin 43½°.

Jan. ye 19th ♃ We stand on & off all day & night & the next morning. In the morning high Land was seen to the SE.[6] At the Extremity of the Isle is a small Isle.[7] Vast Flights of Shags come off, great Quantities of blue Petrels are observed, & several other birds as before. Clear weather. The Thermometer at 37½°, in my Cabin 42°.

Jan. ye 20th ♀ One Shag was so shot that he fell into the Ship. They are of the kind I had called *Pelecanus carunculatas*.[8] Yellow billed

[1] Light-mantled Sooty Albatross.

[2] Wilson's Storm Petrel. Since Forster, George and Sparrman all went on this expedition, landing three times, it is clear that all three worked independently, later perhaps comparing notes with Cook, who seems to have drawn heavily on them for his natural history (*Journals*, II, 622–3).

[3] This volley George (II, p. 529) tells us, perhaps with some incipient republican humour, gave 'greater weight to this assertion [of possession]; and the barren rocks re-echoed with the sound, to the utter amazement of seals and pinguins, the inhabitants of these newly discovered dominions'.

[4] Perhaps Cape Vahsel.

[5] Forster is wrestling here with the problem of how glaciers and ice islands (bergs) could come from anything but a continent. Cook was having the same problem (*Journals*, II, 625).

[6] Cf. *Journals*, II, 626.

[7] Cooper Island. Cook was now off the south-eastern end of South Georgia. To follow the ship's navigation see *Journals*, II, 623–5.

[8] King Cormorant *Phalacrocorax albiventer albiventer*.

Albatrosses, whiterumped Petrels, Pintadas & other Birds attend the Ship. We are allmost becalmed & though there was a little wind, we brought to during night; in the morning we made again Sail along the South Side of the Land, till we saw at distance a point, which we had seen on the other side[1] & therefore we turned about & stood off again, for the high Land we had seen two days ago, to the SE. We were again becalmed. The Thermometer at 40°, in my Cabin 43°.

Jan. ye 21st ♄ At noon we got a fresh breeze, which in a few hours increased in a strong gale, so that we were obliged to close-reef our top Sails; & even soon to hand them, & strike the top Gallant Yards. In the Evening the wind abated; after midnight we got a calm & had rain & foggy weather, all the morning very little wind. Vast Numbers of blue Petrels attend the Ship. The thermometer at 39°, in my Cabin 49°.[2]

Jan. ye 22d ☉ Still foggy & very little wind, & this continues all the night & next morning. Great Numbers of blue Petrels, & yellow billed Albatrosses are observed; I saw in the morning several Pinguins,[3] of a middling Size, long pointed Tails, black above, white below, the white goes from the bill above the Eyes to the Sides of the Neck, Breast & Belly. Their cry something like that of a Goose. The Thermometer at 35°, in my Cabin 45°.

Jan. ye 23d ☽ We find the weather still foggy & are uncertain where the Land lies, which was seen, when we were at the New Isle.[4] We are obliged to stand on & off, & grope as it were in the dark. In the morning we saw a Seal, Pinguins & several hundreds of Shags. About noon we saw the breakers scarcely half a mile a head in a clear interval, & saw several Rocks & some Land behind it. Our Officers say we have gone round this Land. We immediately hauled our wind. The Thermometer at 37½°, in my Cabin 44°.

Jan. ye 24th ♂ The weather moist & foggy, almost calm. Stand on & off. In the morning we saw vast Flights of Shags & Pinguins were seen round the Ship. It cleared up in the beforenoon & we saw the land[5] on our Larboardside, though but in a fog. The Thermometer at 39°, in my Cabin 49°.

[1] Cf. Cook, *Journals*, II, 625. They were south-west of Cape Disappointment off which lie the Green Islets, first seen, George (II, p. 531) tells us on 16 January.

[2] Again we lack the usual summary of a new discovery. Cook (*Journals*, II, 625–6) and George (*Voyage*, II, 532–3) give one. For the naming of this discovery see p. 723, n. 2. below.

[3] Perhaps Gentoo Penguins.

[4] This 'land' was seen on 19 January, apparently first by Clerke.

[5] Clerke's rocks about 35–40 miles ESE of Cooper's Island. See *Journals*, II, 628, n. 1.

Jan. ye 25th ☿ In the Evening we had a clear interval & saw both Lands, the Isle we had gone round & the single we had been groping for in the Fog.[1] We saw Shags & Penguins, vast flights of blue Petrels & yellowbilled Albatrosses. In the morning at 4 o'clock, we made our course East & E.b.S; a great Swell comes from the Northward. The fog continues. The Thermometer at $38\frac{1}{3}°$, in my Cabin 48°.

Jan. y^e 26th ♃ We have a fine fresh breeze & it clears gradually up. The next morning the Course SSE & SbE. Saw several blue Petrels & yellow Albatrosses. The Thermometer at 44°, in my Cabin 48°. Till this day we had at our Table fresh Meat from the Penguins & Geese, which we had roasted & put into melted Lard. Now we return to the old Diet of Salt Meat. But the hopes that we shall in about 6 weeks be at the Cape & there refresh, makes all easy.[2]

Jan. y^e 27th ♀ The wind aft & we go on very well having a great Swell following us. Saw blue Petrels, yellowbilled Albatrosses, & several Fulmars,[3] with a Pinguin. The Thermometer at $38\frac{1}{2}°$, in my Cabin 44°.

Jan. y^e 28th ♄ We altered the course at noon, going again eastward on account of the thick fog that came on. It cleared up soon & we went Southward again. In the Evening several Fulmars were seen, which in high Latitudes are forerunners of Ice, & likewise some Pinguins[4] were observed, & at last between 6 & 7 o'clock we saw two large Ice Islands & a good many loose Ice. We were then a good while going East on acc^t of the Fog.[5] Fog & wet weather continue all night. This morning several Ice-Islands were seen. We observed several snowy Petrels & still more blue ones, & some Pintadas. The Thermometer at 35°, in my Cabin 42°. Saw several Whales.

Jan. ye 29th ☉ The Ice Islands still surround us. The Course ENE.

[1] Here we might note that Hodges also attempted some views of South Georgia, receiving for them – especially the one engraved by S. Smith for Cook's *Voyage towards the South Pole*, pl. XXXIV – George's high praise for his 'very masterly' execution, 'in that great style which is peculiar to him, and which animates all his views of savage countries' (*Voyage*, II, 530). Beaglehole reproduces two Hodges views of South Georgia as figs 76 and 77 in *Journals*, II.

[2] Cf. George's comments on the same subject, *Voyage*, II, 534.

[3] Antarctic Fulmar.

[4] Perhaps, in this latitude, Chinstrap Penguins *Pygoscelis antarctica* (Forster, 1781).

[5] Cook, on this day, ventured 'to assert that that extensive coast, laid down in Mr Dalrymple's Chart of the Ocean between Africa and America, and Gulph of St Sebastian does not exist'. To his predecessors, however, he gave the credit for leading him to the discovery of South Georgia. See *Journals*, II, 629.

We saw much Ice & went WNW. Fulmars, Snowy Petrels & blue ones are seen. The Thermometer at 35°, in my Cabin at 40½°.

*Jan. ye 30th* ☽ The wind freshened, we see Whales, white & blue Petrels, several Pinguins & large Pieces of Ice. In the morning foggy. We have several Patients, who are afflicted with colds & Rheumatisms & are suddenly taken with fainting Fits, probably for want of Animal Spirits, all the organic nourishing particles of our Food being now almost destroyed by the long keeping.[1] The Thermometer at 35°, in my Cabin 39°.

*Jan. ye 31st* ♂ Still foggy, & the Air moist. The Capt will no more go to the South & wants to come from the West upon *Bouvets* Land,[2] so that he may not miss it, in order to see how far this Land is true or not. In the night we passed many Ice Islands & Pinguins, & about 4 o'clock in the morning we saw a great deal of small loose Ice driving in a compact body: at 7 o'clock we saw Land NEbN,[3] & going towards it till 8 o'clock we sounded & had bottom 170fth.[4] We then put about, & hardly had we done that, when we saw again Land to the SSE,[5] which we had it seems passed near enough in the Night. The Land a stern or to the North, was a high projecting Rock & behind it were immense high hills far beyond the clouds, all covered with Snow.[6] We saw the Shores with Snow & before it Ice. The Land a head was covered with Snow. We saw white, blue, & whiterumped Petrels, Pintadas, Fulmars, Shags & Pinguins. The Thermometer at 35½°, in my Cabin 41½°.

*Febr. ye 1st* ☿ At one o'clock afternoon we put about the Ship &

[1] George (II, p. 535) reports this, adding that the crew 'were at present thoroughly tired of this dreadful climate, and exhausted by perpetual watching and attendance, which the frequency and sudden appearance of dangers required'.

[2] See p. 195, n. 1 above and *Journals*, II, lii–liii.

[3] Turning now to Milton to support his view of the wild unexpected new land before them, George (II, p. 535) recounts something of the consternation this discovery invoked since, 'as we steered to the northward, we were in hopes of soon reaching a milder climate, fully persuaded that no further obstacles lay in wait to try our patience. But we were again doomed to experience disappointment, and discovered another frozen country...'.

[4] Cf. *Journals*, II, 631.

[5] 'This being the southernmost extremity of the land [of all that now newly discovered] my father named it Southern Thule, a name which captain Cook has preserved', *Voyage*, II, 536. There are three islands Thule, Cook and Bellingshausen, the most southerly part of the South Sandwich Islands.

[6] Bristol Island, called by Cook Cape Bristol. It rises to 3600 feet. George (II, p. 536) writes that 'it was agreed by all present, that the perpendicular height of this mountain could not be far short of two miles'. See Hodges's view, *Journals*, II, fig. 78.

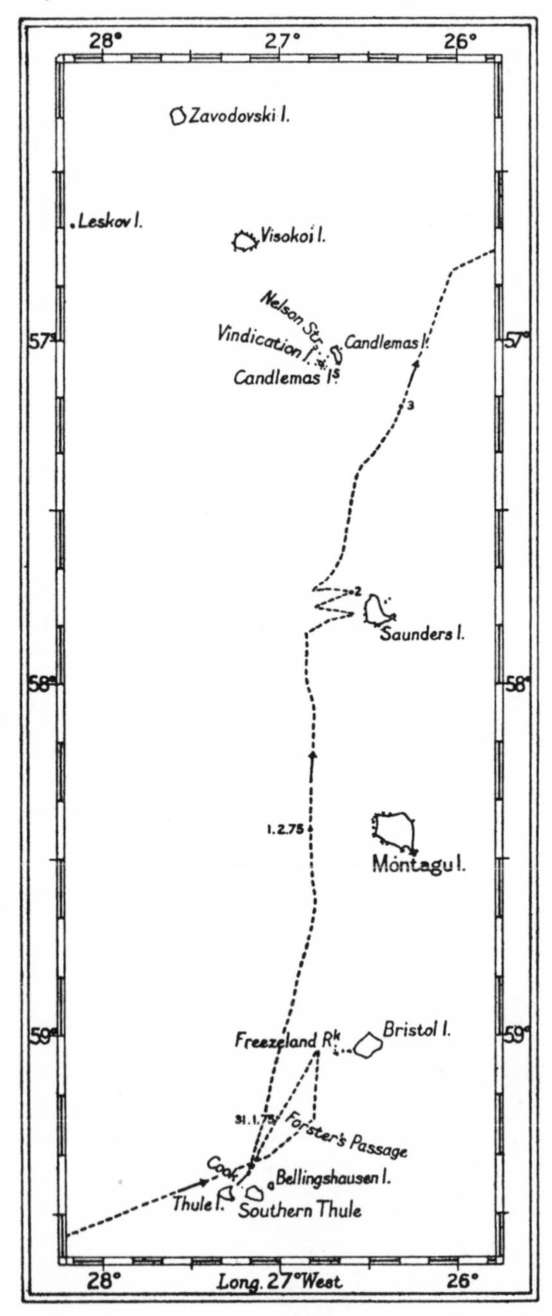

Figure 44. The South Sandwich Islands ★(82).

stood NBW & as far as the wind would allow. At about 5 o'clock we saw the Rock which projected before the Land (& which was called *Freezland's-head* after a Foremast-man of that name)[1] right a breast to leeward at about 4 leagues distance. But is soon grew hazy again & after six o'clock it snowed. We saw yellowbilled Albatrosses, Fulmars, Pintadas, white, blue & whiterumped Petrels, with many Pinguins about the Ship. We endeavour to get to the North of this Land, for fear if we should go on its South Side to the Eastward, we might not be able to come out again, or at least have much to beat to windward in a bad Season & dark nights.[2] It is enough to know the Extent of its Northern shores. Perhaps it is not so large neither as we are now afraid of. Before we tacked about 1 o'clock, we saw the Southern Land bearing from SbE to EbN in various hills, but in a haze at a good distance. We had very little wind all night & came in the morning abreast of a land probably connected with the former by a deep bay.[3] In the beforenoon almost calm. The same birds as before. The Thermometer at $33\frac{1}{2}°$ in my Cabin $40\frac{1}{2}°$.

Febr. y^e 2^d ♃ We had very little wind all night, in the morning we stood East for the furthermost Land,[4] but could not weather it, & put therefore about. Observed white & blue Petrels & Pinguins. It grew in the beforenoon foggy & misty. The Thermometer at $35\frac{1}{2}°$, in my Cabin 40°.

Febr. y^e 3^d ♀ We tack all the Afternoon, towards night it grew clear again. We saw vast Numbers of Pinguins passing the Ship. Saw blue Petrels, Fulmars. In the morning we saw on our larboard bow 2 Isles,[5] which had been seen the day before in the beforenoon through the fog. The Land we saw yesterday, being now astern. We go NbE$\frac{1}{2}$E. The Thermometer at 35°, in my Cabin 41°.

Febr. y^e 4th ♄ We have very little wind. Several Ice Islands in Sight. Pinguins, Fulmars, Pintadas, blue & whiterumped Petrels in sight. Next morning calm. Hoisted a Boat out. Tried the Current, found none.[6] Shot several antarctic Pinguins, a Fulmar, a Pintada & 2

[1] Samuel Freezland, A.B.; from Holland according to Cook's muster roll (*Journals*, II, 881). But George called him a German and, presumably, he would know one. They were now naming Cook's 'Freezlands Rocks' the three high standing rocks west of Bristol Island.

[2] They thought, therefore, that they could become embayed. This supposed bay Cook called 'Forsters Bay', now Forster's Passage. See *Journals*, II, 632.

[3] This was Cook's 'Cape Montagu', now Montagu Island. See ibid, 632–3.

[4] Saunders Island.

[5] Undoubtedly the Candlemas Islands. Forster, we must admit, is not very clear on his sightings of these islands. George did better and also got Cook's names right.

[6] See *Journals*, II, 635.

blue Petrels. Saw a large common Albatross. The Thermometer at 36°, in my Cabin 42°.

Febr. ye 5th ☉ The Breeze freshened & we go on at a fine Rate; white & blue Petrels are seen. We had some Snow. We are come to the last Cask of *Sower-krout*, the best preventative against the Scurvy. It is very remarkable, that the People in the Dolphin under Commodore *Byron* disliked both portable Soup & *Sowerkrout*, of which latter Eatable, they had but two Casks & they were brought back to England: Whereas we found the *Sowerkrout* so good, that we emptied about 60 Casks,[1] & 60 boxes of portable Soup, of 2 Canisters each at 25 lb. Which clearly proves, how much prejudice can operate upon the minds of people. In the Endeavour but few would eat Sowerkrout, but as some of the Crew in the Endeavour came into the Resolution they set the Example to the Rest & all ate very heartily both portable Soup with Pease & Sowerkrout, to which latter we must ascribe the preservation of the Crew from the Scurvy, though we have been longer out at Sea, from any European Port or Settlement & Refreshments, than any other ship whatsoever. For which reason it deserves to be recommended to the Consideration of the Lords & Gentlemen that are at the head of the Brittish Navy, whether it would not in future be useful to introduce the Sowerkrout & its use into the Navy. The Ship pitched very much. The Thermometer at 36°, in my Cabin 41½°.

Febr. ye 6th ☽ The Course is still SEbS & thereabouts. The breeze fresh. Saw sooty Albatrosses, white Sooty, blue & whiterumped Petrils, Pintadas & Fulmars. The Thermometer at 37° in my Cabin 42°.

Febr. ye 7th ♂ We find here the Northern winds cold, & the Southern ones mild, contrary to what might be expected; observed Fulmars; blue & whiterumped Petrils, but few in number. The wind aft, the Course East. In the night tacked North & South. The Thermometer at 37°, in my Cabin 41°. Saw Ice Islands.

Febr. ye 8th ☿ This Wind seems to conduct us nearer & nearer to the end of our Carreer. We have already passed that Meridian we habe been West of *London* before, & are also now round the Globe.

[1] 'and the want of it was severely felt from the captain down to the sailor. It enabled us to eat our portion of salt meat, of which it corrected the septic quality. The wish for a speedy release from this nauseous diet now became universal...', *Voyage*, II, 541. Cf. *Journals*, II, 640 and Forster's account of the preparation and efficacy of sauerkraut in *Observations*, pp. 628–31.

I suggested to *Capt Cook*, to call the First Isle we have met with here to the South, *South Georgia*[1] & to put on the Map representing it, *Horaces* verse

Tua sectus orbis nomina ducet.[2]

with some Emblematical drawing, which he liked very much. To the Map representing the Southern Hemisphere & our Ships track on it, *Mr Hodges* added the Figures of *Labour* & *Science* supporting the Globe, to which I added the motto from *Virgils Aeneis* Æn:II:708.

Ipsa subibo Humeris, nec me labor iste gravabit.[3]

For though *Labour* supports the Globe with the utmost Exertion of power, *Science* seems to do it with great Ease. The wind gradually abated, & in the beforenoon very little was left; the same birds attend. The Thermometer at 36°, in my Cabin 41°. Saw Ice Islands: Snow.[4]

Febr. ye 9th ♃ Saw common & Sooty Albatrosses, blue & white-rumped Petrels, passed Ice-Islands. Calm in the morning. The Thermometer at 36°, in my Cabin 44°.

Febr. ye 10th ♀ Calm. Saw Ice Islands, blue & common white-rumped Petrils, Pintadas & Fulmars. In the night a fine breeze sprung up: the Course East. The Thermometer $32\frac{1}{2}$, in my Cabin $40\frac{1}{2}$.

Febr. ye 11th ♄ The fine breeze & fine weather continue. The wind falls, & Snow in the morning: blue & whiterumped Petrels about the Ship. The Thermometer at 33°, in my Cabin $40\frac{1}{2}$°.

Febr. ye 12th ☉ Very little wind, if any: almost calm. Saw many

[1] This is corroborated by George (II, pp. 525–6) except that he wrote 'Southern Georgia' which reverses, as it were, Beaglehole's 'minor point' of *Journals*, II, 625, n. 4. J. R. Forster seems to have had the honour, therefore, of suggesting the name that stuck.

[2] Which translates 'half the world will bear your name'. Irony, we may take it at this stage of Forster's Anglophilia, was not intended. The quote, also in George (II, p. 525), is from Horace's *Odes* III, 27, l. 75. This poem concerns Europa, an unfortunate girl carried off to Crete by Zeus in the guise of a bull. As she bewails her lot, the goddess Venus tries to comfort her with these words. The Romans, with a restricted geographical knowledge, no doubt saw Europe as 'half the world' (*sectus orbis*).

[3] 'I (myself) will take you upon my shoulders; for me this task is no burden (but a labour of love).' In the original Aeneas is offering to carry his aged father, Anchises, out of burning Troy as the Greeks pour in. Forster alters *Ipse* (masculine) to *Ipsa* (feminine) referring to 'Science'. Of Hodges's device on the map I know nothing. Cook, we must presume, would scarcely countenance this seriously.

[4] With the claims of 'science' so much to the fore and the 'end' of their discovery career near, Forster again surprisingly fails to give the normal summary of findings, especially upon the polar continent, its implications and its existence or non-existence, to which Cook (*Journals*, II, 636–8) and George (II, pp. 539–40) addressed themselves. The *Observations* (pp. 67–8), of course, redressed this, as I have shown in the 'Introduction'.

Ice Islands. Few birds attend the Ship. The Thermometer 34½°, in my Cabin 42½°.

Febr. ye 13th ☽ A Great Swell from the South & calm. Course East. In the night a fine Breeze from the South, very cold, but very few blue Petrels are Seen. The water in the Skuttle – But on deck covered with Ice. The Thermometer at 8 o'clock 32°, in my Cabin 39°. Saw Ice.

Febr. ye 14th ♂ The breeze freshened, the Course still East. The wind freshened, reefed TopSails. It Snows in the Evening. The wind changes into a fresh Gale, with Squalls of Snow now & then. Saw a few blue & one white snowy Petrel & one common Albatross. Passed several Ice Islands. The Ship pitches on account of the heavy Sea coming upon our bow. The Thermometer at 31½°, in my Cabin 37°.

Febr. ye 15th ☿ The Gale fresh. Saw some blue & whiterumped Petrels & some Fulmars. Passed Ice Islands. The Thermometer at 34½, in my Cabin 37½°.

Febr. ye 16th ♃ Bore away at noon. Course NEbE. Having passed the Meridian of London, we go now it seems in quest of *Bouvet's Land*, for the Captain intends to fall in with it from the Westward that he may not miss it, & may be able either to confirm or to deny positively its Existence.[1] The wind falls gradually & during night hardly any. Saw whiterumped & blue Petrils, Fulmars & Pintadas. The Thermometer at 34½, in my Cabin 42½°.

Febr. ye 17th ♀ Mild weather, hardly any wind, a great Sea, the Ship rolls, so that I have had hardly any sleep these 3 nights passed. Towards night a fresh breeze sprung up from NE & went farther & farther to the South; we went first SE, then North & gradually NEbE. Some pretend to have seen a Pinguin, & heard the croaking of several, but others saw at the same time several backfins & heads of Porpesses, which perhaps might be mistaken for Pinguins. Several Fulmars, blue & whiterumped Petrels, had Snow & Sleet. The Thermometer at 33°, in my Cabin 38°.

Febr. ye 18th ♄ A fine fresh breeze, same Sleet & Snow during night, course East & EbS. A few blue & whiterumped Petrels appear; saw several Ice Islands. The Thermometer at 34°, in my Cabin 38½°.

Febr. ye 19th ☉ The breeze fresh & the Course the same, saw many Ice Islands, blue & whiterumped Petrels & a Fulmar. In the

[1] Cf. *Journals*, II, 640–1.

morning at 5 o'clock watch there was an appearance of Land a head, at 8 o'clock it disappeared & having run more than 12 leagues towards it at noon, nothing could be seen.[1] The Thermometer at 34°, in my Cabin 39°.

Febr. ye 20th ☽ It was all day snowing & sleeting. The course EbS & ESE. At 6 o'clock NbW & NNW. In the morning again NNW & towards noon EbS. Foggy, thick weather, few or no birds attending, saw an Ice Island. The Thermometer at 34½°, in my Cabin 38½°.

Febr. ye 21st ♂ Saw a common Albatross, several Shearwaters, blue & whiterumped Petrels. Course ESE. In the morning clear weather, saw an Ice Island. We have now passed over the place where Bouvet lays down his *Cape Circumcision*, which therefore must of Course have been an Ice Island, & we are several degrees of Longitude beyond it, & have gone in the same Latitude, so that we must have seen it, if really such a Land exists; we shall therefore soon, as we hope, hawl up to the North for the *Cape of Good Hope*, & can now consider the Expedition as finished.[2] The Thermometer at 35°, in my Cabin 40°.

Febr. ye 22d ☿ Fine Sunshine & mild weather, the Wind aft. In the morning calm. Saw an Ice Island, and a few Petrels. The Thermometer at 35½, in my Cabin 40°.

Febr. ye 23d ♃ The breeze fresh. At 3 o'clock P.M. SE Course. Saw Ice, & a few Petrels. The Thermometer at 35°, in my Cabin 40½°.

Febr. ye 24th ♀ The breeze still fresh. We go still East, & at 4 o clock in the morning northward, for we have now intersected our first track, we made 2 years ago, when we fell in with the ice, & also entirely circumnavigated the Globe. Very few blue & whiterumped Petrels appear. The Thermometer at 35°, in my Cabin 40°.[3]

[1] It was, says Cook (*Journals*, II, 641), a 'fog bank'.

[2] Cook did not dismiss affairs so lightly and again becomes more the philosopher than Forster in matters geographical. He carefully weighed the pros and cons for Bouvet's Cape Circumcision and continued searching for it in the same approximate latitude for another seven degrees or so to the east. He had, of course, sailed passed to the south of Bouvet Island (lat. 54° 26′ S, long. 3° 24′ E). George echoes Cook's erroneous conclusion that Bouvet 'saw only a field of ice, with such huge mountainous islands of ice upon it, as we fell in with on the 14th of December 1772' (*Voyage*, II, 542–3). Cook seems to have been persuaded by some of his officers – or at least by their belief in land – to continue to search for some days further to the east. See *Journals*, II, cv–cvi and 642–3.

[3] Cook (*Journals*, II, 643–6) pauses here to consider at some length his conclusions on the southern continent – especially the geographical and philosophical reasons for its existence – and on the formation of icebergs and their movements. We must regret, while still praising (as Beaglehole does) Cook's farsightedness here in the matter of icebergs and their origin, that Forster did not introduce any of his reasonings and ideas on the subject. As I have pointed out elsewhere, they certainly rival, if not overhaul those of Cook. See eg. *Tactless Philosopher*, pp. 144–50, *Observations*, pp. 43–102 and 'Introduction'.

Febr. ye 25th ♄ The breeze increases into a stiff gale, hand the Top-gallant Sails, double reef top Sails, & at last go under our Courses; the Ship has much rolling from the great Sea. A few Petrels attend the Ship. The Thermometer at 37°, in my Cabin 41°.

Febr. ye 26th ☉ The wind more moderate, but however we have still a fine breeze. The wind comes more a head & we go on briskly. Saw a few blue & whiterumped Petrels & two antarctic Shearwaters (*Procellaria inexpectata*).[1] The Thermometer at 38½°, in my Cabin 44°.

Febr. ye 27th ☽ The wind comes more round, tack twice. In the Night the wind mends. Saw but few bird. The Thermometer at 40½°, in my Cabin 44½°.

Febr. ye 28th ♂ The wind still won't let us go North but only NE & even EbN; tacked twice during night. Saw blue Petrels, a small black & a common Shearwater. The Thermometer 46°, in my Cabin 49°.

March ye 1st ☿ Though we still go something Eastward, we gain however some thing upon the Latitude, for we were at noon in 47° 58′ S. Latit. & hope soon to fall in with the East & S.E. winds & then soon to reach the Cape of good Hope, perhaps in 10 or 12 days or in a fortnight at farthest. The bad wind continues all night. Some rain before noon in the morning. Saw common Albatrosses, Quebrantahuessos, a Port Egmont-Hen, common & black Shearwater, blue & whiterumped Petrels. The Thermometer at 49°, in my Cabin 51°.[2]

March ye 2^d ♃ About noon the wind came more aft & we can now steer a NNW course, which we hope will bring us in a few days to the Cape. In the morning & before noon hard rain. We saw a Port Egmont Hen, which chased all the large Albatrosses, which came in Sight, allways endeavouring to come under its belly, till the poor Albatross was obliged to alight on the water, & then the Port Egmont Hen went to another Albatross. The Thermometer at 43°, in my Cabin 53½°.

March ye 3^d ♀ After having had a very bad wind & a deal of rain we could at last again proceed to the Northward. Saw many common Albatrosses, large black Shearwaters, blue & whiterumped Petrels. The Thermometer at 46½°, in my Cabin 50½°.

[1] Mottled Petrel.

[2] Cook (*Journals*, II, 647) is more cheerful about morale than George Forster (II, pp. 543–4).

March ye 4th ♄ We are still 11 Degrees Latitude & some more Longitude from the Cape, & hope not to arrive there before the middle of this month. A good many common & black Shearwaters, some blue & whiterumped Petrels fly about. Squally, hard Gales. A great Sea from the West. Thermometer at 42¾°, in my Cabin 47°. Saw 2 Whales.

March ye 5th ☉ The wind from the Northern Quarter; we run WbS, West WbN & WNW. Saw black & common Shearwaters, blue & whiterumped Petrels, & a common Albatross. The Thermometer at 52°, in my Cabin 57°.

March ye 6th ☽ The wind mends in the afternoon but during night again becomes fowl; we steered SWbS & therefore went upon the other tack in the morning. The same birds attend. The Thermometer at 52½°, in my Cabin 60°.

March ye 7th ♂ The preceding night one of the two Otahaitee Sows died; she was with pigs, & near the time of farrowing: there are suspicions that she was killed by the people. The only goat we have likewise fell sick, so that it seems the people are determined not to let a living Quadruped on board: & one of the Capts Dogs disappeared some weeks ago.[1] The wind & course mended over night. We go N & NbW. Saw common Albatrosses & the same Birds as on ye 5th. The Thermometer at 52°, in my Cabin 55½°.

March ye 8th ☿ If this wind stands we may in 8 or 10 days reach the Cape. We were obliged to tack in the Night, because the wind went more to the Northward. Saw common white & brown Albatrosses, which are commonly less & either young ones or a different Sex or perhaps some Variety, together with sooty & yellowbilled[2] ones. The black & common Shearwater, & the blue & whiterumped Petrels. The Thermometer at 60°, in my Cabin 62°.

March ye 9th ♃ The change & mildness of Climate causes a relaxation in our habits & loss of appetite for the Salt provisions, spasms, Cholics & winds. Saw the same birds as yesterday. The wind still northerly. The Thermometer 62½°, in my Cabin 66½°.

March ye 10th ♀ The wind falls. Comes on in the night but still foul. The same birds attend. The Thermometer 62½°, in my Cabin 66½°.

March ye 11th ♄ The Spirits & too warm Expectations of all our too sanguine Gentlemen, to see the Cape in a few days are all fallen,

[1] Cook is silent on this alleged slaughtering.

[2] Possibly, in this vicinity, the Yellow-nosed Mollymawk *Diomedea chlororhynchus* Gmelin, 1789.

many bets lost, & none will venture to lay any thing, unless at a month distance. All the Effects of the foul Wind![1] How difficult it is to bear disappointment with any degree of philosophical temper. We had a rainshower about 3 o'clock in the Afternoon, & I expected soon a Change of wind, which really happened, we put about & go NW. We saw vast Quantities of common Albatrosses of all hues & colours from being all over of a rusty brown, to a white with black wings; they have all the tips of the wings below black & the rest white. Very few black & common Shearwaters, blue & whiterumped Petrels appear. In the morning vast Quantities of Porpesses passed the Ship, all going to the Eastward & there are some that will know we shall soon have a wind from that Quarter. The Thermometer at 54°, in my Cabin 59½°.

March yᵉ 12ᵗʰ ☉ Very little wind & at last almost calm. A good many Albatrosses appear & the same Petrels & Shearwaters. Saw a Sunfish (*Tetradon mola*)[2] above brown, white below, truncated body behind, about 4 feet long, & thick in proportion. The Thermometer at 50°, in my Cabin 56°.

March yᵉ 13ᵗʰ ☽ A boat was hoisted out, & 2 Lieutenants went out shooting & brought 4 Albatrosses & 16 Shearwaters (*Procellaria fuliginosa & inexpectata*).[3] We got after a calm. At 5 o'clock in the morning a faint breeze & we go NNW & NbW. The Thermometer at 60°, in my Cabin 63½°.

March yᵉ 14ᵗʰ ♂ The breeze fresh & we are now standing directly for the *Cape* & hope to be soon there; though every heart throbs with Joy at the approach of this place, where we shall lay off partly that miserable life we now lead; I am however every moment more & more apprehensive & in proportion as we come nearer: for I do not know, what news I shall have there from my Wife & Children, from my Friends & Patrons. I am allmost sure, Friends I shall have lost in the Course of 3 years, but none acquired, which therefore is pure loss. Those therefore who send people out upon such a long Expedition do not think, that we lose so many valuable connexions in Life. I am no more young, if I should be unfortunate enough to have lost in my Absence my best Friends & Patrons, I must begin life as if it were again, which naturally must cast a damp upon my Spirits, which are after such a tedious cruize none

[1] The weather rather than the internal human variety, presumably!

[2] Possibly the sunfish *Mola mola*. There is no drawing or description.

[3] Cooper records this in *Journals*, II, 650, n. 3.

of the highest.[1] We see few birds & those we see are chiefly the black Shearwater. Thermometer at 67½°, in my Cabin 71°.

March yᵉ 15ᵗʰ ☿ Changed cloth as it grows very warm: & we may justly observe that warm & cold are only relative Ideas: for the Indiamen coming from hot Climates always complain of the pinching cold in the neighbourhood of the Cape; but coming from the South we find it rather warm. The wind bad & very high. We cannot lie better than NNE. Have a Head-Sea. A few large Albatrosses & black Shearwaters attend the Ship. This night the Capᵗ, my Son & I got a sore Throat. The Thermometer at 70½°, in my Cabin 73°.

March yᵉ 16ᵗʰ ♃ The wind something abated, but still bad. Some Gannets are seen, & a Seal passed the Ship. At 6 o'clock in the morning a homewardbound Indiaman was seen standing on the other tack, & after breakfast we lost sight of her. At about 10 o'clock we saw another Indiaman: she came on the other tack & we stood in for her. We hoisted Dutch colours & she did the same; then we hoisted English Colours & fired a Gun to leeward, but she kept hers. We gain something upon her, as it is thought, that she makes more leeway.[2] The Thermometer at 69°, in my Cabin 71½°.

March yᵉ 17ᵗʰ ♀ We got a great Squall, & in the Night stood on. The next morning we found our Dutchman a good deal nearer, & had her in Sight all day & very little wind. Saw several yellowbilled Albatrosses. Sounded 55 fathom bottom. The Thermometer at 70°, in my Cabin 71° – caught a *Pollack*.[3]

March yᵉ 18ᵗʰ We stood on & saw the Land on our StarboardSide. In the Night we observed 3 fires on Shore, one very large. We saw still the Dutchman,[4] hoisted a boat out, in order to get news

[1] Was this, we might ask, a deep-seated foreboding of difficulties to come? George made his parent's apprehensiveness and uneasiness the feelings of all on board 'who had left behind them relations and parents...', *Voyage*, II, 544.

[2] On this day Cook, as instructed, demanded logs, journals, charts and other papers from his officers and petty officers and instituted a search among the men for theirs. He also warned 'the whole crew not to devulge where we had been till they had their Lordships permission so to do', *Journals*, II, 652. 'Those who did not belong to the military establishment', noted George (II, p. 545), 'were not subject to this restriction, but preserved their papers, being only requested not to divulge the particular situations of our late discoveries, previous to their arrival in England'. Forster, as we know, was not the only one to break this request with his letters to Linnaeus and Barrington from the Cape. The non-military gentlemen were the two Forsters, Wales and Hodges.

[3] Possibly *Gadus pollachius* of *Descr. Anim.*, p. 315 (name only). There is no drawing.

[4] The 'Bownekerke Polder', Cook notes, a Dutch Indiaman under Captain Cornelis Bosch whom Cook thought generous with his frugal fare but George thought very poor indeed therewith. See *Journals*, II, 652 and *Voyage*, II, 546.

from Europe. We sailed & rowed about 3 hours & then came up with her. We heard that every where was universal peace, that 18 months ago the Russians & Turks were still at war,[1] & that the English Crown had taken the Forts & territorial Possessions from the English E.I. Company & had sent Sir John Clavering as Governor General to Bengal, & other Governors to the other Forts.[2] We were likewise informed that there had been a Ship from the South Sea coming at the Cape, that she arrived on St Patricksday 1774 & went to England in April, that she lost in N. Zeeland a Boatscrew with a Midshipman & Coxswain, who were eaten by the Natives.[3] We soon returned on board, & went to our Dinner. The Thermometer at 71°, in my Cabin 72°. Saw several yellow-billed Albatrosses & Gannets.

*March ye 19th* ☉ Saw besides the Dutchman, 2 Swedish, one Danish & one English Ship. Saw the shore in the Evening. Very little Wind, nearly calm. In the morning we saw the English Ship bear down upon us, we hoisted our Colours & met her, & hoisted a boat out & I went with others on board of her, where I wrote a letter to the Honble Daines Barrington[4] & my Wife. We dined on board of her. She was the *True Britton* Capt *Broadley* from China. We heard of the Adventure's safe return & of the Expedition under Capt *Const. Phipps*[5] to the North East: during our stay on board the Wind freshened & we came off again: The Thermometer at 70°, in my Cabin 72°.

*March ye 20th* ☽ The Wind a Gale; we stand in for the Land, & tack in the Evening but have lost the Advantage; the Wind falling off. Saw a Rainbow caused by the Moon. Next Morning we were off Cape *Agulhas*. During night the wind abated, but the swell great

[1] Forster is the only one to note this and the Indian intelligence below.

[2] Forster is referring to Lord North's Regulating Act of 1773 (13 Geo. III, c 63) whereby Warren Hastings was made first Governor-General in Bengal with powers over the governors of the other two presidencies. It was specifically enacted that lieutenant-governor John Clavering would be one of Hastings's first four counsellors. The 1773 Act remodelled the powers of the Company, placing it completely under Parliament's control, and, although it proved ineffective, it was important as the first participation of the English Government in the administration of India. Forster seems to have got a garbled version of the facts. Clavering (1722–77) bitterly opposed Hastings in India.

[3] This was the *Adventure*, which arrived at the Cape on 17 March, refitting and refreshing until 16 April. For Cook's reaction to the news see *Journals*, II, 652–3.

[4] Barrington was clearly intended to play the key role in Forster's advancement on his return to England.

[5] See p. 166, n. 2 above. Clerke and a midshipman were the 'others' who went aboard the Indiaman with Forster to enjoy 'hearty hospitality' and 'a *plain* dinner' of fattened Chinese quail and goose (*Voyage*, II, 546–7).

& the Ship pitches heavily. The Thermometer at 65, in my Cabin 67°.

*March ye 21st* ♂ We have got in the Night a terrible hard Gale. We saw in the Morning the Land, & can just lay up for Table Bay. The wind falls gradually & we stand in, & set all sails. Saw many Gannets. The Thermometer at 66½°, in my Cabin 67°.

*March ye 22^d^* ☿ We reckon ourselves 7 or 8 leagues off at noon, but go nearly 2 leagues per hour, & hope therefore to come into Table Bay to night & perhaps even ashore. But our hope fails, the wind falls & night comes on, we see fires on the Table Mountain, where they burn old Grass, that new one may spring up for their Sheep. We saw several Ship in Table-Bay & 2 went out to Europe. To morrow we hope early to go ashore. Uneasiness seases me about my poor Family! God knows best, what will be my lot!

Early in the morning we stood into the Bay & had little wind. A boat from the *Ceres* East-india-man Capt Knewte[1] came on board with the 4th mate, offering us assistance. As it had the Appearance that we should come in late, I went off in the boat of the Indiaman & went ashore. I got a few letters, which though not quite fresh, let me however know, that my Family was well a year ago.

I went to Mr Brand's house & took there up my Lodgings:[2] & found there Capt *Knewte*, who intended to go in 2 days to Europe. I paid my Visits to the Governor & principal people, who have been kind & civil to me last time.

Here I break off my Journal at the Cape, as I intend to put my Remarks on the Cape of Good Hope all together, & will there describe the Country, Town, Government, Manners etc.[3] & will therefore resume my Journal from our going away.

[1] This obliging gentleman, who took copies of Cook's journal, charts and drawings ahead to the Admiralty, appears as Newt in George's *Voyage* and Newte in Cook.

[2] '...where we were received with that hearty welcome, which always makes men forget national characters, and convinces them, that real worth is not confined to certain climates or nations', *Voyage*, II, 548. For Brand see p. 183, n. 1, above.

[3] I have not located such an account. George (II, pp. 548–55) gives a brief résumé of their activities at the Cape when Forster made natural history excursions to False Bay, to the Dutch East India Company's garden and menagerie and gathered many other materials for his later zoological work on South African fauna. They also gained considerable intelligence about recent French and Spanish voyages of exploration in the Pacific from Captain Julien Marie Crozet (1728–82), Marion du Fresne's second in command in the *Mascarin* (1772–73). Crozet was at the Cape bound for India. For Cook's discussion of the French news and activities at Cape Town see *Journals*, II, 655–60 (esp. the annotations) and for Forster's work there *Tactless Philosopher*, pp. 128–9 and 288–90.

We found here, that by going by the East round the World, we had gained a Day: as all the other Ships that had gone to the West had lost one day. The Ships gone on this Expedition are the first that are gone by the East round the world.

. . . .

April ye 27th ♃ Having refitted, caulked & rigged the Ship & taken in water & the necessary Provisions, we began to think of going on board, & therefore came about 9 o'clock on board with the Capt.[1]

April ye 28th ♀ At noon *Capt Rice* in the Dutton East India-man hove the Anchor & went under Sail & we seeing this, followed his Example, when the breeze extended to our ship. When we had saluted, & got the Salute returned from the Fort, we came a breast of the Spanish Fregatte the *Juno*, Commanded by Capt Don *Juan Arraos*, returning to Europe from the Manillas, & we were saluted with 9 guns,[2] & we had hardly returned the Salute, when the Danish East India Man Capt Hanssen saluted us with 11 guns, which we likewise returned. We saw immediately after the Juno & the Danish Ship under Sail & pass us by. We went through the Northern Entrance of the Harbour of Table Bay between the North-Shore[3] of Africa & Robben Island. We saw a Dutch Ship at Anchor under the Isle, before the few Houses on this Isle, allotted to the Exiles & people who are banished to this place, & at the name of which every Dutchman at the Cape shudders.[4] We cleared the Land before dark & found that we were the worst sailing Ship in Company. Early in the morning we lost Sight of the English Ship & the Spanish Ship was gaining more & more. This morning we found a Man in the hold a Hannoverian by birth, who had been engaged in the Dutch Service & wanted now to go home, & by means of one of our Sailors had been concealed;

[1] Taking leave here, too, of Anders Sparrman, who elected to spend another year exploring 'the unknown interior', extending the botanical work of his fellow-countryman Thunberg among other things. There is no evidence to support Elliott's comment that Sparrman quit Forster's scientific retinue here because he conceived 'himself not handsomely treated'. See *Journals*, II, 659, n. 3 and *Tactless Philosopher* for a fuller treatment of the relationships between Sparrman and the Forsters.

[2] These Spaniards Cook 'shunned...on all occasions', notes George (II, 554), 'from what motives we were at a loss to determine'. Wales, however, consorted with them, especially over matters astronomical and chronometrical. Even the unexpected Spanish salute was only returned 'a full quarter of an hour afterwards'.

[3] He means, of course, the south shore.

[4] Cf. *Voyage*, II, 556.

Figure 45. Antelopes of the Cape.
Antilope oreas
Drawing by George Forster in B.M. (N.H.) – 'Zoological Drawings', ff. 26 & 30.

Figure 46. The Spring-haas of the Cape. *Yerbua capensis*, now *Pedetes cafer*.
Drawing by George Forster (March–April 1775) in B.M. (N.H.) – 'Zoological Drawings', f. 13.

as this had been done without the Capt leave, both were punished with a dozen at the Gangway.[1] The breeze fine & aft, the weather cool: the Thermometer at 63½°.

*April ye 29th* ♄ Capt Rice lowered his Topgallant-Sails & took his Studding-Sails in order that we might come up with him & sail in Company. We had the same wind & weather, saw Albatrosses & black Shearwaters. The Thermometer at 62½.

*Apr. ye 30th* ☉ We are still in Company with the *Dutton* & have so much gained upon the *Juno* that she was next morning abreast of us, though much to the Northward. The same breeze & weather. The Thermometer at 62½°.

*May ye 1st* ☽ The *Dutton* in Company. The *Juno* a stern. Fine weather. No birds seen. The Thermometer 64½°.

*May ye 2^d^* ♂ An easterly breeze. Fine weather. No birds seen. The Thermometer at 65°.

*May ye 3^d^* ☿ Fine weather. It grows warmer. My Animals begin better to eat: & give me hopes of carrying them safe to England, at least a good many of them. One of my Auk Perroqueets was killed by his antagonist.[2] The Thermometer at 66½°.

*May ye 4th* ♃ The wind abates. One of my Cape Ibis's died. The Thermometer at 67°.

*May ye 5th* ♀ Cloudy. Calm. Rainy in the morning. The Thermometer at 68°.

*May ye 6th* ♄ After some rain we got a fine breeze & sail well. The Thermometer at 64½°, a black Shearwater & the Puffin[3] seen.

*May ye 7th* ☉ The breeze still fresh. The second Cape Ibis died & one of my small Moss birds. The Thermometer at 66°.

*May ye 8th* ☽ The breeze continues. The weather fine. A couple of black Shearwaters attend the Ship. The Thermometer at 66°.

*May ye 9th* ♂ The same breeze & weather & birds. The Therm. at 67°.

*May ye 10th* ☿ Very little Wind. Saw some black Shearwaters. The

[1] This was John Hendrick, A.B., entered on 1 May 1775. See *Journals*, II, 883. 'He soon proved to be', wrote George (II, p. 557), 'one of the most industrious men in the whole ship, and gave our crew a good idea of their Hanoverian fellow-subjects'. In the *Reise* (II, p. 433) George, obviously peeved at Cook's failure to protect one of King George's German subjects, gives us more information about this amiable hardworking fugitive from the Dutch service into which he had been pressed.

[2] For the extent and variety of Forster's South African specimens embarked at Cape Town see *Tactless Philosopher*, esp. pp. 128–9 and 290.

[1] Perhaps the Manx Shearwater *Puffinus puffinus* (Brunnich, 1764).

whole Sea was covered with the *Helix ianthina*,[1] which had a great many small bags full of Spawn sticking to its body & supported by a light frothy substance consisting of a thin Membrane full of Air. The Thermometer at 68°. Some Bonitos were seen, & flying Fish, & a Grampus.

May ye 11th ♃ The Sea still had the same Quantity of the purple shell. Calm hardly any wind. The Thermometer at 69°.

May ye 12th ♀ Still calm weather. Saw some Dolphins. The Therm. 69½°.

May ye 13th ♄ Got in the night at last a fine breeze. Saw still some Dolphins: & a couple of black Shearwaters. The Thermometer at 70½°. One yellow Bird died.

May ye 14th ☉ Saw several flying Fish & Bonitos. The same breeze. The Thermometer at 71°.

May the 15th ☽ On the next morning early we saw the Island of St Helena which seemed to be a high rocky barren Land. However we could discover inclosures & Trees by our Glasses. The Thermometer at 71½°.

May the 16th ♂ This Island was first discovered by the Portugueze Don Juan de Nova[2] on his return from India in 1502. The famous *Halley* was there in 1677[3] & Mr *Maskelyne*,[4] the present Astronomer Royal in 1761: so that its Longitude & Latitude is very well settled. It has none of the most promising appearances. When we came under the high Rocks of the Isle we were becalmed, & obliged to hoist the boats out in order to tow the Ship in. One boat went to the Fort to acquaint the Governor of our arrival. It was about 12 at midnight when at the finest moonlight we dropt the Anchor. Next morning we were saluted by the Fort & returned the Salute & the same was done by & to the Dutton East Indiaman. We moored & worked deeper in. The Rocks are so

[1] Presumably *Janthina janthina* (L.) or *J. globosa* (Swainson). Not in *Descr. Anim.* and there is no drawing. These were closely observed by Banks in the *Endeavour*. See J. Banks, *ENDEAVOUR Journal* (London and Sydney, 1962), II, 171 and Dance, 'Cook Voyages and Conchology', 1971, p. 363.

[2] João da Nova Castella, who discovered the island on 21 May 1502.

[3] He was actually in St Helena from 1676 to 1678 cataloguing the stars of the southern hemisphere and organising them into constellations. He computed the comet named after him in 1682. From 1713 he was secretary to the Royal Society and from 1719 astronomer-royal. See also p. 711, n. 2 above.

[4] Nevil Maskelyne (1732–1811), astromomer-royal since 1765, 'moving force of the Board of Longitude and of the Royal Society on its astronomical side, and intimately concerned with the great voyages'. He had been at St Helena in 1761 observing the transit of Venus. See *Life of Cook*, pp. 101 and 116.

barren, cavernous & dreary, that in reality a small addition of Snow might even outdo the eremitic, dead, & desolate Appearance of *Terra del Fuego*, though nothing can match the terrible scenes of *South Georgia* & southern *Thule*. We shall in the morning go ashore. We landed at a new constructed landing-place with Stairs, which however has the inconvenience of being much subject to a very high Surf, from thence You go between the steep Side of the impending Rock & a parapet-wall to a Gate with a draw-bridge, defended by some small batteries, & leading to a very large battery fronting an Esplanade & a shady fine walk under an avenue of Banian Trees (Ficus religiosa Linn); we passed at its end a Gate & went to the Governors-house, which is again fortified, & makes a little castle. Mr *Scottow*[1] the Governor received us with that politeness, which the known Goodness of his benevolent heart & candour constantly animate: we were invited to dine with him. The Ladies from on board the Dutton[2] likewise paid the Lady of Mr *Scottow* the visit & we dined all at the Governors. I took my Lodgings at Mr *Mason's* a Planter of this Isle, where I met with good accomodations & a friendly host.[3] We paid likewise our Visits to Mr *Corneille* the Deputy-Governor[4] & to Mr *Basset*, a Member of the Council, & Mr *Rangom* likewise one of the Council,[5] & it was with him, that the Passengers in the Indiaman lodged. We made enquiries about the Fish & Birds of the Country.[6]

[1] John Skottowe – 'this worthy and generous veteran, who has been crippled in his country's service' (*Voyage*, II, 558–9), proved a worthy and lavish host. He endeared himself particularly to the Forsters by facilitating their 'researches as naturalists'. As Beaglehole notes, Skottowe was the son of Thomas of Great Ayton, Yorkshire, on whose property Cook's own father, James senior, had been 'hind' or foreman when the future navigator, as a boy, had had his modest fees paid to the Postgate School in Ayton where he learned the rudiments of writing and arithmetic and also his catechism. See *Life of Cook*, pp. 4–5 and 440.

[2] For the 'several persons of Note' in the *Dutton* see *Journals*, II, 660 and *Voyage*, II, 558, note.

[3] He was also, George intriguingly adds, 'a very worthy old man, to whom this settlement owes some of its best and most amiable inhabitants'.

[4] The lieutenant-governor from 1769, Daniel Corneille.

[5] George spares his readers this social list.

[6] Four lines are erased here. Surprisingly there is no special account of the 'elegant dinner' and company they enjoyed at the Governor's table on the first night at St Helena. This social gathering impressed itself upon George for its spirited, informed conversation giving 'a convincing proof, that the means of acquiring useful knowledge, from a store of good books, were by no means neglected among the inhabitants' (*Voyage*, II, 560). One good book they had all read was Hawkesworth's mutilation of Cook with its embarrassing exaggerations about St Helena. George hereafter reserved some caustic barbs for that 'Compilation': this, of course, did not please William Wales. See also *Journals*, I, ccxlv–xlix and II, 661–2.

May ye 17th ☿ It rained all the morning a small misty Rain, coming down the Valley from the higher parts of the Isle. The honble Mr *Stuart*,[1] Capt *Cook* & my Son took a ride into the Country[2] & I stood in the Valley on account of a Headache which plagued me. I visited a small Garden the Governor has in Town with a few flowering Shrubs & plants, amongst which I observed Roses & the *Melia Azederach* Linn: besides it I saw a large *Barringtonia*-Tree, & some of the *Terminalia Catappa*. I went likewise to the Companies Storehouses. In the Afternoon paid a visit to Capt *Tippet* Chief Engineer of the Isle & Commander of the Artillery, & got acquainted with the Revd Mr Robt *Carr*, Clergyman of the Isle, both Men of an open, agreable & admirable Disposition: the last being ready to collect various Curiosities for his Friends in England.

May ye 18th ♃ Breakfasted with Mr *Carr*, & rode into the Country to the Governors Garden, in order to dine with him there. The Cavalcade was numerous, Mrs *Graham*[3] was carried up in a Chair. The Road goes on the Sides of what the Inhabitants call Ladder Hill. This Road is of an easy ascent, 9 Foot wide, has on one Side the Natural Steep Rocks, & on the other a parapet-wall 3 feet high, made of such common stones, as the hill affords. It goes zigzag & brings you in less than a Miles distance to the brow of the hill, where the precipice ends. This road has been built by the present Governor & executed by Capt *Tippet*. It is really very fine, & may be used even for 2 wheeled Carriages, if they be not too wide. It were to be wished the parapet wall were every where of equal goodness, for where the Road wanted a good Foundation, there only it is made with Good Mortar, & in all the remaining parts, with a gritty, gravelly, crumbling Clay, for which reason the few Carts which are used dayly pull down some parts of this wall. The old road is shorter, has more zigzags, is steeper & connects with the new & is used by the Slaves & other people walking on

[1] Frederick Stuart (1751–1802), son of the John Stuart, Earl of Bute, and a passenger in the *Dutton*.

[2] They were all impressed with the interior. George (II, pp. 561–4) gives a good description of the prospects and the general geology, calling, for the latter, Raspe to his aid when discussing volcanoes and sharply criticising Hawkesworth's 'unfortunate... remarks on Nature, as well as... his philosophical digressions', when he, it seems, had often misunderstood Buffon and other authorities like the Dutch ethnographer Cornelius de Pauw (1739–99), from whom he had also copied without due acknowledgment.

[3] Another passenger in the *Dutton*, wife of John Graham, 'late in the council of Bengal'. See *Voyage*, II, 558, note.

foot. All the time we were ascending, we had a fine prospect down into the Valley & could see every soul stirring in the Street: & a fine Plantain-Garden & a few Banian-Trees planted along the Rivulet of the Valley, enlivening the otherwise dreary Scene. The Ships & Boats in the Road & likewise *Mundy-Fort* or Battery can be seen from this Road. The hill on Top has a more gentle Slope going more up to the SW, but as far as the Eye reaches all is still a desart, hardly varied here & there by a Purslane,[1] a Cotula[2] (perhaps the *Anthemoides*) & a *Reseda*. All the rest are heaps of a brown Marle-Stone, half burnt & mixed with Slags & a Soil formed by the dissolution of this Marle-Stone. For about a mile and a half we ride up the hill: however a few solitary Goats & straggling Sheep are seen feeding. Higher up we observed deep Gullets formed on the Sides of the Hill by the strong Rains. When we came to the top of the hill the scene was suddenly altered. You see a great Extent of country, Hills divided by Valleys & the whole covered by a most agreable Verdure. On the Right we saw the *Chapel* on a rising Ground, wherein every fortnight Service is kept, & on the left the Eye was delighted with the Sight of a delicious fertile Valley called *Chappel-Valley*; here the fields are regularly divided by Stone-enclosures, now & then an agreable house appears, surrounded by gardens, Orchards & Plantations. All the Pastures had black Cattle & Sheep. The less fertile Spots are all overrun by the *European-Furze*[3] which though imported, thrives well & affords fuel for the Inhabitants, which shoots sooner up than the Native plants of the Isle. All the Valleys have a little Stream purling down. The hills being in the midst of the Isle very high, attract the Clouds & afford by their moisture & constant Supply for these little Rivulets, which are allways shaded by some Trees & fringed by the snowy Flowers of the *Calla Æthiopica*. At a distance to the South-East we saw Long-hill, which we had observed coming in, crowned with a great many Trees, of a kind, which the Natives call the *Gumwoodtree*.[4] It was not in Flower, but I saw however from the remaining dry *Receptaculum*, that it is a Syngenesist: its wood is white, very hard & tough, & exudes a kind of ambercoloured Rosin, wrongly called Gum by the Natives. There is another sort, which is called the *Bastard-*

[1] *Portulaca oleracea* L.
[2] *Cotula microcephala* D.C.
[3] *Ulex europaeus* L.
[4] *Commidendrum robustum* D.C.

Gumwood,[1] or *white-Wood* & we found it to be a new *Aster*, together with another Tree, which the Inhabitants call the *Greater-Cabbage-Tree.*[2] The lesser Cabbage Tree[3] forms a New Genus, & perhaps a *Monadelphist* will prove an other New Genus. We saw a good many European common plants, as Chickweed,[4] Groundsell[5] etc, which I suspect were imported with European Garden-Seeds. We came at last to the Governors Garden house, situated at the Upper End of a declivity which terminates in a Valley opening to the Sea West of the Road for Shipping. There is a genteel House with a couple of Appartments. Thyme,[6] Myrtle,[7] Roses, Hibiscus Rosa Sinensis, white Lillies, scarlet Geraniums, & other flowers were scattered here & there; a fine walk along a wall inplanted on both Sides with peaches, which are of an orange-colour & a flavor different from our European ones; when perfectly ripe they are excellent. A large American willow beard live Oak (*Quercus Phellos Linn*)[8] makes a fine Appearance, & is a proof that its growth would succeed in this Isle. Wines have been planted several Times without success, so as Cherries & other fruit of that kind, Apples are here & there growing: Cabbages grow here well in other Seasons, but when they are most wanted at the return of the Shipping from India, they are devoured by small Caterpillars & other Insects. Potatoes, Pease, Kidney-Beans, Great Windsor Beans, Carrots, Lettices etc are pretty good together with Artichokes, Asparagus, Cucumbers, etc. Of the *Sophora capensis*[9] I saw a Tree, but it will not bring Seeds though it flowers copiously. The European Garden Seeds must be renewed, because they degenerate, for which reason the Company has wisely ordered that each Ship touching at the Cape should import from thence to St *Helena* the value of 5£ Sterl. in Garden Seeds, which is commonly complied with, but the choice of the Seeds is left to the people at the Cape; who send very little Pease, Beans & Kidney Beans, or of other useful things & make the rest up of Mustard, Cresses & Reddishes, things which now are growing wild on the Isle. The Pastures have a fine Turf &

[1] *Aster gummiferous* Hook. f.
[2] The He-cabbage tree is the Greater cabbage tree *Pladaroxylon leucadendron* Hook. f.
[3] The She-cabbage tree is the Lesser cabbage tree *Lachanodes prenanthiflora* Burch.
[4] This common name is applied to a number of genera.
[5] *Senecio vulgaris* L.
[6] *Thymus vulgaris* L.
[7] *Myrtus communis* L.
[8] The common name in the United States is willow oak.
[9] *Virgilia capensis* (L.) Poir.

continual Grass; so that we suspected the Isle could feed at least as many Cattle again, but we were told by the Inhabitants that the Grass must be spared now towards their Winter Season, for Grass would not grow again up during Winter, & if they had not spare Fields with Grass to put the Cattle in, they starve in Winter. They can however still increase their Stock, for there are now only 2600 Heads of Cattle in the Isle, & they might be increased to 3000, without distressing the Cattle. The beef is delicate, juicy & tender but as there is a constant demand for it here, it is rather killed too young, before it gets a good consistence something like a good English beef, for now it is rather like overgrown Veal. Having been here agreably entertained, we returned to the Valley & it was quite dark, when we came down.[1]

*May ye 19th* ♀ This day we took again a ride into the Country to a house belonging to Mr *Mason*. We found other parts with new Valleys affording fine Views & charming plantations. We went up to the top of a high hill, which together with *Diana's Peak* makes the Saddle & most elevated part of the Country: unhappily it rained. We saw however *Sandy Bay*, where there is a Battery under our Feet, & two Rocks, one called *Lot* & the other *Lot's Wife*. We saw several Covey's of Partridge which I found to be the common *redlegged* one,[2] & it is thought to be a Native of the Place, with a very small kind of Dove, which is blue.[3] The European Pheasant (*Phasianus colchicus* Linn.) is introduced into this Isle by the present Governor with the *Guinea-Hen*[4] & will in a few Years grow very numerous, for at present there is a penalty of 5£ Sterl. for killing them, till they multiply to such a degree that they may become common Game, which period in all probability is not very far off, for we saw a good many in this Excursion. The Ricebirds (*Loxia oryzivora*)[5] are imported & grown pretty numerous. *Rabbits* are likewise in plenty, we saw several. We came after a ride between 6 or 7 miles to a house at the Upper End of an Agreable Valley & found there a fine Garden containing good Greens of all kind, especially the *Eddoes* which the Inhabitants cultivate wherever Water is to be gotten to moisten them. Mr *Mason* has

[1] The aforegoing description is drawn on heavily by George in *Voyage*, II, 565–7.
[2] Probably the Red-legged Partridge *Alectoris rufa* Linnaeus, 1758, although probably not native to St Helena.
[3] Identity not known.
[4] Helmeted Guineafowl *Numida meleagris* Linnaeus, 1758.
[5] Java Sparrow *Padda oryzivora* (Linnaeus, 1758).

begun to plant Indian-corn, which formerly has been sowed in greater Quantities, but is now almost lost in the Isle: but it is said, the numerous Rats & mice destroy vast Quantities of it.[1] I believe that kind of Rice, which grows on dry hills in India & China, mentioned by M^r^ *le Poivre*[2] & in the Voyage of the *Endeavour* deserves to be introduced into this Isle. We returned in the Evening & after dressing we went to the Governors House, where Mr *Graham* gave a ball to the Ladies of the Place, to which we were likewise invited. The Assembly was numerous & brilliant by the really great number of fine women, Natives of this happy Isle, whose fair Complexion, fine Shape & features & agreable, easy lively manners, & ready parts makes them equal to the fairs ones of any Country.[3] The Company broke not up before 3 o'clock in the Morning.

*May ye 20th* ♄ We examined some plants & Fish & went in the Evening again to a Ball, given by Mr *Laurel*,[4] graced by the same Ladies & conducted with the same taste & followed as the former by an elegant Supper. The Dances ended at midnight: We returned to our Lodgings at about 2 o'clock.

*May ye 21st* I went to Church & heard a sensible Sermon, full of good materials, expressed in an elegant style & delivered in a proper manner by Mr *Carr*: we dined again at the Governors & after dinner we im̄ediately embarked. The Anchor was weighed, the Sails set, & we left, after being saluted, & having returned the Salutes, this happy Isle. The *Dutton* will be for a day or 2 with us in Company, but must alter his course to avoid the Isle of *Ascension* by a new Regulation of the E.I. Company, because the American & especially New England Vessels now begin to go to *Ascension* under pretence of Whale-Fishing but in reality in order to buy goods from the English & other E.I. Ships.

The Isle of *St Helena* bears the plainest proof of the assertion

[1] George (II, pp. 567–70) adds some useful information on this day's excursion to Mason's country house and has tended to transpose the order of observations from his father's Journal.

[2] Pierre Poivre (1719–86), botanist, formerly a missionary in Canton and Cochin-China. After spending some time in Batavia learning about the Dutch monopoly in the spice trade, he led a French expedition for the Companie des Indes to Cochin-China to get plants for the Île de France (Mauritius). His first efforts to acclimatise plants were thwarted by nature and authority but later, as superintendent of Île de France and Bourbon, he had enough influence to organise his own scientific expeditions using his nephew Pierre Sonnerat (1749–1814) as the principal scientist.

[3] Both the younger Forster and Cook are enthusiastic about the 'celebrated beauties of St Helena'.

[4] Another passenger of note in the *Dutton*.

that the high solitary Islands in the Great Ocean owe their Origin to a Volcano, or that at least the Soil of the Isle has undergone great Changes from a violent Fire.[1] All the Stones are honey-combed & look like Dross & Slags: some are ponderous, others very light. All are dark & look sooty & more or less brown or black. They moulder & crumble in pieces; being long exposed to the Air. We found some Limestone, Dunstone, & Soaprock or French-Chalk, & a brown ochraceous, gritty clay.[2]

The Soil seems to be fertile & rich enough for Cultivation, & I have reason to believe that the abovementioned kind of Rice, together with Indian corn will succeed very well & afford a great part of the food requisite for the Islanders, without even diminishing the Pastures. I have likewise reason to suspect, that the *Snail-grass* or *Lucerne* or *Saint-foin*, (*Medicago polymorpha* Linn.)[3] when regularly cultivated must turn out to good account, in affording finer pastures for black Cattle, & providing even in winter a plentifull Crop of Food, & that by this means the Inhabitants would be enabled to keep at least 3800 or 4000 head of Cattle, for it would grow & thrive well in the stony Soil, which now is entirely barren.

The Importation of Asses from Senegal, would in my opinion be of great utility to this Isle, for this kind of Asses seems to be best calculated for this Climate, for its high hills, & make

[1] St Helena is, of course, volcanic and has been greatly affected by subaërial and marine erosion. The principal ridge of the island, including Diana's Peak (2704 feet) and High Peak (2635 feet), to which Forster earlier refers, formed the northern rim of the ancient crater, whereas the southern rim has been completely removed, its debris forming the shallow sea bottom to the south-east of Sandy Bay, which is itself, hypothetically, the centre of the old crater. Forster came very close to indicating the future theories and research on St Helena in *Observations* (pp. 154–5) when he wrote of the island that 'there are every where the most evident marks, of its having undergone a great and total change from a volcano and earthquake, which perhaps sank the greatest part of it in the sea'. The island has many intrusions of dykes and basalts. Cf. Forster's work with that of C. R. Darwin in *Geological Observations on... Volcanic Islands...* (London, 1844).

[2] St Helena is the emergent summit of a well-dissected 'basaltic doublet', a composite volcano composed of several superimposed shield volcanoes, probably of Miocene age, with phonolite and trachytic domes, intrusive dykes and pipe-like plugs of alkaline rocks. Forster's limestone is calcareous dunesand composed of shell fragments. 'Dunstone' (see p. 142, n. 1 above) was formerly used for several rocks of dun colour: bedded ironstone (Derbyshire); fireclay or underclay (Wales), magnesium limestone, shale, or amydaloidal spilite (Plymouth). Soaprock (soapstone) or French chalk is steatite or talc, generally associated with metamorphic rocks such as occur at St Helena only as dumped ship's ballast. George (II, pp. 650–1) reported that the rocks on the higher slopes differ from those in the valley and include stratified clay, limestone and soapstone. If so these must be weathering products of volcanics, which alone reach the summits.

[3] Snail clover = purple lucerne = sainfoin, *Medicago sativa* L. Common saint foin = lucerne, *Onobrychis viciifolia* Scop.

transportation of Vegetables & fruit to the valley more easy: nay these Asses might be rode upon; for *Adanson* describes them as very little inferior to a good Horse.[1]

The Cultivation of Garden Stuff should be likewise recommanded to the Inhabitants, especially the *Phaseolus Mungo* or *Lack-tao* of the Chinese, whereof *Bowen*[2] prepares his *Sago*. Plantations of the American live Oak, the Terminalia Catappa & the Barringtonia would supply sooner & more wood, than the slow growing Gumwood-Trees & Cabbage-Trees, & thus make fuel cheaper. Fishing with hook & Line is common enough & supplies the Inhabitants with a fine fresh Meal, on account of the scarcity of Beef & other fresh Meat in the Isle: but many more might be caught in rocky places, where they cannot angle by Fish-pots & by growing food with the braised green fruit of the *Barringtonia*, or the *Vicia Piscidia* & the *Lepidium Piscidium*.[3]

The number of Inhabitants amounts to about 1800 or 2,000, Slaves included; the Soldiers make about the fourth part of this Number. One third are Slaves, the rest make the Inhabitants & their Families. The East-India-Company make use of this Island for a place of banishment of such people in India as oppose their measures in any way. There are now several Bramines, who were suspected to hinder somewhere in India the Success of Trade, & they were seized & transported hither, where they have in the middle of the Country a House & some Land & Gardens, with Servants to serve them, & all the Provisions & Necessaries allowed them by the Company. The Current Coin of the Isle are chiefly Pagodas & Rupees, though English coin is likewise taken: Spanish Dollars go for 4^{sh} 6^{d}, a Pagoda for 8^{sh}, a Rupee for 2^{sh} 3^{d}.

Though the Climate here is warm, on account of the Vicinity of the Sun, they have however no Thunder & Lightning & the winds mitigate the Air; the moisture attracted from the Clouds likewise diminish the heat, & cause that the Inhabitants & especially the women are so fair as ever a European can be: nay

[1] This last note on asses is in the margin of VI, f. 113. The authority referred to is Michel Adanson (1727–1806), French naturalist, and author of *Histoire naturelle du Sénégal*. . . (Paris, 1757). The reference here is to p. 117 of this work. Adanson was in Senegambia from 1748 to 1753. George also has a note.

[2] See *Voyage*, II, 567, note. Interestingly it was the introduction successfully of the New Zealand flax to St Helena in 1907–08 which led to the island's economic recovery.

[3] Cf. Cook (*Journals*, II, 662–4) on the state and prospects of St Helena. See also S. L. Olson, *Palaeornithology of St Helena Island, South Atlantic Ocean* (Smithsonian Contributions to Palaeobiology, No. 23, Washington, 1975) for a more recent scientific introduction.

the Sex have a bloom of health & a delicacy of complexion, which proves the healthiness & excellence of their Climate beyond any doubt. I am allmost tempted to believe that more Females are born here than males; from what I saw in the Families which in my Opinion is at the Cape quite out of all Question, so that perhaps Tropical countries or in their Vicinity are calculated for Polygamy, so as the temperate ones for Monogamy.[1] The Company has built a new, neat Church, which was allready ordered to be erected when Capt *Cook* was here in the *Endeavour*: & everywhere the Company erects good & new buildings for the Use of their own Servants. The Fortifications are in good repair, & I am apt to believe that in case an Ennemy should attack the Isle he would be ill received for he must first pass the Fire of *Banks's Fort*, where one Battery is high, the other on the waters-Edge, *Prince Ruperts Fort* comes next at the bottom of *Ruperts-bay*. The next is *Mundy Fort* & then is a good battery in Front of *James's bay* or *James Fort*,[2] so that if a Ship intends to silence this last, she must be exposed to the Fire of all these Batteries, & runs a chance to be disabled before she comes up; nor can any thing be undertaken against the Isle before *James's Fort* is taken. The Natives use wheel barrows, but seldom; & the garrison has a large Cart for to fetch Stones with from the Sides of Ladder-hill for to build with. Every thing in this happy Spot seems to be contented & thriving under the influence of the Governor, who seems to have the Good of the Country very much at heart, & to promote every scheme tending towards it.

May y^{e} 22^{d} ☽ We came on board in a very rainy weather, & having weighed, soon removed from the Isle. It rained all night, & we never saw it any more, it being hazy next day. The Thermometer at $70\frac{1}{2}°$.

May y^{e} 23^{d} ♂ The *Dutton* still in company, the weather still now & then rainy. The breeze fine & fresh. Lost one of my *Surikatyes*, a *waxbill* & had two small Redbeaked Ducks[3] killed by the Dogs. The Thermometer at $71\frac{1}{2}°$.

[1] This theme is pursued by George (II, pp. 569–70) as being of interest to 'philosophers [who] could not fail to draw many inferences from thence relative to the domestic life of various nations'. As early considerations on fertility and population trends the Forsters' ideas are not to be disparaged. The theme is pursued at great length in *Observations*, pp. 423–34.

[2] The town was Jamestown.

[3] All part of his South African 'Livestock', some of which is enumerated in a letter from Solander to Banks, 14 August 1775 (Mitchell Library, Banks and Solander Corresp., As 24) f. 237.

May yᵉ 24ᵗʰ ☿ In the Afternoon a Shower of rain; we had fine wind, saw some flying Fish, & some few Manks Petrels or common Shearwaters. The Thermometer at 72½°.

May yᵉ 25ᵗʰ ♃ Went about Noon on board the *Dutton* in order to dine there according to an Invitation we got from these Gentlemen at our departure from *Sᵗ Helena*. In the Evening returned on board & we left them,[1] & steered for *Ascension*. Saw flying Fish & two Shearwaters, fine breeze. Therm. at 74°.

May yᵉ 26ᵗʰ ♀ The weather mild, the breeze fresh. Saw some flying Fish & Shearwaters. Therm. at 75°.

May yᵉ 27ᵗʰ ♄ The same weather & breeze. Great many flying Fish, & a couple of Albecores are seen about the Ship. A booby was seen early in the morning. The Thermometer at 77½°.

May yᵉ 28ᵗʰ ☉ We saw in the Afternoon several Man of war birds,[2] Tropic-birds[3] & 3 kinds of Boobies,[4] a white one with black wings, a quite greyish brown one, & one of the same colour with a white belly. We observed flying Fish. But we could see no Land in the Evening tho' every one almost expected to see it before night, brought to during night, made sail in the morning. Saw at 6 o'clock the Isle about 10 leagues distance in a haze. A great many Man of war birds appeared in proportion as we came nearer to the Isle, together with Terns, Boobies & Tropicbirds. The Thermometer at 77½.

May yᵉ 29ᵗʰ ☽ In the Afternoon we saw when abreast of the Isle innumerable Boobies & Man of war birds. I shot of each kind one. Two of the Man of warbirds had a red bunch under the Chin, which we thought was artificial, but others thought accidental, by the dilation of some burst Vessel. I will endeavour to shoot one of them tomorrow: we left at a bay to windward a party of Men: when we were in *Crossbay*, we left 2 other parties ashore. A kind of blackish brown Fish was caught, called by Osbeck *Scomber Ascensionis*[5] & by *Linnaeus* Sc. *Glaucus*[6] but the latter confounds

[1] Cook gave Captain Rice a packet of his officers' journals to take to England. See *Journals*, II, 665.

[2] Ascension Frigate Bird *Fregata aquila*.

[3] Both the Red-billed Tropic-bird *Phaethon aethereus aethereus* Linnaeus, 1758 and the White-tailed Tropic-bird *Phaethon lepturus ascensionis* (Mathews) breed at Ascension Island.

[4] Three species of Booby have been recorded at Ascension viz: Brown booby *Sula leucogaster* (Boddaert, 1783); Blue-faced booby *Sula dactylatra* (Lesson, 1831) and Red-footed booby *Sula sula* (Linnaeus, 1766).

[5] *Scomber adscensionis* in P. Osbeck, *Voyage to China* (London, 1771), trans. J. R. Forster, I, 266.

[6] C. Linnaeus, *Systema Naturae* (10th ed., 1758), p. 298. This combines Osbeck's *adscensionis* of 1757 with an Artedi description and names the result *Scomber glaucus*.

two fish. The one of which is a *Gasterosteus* & is the *Glaucus*. The *Scomber ascensionis* is new.[1] A good many small Horsemackrel[2] were caught & one *Gasterosteus Glaucus*.[3] The country looks dreary & one might trace the crater of a Volcano, which forms a circle of red hills formed of red cinders, & on one side is a rough plain from this Crater perhaps formed by Lava & pummice-Stone. We saw however a few green Spots, covered thinly by a faint Verdure. When we came a shore we found no Verdure, but all one barren solitude:[4] The shore consists of Shellsand, the hills & interior parts of a kind of brown, porous, light Stone looking like Dross or Cinder. These Stones gradually decay & form a kind of coarse Gritty Sand. Here & there are Strata of a yellow Ocker & in other Spots a red Slaggy Stone, perhaps a Scoria of Copper & Iron. I found but one piece of Iceland Agate. The highest hill in the Isle seems to be of a Structure quite different from the rest, for it is white at a distance.[5] We found a great many Man of War birds sitting on one white Egg of the size of a Goose-Egg, or larger. They have all no red bags under the blueish, lead-colored bill: this is common to the quite black-ones & those with white bellies; the young ones have no red bags, & their feet are only have webbed, & red, but the old birds have sootcoloured feet & red only below. The white Booby has black quill feathers in the wings & the old ones have likewise black cuneated Tails; Yellow bills with a blackish hue towards the Membrane on the Naked face, & yellow Legs. Younger birds have red feet, & lead coloured bill, yellowish towards the Face & a white Tail. They had one or two Eggs. We found the grey Booby only near the Seaside on the rocks. Tropicbirds & quite white Eggbirds[6] are likewise here. Towards

[1] *Scomber ascencionis* of *Descr. Anim.*, p. 412 and George's drawing No. 226.

[2] *Scomber trachurus* of *Descr. Anim.*, p. 413 and drawing No. 223 (Dusky Bay).

[3] *Gasterosteus glaucus* of *Descr. Anim.*, p. 5 (St Jago) and also George's drawing No. 225 as *Scomber glauca*, Ascension I., 28 May 1775. See also p. 154, n. 1 above. See also Cook's natural history description of Ascension (*Journals*, II, 666).

[4] 'The dreariness of this island surpassed all the horrors of Easter island and Tierra del Fuego, even without the assistance of snow', *Voyage*, II, 572. George, however, gives a good account of the geology. This account is again worthy of comparison with Darwin's chapter (III) on Ascension in *Geological Observations* (1844). See also *Observations*, pp. 152–4.

[5] Ascension is a young volcanic island, a composite cone with many vents, made up of scoriaceous basaltic flows and of trachytic masses either intercalated with or overlying the basalts. Locally there are extensive pyroclastics. See R. C. Mitchell-Thomé, *Geology of the South Atlantic Islands* (Berlin, 1970). Concerning the terms which Forster uses, 'dross' is the scum or slag on molten ore or metal, which solidifies as a lightweight porous rock (like coke) and 'Iceland agate' is a variety of obsidian or volcanic glass, probably associated with trachytes. One of the trachyte domes is still called White Hill and another Green Mountain. See also p. 747 below.

[6] White Tern *Gygis alba alba* (Sparrman, 1786).

noon we went on board: & heard that 6 Turtle had been turned the preceding night.

May ye 30th ♂ There came an Acct that to the East of our Anchoring-place, there is a wreck of a Ship: as we wanted wood, the Capt thought best to take some of the wreck, & to try for more Turtle. When it was darknight, we saw a small Ship coming directly for us, we haled her several times & at last she answered; she came from New-York. A Lieutenant went on board of her, & brought Acct that the Ship was the *Lucretia* from *New-York*,[1] the Masters Name *Greaves*: that he had been at *Sierra-Leon* & was now come a turtling, for to go to the windward Isles with Turtle, & that he had taken us for a French East Indiaman. It appeared likewise from his talk, that he had expected to see East-India Ships here, & to trade with them. The India-company had wisely ordered, that none of their Ships should touch at Ascension, but steer directly NW from St Helena, which has disappointed these Smuggling-traders for this year; but next year they will Cruise off St Helena in the track of the Ships & thus elude this regulation.[2] It is amazing with what spirit & boldness these Americans with a small one-mast Sloop, & 8 men in her traverse the vast Atlantic Ocean beyond the Equator: besides what boldness they use to infringe the Laws, for *Sierra-Leon* is by no means a place they are allowed to go to, by the Act of Navigation & those which are annexed to it. Nay here it appears likewise, what these people think of their own Non-Importation-Schemes & Regulations made by their Great Continental Congress: they forbid the Importation of all India goods & some go to fetch them beyond the Atlantic & the Limits prescribed by Law for the Term of their Navigation. It appears hereby that these people, who are grown up in the Forests & wilds of America & who have hitherto been kindly treated & fostered by the Mother-Country, who at a vast Expence of Blood & Money removed the terror from their Backs, the French in Canada, will not bear any regulations made by the Legislature to lighten the burden of domestic Debts contracted for the American's Sake, nay that they are grown inflexible, unruly & licentious from the habit they Contract in these Wilds of being

[1] '...a Sloope of about 70 Tons burdthen', *Journals*, II, 667.

[2] Cook sets down his views of the new regulations and chance trading in *Journals*, II, 665 and 667. The former he approved of but the latter he did not. Greaves (or Greves) was 'a sencible intillegent man' upon whose evidence Cook relied for part of his account of the interior of Ascension.

under nobodies controul, & never to live under the gentle curb of civil & Social Life, the Laws of a free people, made by the just Legislative power. (But this Excursion is only accidental).[1]

The next morning I took a long walk ashore to the high white hills. For the hills situated near the place where the Ship lies in *Cross-Bay* bear the most evident Signs of being thrown up by a Volcano. There is a plain surrounded by conic hills of a reddish cast, which consist entirely of small Ashes & gritty dissolved Slags, some of which are black, others ochraceous-yellow, others red.[2] These hills include a plain which is about 2 miles over; covered by black gritty Slag-Ashes, & sometimes yellow-Ochre Dust: over all this plain you see at 30 or 60 yards distance little hummocks about 10 or 20 feet high of very rugged Slags & Cinders full of pores; in short Lava, some of which we can trace towards the Sea, where it forms the most sharp, craggy Rocks I ever saw in my Life; lying in such irregular Masses, intersected by deep gullies, that you easily may from thence infer they were once in a fluid State & in a state of Fusion. All these Slags & Lava ring like bells, so that if a piece is broken off & thrown down the sides, it gives a sharp clank or ringing Sound. Beyond these hills surrounding this described plain, we see the highest peak in the Isle, attracting the clouds, lying SE & E from *Cross Bay*, which at some Seasons must yield an immense deal of Rain, which appears from the deep gullies coming in every direction from this Peak. This Hill has a different appearance from all the other hills in the Isle, which in general are either Masses of Lava, or cones of Ashes & cinders, for it is divided in various bodies, which all connect & form but one body & are at last crowned by a still higher oblong Summit: This Hill is white & consists of a gritty tophaceous Stone concreted by

[1] Accidental or not this excursion is an interesting comment upon both Forster's political awareness and his now very short-lived British patriotism, a quality soon to be dissipated after this voyage. George notes that they had devoured 'heaps of old gazettes' at the Cape to discover 'the history of those years, during which we had been banished, as it were, from the world', and they were thus reasonably abreast of events in and concerning the North American colonies. The first skirmishes of the American War of Independence at Lexington and Concord (April 1775) were, of course, only just 'news' in the English papers of May 1775. Significantly George left out this political comment from the *Voyage* for, by 1776–77, the Forsters' attitude towards this struggle was radically changed. For Forster's attitude to the North American revolution see *Tactless Philosopher*.

[2] Basaltic flows and pyroclastics are commonly red in colour where lava has been partially oxidised on contact with the air. Modern maps of Ascension show cones named Mountain Red Hill, Sisters Red Hill, South Red Crater etc. Porous scoria and ash of variable colour are characteristic of basaltic lavafields where a wide variety of structural features (e.g. tumuli, lava tunnels) are commonly associated with basaltic flows.

marle, & some Sand: it is covered by parts of this Stone dissolved into a kind of Earth, which however is covered on its lower outskirts with common *Purslane*,[1] & the higher parts have here & there *two kinds of Grass*: the *Aristida ascensionis* & *Panicum sanguineum*.[2] I saw on the outskirts, in the Lava-hills a *Fern* & a *Lonchitis* between the Rocks, & in two places I saw very young Plants of an *Asperifolia*[3] as I presume: among the Cinders on the plain, grows a *Spurge*[4] & these are all the plants I saw, with two kinds of *Lichens* on the Stones. About this hill several herds of wild Goats are eating the fine Purslane. They are shy &c retired immediately into the higher parts of the hill, when we approached. In one parcel were 10, in another I saw 5, & still other 5 appeared in another flock, & I chased 3 on the summits of the Lava-hills on the foot of the great white Hill. I suspect therefore not without some reason & probability, that this white Peak is one of the primigenious Lands, that the part which is now so desolate contained some Pyritical Matters set by water in fermentation & lastly a fire, which burned as long as any combustible Strata were met.[5] The mineral Substances were melted into Slags & some quite dissolved into Ashes. The Volcano threw up the conic hills, the Lava went down to the Sea in various directions & when all combustibles were consumed the Crater was filled gradually with Ashes & cinders washed down the hills & the boiling Slags remained as they had been boiling up by the internal heat formed in various hummocks.

We were told by the Master of the New York Vessel that there is a Spring somewhere on this high Peak falling down a great Precipice, where it is at once lost & absorbed by Sand & Sun: we did not see it however. The Same Master of the New-York-Sloop told that a Bermudian Sloop had been here & taken in a great Number of Turtles & besides those had turned & killed more than 100 of them merely for the wanton gratification of having their Eggs, leaving the Meat to rot on the Shores, of which some were seen by us. A cruelty hardly to be believed, if the performer had not bragged of it himself, & several had seen the Vestiges of this

[1] *Portulaca oleracea* L. See *Journals*, II, 666, for further botanical annotations.

[2] Respectively *Aristida adscensionis* Linn and *Panicum sanguinale* Linn.

[3] *Aspera muralis*? The genus *Aspera* has been sunk in *Gallium*.

[4] *Euphorbia origanoides* Linn.

[5] This combustion view of vulcanicity was later abandoned by Forster. See e.g. *Tactless Philosopher*, pp. 311–16.

cruel Epicurism, which must of course vastly diminish the numbers of these Creatures useful to Navigators.[1] Having eaten something of a Fowl at the Foot of the hill near a single high Stone close to the dry torrent we emptied a bottle & I wrote on a piece of paper, which I rolled up & put into the bottle, corking it afterwards up the following Words: *His Britannic Majesties Sloop Resolution, that sailed eastward round the world Capt Cook Commander. May ye 30st 1775. John Reinhold Forster F.RS. George Forster.*

May ye 31st ☿ We returned gradually to the Sea-shore, which is about 5 miles from the Foot of the white Primigenial Peak, the road going over fields of black gritty small cinders & Slags, between hillocks of large Slag-masses. The Sun reflected from these brown plains, burnt our Faces, Necks & breasts most cruelly. When we came to the Sea-shore we bathed & found ourselves much refreshed & returned on board. The next morning Capt Cook took with the first Lieut & me another walk towards the same hills, but we could not reach them as dinner time drew near & the Capt on acc^{t} of a *Lumbago* & I from my yesterdays Excursion were both much tired.[2] The New York Sloop sailed away at day break, in quest of India-Ships.

June ye 1st ♃ In the Afternoon we took the boats in, weighed & set sail again. Leaving this barren Island, which with very little trouble might be settled & made a very useful place of refreshment.[3] For this purpose nothing is wanting but water & wood. I am persuaded that if the common Furze, which thrives so well at St *Helena* were planted on this Island, it would no doubt equally thrive here: & were these Furzes first every where growing, Grass & other plants would no doubt immediately after grow between them, form a coat & of course gradually form a Soil of Mould capable of bearing more & more plants. The more the Surface of the Earth is covered with plants, the more would they not only evaporate but even attract the moisture of the Air, & keep it within the Soil & consequently if any Springs are in the Isle, they would soon increase their Water & perpetuate their Supplies. That plants

[1] Cook, too, was outraged by this wanton behaviour. See *Journals*, II, 667. The turtles, for which Ascension is celebrated, were probably the Green Turtle *Chelonia mydas* (Linn.).

[2] Cook, as might be expected, makes no reference to this indisposition, or, indeed, to the abortive excursion.

[3] This the island was destined to become, useful as a naval victualling station, sanatorium and store depot. The British took possession of Ascension in 1815 after the arrival of Napoleon on St Helena.

will & can grow within the Ashes & Cinders of a Volcano is very well known from the cultivated Spots on the *Vesuvio* & *Mongibello* in Sicily, & from what we have seen at *Tanna* in the *South-Seas*. After Grass & Water were more plentifull in the Isle certainly many a Tree would soon grow up & thus afford fuel. So that cattle would thrive here, & afford the Navigator a new place of refreshment in this vast Atlantic Ocean & perhaps assistance to a Ship in distress: for the Ship whose wreck we found had marks upon it of being burnt, & that the people run her ashore in order to save their lives: however though they may have been saved, the poor wretches must have undergone a world of distress & misery: without Shelter against the parching Sun & the frequent Showers of rain, without a regular supply of fresh water, or fuel. Humanity feels at the memory of these disasters more than most eloquent Man's pen can describe. My heart shudders at the bare remembrance, gives its tribute of sorrow in a trickling tear & incapable of painting the object to advantage it remains silent upon this Scene of wretchedness.[1] Saw flying Fish & next morning saw some Man of war birds soaring in the Air & a couple of Terns swimming on the Water. The Thermometer at 77½°.

June yᵉ 2ᵈ ♀ The course being since 8 o'clock in the morning altered to WNW, some suspect we are going to the Isle *Fernand Noronha*,[2] & now at noon we go WbN½N. Saw several Man of war birds & flying Fish. The Thermometer at 77½°.

June yᵉ 3ᵈ ♄ The breeze freshen's, many Albecores & flying Fish about the Ship. I got an Eruption & a kind of Fever from the heat in Ascension; & now today a loseness. It rained 2 hard Showers during night. Saw a black Shearwater. The Therm. at 76°.

June yᵉ 4ᵗʰ ☉ We saw a grey Booby, several flying Fish & Albecores jumping out of the Water. The Therm. 77½°.

June yᵉ 5ᵗʰ ☽ Saw again a grey Booby, plenty of flying Fish. The breeze fresh: fine weather, very hot. The Therm. 79½.

June yᵉ 6ᵗʰ ♂ Saw Flying Fish. Several of our Ships Company get Fluxes & Rheumatisms, so as nearly to be contracted. The breeze & weather fine. The Therm. 80°.

June yᵉ 7ᵗʰ ☿ Flying Fish seen. Fine weather & breeze. Therm. 80°.

June yᵉ 8ᵗʰ ♃ Saw at 2½ P.M. an immense Quantity of Porpesses, one was struck & broke the Line. We had altered the course at

[1] George omitted this lachrymal outburst.
[2] Cook made for this island to determine its longitude. See *Journals*, II, 668.

noon from WbN½N to NW. Saw next day 3 Man of war birds. The Thermometer at 79½°.

*June ye 9th* ♀ Altered the course at noon. Course West: in order not to miss the Isle of *Fernando Noronha*, which the Capt it seems will make, perhaps in order to get water & wood which latter we stand much in need of.[1] These two last days the Capt ordered the Log not to be hove & set *Foxton's* new Patent-Log a going, but it goes much too short, so that we may with great certainty pronounce, this otherwise ingenious invention to be of little utility. For when the Worm or Log is driven into the whirlpools caused by the wake of the Ship it stops, which slakens the Log-Line & the Machine is for that time at a stand, & then the Ship at last going forward the Stray-Line is stretched again & sets the Machine a going.[2]

Fresh wind all night. Saw Man of war birds, Terns, flying Fish & Albecores jumping out of the Water. The Therm. 79½.

*June ye 10th* ♄ Were willing to hawl more up for the Isle of *Fernand Noronha*, when from the Deck the Isle was seen, tho' the Midshipman at the Masthead saw nothing: owing to the Caprice of the first Lieut. who allways sends such young Men at the Masthead, who are under his private displeasure, this now there being shortsighted & could not see the Land, though we were not above 6 or 7 Leagues off.[3] But the first Lieut. often sent some shortsighted people to the Masthead for to gratify his private resentments; so much is power abused by weak men! Even to serve a private pique. But the kings service is less important in the Eyes of such mean groveling Souls.

The Isle has a singular appearance; at its South West End is a small rock looking at a distance like a bottle; in the middle of the Isle is a large Peak looking like a Church Steeple & to the East of that there is a broken Land & a large Rock. The hills when we came nigh, were clothed with trees, & had agreable Verdure. We saw two Castles, one on a high Eminence with a flagstaff & another opposite to it. We then went round the East point in order to get into the harbour. When we came abreast of the harbour we discovered at once 5 Forts & the colours hoisted. A little while

[1] Cook, it seems, was not confiding much to his naturalist.

[2] Cook had got Foxon's hydrometer from Captain Rice of the *Dutton* at St Helena. Forster, here rather earlier than Cook (*Journals*, II, 665, n. 2), categorically dismisses this prototype of the perpetual log which became widely adopted in later years.

[3] I can find no evidence to show who this myopic midshipman was or to give any clue as to why, at this particular time, Cooper had again become the target for Forster's anger.

after they made some signal or other & fired a Gun. When we hawled the Wind & stood NNE, we fired likewise a Gun to leeward & took thus leave from these *Senhors* at a Distance. The Eastermost Fort is small, stands on a plain at the back of a larger one & is I believe to hinder the Landing from the opposite South East side of the Isle; more to the North is on an elevate[d] Rock a fine large Fort; in the harbour we saw some Rocks & on a more elevate[d] Rock is the highest Fort, behind which in a Valley, I saw the Front of a Church; still more to the West, near the Water's-Edge is another small Fort, & a great way westward of all in another harbour, as I suspect, we discovered another Fort. Don *Antonio de Ulloa*[1] says, there are still 2 more Forts, & thus this small Isle, which is not 2 leagues across, is defended by seven Forts & according to *Ulloa* by about 1000 Men: which must of course be very expensive. If the Portuguese intend to keep only possession of the Isle, they might as well do it by keeping a Serjeant with 20 Men, just enough to hoist a Flag & to shew that it belongs to the Crown of Portugal. Whereas all these expensive Forts & Garrisons will not in the least deter an Ennemy from striking a stroke on the Continent, where *Rio-Janeiro* the Capital would be by far more important, & tempting for an Enterprize of that Nature, as it has at its back a bay where troops might be landed, where no Fort can hinder them, & where they might at once come at the back of the City & all its famous Forts, & facilitate an Enterprize, which would draw after it the Conquest of a rich Province. The situation of this Isle might in a long war no doubt distress the Portuguese in giving a place of Rendezvous to the Ennemies Ships & a place for Hospitals & Stores & a retreat for Privateers; but if *Rio Janeiro* were taken, it will serve at once all these purposes, & the Armaments must be for the one and the other place allmost equal, nay if you will first take *Fernando Noronha*, in order to pursue from thence the Conquest of the Brasils & its Capital the Equipment must of Course be greater in order to keep both; whereas if you strike the great Stroke at once at the Capital, this little unimportant [Island] may by the cruising of a couple of

[1] Ulloa (1716–95) was, notes Beaglehole, more a scientist than a sailor. The source of Forster's (and Cook's) intelligence on this island is probably one of the English editions of Ulloa's *Voyage to South America* which appeared in Spanish in 1748 and in English translation first in 1752. As a scientist, 'though not himself deep or exact in research' but withal 'one of the ornaments of the intellectual renaissance in the Spain of his day' (Beaglehole in *Journals*, II, 670, n. 2), Ulloa would certainly have been read and hence known by the elder Forster in some depth.

Ships be so distressed for Provisions, which must all come from the Main, that they must soon surrender, without a regular siege or Armament.[1]

We saw several Man of war Birds & grey Boobies with white Bellies (*Pelecanus Sula*). Had Squalls & Rain at intervals. The Therm. 81°.

June ye 11th ☉ The wind fresh, during all night heavy Showers of Rain & Squalls. The Turtles we have hitherto had begin to pine & would die, did we not kill them, to prevent them dying. The Therm. 80½°.

June ye 12th ☽ We were at Noon about 12′ South of the Line & shall therefore repass into the Northern Hemisphere this very Afternoon. The Squalls still continue. The Therm. 80½°.

June ye 13th ♂ Still Squalls coming on. Saw flying Fish. The wind draws a head. The Therm. 81½.

June ye 14th ☿ Squalls & Rain. The wind still more a head; Course NW. NNW. NbW. Saw several Porpesses, & Albecores jumping out of the water. Therm. at 79½°.

June ye 15th ♃ Little Wind & Squalls with heavy Showers of Rain together with Thunder & Lightning. A small Porpesse of the kind called the *antient Dolphin*[2] was struck & immediately shared out among the people. Vast Quantities of Albecores jump out of the Water. The Thermometer at 78°.

June ye 16th ♀ Calm, heavy Showers of rain; 3 Sharks were caught & a good many Sucking-Fish were sticking to them. Saw Albecores jumping out of the Water. The Thermometer at 77½°.

June ye 17th ♄ Still calm: a Rain during night & next morning. The Thermometer 78½°.

June ye 18th ☉ Still calm: caught a Shark, & 3 Sucking-Fish sticking to it. Heavy Showers of Rain during night. Saw several Albecores & other Fish playing about the Ship. Caught another Shark. Therm. at 77½°.

June ye 19th ☽ Still calm & several Showers of Rain. Saw several Albecores jumping about the Ship. About 7 o'clock we got a breeze, which continued even to 10 o'clock, when I went to bed, so that we have hopes, of being at last delivered of these calms.

[1] We are reminded vividly here of Forster's course of lectures offered at Warrington Academy in the summer of 1768 on fortification, gunnery and tactics, 'collected from the best writers on those subjects, antient as well as modern'. See *Tactless Philosopher*, pp. 60–1. Cook's view of Fernando de Noronha was more that of the navigator (*Journals*, II, 669–70).

[2] Presumably *Delphinus delphis*.

The wind continued all night, but in the morning very little of it was left. The Thermometer at 80¼°.

*June ye 20th* ♂ Saw vast Quantities of Albecores. At about 6 o'clock P.M. the Wind freshened & we got all night a fine breeze. We had in the Afternoon several Showers of Rain. Saw in the morning a single Shearwater, & several Albecores & Bonitos, & flying Fish. The Thermometer at 81°.[1]

*June ye 21st* ☿ The breeze fresh, goes more a head; Albecores & Bonitos in vast Numbers about the Ship. In the Evening the breeze freshened still more. The Thermometer at 80½°.

*June ye 22^d^* ♃ The breeze still fresh. Albecores & flying Fish in great Shoals, a Dolphin was seen about the Ship. The Thermometer at 80°.

*June ye 23^d^* ♀ The breeze fresh. Saw more than 20 Shearwaters, good many Albecores & flying fish. Rain in the morning. The Therm. 79½.

*June ye 24th* ♄ The breeze fresh, clowdy; still Albecores & flying Fish are seen. Next morning about noon it cleared up. The Therm. 77°.

*June ye 25th* ⊙ The breeze fresh, cloudy: Saw a flying Fish & a Shearwater. About 11 o'clock A.M. saw an outward boun[d] Ship, which afterwards hoisted Dutch colours, going probably to *Surinam*. She was very large. The Therm. 77°.

*June ye 26th* ☽ The breeze still fresh. Commonly in the night the wind goes more to the East, & lets us go more North, but in the beforenoon the wind comes more round & we must go WNW or NW or NNW. This seems to be caused chiefly by the Sun, which being still a head of us, rarefies during day the Air under him, which of course must alter the course of the current of Air or Wind, going to replace the Equilibrium. The Thermometer at 77½°. Saw a Shearwater, had rain & Squalls.

*June ye 27th* ♂ The breeze still the same. My *Yerbua Capensis*[2] died

[1] Cook now ordered the distilling apparatus to be set up again primarily to obtain fresh water. Forster seems to have lost interest at this time. See *Journals*, II, 671–2 and pp. 160–9 above.

[2] See *Descr. Anim.*, pp. 365 and 368 and George drawing No. 13. Forster's paper on the animal (1778) is dated May 1777 and includes a folding plate based upon George's drawing. Sparrman also wrote a supplement to this paper and Buffon apparently used George's drawing for his description of *Dipus capensis*. It is now the Spring-haas *Pedetes cafer*. There is a gouache copy of it (No. 2) among the Forster drawings in the Forschungsbibliothek, Gotha. See *Tactless Philosopher*, pp. 129, 185, 290, n. 31 and 344 and Whitehead, 'Forster collection of zoological drawings', pp. 37 and 46. The London drawing is reproduced in A. MacLean *Captain Cook* (London, 1972), p. 111.

this night. The wind goes more upon the whole to Eastward. The Thermometer at 76½°.

June ye 28th ☿ The breeze fine. Saw some flying Fish & Gulphweed. The Thermometer at 76½°.

June ye 29th ♃ Saw flying Fish. The breeze stands. The Therm. 77½°.

June ye 30th ♀ Saw in the Night at 2 o'clock a Ship close to ours, which probably was going to the West-Indies. Saw a good deal Gulphweed[1] floating: & a bird was observed at a distance, perhaps a Tropic-bird. The Thermometer at 76½°. Passed at 5 o'clock P.M. the Tropic of Cancer.

July ye 1st ♄ The same breeze. The Thermometer at 75°.

July ye 2d ☉ The breeze fresh. Saw many Gulphweed floating. The Thermometer at 74°.

July ye 3d ☽ The breeze fresh & permits us to go NNE. Some Gulphweed seen. At noon the breeze faint. The Therm. 73⅔°.

July ye 4th ♂ The breeze fell & we had Calms & alternating Squalls but in the morning the wind freshened; A good many Gulphweed seen. Some Rain during night. The wind SEbE. The Thermometer at 73½°.

July ye 5th ☿ The breeze falls & now & then freshens again. Saw Gulphweed. The Thermometer at 73°.

July ye 6th ♃ A dead Calm & warm weather. The Therm: at 74°.

July ye 7th ♀ As perfect a Calm as ever was seen. In the morning at 5 o'clock we had a faint breeze. The Therm. at 75°.

July ye 8th ♄ Hardly any wind. In the Evening towering clouds to the West. In the morning a faint breeze sprung up. Towards noon calm. The Therm. 73½°. Caught at 5. P.M. a Dolphin weighing 13 pounds.

July ye 9th ☉ Calm at noon, some few drops of Rain. The wind came more aft in the morning, & freshened. The Thermometer at 75°.

July ye 10th ☽ The breeze freshen's. The Course NEbE. We approach gently the *Western Isles* or *Azores*, whose Situation is looked upon as not yet well settled; we shall perhaps have an Occasion to do it by some good Astronomical Observation.[2] If we go ashore, I shall have an Opportunity to see the Products of the Country. The breeze still fresh. Saw some flying Fish. The Thermometer at 76½°.

July ye 11th ♂ The Course ENE & in the Evening we got a fresh

[1] *Sargassum bacciferum*. See *Journals*, II, 673, n. 1.
[2] Cf. *Journals*, II, 673–4.

Gale; we altered at 10 o'clock P.M. the Course to EbN. The Gale fresh all night & next morning. The Thermometer at 76°. Saw a Ship in the morning.

July ye 12th ☿ The finest strong Gale. Saw some flying Fish. The Therm. 75°.

July ye 13th ♃ The Course E.b.S. The Gale still fresh. saw at about 2 o'clock P.M. a Snow standing eastward. Expect soon to see some of the *Azores*. In the morning the wind abated. We saw about 4 Ships. The Therm. 72½°.

July ye 14th ♀ About 4 o'clock P.M. we saw Land, on our Larboard-bow supposed to be *Fayal*. We changed Course at 7 o'clock, go ESE. *Pico* we cannot yet see. Tacked during night.[1] Stood into the Road in the Morning. Came to an Anchor about 8 o'clock in a place shewn us by the Master of the Port, who came off on purpose in a boat. We found a small Portuguese Snow in the harbour just arrived from *Para*[2] & the River *Maragnon*, having been intended to bring provisions to the Cape Verd Isles but she missed them: a small American Vessel was here & a French Frigatte comãnded by M. *d'Estelle* coming from St Domingo, going to Madeira & the Canaries for Wine. We were complimented by M. *d'Estelle's* 2d Lieutenant M. *de St Michel* & his Services offerred. He told the Kings troops had had a Skirmish with the Provincial Troops in N. America, wherein 8 were killed, that 14 Sail of the Line blokaded the Port of *Boston*[3] & that several Frigates cruized & took all N. England Vessels; that one stood here several times in, but se[e]ing the French Frigatte & mistaking her for an English Ship, stood out again. We saw our Ship well moored & we did not salute the Fort, because they never return an equal number of Guns.[4] The Therm: at 73°.

July ye 15th ♄ We went immediately after Dinner a shore, to Mr Thom. *Dent* the Consul,[5] & with him saw the town & some of the Monasteries. There are 2 forts, one on the South side of the

[1] Cook records that they saw Pico before night fell. They anchored in the Bay of Fayal.

[2] Now Belem in the Para Province of Brazil.

[3] We might recall here that the first important battle of the revolutionary war had been fought at Bunker Hill, Boston, on 17 June 1775, just one month before.

[4] Cook had problems with both saluting and port charges. See *Journals*, II, 673–4. They received no salutes, notes George (II, p. 583) because 'the cannon rested on rotten carriages, which it was prudent not to expose to the shock of a discharge' and because powder was too expensive! See p. 757 below.

[5] He was, in fact, deputy or vice-consul. The Forsters, Wales and Hodges lodged with him in Villa da Horta, the town.

town & another to the North of it; the first is the principal one. The Road is open to the South & SE winds, which blow sometimes hard in winter; but the bottom is a good sand & in Winter even English American Ships ride here with 4 or 5 Anchors, but chiefly they come in Summer when it is pretty safe: there is a Hill making the North point of the Road, called *Punta da Esplamayu* & to the South is a Hill called *Monte da Guia* which has a battery & on top a watch tower; this Hill connects with the Isle only by a narrow Neck of Land, beyond which there is another harbour to the SW which is ½ mile broad & 2 miles long: along the *Monte da Guia* is deep water close in shore: on the NE Side it shoals; it might be improved by an Arm going out at Sea to Shelter the Place; they call it *Porto Pim*, which is corrupted from *Fim*, because it is the last good port to the South & West on that Side.

There are some batteries even to defend this port, but they are decaying, & not repaired. The Garrison consists of a Company of Soldiers of 100 Men, of whom only 40 are really existing. The large Guns in the Forts are standing on old rotten Carriages. A Capt is Governor of the Fort.

The Town is called *Villa da Horta* & extends along the Seashore at the bottom of the Road & is about 1 mile & one quarter long, but hardly more than one principal Street, & a couple meaner ones make up its breadth, which is on the slope of a hill. There are three Parish-Churches in Town; the principal of which is called *Matriz* & stands on the North Side of the Town, another Parish is quite on its northermost Extremity; & the third is beyond the Fort to the South near *Porto Pim* & is called *Nossa Senhora da Angustias*. The Churches have allmost all the same Structure & ornaments viz: a great Altar opposite the Entrance at the bottom of the Church, & two smaller Altars on each Side. A gallery opposite the Great Altar, & commonly 2 Pulpits one opposite to another, where two Preachers at a time, as I was told, undertake in one the Cause of God Almighty, & that of the Host of Angels & Saints, & in the other that of Lucifer & his host & the poor Devil is certainly to be fairly beaten every time. The Altars are sculptured & ornamented with a great Deal of trifling tinsel; some are made of Cedar-wood, & perfume the whole Church with the Fragrancy of the wood.[1] Besides these Parish Churches there are about 6

[1] These observations are transposed to a later stage of *Voyage*, II, 600.

more belonging to Monasteries. The Franciscan Cordeliers have a Monastery & a Church dedicated to S[t] *Francis*. There are about 20 Priests in the Monastery, & several Lay Brothers. These Reverend Fathers teach Rhetorics, Philosophy & Divinity. The next Church is that which formerly belonged to the College of Jesuits, it is by far the best building; & the King has appropriated the College for the School of the Isle, & the rest for a Court of Justice. The third is the Church of *Nossa Senhora da Carmel* & in the Monastery annexed to it are 12 Carmelite Priests & several Lay-Brothers. The last to the North is built pretty high on the Side of a hill dedicated to *St Antonio* & has a Monastery of 12 Capucian Priests with several Lay-Brothers.

There are 2 Nunneries in this Town. Near the *Matriz* Parish Church is that of the order of *Sta Clara*; their Church is dedicated to *San João*. It consists of about 140 or 150 Nuns & as many Servants. The Nuns wear white Callico-cloth below & a kind of brown Serge-Cloak over it, & white coëffes, that are very singular. The next to them in a lower Situation of the hill, are the Nuns of *Nossa Senhora de Concepção*, of which there are about 80 or 90 & as many Servants. These wear all white cloth & Cloaks, but on their breasts is fixed a blue silken orb with a silver plate – Image of *Nossa Senhora*.

The Friars are the most ignorant Fellows, I ever met with: they cannot connect 3 words of Latin, without stuffing 6 words of Portugueze in: all use Snuff, & are Traders; one Reverend Father offerred me a Pipe of wine for Sale. As we were Foreigners, we had no Occasion of being introduced into Company of Ladies, for it is only then, when one is upon a very good Footing with the Master of the House, that one has the pleasure to converse with the better Sort of Ladies. We took also the first opportunity to see at least the Nuns, who are very desirous of seeing company & as soon as You come to the Grate, there are immediately some present to take up the Conversation which was very insipid, as we did not understand their Mother-Tongue, nor they any other besides. They commonly presented us with some cakes or sweat-Meets, Custards etc. & lastly desired us to buy their Flowers. If their Industry were directed to something which might be useful to Men or Women, as in making Garters, Mittens, Purses, Portugueze Caps, then would it be a pleasure in purchasing some such trifles; but miserable Tinsel-Flowers made everybody backward to purchase them, & to throw away money upon things which are absolutely useless. They are for the greatest part old, some young ones, are not quite disagreable, & their Complexion is fairer than one should expect from Portugueze.

But the Situation of these Isles, in the middst of a large Ocean & perhaps the mixture of the Portugueze blood with that of the first Inhabitants of this Isle of Fayal viz. the Flamish people, contributes towards making their complexion less swarty, than that of the rest of their Countrymen in Portugal & Madeira. They have fine sparkling black Eyes, & often fine Teeth & very fine hands, are very slender in the waist, which we could see, when they threw their Cloaks back. They seem to be very amorous, in the spite of their Cloisters & double Grates. Their speech is very singing, & soft. If the Stories told us are true, they are even very libidinous, & not being able to satisfy their desires with Men, they endeavour to do it effectually one way or other. These are the miserable effects of bigotry & false notions of sanctity in religious matters, & of the violence & arbitrary powers of parents & families in confining so many poor victims in these places, where instead of becoming the models of piety, devotion & chastity they degenerate into the most miserable profligates in morals, pine away their wretched life, & become entirely useless to that society, for which they were originally destin'd useful Members. But the ambition of the great Families & the false Notions of derogating from their Nobility by letting their Daughters marry Men of an inferior Rank, have blinded Mankind and led them astray in various Countries: in Portugal & in Roman Catholik Countries this Prejudice condemns so many poor Girls to a perpetual Prison, & in England & other Protestant Countries it makes so many old Maids, the greater Part of which are become a Nuisance to Society by their Eagerness for Cards & Scandal.[1]

We stood this day ashore,[2] & next morning we took a walk into the Country, which we found to be highly cultivated; all the Fields are inclosed by dead Walls made of large Stones & Moss laid between them; in some places they are made of Mortar. They

[1] This long critique of religion, manners and prejudices was drastically condensed and its blows softened or omitted by George (II, pp. 584–5).

[2] George gives us a clearer picture of the sequence of each day's events. One suspects that Forster wrote up his Fayal journal at one or two long sittings. Before setting off on their country walk they visited an English widow, Mrs Milton, mother of William (or Thomas), one of Furneaux's men lost in the murders of Grass Cove, Queen Charlotte Sound. See *Voyage*, II, 586–7.

cultivate chiefly Wheat, which is here bearded, & very free of weeds, has fine ears, but stands not very thick, nor is its Straw very long. They cut it here short, bring it immediately in small Sheaves to the Thrashing Floor & have it trod out by Oxen, dragging a Board over it, with sharp Flints sticking in it; the Driver always stands on it, to give it more weight. They pull up the remaining Straw & Stubble & lay it regularly in rows to dry & use it for thatching Cottages & Stables, & other Outbuildings: the other Houses being commonly tiled. Besides Wheat, they sow Barley, but all the rest of the Land is taken up with Plantations of Mayz, which they grow even under the large Chestnut-Trees of which we found several Clusters: where no Trees stand, there they plant between the Mayz, French-Beans. The Barley we found housed; the wheat was likewise either cut or housed & but few was more standing. In some Fields near Houses we observed Cucumbers, Gourds, Water Melons & Melons planted, & here & there some Safflor, which they employ to die their Dishes yellow with. Here & there we found Copses of wood, consisting chiefly of Asp, some Chestnut, which they use for the Fruit & some other Shrubberies especially one Evergreen which they call *Faya*,[1] & from whose Quantity the Isle was called *Fayale*. I suspect it to be Beach, but I will not be positive. I saw neither Fruit nor Flowers on it. They have near the Houses Orchards of Lemons, Limes, Oranges, Plumbs, Abricocks[2] & Figs, Pears & Apples. They have good & many Potatoes, but sell them Cheap, because they do not like them, tho' they are obliged by a Law to plant them. Cabbages are rare but fine, Carrots degenerate & become white, for both they must have every year from Europe fresh Seeds. Their Onions are large & excellent, & they have plenty of Garlick. They cultivate likewise some Wines, but hardly can ever any good Wine be made of nor exceeds the Quantity made on the whole Isle a few Pipes. There is a kind of Nightshade *Pomua Amoris*[3] which they eat & is called *Tomatos*. They give the same Name to a kind of *Physalis*,[4] with a fine tart fruit similar in taste to a Currant when ripe. Great many Strawberries came every day to Town. They have small Oxen, the Beef is however good: tho' they be all employed to draw their Ploughs & Carts, which are of a curious

[1] *Myrica faya* Aiton.
[2] Directly from Portuguese albricoque; also formerly apricock.
[3] *Lycopersicum esculentum* Mill.
[4] *Physalis peruviana* L.

Construction, for the Wheels are made of 3 pieces of plank, bound by Iron as ours are, very strong & fastened to an Axle-Tree which is moveable together with the wheels & turns in a round hole of a square piece of wood joined to the Cart above, which has a triangular or rather pentagonal figure. These Carts make a terrible noise, enough to make a Man deaf. (Myrtle grows likewise wild here). I saw but few & small horses, & some good Mules. Their Goats & Sheep are small & Lean, but the Mutton is well tasted, tho' no Ram is ever castrated in this Isle. They have longlegged & longsnouted tolerable Hogs, great many Cocks & Hens, some Geese & Ducks, & keep great many Blackbirds,[1] Canarybirds[2] & black Flycatchers (*caflis Vinagriadus*) in Cages of curious Construction. In the interior parts of the Isle on the Summits of the hills are *Hawks*,[3] of a small kind; but I could get none, to settle the Species, which they call *Açores*, which formerly were more numerous & gave to these Isles their Name.

We found everywhere a numerous & industrious people, not very tawny, nor tall, lean, with large Feet, strong Cheekbones: black strait or somewhat curled Hair, fine black Eyes, good teeth & tolerable Features. Men wear Jackets, Linnen Drawers & Breeches over it; some go barefooted, others have Boots, others Cloth-stockings reaching to the Instep only: & when in State in Town a large Cloak & a large Hat. Women have their Hair tied up, & the lower Sort have large Hats; & a kind of linnen Cap with a long Lapel: unmarried ones go with their Hair only; a Corselet & Pettycoat make the whole Dress, when they go out, they have a Cloak tied round the Waist, & going over the head like a Veil, leaving just an opening for the Eyes to look through.

Though the Country is so happily cultivated & populous, nothing can give an Idea of the fine Prospects it affords than the varied & fine Scenery itself we had before our Eyes in various Situations, to which the Sea, the Town below us & the Sight of the equally finely cultivated Isle of Pico opposite to us, contributed not a little. The Country is full of Quails,[4] Rabbits & wild Pigeons.[5] The first are heard every where. We returned towards Noon very much fatigued.

[1] *Turdus merula azorensis* Hartert, 1905.
[2] *Serinus canarius canarius* Linnaeus, 1758.
[3] Probably the Azores Buzzard *Buteo buteo rothschildi* Swann, 1919.
[4] *Coturnix coturnix conturbans* Hartert, 1917.
[5] Probably the Rock Pigeon *Columba livia atlantis* Bannerman, 1931.

July ye 16th ☉ In the Afternoon my Son took another long walk into the Country.[1] I stood at home & collected various Accounts of the Country & Isles.[2] We had towards night a Rain, which it was said would be worth at this time several 1000 to the Inhabitants, as this moisture would swell the Grapes, which else would remain small & indifferent. Towards Evening there was an Illumination on the Front of the Carmelite Church. Next morning we visited several Churches, the Music in the Carmelite-Church for the high Mass was thought to be Tolerable.

July ye 17th ☽ In the Afternoon we paid the Nuns of the Sta Clara another visit. We saw afterwards a Procession where all the Clergy of the Town & the *Beneficiati* of the Isle assisted. A good many Principal People in black Gowns & Cloaks walked in the Procession & at last the Host came.[3]

Next morning I took again a walk into the Country to a little Garden House of Senhor Joseph Ignace de Sousa Doctor of Cannon-Law, which is situated on the Slope of a high Hill, from whence we had a charming Prospect towards a little agreable Village called *Nossa Senhora da la Luz*, surrounded by a most fertile & picturesque Valley. Beyond this Valley begins the Ascent of a ridge of Hills, conducting to the highest part of the Isle. About 9 miles from town, there is a Valley on the top of these Hills; it is circular & has about 2 Leagues circumference & is quite

[1] In the company of Wales, Patten, Hodges and Gilbert towards the village of Nossa Senhora de la Luz. On this excursion Wales and Gilbert fell behind the other three who encountered in a stream hollow some local 'young girls' drawing water and preparing flax. For the younger men it has been a fatiguing yet enjoyable day among 'romantic hills and groves'. See *Voyage*, II, 590–2.

[2] 'During my absence my father had conversed with several Portuguese, especially with the clergyman', whom they had met on their first evening at Fayal at Dent's house, and 'who spoke Latin better than all the friars in the different convents, and appeared to be a very intelligent man, whose inquisitive turn of mind had got the better of many prejudices which were common among his countrymen', *Voyage*, II, 585 and 592. This literary gentleman would have soon attracted Forster, hungry for information. The summary of the intelligence gained is given below, pp. 763–8 and by George (II, pp. 592–600).

[3] From George we get another interesting glimpse of Forster's (and perhaps his earlier) militant Protestantism as the host passed them by: 'The commercial intercourse with the North-Americans seems to have abated the spirit of persecution, of which the church of Rome is sometimes accused in other countries. When the host passes, no person is insulted, who does not choose to perform an act of adoration; and strangers in particular are treated with a degree of civility in this subject, which they do not meet with in the polite but slavish metropolis of France', *Voyage*, II, 600–1. This comment on Paris springs almost certainly from the elder Forster's disillusionment with that city during his visit there in September 1776. George, working on the writing of the *Voyage* back in London, would have imbibed his father's anti-Gallic feelings in time to enter them into the *Voyage* text. Perhaps he had no choice in the matter! See *Tactless Philosopher*, pp. 164–5.

excavated & very deep & at its bottom is a Lake of fresh Water; all this is called *La Caldeira* or the *Kettle* on account of its figure, & the Natives say, that in case the Peak of *Pico* should be taken off, it would just fit in this conic hole. The water is not deep, for it reaches only to a Mans Arms, as some English Gentlemen Experienced, who went into it for bathing. The Sides are clad with a fine Verdure & the Sheep grazing on it are very wild; if a Set of Gentlemen go there on a party of pleasure to shoot Rabbits, Quails & wild Ducks,[1] they frequently kill a Sheep or two for their Consumption with their Guns, & their Masters come perhaps in a Month or two to enquire for the payment: from the NW brim of this Caldera the Sea is very nigh & the Shore a precipice.[2]

We returned towards noon very much fatigued to town.

*July ye 18th* ♂ In the Afternoon I had a Visit paid me by Padre *Joaõ de Buys* & another Clergyman, & likewise by Dr *Sousa*; they talked both French & the latter some English. They had read a good deal & collected a tolerable Collection of books, & one had the Abridgment of the Phil: Trans: They conversed very agreably & gave me several useful Informations relative to these Isles.[3]

The next morning I repaid my Visits & took leave of this Island, going to dinner on board with the Consul one Padre Francisco H. Omi, a Captain Suarez in the Land Service & a Captain of a Ship called Chaviers, & one Senhor Ignace Davilla Bethincourt.[4]

*July ye 19th* We sent our Guests in the Evening on board, had unmoored & next morning at 4 o'clock, we had weighed & set Sail with a fresh wind.

The Açores were first discovered by the Flamish about the Year 1439[5] & they settled at Fayal, & from thence these Isles are called

[1] Probably the Mallard *Anas platyrhynchos platyrhynchos* Linnaeus, 1758.

[2] For further comments on the calderas and vulcanicity of Fayal and the Azores see *Observations*, p. 154; *Voyage*, II, 602 and p. 766 below. Later, when writing up and expanding upon these observations for the *Voyage*, George had the services of R. E. Raspe to call upon and, concerning the volcanics of the Azores, he relied heavily upon this fugitive 'man of science and genius'. The obvious vulcanicity of the Azores seems to have confirmed Forster in much of his thinking on this topic.

[3] George, as usual, went his own way, this time to the 'covent of St Clare' with the French consul.

[4] These gentlemen impressed with their 'easy and chearful...conversation...the reverse of that haughty taciturnity which is the general character of the Portuguese nobility at Madeira', *Voyage*, II, 604.

[5] The question of the 'discovery' of the Azores group was a historically vexed one, since, certainly, the Arabs knew about them in the twelfth century and a Genoese chart of 1351 shows them. The Fleming van der Berg of Bruges is said to have been driven to them in 1432 and, perhaps influenced by this, the Portuguese navigator G. V. Cabral reached Sta Maria in the same year.

in some Geographies the Flamish Isles, & a Parish in the Isle of Fayal is still called Flamingos. In the Year 1447 or 1448 these Isles were discovered by the Portugueze from the other End, for they saw first S[ta] Maria, then S[t] Miguiel & lastly *Terceira*. In the Year 1449 *Don Gonzalo Velho Cabral* Commander of *Almuros* settled on *Terceira* & founded the town of *Angra* which from the *Bay* or *Road* it was built near to got its name. The Isles of *S[t] George*, *Graciosa*, *Pico* & *Fayal* were likewise seen & gradually settled but *Flores* & *Corvo*, which were thus called from the Quantity of *Flowers* & *Crows* found there, were discovered after them all.

These Isles stand now under a Governor General residing at *Terceira* in the *Cidade of Angra*. The present one is called *Don Anton da Almada*, he is very much liked, on account of his goodnature & averseness to Extorsions & oppression: he has spent all his Income & more; so that he is reputed to be in debts, having allways lived in great splendor & state in a fine Palace, which is destined for all the Governors. He has been six Years in this Place, tho' the other Governors seldom stay longer than 3 years. His successor *Don Luis de Tal Pilatus* is daily expected in a Man of War from Lisbon together with a new Bishop & a Juiz for Fayal. The Governor has all political & military departments under him, together with the revenue. The Bishop of *Angra* has a College of 12 Canons at his Cathedral & all the Clergy of the 9 Isles stands under him: his income is in Trigo or Wheat, of which he has 300 Muys yearly, of about 4£ 1[sh] Sterl. each in cheap years, & in dear ones it brings of course more in. At the lowest value therefore he has 1200£ Sterl. a year. Fayal & all the other Isles have separate Chiefs called *Capitan Mõr*, who are a kind of Under-Governor & direct the Police, Militia, & Revenue. The Law-Department is under the *Juiz*, whereof each Isle has one; from him the Appeal goes to *Terceira*, to a higher Court & from thence the last Appeal goes to Lisbon. The Natives of these Isles are said to be quarrelsome & constantly at Law with one another.

1. The Isle of *Corvo* is the least, & contains scarcely 600 Inhabitants, its chief Production wheat, & bacon; it exports very little, but has no wine.

2. The Isle of *Flores* is something larger, more fertile & more populous. Its Inhabitants amount to about 5000. They export yearly about 500 or 600 Muys of Wheat, of 24 Bushel each, & some Bacon; but fetch their Wine from *Fayal*. Many years ago a Spanish

great & rich Man of war was lost upon this Isle; however the Crew & Treasure were saved. These Spaniards introduced the French disease[1] into Flores, where it never was known before, because their money bribed almost every woman in the Isle: & to expatiate these Crimes they left a considerable Sum to build a Church of, which is the most splendid & considerable building now in all the Isles. However the evil has taken since that time so deep root in this Isle, that there is hardly an Individual free of it, & great many perish of it in a most miserable manner, since no Physician on that Isle is living, who is capable of curing it. They come therefore frequently to Fayal to be cured.

3. *Fayal* has a Capitan Mõr; the present one is called *Senhor Thomas Francisco Brum de Silveyra* & is reckoned very covetous; for which reason he lives in the Country, in order to avoid showing any civilities to Strangers or others. His Father was a curious Man & collected Materials for the History of the Açores, especially all the Mst works of Dr *Fruttuoso* from St *Miguiel*. The Clergy is under an *Oviedor*, who at present is the Vicar of the *Matriz*; there are 12 parishes in the Isle & about 15,000 Inhabitants, 5,000 of which are in the *Villa*, the rest in the Country. They have a *Juiz* for the decision of matters of Law.

Learning is at present at a very low ebb in Fayal, the Açores & Portugal in General. When about 2 or 3 years ago a French Ship with 2 Astronomers on board came to Terceira, the Governor would not let them land their Instruments & make Observations. Ever since the last war the Portugueze print no more any News Papers, that no News of their own country should be known. They read now Spanish ones. What Barbarism! & false Politics![2]

The king laid about 2 years ago an Impost of 2 Reys per Canari[3] upon all wine made in Fayal & Pico, for the Support of 3 Teachers of their Youth, to be established at Fayal after a previous Examination at Lisbon. This makes about 1 Shilling Sterling per Pipe & as about 20,000 Pipes are made every year, it amounts to

[1] George calls it by its less euphemistic name: venereal disease.

[2] This note on the French scientific expedition and Portuguese politics is in the margin of VI, f. 147. The expedition referred to, as George (II, 595) makes clear, was that of Fleurieu in the *l'Isis*, which carried Pingré as the principal astronomer. See p. 152, n. 1 above on the evidence encountered at Cape Verde Islands of the same expedition. Wales had no such problems at Fayal since he set up his instruments in the garden of Thomas Dent, vice-consul and host. See *Journals*, II, 674 and 679.

[3] A *rey*, George obligingly informs us, was worth one twelfth of a penny and a *canari* was 'somewhat larger than a gallon'. (*Voyage*, II, 595, note).

about 1000£. Sterl. & would allow 333⅓£. Sterl. for each of the three Professors, but unfortunately this money is diverted into a different Channel, & the Soldie[r]s employed at Fayal get now their pay from thence & the Inhabitants are still obliged to pay for the Education of their Children; for there is now a Professor without Salary, who got the Chair having undergone the Examination, but he teaches nothing but a few Scraps of Latin. There is likewise another Impost of 2 *p.* Cent laid upon all Exports, for to maintain the Fortifications at Fayal, which for all that are decaying: & the money goes to Terceira where it is employed for some other purpose.

The king has besides the Farm of the Tobacco which brings a considerable Sum every year: & likewise the Tenth of the Productions of all the Isles. They grow chiefly Wheat & Mayz on Fayal, & some Flax. In good years they export some wheat to Lisbon: 2 years ago 3 Ships went out loaded with wheat.

As Fayal has a tolerable Port, all the trade of these Isles is in the hands of the people at Fayal. The wine raised yearly at *Pico* goes under the Name of Fayal-wine to North-America & Brasil, & several Vessels come there to fetch it. The best wine costs about 4 or 5£ Sterl. a Pipe; & is tart & when kept a few years is a very good wine, but the common sort is between 3 & 4£ the Pipe. The sweet wine, called *Passada*, is about 7 or 8£ the Pipe; but the French Officers in the Fregatte La Pourvoyeuse[1] paid extravagant prices, & bought all the Passada-wines for 10 & 12£. Sterl. up. Beef & Mutton are cheap but not very good. The Isle is 9 Leagues long from *Castel Branco*: & about 4 broad.

4. The Isle of *Pico* has its name from the Peak or high hill on it,[2] which is always capt with Clouds & but seldom free of it. It is the Thermometer & Barometer of the people at Fayal. On its Summit a constant Smoke comes out between the Rocks, according to Capt Chavires, who had been on its Summit, & several people assured me, that the Smoke may be distinctly seen from *Fayal* early in the Morning on some clear days. It appears also from thence that it has a subterraneous Fire, & as these Isles are subject to Earthquakes, (for they had one about 3 weeks before our Arrival). It is not improbable, that one day or other *Pico* may become a Volcano. The *Caldera* on *Fayal* seems to be the Crater

[1] Which Cook names as the *Pourvoyeur* (*Journals*, II, 678).
[2] Pico alto, some 2320 metres high.

of an old Volcano.[1] This Isle of Pico is however not only the greatest of all the other Isles but it has likewise the greatest Fertility & Population. There are about 30,000 Inhabitants on it. It has no Corn-Fields, for every part of it is converted into Vineyards, which on its gentle Slope have a Charming appearance. They get all their Corn & other necessaries from Fayal. In the time of the Vintage, more than half of the Inhabitants of Fayal emigrate to Pico with their Wives, Children, Cattle, Cats & Dogs & even Chicken. A vast number of grapes, more than would make 3000 Pipes of Wine are then eaten. Some Years ago the Vintage was more advantageous than of late: for then they made 30,000 Pipes of Wine, nay in one year 37,000 but since late a Disease has befallen their Vines, causing the Leaves to fall off in the time, when the Grapes want most Shelter, which exposed them too much to the Sun & caused little & bad wine. The Vines have since recovered & they make now commonly 18,000 or 20,000 Pipes of wine a year. That part opposite to *Fayal* is chiefly the property of people at *Fayal* & yields the best wines; of those on the opposite Side, they make chiefly Brandy, reckoning 3 or 4 Pipes of wine, to distill one of Brandy from.

5. St *George* is steep & high, bears a good deal of wheat & very little or no Wine at all, & has about 5000 Inhabitants.

6. *Graciosa* has a more gentle Slope, than the former, & grows a good Deal of wheat & even some wine but of a very low Quality, so that they employ 5 or 6 Pipes of wine to make one of Brandy. The two last Isles have some Pastures & export some Cheese & Butter. The Isle of Graciosa has about 3000 Inhabitants.

7. *Terceira* is the largest Isle after *Pico*, highly cultivated with wheat Fields, & some but bad wine. The Residence of the Governor General & the Superior Court of Justice with the See of a Bishop give it some Importance. They export some Wheat in good Years to Lisbon. There are about 20,000 Inhabitants on it.

8. St *Miguiel* (discovered 1444) is likewise of a great Extent, very fertile & very populous. They cultivate no wine, but so much more wheat & Flax, of which they manufacture such a Quantity of a coarse Linnen, that about 3 Ships Cargoes of it go yearly to the Brasils. The Linnen is about 2 Feet broad & the Vara[2] of

[1] Cf. *Voyage*, II, 602.

[2] The so-called Portuguese yard, about 85 cm.

common Cloath costs about 1^{s} ^{h} 6^{d} which in my opinion is dear. There are about 25,000 Inhabitants on it. The *Cidade de Ponte de Gada*[1] is on this Isle.

9. St *Maria* is the Southermost of all the Açores so as *Corvo* is the Northermost. They have a good deal of wheat, but their chief Manufacture is a kind of common, coarse Earthern ware of Pots & Jars & other Utensils. Lately they have built one or two small Ships of their own wood & about 5000 Inhabitants are reckoned to be on this Isle: discovered 1432.

These are the Chief Remarks I could collect about these Isles during the few days of our Stay at Fayal. There are some old noble Families settled on these Isles, but I had no time to enquire after all their Names.[2]

We had a fresh wind & approached from the Isle of St George, having past the Eastermost Extremity of *Fayal*, which is high & a bluff point. *Pico* seemed to have a gentle slope, except where the Peak begins, which almost terminates in a point. *St George* has steep & bold Shores & was only on top cultivated: its NW point look much like Port Jackson in N. Zeeland. *Graciosa* has a little Rock to Leeward, & is gently sloping. When we came under St George, the Isle broke the wind & we were near becalmed. The Thermometer at 73°.[3]

July ye 20. ♃ We recovered soon the fine breeze again & saw at noon Terceira. At 3 o clock we were along side of its North part & saw the finest inclosures & Marks of the highest Cultivation. We got some Rain & soon after a Contrary Wind. We observed an Eggbird & a Shearwater.[4] The Thermometer at 71½°.

July ye 21st ♀ The wind still North more or less. The Course EbS, East & EbN. The next morning we saw several large Albecores along Side of the Ship one of which was struck, but came off from the Grains, a Port-Egmont-Hen or Skua[5] was observed, & a Shearwater. The Thermometer at 70½°.

[1] Ponta Delgada, capital of the Azores.

[2] 'I flatter myself', wrote George (II, p. 600) who followed his father very closely in this summary of the islands, 'that the above particulars, though insufficient to give a perfect idea of the Açores, will not be unacceptable to my readers, especially as these islands, being seldom visited by Europeans, are little known, notwithstanding their short distance from us'. Cook's description is very short since, he surmised, 'a better account of these Matters may be had...any day in London from the English Merchants who have resided upon them than any I can give'. His main intention in calling at Fayal lay in letting Wales determine the rate of his chronometer and 'to fix with some degree of certainty the Longitude of these Islands'. See *Journals*, II, 675–8.

[3] Cf. *Journals*, II, 681–2.

[4] Perhaps a Manx Shearwater.

[5] Presumably a Great Skua.

July y^{e} 22^{d} ♄ The wind abated, in the morning calm & change of wind. Alter the Course to ENE. Saw a Shearwater. The Thermometer at 68°.

July y^{e} 23^{d} ☉ Fine breeze. Saw a bird like a Gull flapping its wings. The Thermometer at $67\frac{1}{2}^{\circ}$.

July y^{e} 24th ☽ The breeze fresh: & our hopes of seeing in 10 or 12 days the shores of England increase every moment & gladden our hearts. We have a terrible Swell from the West, & the Ship rolls very disagreably. The Thermometer at 68°.

July y^{e} 25th ♂ The Ship rolls Gunwall to: but the Breeze is still fine & favorable. The Swell continues. In the night we had some Squalls. The Thermometer at $65\frac{1}{2}^{\circ}$.

July y^{e} 26th ☿ The breeze fresh; saw a Shearwater. Had several Squalls. The Thermometer at 63°.

July y^{e} 27th ♃ The breeze still continues. Squally. The Thermometer 63°.

July y^{e} 28th ♀ The same Gale stands. See Porpesses & a small bird. The colour of the Sea changed, supposed to be in Soundings & about 50 Leagues off the Lizard. The Thermometer $63\frac{1}{2}^{\circ}$. Saw the Day before in the Afternoon a Ship standing Eastward.

July y^{e} 29th ♄ The same fine Gale. Pass in the Morning the Lizard. Saw all the beforenoon vast Number of Ships plying to windward in order to get out of the Channel. Had Squalls. The Thermometer at $62\frac{1}{2}^{\circ}$.

July y^{e} 30th ☉ The same Breeze. Saw at 4 o'clock Eddystone Lighthouse & Start Point, the first part of Englands happy Shores. The numberless Ships & finely cultivated country we see make our hearts Glad, being a Sight from which we were weaned 3 tedious long years.[1] Our Hopes & Joy now get every moment new food & new Increments & we expect to morrow in the Afternoon to be at an Anchor at farthest.[2]

[1] Cook summarizes it more closely: 'Having been absent from England Three Years and Eighteen Days in which time I lost but four men and only one of them by sickness', *Journals*, II, 682. George, in his closing paragraph (*Voyage*, II, 604–7), gives a much longer overview of this epic voyage.

[2] They anchored at Spithead 'a little before noon' on Sunday 30 July. The same day the Forsters with Cook, Hodges and Wales posted to London. See *Journals*, II, 682 and *Voyage*, II, 604.

APPENDIX I

by Phyllis Edwards

George Forster's Plant Drawings from Cook's Second Voyage in the Department of Botany, British Museum (Natural History), London

As a result of the withdrawal of Banks and his suite there were no official artists on Cook's second voyage. J. R. Forster intended to adopt the pattern of natural history description followed by Banks and Solander on the first voyage, and this was one of the reasons why he requested the Admiralty to allow him to take his son George with him. George was a competent draughtsman, and his father wanted him to record the new plants and animals they would encounter. He was not a professional artist and one cannot compare his finished drawings with those of Sydney Parkinson. Most of George's 301 drawings, now bound in two volumes housed in cabinets in the main library of the Department of Botany, British Museum (Natural History), are in pencil or ink; some have a colour wash, and thirty-one are in full colour. Some have been executed with much greater care than others, and a few bear an inscription such as 'sketched Aug. 1772', or 'painted Feb. 28 1773'. Banks purchased this set of drawings from J. R. Forster after the voyage for £420, and with the Forster zoological drawings now in the Museum they are considered to have formed Banksian MSS 6–9.

George Forster and Sparrman prepared the text for the Forsters' *Characteres generum plantarum quas in itinere ad insulis maris australis collegerunt descriptserunt, delinearunt* while on the voyage. In the preface to this work it is stated, 'to assist our memory we began describing and illustrating the characters of the new genera in a separate book.' Sprengel claimed that he had the original drawings for the *Characteres*,[1] possibly the separate book referred to in the Forsters' preface. The illustrations in the *Characteres* are of the

[1] K. P. J. Sprengel, *Geschichte der Botanik* (Leipzig, 2 vols, 1817–18), p. 342.

detailed structure of the flower only, whereas the drawings in the Banksian collection are of the whole plant to which the floral details as given in the *Characteres* have been added.[1]

George Forster planned a major work on the botany of the voyage, 'Icones Plantarum in itinere ad insulis maris australis collectarum', but it was never published. However, 131 engravings were made, and some pulls taken from them. Only two sets of these pulls are known. Aylmer Burke Lambert (1761–1842) acquired a set, and at the sale of his library in 1842 the set was bought by Bolm. This is probably the set sold by Friedlander in 1869 to the Botanic Gardens in Leningrad. The other set of 129 engravings is bound in with the Banksian collection of drawings. The two sets are thus not quite identical; the two engravings missing from the Banksian set are tab. 130 *Gentiana saxosa*, and tab. 131 *Forstera sedifolia*.

In the lists of George's plant drawings from the Banks Collection set out below, the plants are arranged by country (the Madeira and Cape Verde plants are listed in the text, pp. XX, XX). The manuscript name on the drawing is given in the left-hand column, the modern name in italic in the right-hand column. Much of the latter information has been taken from recently published works listed at the end of the Appendix, but I must also acknowledge the kind assistance of Dr Lucy B. Moore MBE, formerly Senior Botanist, Botany Division, DSIR, Lincoln, Canterbury, New Zealand and Dr Eric J. Godley, Director of the same Division, for work on the New Zealand species; and of Dr B. C. Stone of the University of Malaya, Kuala Lumpur, for assistance with the South Sea identifications.

NEW ZEALAND

Agrostis ovata *Echinopogon ovatus* (Forst. f.) Beauv.
Ancistrum diandrum *Acaena anserinifolia* (J. R. & G. Forst.) Druce
Andromeda rupestris *Gaultheria rupestris* R. Br.
Anthoceros univolvis ??
Anthoxanthum crinitum *Dichelachne crinita* (Linn. f.) Hook. f.
Arnica oporina *Olearia oporina* Hook. f.
Arthericum cirratum *Arthropodium cirrhatum* R. Br.

[1] See figs. 6, 11b, 16 and 36b above.

Aster holosericeus *Celmisia holosericea* (Forst. f.) Hook. f.
Avena filiformis *Deyeuxia forsteri* (Roem. et Schult.) Kunth.
Calea leptophylla *Cassinia leptophylla* (Forst. f.) R. Br.
Calendula pumila *Lagenophora pumila* (Lagenifera) Cheeseman
Campanula gracilis *Wahlenbergia gracilis* A. DC.
Carex uncinata *Uncinia uncinata* Kukenthal
Carpodetus serratus *Carpodetus serratus* J. R. & G. Forst.
Chenopodium triandrum *Rhagodia triandra* (Forst. f.) Aellen
Cineraria repanda *Brachyglottis repanda* J. R. & G. Forst.
Cineraria rotundifolia *Senecio reinoldii* Endl. ex. Hook.
Clematis hexapetala *Clematis forsteri* Gmelin
Coccoloba australis *Muehlenbeckia australis* Meissner
Convolvulus tuguriorum *Calystegia tuguriorum* (Forst. f.) R. Br. ex Hook. f.
Coprosoma foetidissima *Coprosoma foetidissima* A. Cunn.
Craspedia uniflora *Craspedia uniflora* Forst. f.
Dicera dentata *Elaeocarpus dentatus* (J. R. & G. Forst.) Vahl.
Dichondra repens *Dichondra repens* J. R. & G. Forst.
Dracaena australis *Cordyline australis* Hook. f.
Dracaena indivisa *Cordyline indivisa* Steudel
Epacris fasciculata *Styphelia fasciculata* (Forst. f.) Sleum.
Epacris longifolia *Dracophyllum longifolium* (J. R. & G. Forst.) R. Br.
Epacris pumila *Pentachondra pumila* R. Br.
Epacris rosmarinifolia *Dracophyllum rosmarinifolium* R. Br.
Epilobium rotundifolium *Epilobium rotundifolium* Forst. f.
Euphorbia glauca *Euphorbia glauca* Forst. f.
Euphrasia cuneata *Euphrasia cuneata* Forst. f.
Forstera sedifolia *Forstera sedifolia* Linn. f.
Gahnia procera *Gahnia procera* J. R. & G. Forst.
Gaultheria antipoda *Gaultheria antipoda* Forst. f.
Gentiana montana *Gentiana montana* Hook. f.
Gentiana saxosa *Gentiana saxosa* Forst. f.
Gnaphalium involucratum *Gnaphalium involucratum* Forst. f.
Gnaphalium lanatum *Gnaphalium lanatum* Forst. f.
Gnaphalium trinerve *Gnaphalium trinerve* Forst. f.
Griselinia lucida *Griselinia lucida* Forst. f.
Haloragis alata *Haloragis erecta* Schindler
Hedycarya dentata *Hedycarya arborea* J. R. & G. Forst.
Hydrocotyle moschata *Hydrocotyle moschata* Forst. f.

Laserpitium aciphylla *Aciphylla squarrosa* J. R. & G. Forst.
Lepidium oleraceum *Lepidium oleraceum* Forst. f.
Linum monogynum *Linum monogynum* Forst. f.
Lobelia angulata *Pratia angulata* Hook. f.
Loranthus tetrapetalus *Elytranthe tetrapetala* (L. f.) Engl.
Lotus arboreus *Carmichaelia arborea* (Forst. f.) Druce.
Melaleuca florida *Metrosideros fulgens* Sol. ex Gaertn.
Melaleuca perforata *Metrosideros perforata* J. R. & G. Forst.
Melaleuca diffusa *Metrosideros diffusa* A. Cunn.
Melicope ternata *Melicope ternata* J. R. & G. Forst.
Melicytus ramiflorus *Melicytus ramiflorus* J. R. & G. Forst.
Mniarum biflorus *Scleranthus biflorus* (J. R. & G. Forst) Hook. f.
Myosotis spathulata *Myosotis spathulata* Forst. f.
Myoporum laetum *Myoporum laetum* Forst. f.
Ophrys unifolia *Microtis unifolia* Reichenbach
Panax arboreum *Pseudopanax arboreus* (Murr.) Philipson
Panax simplex *Pseudopanax simplex* (Forst. f.) Philipson
Passerina gnidia *Pimelea gnidia* (J. R. & G. Forst.) Banks & Soland. ex Gaertn.
Passerina pilosa *Pimelea tomentosa* (J. R. & G. Forst.) Druce.
Passerina prostrata *Pimelea prostrata* (J. R. & G. Forst.) Willd.
Pennantia corymbosa *Pennantia corymbosa* J. R. & G. Forst.
Periploca capsularis *Parsonsia capsularis* (Forst. f.) R. Br.
Peucedanum geniculatum *Angelica geniculata* (Forst. f.) Hook. f.
Scandia geniculata (Forst. f.) Dawson
Phormium tenax *Phormium tenax* J. R. & G. Forst.
Piper excelsum *Macropiper excelsum* Miq.
Plagianthus divaricatus *Plagianthus divaricatus* J. R. & G. Forst.
Rubus australis *Rubus australis* Forst. f.
Schefflera digitata *Schefflera digitata* J. R. & G. Forst.
Serapias regularis *Thelymitra longifolia* J. R. & G. Forst.
Shawia paniculata *Olearia paniculata* Cheesem.
Sheffieldia repens *Samolus repens* (J. R. & G. Forst.) Pers.
Sisymbrium heterophyllum *Cardamine hirsuta* Linn.
Sisyrinchium ixioides *Libertia ixioides* Spreng.
Skinnera excorticata *Fuchsia excorticata* (J. R. & G. Forst.) Linn. f.
Solidago arborescens *Olearia arborescens* Cockayne & R. M. Laing
Solanum aviculare *Solanum aviculare* Forst. f.

Sophora tetraptera *Sophora tetraptera* J. Miller
Tetragonia halmifolia *Tetragonia tetragonioides* Kuntze
Trichelia spectabilis *Dysoxylum spectabile* Hook. f.
Veronica catarractae *Parahebe catarractae* (Forst. f.) W. R. B. Oliv.
Veronica elliptica *Hebe elliptica* (Forst. f.) Pennell
Veronica salicifolia *Hebe salicifolia* (Forst. f.) Pennell
Viscum antarcticum *Tupeia antarctica* (Forst. f.) Cham. & Schl.
Weinmannia racemosa *Weinmannia racemosa* Linn. f.
Wintera axillaris *Drimys winteri* J. R. & G. Forst.
Xeranthemum bellidioides *Helichrysum bellidioides* Willd.

TAHITI

Adenostemma viscosa *Adenostemma lavenia* (L.) Ktze.
Aleurites triloba *Aleurites moluccana* (Linn.) Willd.
Antirrhinum hexandrum *Lindernia crustacae* (L.) F. v. Muell.
Artocarpus incisa *Artocarpus altilis* (Parkinson ex Z) Fosb.
Ascarina polystachya *Ascarina polystachya* J. R. & G. Forst.
Barringtonia speciosa *Barringtonia asiatica* (L.) Kurz
Casuarina equisetifolia *Casuarina equisetifolia* Stickm.
Commersonia echinata *Commersonia echinata* J. R. & G. Forst.
Croton nutans *Homalanthus nutans* Guill.
Daphne foetida *Wickstroemia viridiflora* Meissn.
Dianthera clavata *Dicliptera ciliaris* Juss.
Dolichos luteolus *Vigna glabra* Savi
Dorstenia lucida *Procris cephalida* Comm. ex. Poir.
Dorstenia pubescens *Elatostemma sessile* J. R. & G. Forst.
Echites costata *Alstonia costata* R. Br.
Epidendrum biflorum *Dendrobium biflorum* Sw.
Epidendrum clypeolum *Liparis clypeolum* Lindl.
Epidendrum crispatum *Dendrobium crispatum* Sw.
Epidendrum equitans *Oberonia glandulosa* Lindl.
Epidendrum myosurus *Oberonia myosurus* Lindl.
Erithalis obovata *Timonius forsteri* DC
Euphorbia atoto *Euphorbia atoto* Guill.
Ficus tinctora *Ficus tinctora* Forst. f.
Galega littoralis *Tephrosia purpurea* (L.) Pers.
Glycine lucida *Glycine tenuiflora* Willd.
Gynopogon scandens *Alyxia scandens* Roem. & Schult. (Forst.)

Inocarpus edulis *Inocarpus fagifer* (Parkinson Ex Z) Fosb.
Ischaemum involutum *Ischaemum involutum* Forst. f.
Kyllinga triceps *Kyllinga monocephala* Rottb.
Lepidium piscidum *Lepidium piscidum* Forst. f.
Lobelia arborea *Sclerotheca arborea* (Forst.) DC.
Loranthus stelis *Loranthus forsterianus* Schultz
Melaleuca aestuosa *Metrosideros collina* (J. R. & G. Forst) A. Gray.
Melastoma glabrum *Lomanodia glabra* (Forst. f.) Ratin.
Meryta lanceolata *Meryta lanceolata* J. R. & G. Forst.
Mupanda frondosa *Mussaenda raiateensis* J. W. Moore
Nelitris forsteri *Nelitris fruticosa* A. Gray
Ophiorhiza subumbellata *Elatostemma sessile* J. R. & G. Forst.
Phyllanthus virgatus *Phyllanthus simplex* Retz.
Piper latifolium *Piper latifolium* Forst. f.
Psychotria speciosa *Psychotria speciosa* Forst. f.
Ruellia fragrans *Limnophila serrata* Gaudich.
Scrophularia pacifica *Premna taitensis* Schauer
Solanum repandum *Solanum repandum* Forst. f.
Spondias dulcis *Spondias dulcis* Forst. f.
Tacca pinnatifida *Tacca leontopetaloides* (L.) Ktze.
Vaccinium cereum *Vaccinium cereum* Forst. f.
Xylosma suaveolens *Xylosma suaveolens* Forst. f.

SOCIETY ISLANDS

Aeschynomene coccinea *Sesbania grandiflora* Poir.
Boerhaavia tetrandra *Boerhaavia tetrandra* Forst. f.
Crossostylis biflora *Crossostylis biflora* J. R. & G. Forst.
Epidendrum fascoila *Taeniophyllum fasciola* Reichb. f.
Epidendrum umbellatum *Cirrhopetalum thouarsii* Lindl.
Epidendrum resupinatum *Microstylis retusa* J. J. Smith
Hibiscus hastatus *Hibiscus tricuspis* Banks ex Cav.
Melastoma glabra *Lomanodia glabra* (Forst. f.) Ratin.
Triumfetta procumbens *Triumfetta procumbens* Forst. f.
Urtica ruderalis *Fleuria ruderalis* (Forst. f.) Gaudich

COOK ISLANDS

Lithospermum incanum *Heliptropium anomalum* Hook. & Arn.
Lythrum pemphis *Pemphis acidula* J. R. & G. Forst.
Rottbolla repens *Lepturus repens* R. Br.

TONGA

Achras dissecta *Mimusops kauki* Linn.
Cerbera parviflora *Ochrosia elliptica* Labill.
Cinchona corymbifera *Tarenna sambucina* (Forst.) Durand
Clusia sessilis *Garcinia sessilis* (Forst.) Seem.
Coffea cymosa *Chasalia fontanesi* DC.
Dais disperma *Drimyspemum forsteri* Meissn.
Fagara euodia *Euodia hortensis* J. R. & G. Forst.
Ficus scabra *Ficus scabra* Forst. f.
Ficus obliqua *Ficus obliqua* Forst. f.
Gentiana arborea *Morinda citrifolia* Linn.
Glochidion ramiflorum *Glochidium ramiflorum* J. R. & G. Forst.
Grewia mallococca *Grewia crenata* (J. R. & G. Forst.) Schinz & Guill. in Sarasin & Roux
Gynopogon stellatum *Alyxia stellata* (J. R. & G. Forst.) Roem. & Schult.
Limonia minuta *Mieromelum minutum* (Forst. f.) Seem.
Maba elliptica *Diospyros ellipticifolia* Stokes var. elliptica (J. R. & G. Forst.) Bakh.
Melochia odorata *Melochia aristata* A. Gray
Mimosa mangium *Acacia laurifolia* Willd.
Mupanda frondosa *Mussaenda raiateensis* J. W. Moore
Oldenlandia foetida *Hedyotis foetida* (Forst.) J. E. Smith
Petesia carnea *Ixora carnea* Benth. & Hook. f.
Pometia pinnata *Pometia pinnata* J. R. & G. Forst.
Portlandia tetrandra *Bikkia tetrandra* (Forst. f.) A. Rich.
Teucrium villosum *Teucrium villosum* Forst. f.
Trichilia alliacea *Dysoxylum forsteri* (Juss.) DC.
Xylosma orbiculatum *Xylosma orbiculatum* Forst. f.

EASTER ISLAND

Paspalum undulatum *Paspalum forsterianum* Fluegge

MARQUESAS ISLANDS

Celastrus crenatus *Celastrus crenatus* Forst. f.
Chiococca barbata *Plectronia barbata* (Forst.) Benth. & Hook. f.
Lophanthus tomentosus *Waltheria tomentosa* (J. R. & G. Forst.) St John
Pisonia inernis *Pisonia brunoniana* Endl.
Solanum repandum *Solanum repandum* Forst. f.

NEW HEBRIDES

Adenanthera scandens *Entada scandens* Benth.
Asclepias volubilis *Hoya australis* R. Br.
Balanophora fungosa *Balanophora fungosa* J. R. & G. Forst.
Baeobotrys nemoralis *Maesa nemoralis* (Forst.) A. DC.
Breynia disticha *Breynia disticha* J. R. & G. Forst.
Ceodes umbellifera *Pisonia umbellifera* (Forst.) Seem.
Chrysocoma purpurea *Chrysocoma purpurea* Forst. f.
Convolvulus coelestis *Ipomoea hederacea* Jacq.
Eclipta prostrata *Eclipta erecta* Linn.
Ficus aspera *Ficus aspera* Forst. f.
Ficus granatum *Ficus granatum* Forst. f.
Geniostoma rupestris *Geniostoma rupestre* J. R. & G. Forst.
Justicia repanda *Anthacanthus repandus* Nees in DC.
Justicia longifolia *Anthacanthus sinuatus* (Vahl.) Nees in DC.
Lysimachia decurrens *Lysimachia decurrens* Forst. f.
Oldenlandia tenuifolia *Hedyotis tenuifolia* Forst. f.
Polyscias pinnata *Polyscias pinnata* J. R. & G. Forst.
Rottbollia coelorachis *Rottboellia coelorachis* Forst. f.
Ruellia reptans *Hemigraphis reptans* T. Andrews
Thalia cannoeformis *Donax sp.*

NEW CALEDONIA

Anthericum adenanthera *Dianella ensifolia* [DC] in Red.
Argophyllum nitidum *Argophyllum nitidum* J. R. & G. Forst.
Casuarina nodiflora *Casuarina nodiflora* Forst. f.
Clusia pedicellata *Garcinia mungotia* Deplanch ex Pierre
Codia montana *Codia montana* J. R. & G. Forst.
Cotula minuta *Centipeda minima* (L.) A. Br. et Aschers.

Dentella repens *Dentella repens* J. R. & G. Forst.
Dianthera pubescens *Dicliptera pubescens* Juss.
Embothrum umbellatum *Stenocarpus umbelliferus* (J. R. & G. Forst.) Druce
Epidendrum tuberosum *Epidendrum tuberosum* Forst. f.
Epidendrum triste *Epidendrum triste* Forst. f.
Euryandra scandens *Euryandra scandens* J. R. & G. Forst.
Hypericum gramineum *Hypericum gramineum* Forst. f.
Lawsonia achronychia *Acronychia laevis* J. R. & G. Forst.
Melaleuca ciliata *Metrosideros ciliata* Smith
Melaleuca virgata *Baeckia virgata* J. R. & G. Forst.
Melistaurum distichum *Casearia disticha* (J. R. & G. Forst.) Gray
Melodinus scandens *Melodinus scandens* J. R. & G. Forst.
Myoporum tenuifolium *Myoporum tenuifolium* Forst. f.
Passiflora aurantia *Passiflora aurantia* Forst. f.
Pometia pinnata *Pometia pinnata* J. R. & G. Forst.
Rhus atrum *Semocarpus atra* Vieill.
Ximenia elliptica *Ximenia americana* Linn.

NORFOLK ISLAND

Blackburnia pinnata *Zanthoxylum pinnatum* (J. R. & G. Forst.) Druce

TIERRA DEL FUEGO

Amellus diffusus *Chiliotrichium diffusum* (Forst. f.) Dusen
Arbutus mucronata *Pernettya mucronata* (Linn. f.) Gaudich.
Arbutus pumila *Pernettya empetrifolia* (Lam.) Gaud.
Berberis ilicifolia *Berberis ilicifolia* L.
Berberis microphylla *Berberis microphylla* Forst. f.
Calendula pumila *Lagenophora nudicaulis* (Comm. ex Lam.) Dusen
Chelone ruelloides *Ourisia ruelloides* (Linn. f.) Dusen in O. Nordensk.
Crassula moschata *Crassula moschata* Forst. f.
Donatia magellanica *Donatia fascicularis* J. R. & G. Forst.
Embothrium coccineum *Embothrium coccineum* J. R. & G. Forst.
Ixia pumila *Tapeinia pumila* (Forst. f.) Baill.
Juncus grandiflorus *Rostkovia grandiflora* (L. f.) Hook. f.

Leantria myrtoides *Myrtus sp.*
Melanthium pumilum *Astelia pumila* (Forst. f.) Banks & Sol. ex R. Br.
Oxalis magellanica *Oxalis magellanica* Forst. f.
Percidium magellanicum *Perezia magellanica* (Linn. f.) Lag.
Phyllachne uliginosa *Phyllachne uliginosa* J. R. & G. Forst.
Plantago barbata *Plantago barbata* Forst. f.
Tussilago trifurcata *Senecio trifurcatus* (Forst.) Less.
Wintera aromatica *Drimys winteri* J. R. & G. Forst.

ST HELENA

Pentapetes erythroxylon *Melhania erythroxylon* R. Br.
Solidago spuria *Commidendrum spurium* DC.
Solidago leucodendron *Senecio leucodendron* Benth. & Hook. f.
Spilanthus arborea *Petrobium arboreum* (J. R. & G. Forst.) R. Br.

ASCENSION

Lonchitis adscensionis *Pteris dentata* Forst. var.

It is necessary to compare this list closely with the set of Forster drawings deposited in Russia. See especially Herder, F. von, 'Verzeichnis von G. Forster's Icones Plantarum in itinere ad insulas maris australis collectarum . . .', *Acta Hort. Petrop.* IX (1886), 485–510; and see also the literature cited in the Bibliography.

The following authorities were consulted for the identification of Forster plants in this Appendix.

Index Kewensis

Guillaumin, A. (1948). *Flore analytique et synoptique de la Nouvelle Calédonie, Phanerogames*, Paris.

Hiepko, P. (1969). 'Von J. R. & G. Forster gesammelte Pflanzen im Herbar Willenow in Berlin', *Willdenowia*, I, 771–80.

St John, H. (1971). 'The date of publication of Forsters' [sic] Characteres Generum Plantarum and its relation to contemporary works', *Naturaliste can.* *98*, 561–81.

Skottsberg, C. (1916). 'Botanische Ergebnisse der Schwedischen Expedition nach Patagonien und dem Feuerlande 1907–1909' *K. Svenska Vetensk. Akad. Handl.* *56*(5), 1–366.

APPENDIX II

Nota rélativement aux Curiosités Artificielles, qu'on a rapportées de la Mer du Sud[1]

Les isles situées dans la Mer du Sud, étant semées dans ce vaste Océan à de très grandes distances les unes des autres, sont habitées par differentes peuplades, dont les moeurs, les fabriques et les outils sont également differens. Ces isles, ainsi que leurs habitans, ont été décrites dans les récits du dernier Voyage autour du Monde, aux quels je m'en rapporte pour les détails nécessaires, relativement aux noms, &ca des differentes isles.

O-Taheiti & isles adjacentes nommées Isles de la Société

1. Les habitans de ces isles se revetissent de differentes sortes de Toiles ou Pagues, fabriquées de l'écorce d'un meurier (*Morus papyrifera*), qu'ils passent autour du corps à plusieures reprises. Ces toiles sont de diverses qualités & couleurs. L'on en pourra fournir de grandes piéces capables de faire des habillements entiers, de plusieures sortes; et l'on fournira des autres espéces des echantillons d'une ou deux aunes en longueur. Tout compté il y a une belle suite de quinze sorte de Toiles, plus ou moines fines.
2. Parmi les Outils & ornémans de ce peuple, il y a une espéce de bouclier, ou plutôt de targe, faite d'un tissu de roseaux, & couverte d'un beau plumage verd-noir, parsemé de trois rangs de dents de réquin, et garni de poil de Chien & de nacre de perle. Puis il y a une *herminette ou hache* de pierre, avec un manchon de bois, pour les usages d'Agriculture; un *Battoir*, ou machine à cannelures qui sert à la fabrique des toiles; des *fils* qu'on a fait

[1] The spelling and inflexions are reproduced as in the original, which is housed in The Alexander Turnbull Library, under Misc. MS 1169. An English translation and commentry has been published recently by Ruth Dawson, 'Collecting with Cook: the Forsters and their Artifact Sales', *Hawaiian Journal of History*, XIII (1979), 5–16.

des cheveux de leurs femmes, & dont ils font un ornément pour leurs danseuses; une *fronde*; un instrument composé de plusieures Coquilles pour servir de *poids* à leurs hameçons; ainsi que plusieures petites choses de peu d'importance.

Isle de la nouvelle Amsterdam
& isles des Amis, adjacentes

3. Les peuples de ces isles s'habillent pour la pluspart d'une natte dont on a rapporté trois espéces très differentes pour le travail, quelques-unes étant travaillées à jour. Ils se revetissent aussi d'une toile fait de l'écorce du mûrier, comme à O-Taheiti, mais enduite d'un vernis & colorée différemment.
4. Leurs ouvrages sont plus variés que ceux des Tahitiens. Nous en avons des *Tabourets* de bois, qu'ils placent sous la tête pour s'y reposer; plusieures espéces de *Massues* ou *Casse-têtes* d'un bois dur, très-joliment ciselées; une *Corbeille* fabriquée des fibres de Cocos, entrelacées de Coquillages; un *peigne* d'un bois blauch-âtre; un ornément de Gorge, des *filets* pour prendre les poissons; les *hameçons* de nacre de perle; un instrument de musique semblable au *Syrinx* des Anciens, &c &c.

Nouvelle Zeelande

5. La peuplade belliqueuse qu'on trouve à la Nouvelle Zéelande n'est pas fort avancée dans les arts. Nous en avons seulem[t] rapporté quelques *hameçons* grossierement travaillés, une *pierre ollaire verte*, très-dure, dont ils font leur hachettes, & une petite quantité du *lin* ou de chanvre dont ils fabriquent leurs habillemens.

Nouvelle Calédonie, &
Nouvelles Hébrides

6. Dans la partie la plus occidentale de la Mer du Sud, nous avons découvert plusieures nouvelles isles, jusque-là inconnues, & habitées par des nations noires, très differentes de tous les autres peuples de la Mer du Sud. Ces nations moins civilisées que les autres, vont toutes nuës, sans le moindre habillement, excepté quelques feuilles, dont ils s'enveloppent les parties honteuses. Ils

portent toujours des armes, c'est à dire *flêches & des arcs*, des *javelots*, & des cassetêtes. Ils se servent d'un petit bout de *corde* assez bien travaillée pour lancer les Javelots avec plus de force & de Justesse. Nouse avons rapportés quelques-uns de ces cordons, et des Armes de toute espéces.

Par dessus les Curiosités Artificielles, nous pourrons encore compter les productions Naturelles, c'est à dire les Plantes de toutes ces isles où nous avons atterré. Notre herbier se monte à six ou sept-cens espéces extremement rares, dont on ne voit gueres des exemplaires dans les Cabinets de l'Europe, & dont deux à trois cens n'ont jamais été vues ou decrites par aucun autre Botaniste.

Londres
ce 17 Fevrier 1778.

Jean Renaud Forster.
Docteur en l'Université
d'Oxford en Angleterre,
Membre de la Societé Royal
de Londres & de la Société
Royale de Gottingue, & de
l'Acad. R. de Madrid.
Correspondant de l'Acad.
des Sciences & de celles des
Belles Lettres et Inscr à Paris;
Membre de l'Acad. R. à
Uppsal, de la Societé
physique de Danzig & celle
de Berlin.
et son fils
George Forster.
Membre de la Societé
Royale de Londres, de
l'Acad. R. de Madrid & de la
Societé physique de Berlin,
& Correspondant de la
Societé Royale de Gottingue.

SELECT BIBLIOGRAPHICAL REFERENCES

I. *Forster Manuscripts*

Journal Holograph MS journal of J. R. Forster in Manuscripts Department, Staatsbibliothek Preussischer Kulturbesitz, Berlin (Hereafter SPK, Berlin). MS germ. quart. 222–227 (6 vols). The text here printed.

Account Holograph MS by J. R. Forster (11 June–30 Oct. 1772); referred to as draft B. From Sandwich Papers in possession of Mr Victor Montagu, Mapperton, Dorset, England.

Catalogue of Curiosities Holograph MS, Pitt Rivers Museum, Oxford.

Descriptiones animalium Holograph MS with later editor's (Lichtenstein's) notes, consisting of three quarto and one folio vols. SPK, Berlin, MS lat. quart. 133–136.

Descriptiones plantarum Holograph MS of botanical descriptions consisting of three folio vols, Bibliothèque Centrale, Muséum d'Histoire Naturelle, Paris, MS 1303–05.

Index Popularum Holograph MS fragments on Pacific anthropology and diseases at sea. SPK, Berlin, MS germ. oct. 79.

Log-book Holograph fragment of log in Universitäts- und Landesbibliothek Sachsen-Anhalt, Halle, MS Yd. F.20.

Nota rélativement aux Curiosités MS listing artefacts from Tahiti, Tonga, New Zealand, New Caledonia etc. in Alexander Turnbull Library, Wellington, Misc. MS 1169. Printed as Appendix II.

Observationes Latin MS notebook by George Forster of plants and animals (26 March–11 May 1773). Bibliothèque Centrale, Muséum d'Histoire Naturelle, Paris, MS 189.

Verzeichnis der Forsterschen Südseesachen MS Catalogue of Forster ethnographical materials purchased by Blumenbach for Göttingen University in Institut und Sammlung für Völkerkunde, Göttingen.

Vocabularies MSS of South Sea Vocabularies by J. R. Forster, SPK, Berlin, MS or. oct. 61–62.

Warrington Lectures Lectures on entomology, natural history and mineralogy delivered by J. R. Forster at Warrington Academy (1767–69), SPK, Berlin, MS germ. oct. 21–22a–b.

(A more extensive list of Forster MSS, Correspondence etc. is printed in Hoare, *Tactless Philosopher*, pp. 373–84.)

II. *Printed Works*

Banks, Endeavour *Journal* *The* Endeavour *Journal of Joseph Banks 1768–1771*. Edited by J. C. Beaglehole. 2 vols, Sydney, 1962.

Beaglehole, *Life* *The Life of Captain James Cook*. By J. C. Beaglehole. London, 1974.

Bougainville *A Voyage round the World....* By Lewis de Bougainville...Translated from the French by John Reinhold Forster, F.A.S. London, 1772.

Buhle, *Literarischer Briefwechsel* *Literarischer Briefwechsel von Johann David Michaelis*. Edited by J. C. Buhle. 3 vols, Leipzig, 1794–6.

Burney, *Private Journal* *With Captain James Cook in the Antarctic and Pacific. The private journal of James Burney Second Lieutenant in the Adventure on Cook's Second Voyage 1772–1773*. Edited by Beverley Hooper. Canberra, 1975.

[*Cook's Journals*] *The Journals of Captain James Cook on his voyages of Discovery*. Edited by J. C. Beaglehole.

I. *The Voyage of the* Endeavour *1768–1771*. Cambridge, 1955.

II. *The Voyage of the* Resolution *and* Adventure *1772–1775*. Cambridge 1961.

III. *The Voyage of the* Resolution *and* Discovery, *1776–1780*. Cambridge, 1967.

Cook, *Voyage* *A Voyage towards the South Pole and round the World. Performed in His Majesty's Ships Resolution and Adventure, In the Years 1772, 1773, 1774, and 1775....* By James Cook... 2 vols. London, 1777.

Dalrymple, *Historical Collection* *An Historical Collection of the several Voyages and Discoveries in the South Pacific Ocean*. By Alexander Dalrymple. 2 vols. London, 1770–1.

Forsters Werke *Georg Forsters Werke. Sämtliche Schriften, Tagebücher, Briefe*. Published by Academy of Sciences of the German Democratic Republic, Berlin.

I. *A Voyage round the World.* Edited by R. L. Kahn. 1968.

II and III. *Reise um die Welt.* Edited by G. Steiner. 1965–66.

IV. *Streitschriften und Fragmente zur Weltreise.* Edited by R. L. Kahn, G. Steiner, H. Fiedler, K-G. Popp and S. Scheibe. 1972.

VIII. *Kleine Schriften zu Philosophie und Zeitgeschichte.* Edited by S. Scheibe. 1974.

XI. *Rezensionen.* Edited by H. Fiedler. 1977.

XII. *Tagebücher.* Edited by Brigitte Leuschner. 1973.

Forster *Characteres generum plantarum, quas in itinere ad insulus maris australis, collegerunt, descriptserunt, delinearunt, annis MDCCLXXII–MDCCLXXV.* By J. R. Forster, LL.D... and George Forster. London, 1776.

Forster *De plantis esculentis insularum oceani australis...* By George Forster. Halle, 1786.

Forster, *Letter to Sandwich* *A Letter to the Right Honourable The Earl of Sandwich...* From George Forster, FRS. London, 1778.

Forster, *Prodromus* *Florulae insularum prodromus...* By George Forster, Göttingen, 1786.

Forster, *Reply* *Reply to Mr Wales's Remarks.* By George Forster. London, 1778.

Forster, *Voyage* *A Voyage round the World, in His Britannic Majesty's Sloop, Resolution, commanded by Capt. James Cook, during the Years 1772, 3, 4, and 5.* By George Forster, F.R.S.... 2 vols. London, 1777.

This work is referred to below as *Voyage* or George Forster, *Voyage* to differentiate it from Cook, *Voyage* above.

Forster, *Reise* *Johann Reinhold Forster's...Reise um die Welt während den Jahren 1772 bis 1775...* By George Forster... 2 vols, Berlin, 1778–80.

Forster *Descriptiones Animalium quae in itinere ad maris australis terras per annos 1772 1773 et 1774 suscepto collegit observavit et delineavit...* By J. R. Forster... Edited by H. Lichtenstein. Berlin, 1844.

Forster, 'Historia Aptenodytae, generis avium orbi australi proprii. Auctore Io Reinoldo Forster LLD', in *Commentationes Societatis Regiae Scientiarum Gottingensis*, III, *Classis Physicae*, III (1780) [1781], pp. 121–48.

Forster 'Mémoire sur les Albatros. Par Monsieur Forster', *Mémoires de Mathématique et de Physique. Présentés à l'Académie Royale des Sciences...*, x, Paris, 1785, pp. 563–72.

Forster, *Observations.* *Observations made during a Voyage Round the World, on Physical Geography, Natural History, and Ethnic Philosophy*... By John Reinhold Forster, LL.D. F.R.S. and S.A. London, 1778.

Hoare, *Tactless Philosopher* *The Tactless Philosopher. Johann Reinhold Forster (1729–1798).* By Michael E. Hoare. Melbourne, 1976.

Huber, *Briefwechsel* *Johann Georg Forsters Briefwechsel. Nebst einigen Nachrichten von seinem Leben.* Edited by Therese Huber. 2 vols. Leipzig, 1829.

Kelly *La Austrialia del Espíritu Santo. The Journal of Fray Martín de Munilla O.F.M. and other documents relating to the Voyage of Pedro Fernández de Quirós to the South Sea (1605–1606) and the Franciscan Missionary Plan (1617–1627).* Translated and edited by Celsus Kelly O.F.M. 2 vols. Cambridge, 1966.

Lysaght, Averil M. 'Some Eighteenth Century Bird Paintings in the Library of Sir Joseph Banks (1743–1820)', *Bulletin British Museum (Natural History), Hist. Ser.*, I, No. 6 (1959), 253–371.

Oliver *Ancient Tahiti Society.* By D. L. Oliver. 3 vols. Honolulu, 1974.

Sparrman *Museum Carlsonianum.* 4 fasc. Stockholm, 1786–89.

Sparrman *A Voyage Round the World with Captain James Cook in H.M.S. Resolution.* By Anders Sparrman. Introduction & notes by Owen Rutter. London, 1944.

Steiner and Baege *Vögel der Südsee. 23 Gouachen und Aquarelle nach Zeichnungen Georg Forsters, entstanden während seiner Weltumseglung 1772 bis 1775.* Edited by Gerhard Steiner and Ludwig Baege. Leipzig, 1971.

Wales [and Bayly] *Astronomical Observations* *The Original Astronomical Observations, made in the course of A Voyage towards the South Pole, and Round the World*... By William Wales F.R.S.... and Mr William Bayly... London, 1777.

Wales, *Remarks* *Remarks on Mr Forster's Account of Captain Cook's last Voyage round the World, In the Years 1772, 1773, 1774, and 1775.* By William Wales, F.R.S. London, 1778.

Whitehead, P. 'The Forster collection of zoological drawings in The British Museum (Natural History)', *Bulletin British Museum (Natural History), Hist. Ser.*, VI, No. 4 (1978), 25–47.

NATURAL HISTORY INDEX

GENERAL INDEX

Abbreviations used: F for J. R. Forster, GF for George Forster